Retail Ma

David Cook
and
David Walters

Retail Marketing: Theory and Practice

PRENTICE HALL
New York London Toronto Sydney Tokyo Singapore

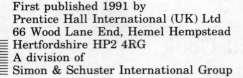

First published 1991 by
Prentice Hall International (UK) Ltd
66 Wood Lane End, Hemel Hempstead
Hertfordshire HP2 4RG
A division of
Simon & Schuster International Group

Typeset in Century $10\frac{1}{2}/12$ pt
by MHL Typesetting Ltd

Printed and bound in Great Britain
by BPCC Wheatons Ltd, Exeter

Library of Congress Cataloging-in-Publication Data

Cook, David, 1939–
Retail marketing: theory and practice / David Cook and David Walters.
p. cm.
Includes bibliographical references and index.
ISBN 0-13-778812-6
1. Retail trade — Management. 2. Retail trade — Management — Case studies. I. Walters, David, 1936– . II. Title.
HF5429.W247 1991
658.8′7 — dc20 90-27808
CIP

British Library Cataloguing in Publication Data

Cook, David *1939–*
Retail marketing.
1. Retail trades. Marketing
I. Title II. Walters, David *1936–*
658.87

ISBN 0-13-778812-6

1 2 3 4 5 95 94 93 92 91

Contents

List of Figures

List of Tables

Preface

There is an increasing interest in retailing as an academic subject and retailing topics are appearing on a number of programmes at varying levels. Our purpose in writing this text is to provide students with a current view of the role of marketing in retailing companies and to demonstrate how retailing strategy is developed and implemented.

The text is in two broad parts. The first considers the role of marketing in a strategic planning context. We argue that marketing should be considered as a support strategy in the context that strategy has a hierarchy of influences. We suggest that once the company has decided on its corporate objectives and strategic direction (the broad means by which objectives will be achieved), it is the company's positioning strategy that conveys the corporate response to its perception of the opportunities offered by the market environment. It is the responsibility of marketing (together with the finance, property, personnel, systems and operations activities) to make this happen. In this context, it is the merchandise, customer service, trading format and store environment, and customer communications strategies that become important to the success of the business.

The second part of the book is a series of case studies/histories, which offer the student an opportunity to use the material in Part One to consider the issues facing the subject companies and the alternative ways in which these may be analyzed and resolved. Cases include a range of both merchandise and service product companies and a range of large and small businesses.

The book will be found to be useful on post-graduate and post-experience programmes in retailing. It has been written following a considerable amount of research among practitioners; and while we suggest that the result is a synthesis of current practice, we must add that the views expressed are ours.

Our thanks are directed towards colleagues who have commented on initial draft chapters and to those practitioners who gave time to discuss issues, which to them may have seemed to be esoteric at the time. However, we hope that they will agree that the bond of academic and pragmatic inputs is of practical value.

We would also like to thank Dee Dwyer and Gillian Naismith for their efforts as their support has made our task much easier.

David Cook
David Walters

PART ONE

The Role of Retail Marketing

CHAPTER 1

Retail marketing as a managerial discipline

Introduction: the environment of retailing

Retailing has become sophisticated in its application of management disciplines to the problems of strategic management and the implementation of strategic decisions. The rapid development of both retailing strategy and retail marketing has occurred because of the emergence of a number of converging circumstances.

Firstly, the growth opportunities of the early 1980s offered encouragement to the well-organized and established multiple retailers. It is interesting to note here that most consumer product markets are predominantly concentrated, and this has resulted in large companies, which either have strong financial resources or have access to them. Concentration also implies the possibility of intensive competition, and this too is a feature of UK consumer goods and services retailing.

The growth opportunities were fuelled by the buoyancy of the early 1980s. The UK economy returned to a growth period after the problems of inflation (and consumer pessimism) of the late 1970s. Social change – specifically the shift in values and attitudes – has had an important influence. The intensifying of individuality, a continuation in the breakdown of formality and authority, resulted in consumer preferences for products to be used as artefacts to express these views. Consequently, social values and attitudes have become consumer values and attitudes and, in turn, opportunities for the progressive retailers. Thus it was that Next, Burton and Laura Ashley saw (and took) considerable growth opportunities during the 1980s. These social and consumer values and attitudes were spread across product markets other than apparel and home furnishings and furniture. For example, we have seen the development of specialist stationery chains (Paperchase), which have offered individualism in stationery, greetings cards, gifts, pictures/prints and posters.

Service-products were given an opportunity for growth. An expansion of the availability of domestic finance led to rapid growth of both financial service-products and retail outlets. The banks and building societies were very active in expanding into adjacent service-product areas, e.g. real estate, travel, insurance, removals, etc. Much of this growth was due to government relaxation of its control over financial services and activities and its encouragement of the growth of a highly competitive service-product sector.

The role of IT (information technology) and information management has been extensive in its impact on the planning and control activities of distribution companies. The impact of EPOS (electronic point of sale) on inventory management and labour scheduling costs is well documented. The full impact of information sciences on strategic planning in those businesses is yet to be seen. However, there is already sufficient evidence to suggest that local marketing and store layout that reflect buying behaviour are but two problems likely to be addressed. The use of IT in product market augmentation, adding value to existing merchandise offers and extending product markets 'electronically' are clearly viable opportunities.

There has been considerable development in the sophistication of sourcing capabilities among the large multiple retailers. This development has been seen in organization structures as well as strategies. The sourcing strategies of large retailers have matched the changing preferences of consumers. The retailers have identified market sources for quality products with facilities to produce exclusive merchandise at competitive costs. They have also developed organization structures which enable these strategies to operate. Most significant is the merging of the buying and merchandising activities, which have become market-led and responsive to shifts in consumer preferences.

The role of operations management cannot be understated. Retailing is intensively competitive and the consumer is becoming increasingly selective. Thus, while competitive advantage is concerned with quality, variety and exclusivity, it is developed mindful of the fact that these are consumer 'desirable' – at a price. It is the function of operations management to deliver the response to the customer cost-effectively; in other words, it is the effective management of resources (capabilities and capacities) to offer an appropriate merchandise range at acceptable prices, at relevant locations and at relevant times for the customer.

Finally, we should consider the role of the customer. It is very clear that the age of mass merchandising is past. It has been replaced by targeting and differentiation. Research has suggested that consumers are not an aggregate mass, but comprise a range of customer groups, each with different preferences. It is understanding the importance of these differences and the extent to which they are shared which offers many retailing companies market opportunity. Preferences differ across customer groups and across product markets. For example, there are clearly discernible differences and preferences across socio-economic, demographic and socio-cultural groups. Equally, the production characteristics, or possibly the market environment characteristics (e.g. climate), of product markets can determine the characteristics of a retail offer. The issues concerning market segmentation and customer profiling are becoming important features in retailers' decision-making.

Positioning: a major element in retailing strategy

Within the business environment the retailer has developed a unique approach to strategy which has been dependent on a marketing philosophy. Retailers are, by the very nature of their business, in direct contact with their customers. This has the advantage of being able rapidly to identify and react to changes in the market-place. It is a very different form of market contact from their suppliers', because the retailer must consider not only the merchandise characteristics of the customer offer but also the store environment (and its location, size, etc.) and the service expectations of the customer. The offer made to the customer is manifested by the company's positioning strategy or statement. It is a visible response to the expectations of an identified target customer group, comprising merchandise, trading format and store environment and customer service, and is communicated in a relevant way to the selected or target customer group. At this point, we propose to define the concept in order that its importance can be considered within the context of the purpose of this book.

Positioning is then:

> the 'strategic' use of corporate marketing resources in response to an identified, customer-based, marketing opportunity. It is based upon the company's distinctive competences which are used to create (or maintain) competitive advantage(s) which reflect the expectations and perceptions of a target customer base. It requires a 'co-ordinating statement' to be made by merchandise selection, trading format and store environment, customer service and customer communications. The more closely the customer can identify with the 'offer' presented,

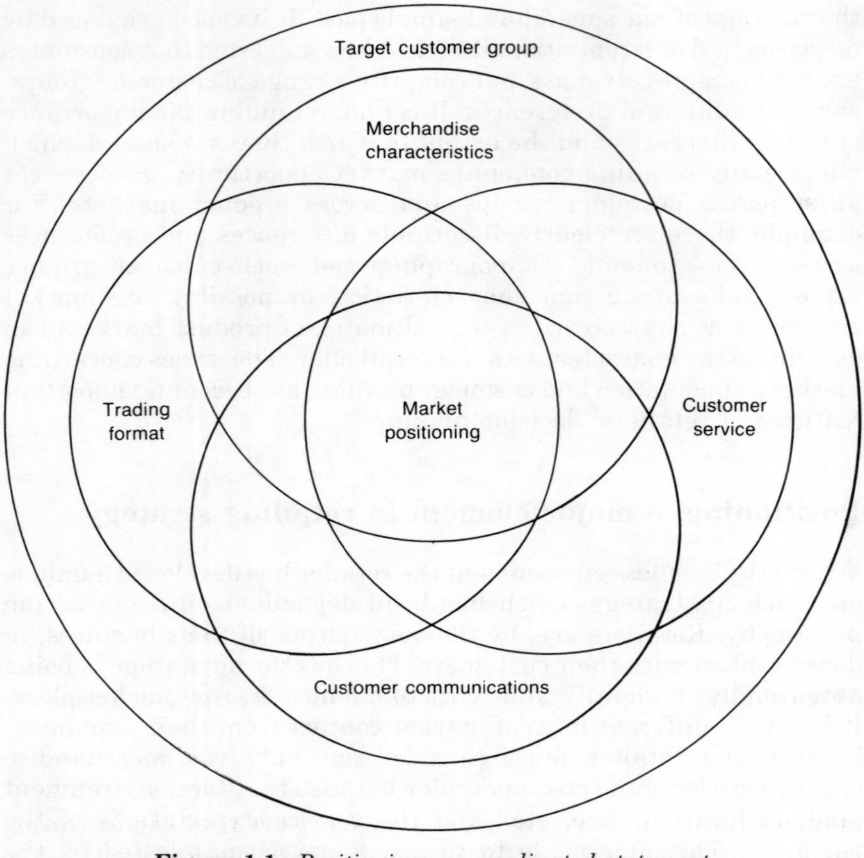

Figure 1.1 *Positioning: a co-ordinated statement*

the more comfortable will the customer be, and will respond in terms of shopping visit frequency, size of spend per visit, the number of items purchased each visit, the 'range' of purchases and thus the proportion of total spend allocated to the favoured store compared to that spent with competitors.

See Figure 1.1 which illustrates this principle.

The retailing developments of the 1970s and 1980s suggested that, to be successful, the retailer should consider the total market carefully and identify segments within it, which shared specific characteristics and which could, if addressed and satisfied, result in the retailer being considered as the major supplier for that customer group. The rapid development of Burton and Next using this approach is well chronicled and requires no repetition. More recent events in the area

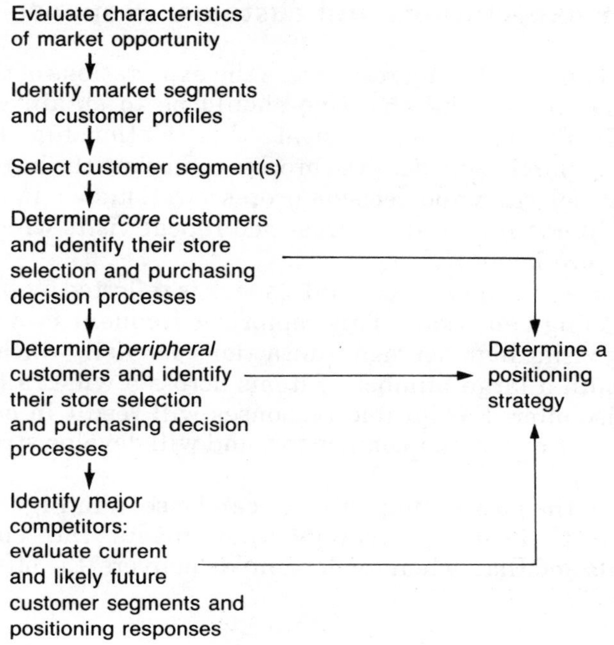

Figure 1.2 *Identifying customer segments (core and peripheral groups) to create a positioning strategy*

of 'niche retailing' have given reasons to believe that specialization can be pursued to too narrow a merchandise base offered, to too narrow a response to customer segment. Consequently, there are some clear lessons to be learned.

In Figure 1.2 we suggest that the initial research identifies both *core* and *peripheral* customer groups, which an offer may be directed towards. The purpose of this is simply to avoid over-specialization. The positioning strategy which may evolve from the research will have identified those aspects of the strategy (i.e. merchandise, customer service, trading format and store environment and communications) that can have major appeal to the core customer group, while also offering some interest to a peripheral group (and thereby producing traffic and revenue), the inclusion of which will not necessarily dilute the impact of the 'positioning statement'. Competitive reaction to current and future positioning strategy should be considered, and areas where corporate distinctive competence can be exercised (and corporate advantage developed) be identified and pursued.

Customer expectations and customer response

The basis of any marketing response is the expectations of the target customer group, and its objective should be to obtain a specific response. In Figure 1.3 we illustrate this relationship. The store selection and purchasing decision process comprises the basic search, comparison, selection and decision process, well known in the buyer behaviour literature. To it we must add repeat visits which reflect customer store loyalty.

The customer response that retailers seek is reflected by store visits and purchasing behaviour. This comprises frequent browsing and purchasing visits, high average transactions per visit, which, in turn, comprise both a large number of items across a wide range of the merchandise offer. Favourable responses will result in credibility for the retailer as a major competitor, and will develop strong store loyalty.

The role of the positioning strategy can be seen in Figure 1.4. By devising a positioning strategy that meets the customers' expectations and that, when implemented, 'delivers' the offer implies

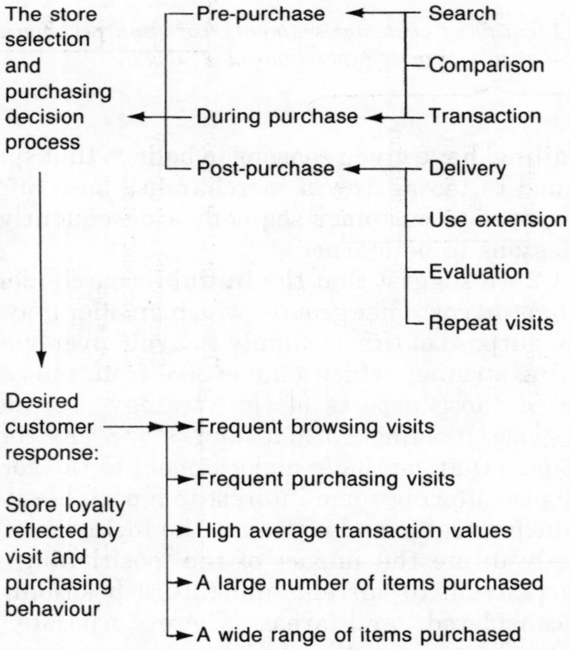

Figure 1.3 *Customer expectations and response*

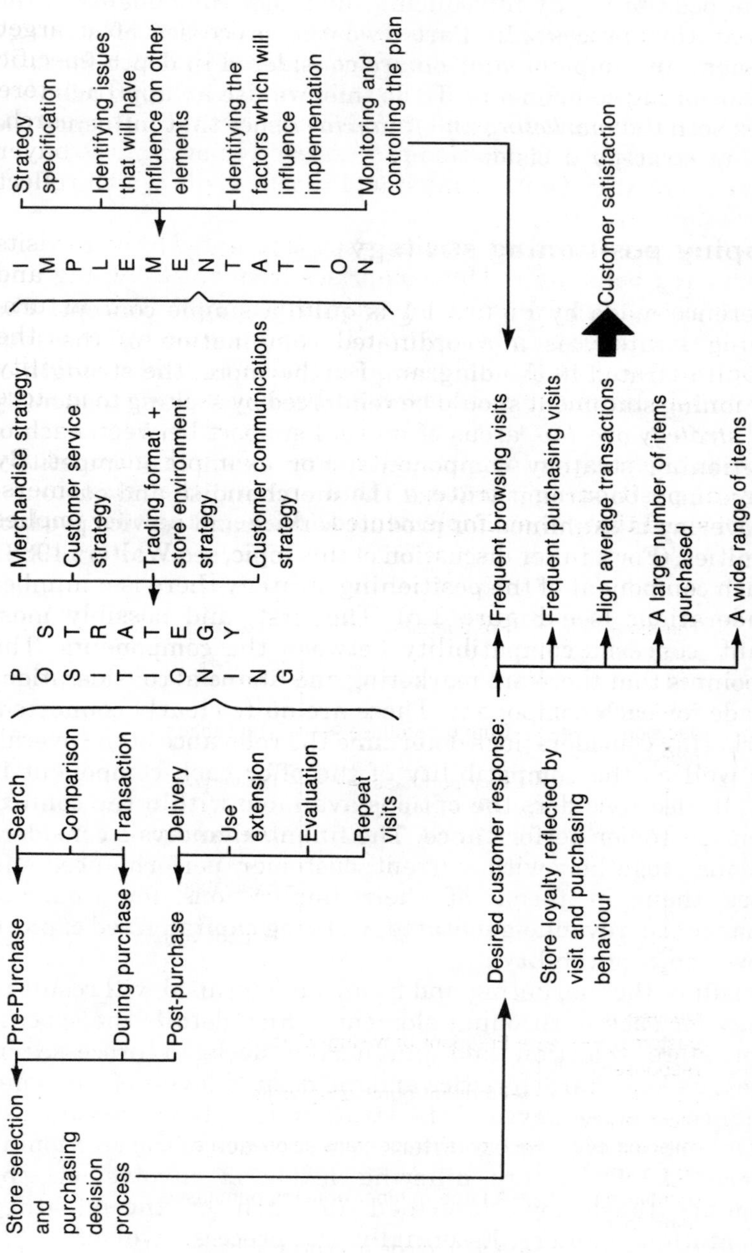

Figure 1.4 *The store selection and purchasing decision process: developing and implementing strategy*

that customer satisfaction is also achieved. Figure 1.4 expands the process of positioning by introducing the major components of the implementation process. In Part Two the processes of strategy development and implementation are considered in depth for each of the positioning components. To do this, we use an approach that considers both the *marketing* and *financial* issues that influence the positioning strategy decision.

Developing positioning strategy

The inference made by Figure 1.1 is quite a simple concept. The positioning strategy is a co-ordinated combination of the four elements illustrated in the diagram. Furthermore, the strength of the positioning statement should be reinforced by seeking to identify areas of *strategy overlap*, areas of mutual support between each of the positioning strategy components. For example, competitive advantage may be strengthened if the merchandise and customer service overlap is examined for product service and service product opportunities. (For a fuller discussion of this topic, see Walters 1988.)

For each component of the positioning strategy there is a number of considerations (see Figure 1.5). The first, and possibly most important, concerns compatibility between the components. The second point is that there are marketing and financial considerations to be made for each component. These are quite clearly connected. The marketing considerations determine the relevance of the overall offer as well as the compatibility of the offer each component is making. It also considers the options available within the context of current customer performance. The financial analysis considers the options, together with current customer performance, and evaluates them in terms of their implications for financial performance (i.e. revenue-generated, working capital, fixed capital, cash flow and profitability).

The result of the marketing and financial appraisal will result in a strategy for each positioning element, which details the specific customer store selection and purchasing decision processes it addresses, its key characteristics and the desired levels of customer performance to be achieved if the strategy is to be successful.

The implementation process differs between each of the positioning characteristics. There are differing levels of involvement by department; these are described in each of the strategy implementation chapters. Essentially, the process involves:

1. Detailing the strategy specification.

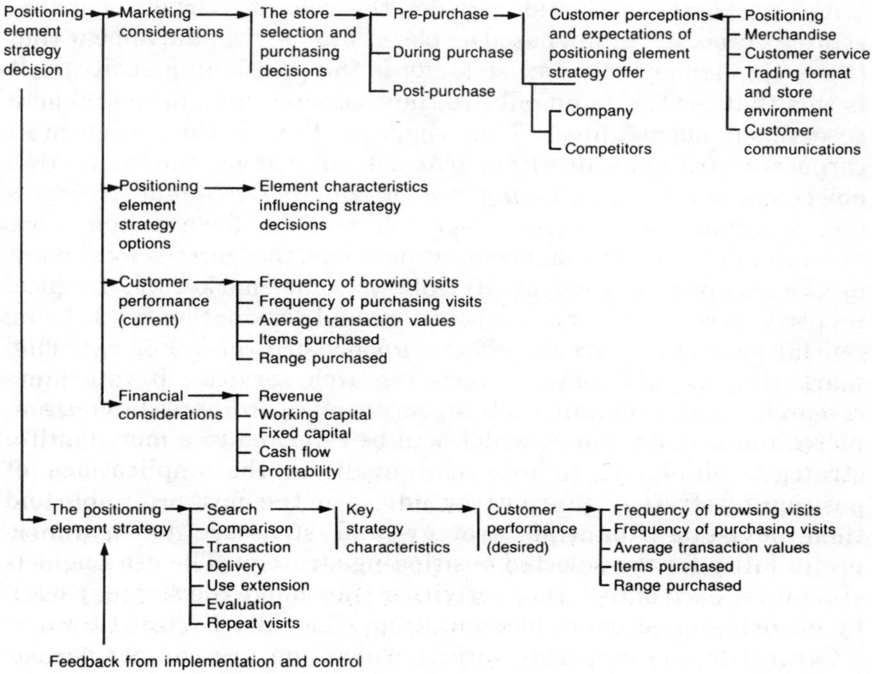

Figure 1.5 *Developing positioning strategy*

2. Considering the issues arising for each of the other positioning elements.
3. Identifying the factors that will influence successful implementation.
4. Developing an operational plan and determining responsibilities and performance requirements.
5. Developing measures for monitoring successful implementation.

Retailing strategy: a process and the role of marketing

Our observations of company strategies suggest that, while the organizational structures developed for their implementation differ, their philosophy and the process used have much in common. It is also true to say that many companies have no formalized strategy formulation process; indeed, many have no formal strategic plans. This is becoming less the case though, particularly for the larger companies.

At this point we should consider the role of marketing in the strategy process. Again, based on observations, it would appear that the overt element of retail strategy is the positioning strategy. It is this that manifests an offer to the customer (an offer based on a researched opportunity). This suggests that within an overall corporate strategic direction, one determined by the company's objectives, it is the *positioning strategy* and its *functional* strategies (i.e. merchandise, customer service, trading format and store environment and customer communications) that are the focal point of the company's strategy. It follows that marketing, finance, property, personnel, systems, operations and distribution, while being crucial for success, are, in effect, *support strategies*. For example, marketing in this context offers research services; it interprets research; creates planning intelligence; and co-ordinates buying and merchandising decisions, which will be reflected in a merchandise strategy. Similarly, finance will evaluate the implications of positioning strategy alternatives, advise on the most profitable and then devise a financial strategy and structure to maximize profitability for the selected positioning strategy. The argument is similar for each of the other activities; they make the strategy work by ensuring effective implementation. (Consider Figure 1.6.)

Central to the corporate direction decision are the companies' objectives. In Chapters 2 and 3 we discuss how these may be considered as critical success factors and how the components to these (their key variables) may be utilized in the planning process. Figure 1.7 lists the five critical success factors common to all retailing companies.

The discussion in Chapters 2 and 3 develops an argument for considering retailing strategy to be a hierarchy of interdependent strategies. The board of directors will decide on the companies' financial and marketing objectives and will consider the implications of these for the company's critical success factors. The board will also express a view on the corporate direction the company should pursue. This will reflect its considered view of opportunities and threats, corporate distinctive competences, the requirements for competitive advantage and an overall view of the risk involved. Thus, they may opt for a relatively low-risk corporate strategy of consolidation and productivity, or they may consider that the opportunities offered by diversification outweigh the risk involved. Clearly, a combination of corporate strategies is possible, provided that both the management and financial capabilities and capacities are available.

The corporate direction may influence the positioning strategy. Clearly, there will be little or no influence if a consolidation and productivity strategy is pursued. However, the functional strategy

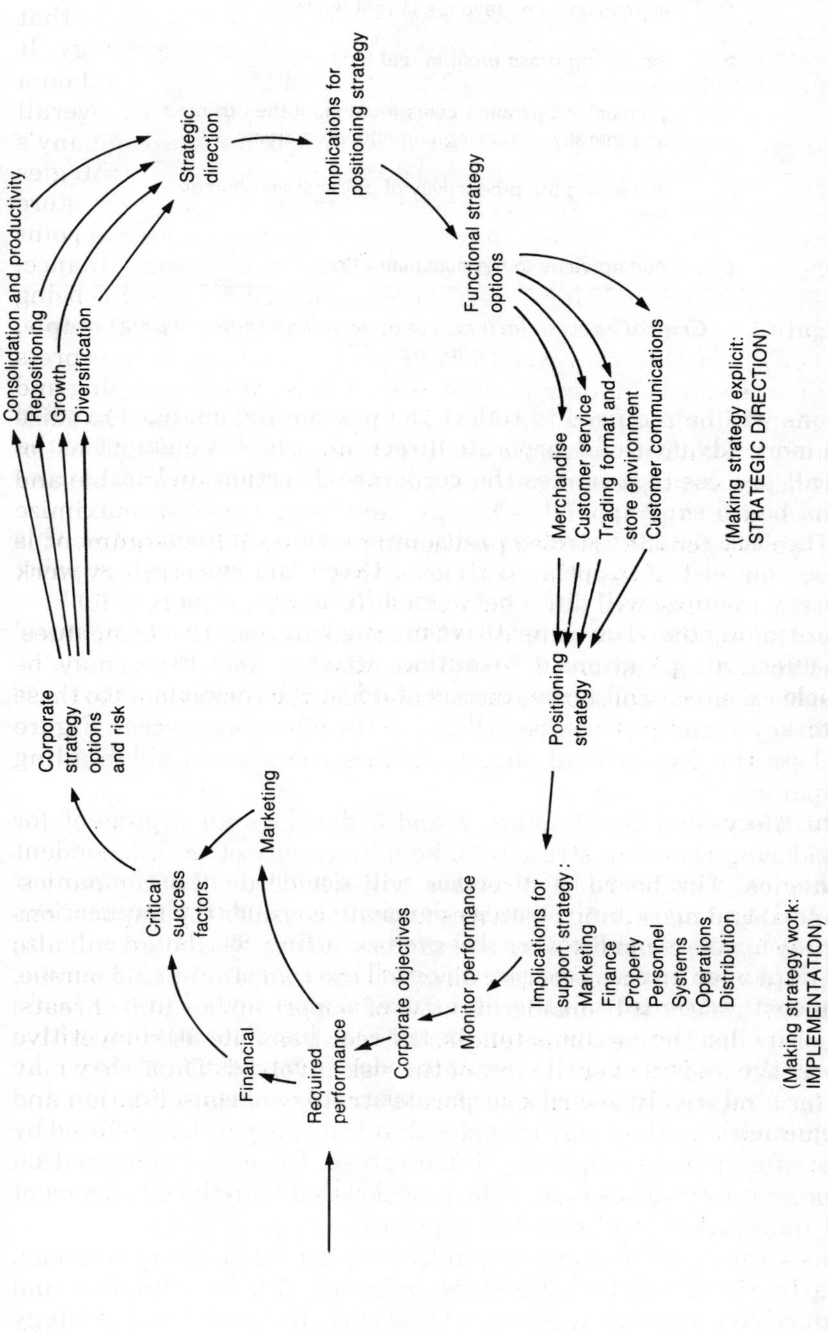

Figure 1.6 *Developing and implementing retail strategy: an overall view*

1. Increasing sales revenue in real terms.
2. Increasing gross profit in real terms.
3. Containing operating costs throughout the business and thereby increasing contribution margins.
4. Increasing the productivity of physical and human assets.
5. Adding value to the customer offer.

Figure 1.7 *Critical success factors: common denominators of successful retailing*

options will be required to reflect the positioning changes implied by a more adventurous corporate direction. It is this element of the overall process that makes the corporate direction and intentions of the board explicit.

To be successful the strategy must be effectively implemented. This is the role of the support strategies. Often the role each support strategy assumes will differ between different forms of retail offers. A positioning based on competitive pricing will require an extremely cost-effective operations/distribution activity. Others (e.g. motor vehicle exhausts and tyres services) find that location is critical for success.

Summary

In this text we offer our view on the role of marketing in the context of retail strategy – both strategy development and implementation. We have, over recent years, observed retailing companies making and implementing strategic decisions. These observations, together with contributions from the literature, are presented in this book. We also offer the reader a number of case histories/studies, which afford the opportunity to examine decisions taken against the background (and the benefit) of the experiences and practices of other companies.

CHAPTER 2

The role of marketing in strategic decision-making

Introduction

For the larger retailer the increased emphasis on corporate strategy has often been led by an increased awareness of the importance of retail marketing. This has led to:

1. Clear definitions of market segments, target customers and retail offers needed to reach them, encompassing merchandise, trading format, customer service and communications.
2. Emphasis on the creation of exclusive positioning through the composition of the retail offer strategy to develop competitive advantage.
3. The development of the retail brand to emphasize the selected positioning, supported by retailer-branded merchandise and services.
4. An awareness of the value of information to monitor markets and customer shopping behaviour for both strategic and operational planning.

We would suggest that awareness of the value of corporate and strategic planning has been preceded by the increasing contribution to retailers' businesses on the part of retail marketing. Examples of this can be seen in the changing role of retailer own-brand merchandise. Initially, own-brands were seen as a means by which low-price alternatives to manufacturers' brands could be offered, together with an opportunity to share (at low investment cost) in the growth markets brought about by manufacturers' product development activities. Subsequently, the retailer own-brand became a major plank for building positioning images to reflect exclusivity, quality and innovation in their businesses.

We make the suggestion, then, that for retailing and retail strategy the role of marketing has been important. It has introduced retailing to the concept of being 'market-led' businesses, orienting their short-, medium- and long-term activities towards maximizing customer satisfaction and towards achieving a high level of performance of those *critical success factors* that are important to all retailing businesses:

1. Increasing sales revenue in real terms by increasing customer visit frequencies, customer transaction size and customer spend across the range per visit.
2. Increasing gross profit in real terms by improved margin management.
3. Containing operating costs throughout the business.
4. Increasing the productivity of physical and human assets.
5. Adding value to the customer offer.

Objectives and critical success factors

If the process or strategic planning is directed towards achieving these factors it is more likely that business decisions will be successful if they are supported by effective marketing decisions.

Each of these critical success factors (CSFs) can be regarded as comprising a number of *key variables.* Many of these will be seen not to be mutually exclusive, and some may not be directly influenced by marketing decisions. Furthermore, one CSF may well be dependent upon another. As a general guide, the CSFs and key variables indicate the main areas where effective operating systems either need to be in place or need to be developed. Examples of CSFs and key variables are shown as Figure 2.1. The interrelationships of key variables with CSFs is suggested by the figures in brackets indicating other CSFs influenced.

Before discussing the process or strategy, we should consider the link between objectives and goals. Hofer and Schendel (1978) suggest:

> We consider goals to be the ultimate, long-run, open-ended attributes or ends a person or organisation seeks, while we consider objectives to be the intermediate-term targets that are necessary but not sufficient for the satisfaction of goals.
>
> It follows . . . that goals are not achievable since they are not bounded. Thus, it is never possible to maximise profits, as there always will be some profitable options that might have been pursued that were not . . . . In combination, though, goals do reflect the purposes (or missions) of an organisation.
>
> Objectives can be realised, however, since they are simply milestones in the never-ending pursuit of goals. As such all objectives have four components: 1) the attribute sought, 2) an index for measuring progress

Critical success factors	Key variables	
1. Increasing sales revenue in real terms by increasing customer visit frequencies and customer transaction size per visit.	Customer stock availability	(2) (3)
	Depot stock availability	(2) (3)
	Branch reorder/replenishment	(2) (3)
	Merchandise selection effectiveness	(2) (3)
	Co-ordinated merchandise ranges	(2) (3) (5)
	Pricing and price competitiveness	(2) (3)
	Customer perceptions of merchandise and service	(2) (3) (5)
	Provision of sales data	(2) (4)
	Merchandise/space control	(2) (4)
	Improved sales forecasting	(2)
2. Increasing gross profit in real terms by improved margin management.	Supplier performance monitoring of availability, terms of trade, merchandise range development	(3)
	Monitoring and adjusting 'in-house' distribution service and costs	(3)
	Optimizing the number of suppliers	
	Sales/stock data	
	Improving contribution from merchandise range	
	Cash controls	(3)
3. Containing operating costs throughout the business and thereby increasing contribution margins.	Review accountability levels (i.e. head office, regional offices, distribution facilities and branches)	
	Identify costs by activity (i.e. head office, regional offices, branches and support activity centres, e.g. distribution)	
4. Increasing the productivity of physical and human assets.	Increasing sales per square foot and employee	(1)
	Increasing contribution per square foot and employee	(2)
	Increasing throughput of distribution facilities (i.e. vehicle utilization, stocktime in depots, picking rates)	
5. Adding value to the customer offer.	Adding service to existing merchandise ranges (e.g. installation services, disposal of replaced durables, wardrobe services in fashion)	(1) (2)
	Expanding merchandise range coverage to include customer perceived added value items (e.g. time and 'energy' saving aspects in convenience food ranges)	(1) (2)
	Offering facilities to encourage customers to spend more time in branches (e.g. crêche facilities, delivery, credit, advice centres, new product information)	

Items in brackets indicate key variables that influence other critical success factors.

Figure 2.1 *Critical success factors and key variables*

toward the attribute, 3) a target or hurdle to be achieved, and 4) a time frame within which the target or hurdle is to be achieved.

This is a useful definition for retail strategy because we can describe corporate intentions in these terms. For example, corporate goals:

- Description of the business mission.

- A positioning statement within that mission.
- An explicit view of the requirements to achieve sustainable competitive advantage.

We shall consider these to be components of corporate direction, together with corporate objectives that are quantifiable and include:

- Volume growth (sales, market (segment) share).
- Efficiency (productivity).
- Resource utilization (ROI, RONW).
- Contribution to owners (dividends, EPS).
- Contribution to customers (merchandise, store environment and customer service characteristics measured by assessing attitudes and perceptions and analyzing purchasing behaviour).
- Contribution to employees (rates of pay, pensions, employment stability, achievement of job satisfaction, exploitation of development potential).
- Contribution to suppliers (sales growth, continuity of supply).
- Contribution to society (charitable donations, wider employment concern support, selective sourcing).
- Contributions to the environment (store design and architecture, energy use, packaging materials specifications, attitude to tidiness).

Thus we can see that within the context of its corporate goals the company must develop a series of objectives, which will guide it towards achieving the goals. Ideally, they will be quantifiable and be set within a time-frame for achievement.

If we can break down the objectives into small but significant features of the business, we shall be able to understand better the significance of the objectives under consideration on each component of the business. This will in turn be useful when considering strategic alternatives, because such an analysis will identify areas of potential strength and weakness that may enhance or constrain the achievement of any objective. For example, where we have the conceptually simple objective of sales growth, we need to consider a number of component issues, such as the merchandise selection and its availability in-store; frequency of customer visits; and customer purchases when in the store. An analysis of these components might uncover areas where performance could be enhanced (by increasing service level, say) or where no room for improvement exists (due to capacity problems, say). Furthermore, consideration of the operational conditions of the components themselves may be useful in formulating a view on the supporting role of marketing. It is here that we can usefully use the concept of critical success factors and key variables because, by matching objectives with critical success factors, the marketing implications can be readily identified.

All retailing businesses have objectives similar to those we identified earlier. They are derived from an amalgamation of planning assumptions. They should have performance monitors to indicate growth and success, which will include targets to:

1. Increase sales revenue in real terms by a specified percentage.
2. Increase the number of purchasing customers per week.
3. Increase the size of average customer purchase.
4. Increase the range of customer purchases.
5. Increase gross profit in real terms by a specified percentage.
6. Adjust sales mix by product type and pack type (with considerations of own-brand participation).
7. Rationalize the assortment (increase product lines where appropriate, reduce and delist those lacking customer appeal and with low demand).
8. Reduce operating costs (or maintain them at an acceptable level).
9. Reduce stockholding (or maintain at an acceptable level) in branches and warehouses.
10. Expand the number (and possibly the size) of branches, or possibly;
11. Rationalize branches (optimal sizes).

Qualitative objectives (often called aims) may include:

12. Exercising better management controls by the provision of accurate, up-to-date and timely data through management information and cost-effective systems that maximize benefit and flexibility and minimize cost and overheads.
13. Improving customer service.
14. Improving product quality.
15. Improving store ambience.

Objectives can be matched with critical success factors, and this is illustrated in Table 2.1. There is likely to be some overlap. For example, objective 7 (rationalize the assortment) has significance for both gross profit improvement (CSF2) and cost-containment (CSF3). Others may exist, depending on the nature of the business.

Hierarchies of strategy in retailing

Before considering the role of marketing in the strategy process, we should consider the role of strategy in retailing in more detail.

The importance of explicit positioning has been discussed earlier. If positioning is seen to be of primary importance in that it indicates

Table 2.1 Linking objectives, critical success factors and key variables

Objectives	Critical success factors	Key variables	
1. Increase sales revenue 2. Increase purchasing customers 3. Increase customer transactions 4. Increase range of customer purchases 10. Expand the number (and size) of branches	1. Increasing sales revenue in real terms by increasing customer visit frequencies and customer transaction size per visit	Customer stock availability	(2) (3)
		Depot stock availability	(2) (3)
		Branch reorder/replenishment	(2) (3)
		Merchandise selection effectiveness	(2) (3)
		Co-ordinated merchandise ranges	(2) (3) (5)
		Pricing and price competitiveness	(2) (3)
		Customer perceptions of merchandise and service	(2) (3) (5)
		Provision of sales data	(2) (4)
		Merchandise/space control	(2) (4)
		Improved sales forecasting	(2)
5. Increase gross profit 6. Adjust sales mix by product group 7. Rationalize the assortment	2. Increasing gross profit in real terms by improved margin management	Supplier performance monitoring of availability, terms of trade, merchandise range development	(3)
		Monitoring and adjusting 'in-house' distribution service and costs	(3)
		Optimizing the number of suppliers	
		Sales/stock data	
		Improving contribution from merchandise range	
		Cash controls	(3)

8. Reduce operating costs (or maintain them at an acceptable level) 9. Reduce stockholding (or optimize) in branches and warehouses 12. Exercise better management controls using cost-effective MIS	3. Containing operating costs throughout the business and thereby increasing contribution margins	Review *accountability levels* (i.e. head office, regional offices, distribution facilities and branches) Identify *costs* by activity (i.e. head office, regional offices, branches and support activity centres, e.g. distribution)	
11. Rationalize branch sizes (optimal sizes, staff and stockholding)	4. Increasing the productivity of physical and human assets	Increasing sales per square foot and employee	(1)
		Increasing contribution per square foot and employee	(2)
		Increasing throughput of distribution facilities (i.e. vehicle utilization, stocktime in depots, picking rates)	
13. Improve customer service 14. Improve product quality 15. Improve store ambience	5. Adding value to the customer offer	Adding service to existing merchandise ranges (e.g. installation services, disposal of replaced durables, wardrobe services in fashion)	(1) (2)
		Expanding merchandise range coverage to include customer perceived added value items (e.g. time and 'energy' saving aspects in convenience food ranges)	(1) (2)
		Offering facilities to encourage customers to spend more time in branches (e.g. crêche facilities, delivery, credit, advice centres, new product information)	

to the selected target market the precise nature of the retail offer, it follows that marketing, finance, property, personnel and systems are facilitating or support activities, which implement the position strategy, comprised of merchandise, service and environment offers combined to make the positioning statement/strategy explicit.

This is an important issue because it suggests three levels of organizational strategy, and within these marketing is seen to be in a supporting role. Clearly, marketing is important in the role of identifying opportunity and monitoring progress towards maximizing corporate returns from that opportunity, but it does so within a hierarchy of strategies.

For our purposes we consider there to be three levels of organizational strategy:

1. *Corporate strategy* is concerned with answering the questions: 'What businesses are we in?' And 'Should we be in them?' It is very much a macro-concept, and is of particular interest to both single format and conglomerate retailers. It relates to ways and means by which objectives may be met by focusing on competing in specific industries or product markets. Defining distinctive competences and competitive advantage(s) is usually the most important component of strategy at this level. Conglomerate retailers, such as Kingfisher (Woolworth Holdings), J. Sainsbury and Sears, may well develop different strategies for each business unit.
2. *Functional strategy* leads to the initiation of activities that interpret the positioning statement or strategy of the company. We discussed the four elements, merchandise, trading style/format, customer service and customer communication strategies, in Chapter 1.
3. *Support strategies* are activities that facilitate or enable the other strategies to be implemented. Thus we have marketing operations, finance and administration, systems, property and personnel strategies. In this book we focus on marketing, and our thesis is that given the interlocking relationships that exist, marketing is closely linked with, and should be developed alongside, business and functional strategies. In this context it is a support or service activity and is very much involved with implementing the positioning strategy adopted by the company.

Strategic options

In developing the options of corporate strategy, whether for the single format retailer or for business units within a conglomerate, a number of critical questions must be asked:

1. Is recent (marketing and financial) performance likely to continue to be satisfactory? If not, are the objectives that have been set realistic?
2. What is an acceptable level of risk?
3. Will existing competitive advantage(s) be sustainable? If not, what is required?
4. Will the current market positioning require change?
5. Which of the following strategic options appear most suitable in order to achieve the objectives for the next planning period (say, five years)?
   (a) *Consolidation and productivity*: increased performance from the existing resource base to provide margin, volume and asset-utilization improvements.
   (b) *Repositioning*: meeting the changing needs of existing customers and related customer segments.
   (c) *Growth*: expansion into related formats, merchandise areas or trading environments, or possibly new territories.
   (d) *Diversification*: expansion into new merchandise areas, new trading environments, customer services or service products; consideration of conglomerate, regional and international activities.

Strategic options, risk and the planning gap

In Figure 2.2 the notion of the planning gap is illustrated. This is the 'gap' left between the projected ideal future performance and the performance that can be expected if no action is taken. The wider the gap the more likely it is that the company will move away from its existing base of knowledge and expertise. Often this is seen as an indication of risk: the wider the planning gap, the greater the risk. It is not suggested that the strategy options are successive or progressive, but they are presented as strategic options that are based on progressively increasing risk. Some examples of each follow.

Consolidation and productivity improvements

Consolidation and improvements in productivity increase performance from the existing resource base (both of physical and human resources) by enhancing both margin and volume improvement.

They can include pricing adjustments, product range adjustments (to achieve greater margins) and outlet rationalization (to achieve optimum branch or department profitability). Such activities are

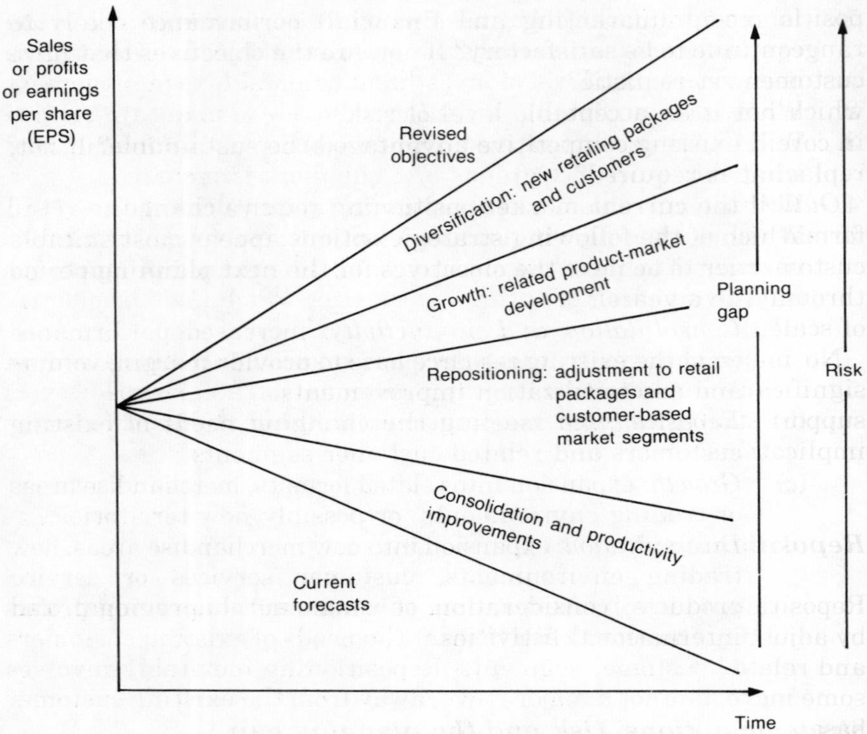

Figure 2.2 *Alternative methods of filling the planning gap (Source: Knee and Walters, 1985)*

conducted within the existing retail product package and customer segment.

Productivity may be increased by improving jobs and work practices to obtain a more effective use of existing staff.

Sales and profit per selling area may be increased by introducing more effective store design, layout and fixturing. Greater productivity from inventing investment may be available by reviewing location and supply chain management.

Price changes (increases or reductions) can be seen to influence performance. Increases may be effected for product groups for which the consumer is price-insensitive (price-elastic products) which fall into the category of luxury, monpoly, exclusive, impulsively purchased. Decreases may be effective for competitive product groups where the customer is price-sensitive (price-inelastic products). Price reductions, however, require a compensatory increase in volume, for without such increases there will be an overall decrease in profit.

Range rationalization, i.e. range adjustments, to meet market position and profit targets by reviewing the assortment (lines in the range) and variety (individual stock keeping units), in order to give customers choice at a level of investment acceptable to management which provides availability of sufficient stock to maintain service in core or main product ranges. The possibility of eliminating and replacing entire product groups and suppliers is included.

Outlet rationalization, i.e. changes in the features of the retail format (store size, layout, location), in order to retain or attract customers and to meet competition; and to enhance productivity through the adoption of optimal store sizes which yield economies of scale.

No major changes to the 'offer' are made, hence there are no significant implications for the functional strategies. However, support strategies, such as operations, are likely to identify major implications.

Repositioning

Repositioning involves expanding revenues and improving profits by adjusting the retail offer to meet the needs of existing customers and related customer segments. Repositioning inevitably involves some move, but not a major move, away from the existing customer base.

As we discussed in Chapter 1, positioning is achieved by adjusting the product mix or market posture, to address the specific needs of a market segment more effectively, and thereby to strengthen its position within a segment. It can involve all elements of functional strategy, but typically may focus on one component such as merchandise and offer improved quality and product exclusivity or variety.

Growth

Growth may be achieved by changes to the retail offer which are either 'product-led' or 'market-led'; by adding ranges to the existing assortment; by increasing the size of new outlets and closing older, smaller branches; by expanding geographically; or by campaigning to win over customers who did not perceive that their requirements had been met. Such requirements could relate to assortment or customer service. The expansion of the outlet base would be to exploit economies of replication where the operating economics of the rationalized stores are maximized.

Example

Product-market development is the major modification of a market position by extending products or markets into related areas. It builds on strengths and develops specializations. The extension could depend on an original specialization or direction.

Success often depends on skilful implementation of a package that meets emerging consumer requirements. Risk and opportunity are reduced by extending areas of existing strengths. Such an approach allows the specialization to be retained as a base for successful product-market diversification. Boots and Woolworth (Kingfisher) are following this strategy with their specialist children's stores.

Product-market development can be a means of modifying the impact of seasonal trading and changing market conditions. Where it does not build on existing strengths, it may be necessary to 'buy in' skills not currently available within the company. A joint venture with a company with complementary skills can be a worthwhile alternative to the risk of untried new employees. This also offers the potential for adding compatible merchandise ranges for which there are no skills within the company. The Sainsbury Home Base venture was one in which overall risk was shared with GB Inno BM, who provided much needed skills in DIY, and with Laura Ashley, who provided a strong element of fashion to the stores.

Clearly, there are strong implications for both functional and support strategies. The extent of the changes will depend strongly on the direction selected for growth.

Diversification

If both the retail format and the customer base are totally changed, the company will move towards being a retail conglomerate. This quite often requires a greater number of different skills and a different view of strategy from those of a specialist retailer.

Diversification is aimed at increasing volume by moving into markets that have no link with the business. It involves the company in new products and new markets, as well as often in selling from new types of outlets.

The numerous problems of a diversified approach include: a clash of disparate corporate cultures; a need to harmonize unrelated management skills; a disparity of customer service offerings; and different approaches to fixed and working capital. This requires a strong but 'hands off' approach on the part of central management. The approach to marketing in this situation is usually to devolve the decision-making and to allow the subsidiary to operate both functional and support strategies within an overall agreed corporate strategy, provided that the required financial performance is achieved.

Strategic options: the influence of the business environment

Any strategic option must be considered within the context of whether or not, in the light of recent performance, it is feasible. It is important to consider the macro-performance of the company's operating environment, i.e. that of the economy, the industry, as well as that of the company. During such an analysis firm indicators or trends may be identifiable which will shape or influence the performance of the company during its planning horizon and consequently determine the size of the planning gap.

Earlier, we suggested that successful retailing largely depended on co-ordinating the functional activities involved in creating an exchange environment. Any corporate strategy must be capable of being implemented coherently by the accompanying functional strategies — merchandise, trading format/style, customer service and customer communications — to achieve a coherent positioning strategy. The role of customer communications is to ensure that the overall strategy is made clear to potential customers (the customer base) and is understood.

Co-ordination across the functional activities will avoid dysfunction across different parts of the retail marketing strategy, which would be misleading to the consumer. Furthermore, such an approach will ensure that integrated planning occurs.

Summary

In this chapter we have introduced the reader to the notion that strategy in retailing companies is likely to be most successful when the company is marketing-led. The growing influence of marketing in retailing has led to an increasing sophistication in their decision-making processes.

The discussion considered the need for the planning process to keep in mind its performance when measured against critical success factors indicating the sales, profit, productivity and added-value performance of the company. Critical success factors were discussed in the context of marketing and financial objectives.

The nature of strategic alternatives, and the need for strategy to be considered at three levels, were both discussed. Corporate, functional and support strategy was explained by considering the primary requirement to be a clearly articulated positioning strategy, implemented by a co-ordinated amalgamation of merchandise, customer service, trading format and communications strategies.

Marketing was described as a support strategy with a service role which included research for market and customer definition, competitive advantage requirements, sourcing alternatives, promotional effectiveness and the levels of consumer satisfaction achieved.

CHAPTER 3

The role of marketing in retail strategy

Introduction

Chapter 2 introduced the notion of a hierarchy of strategies. Three levels of strategy were suggested:

1. Corporate strategy, comprising consolidation and productivity activities:
   (a) repositioning,
   (b) growth,
   (c) diversification.
2. Functional strategy comprising a positioning strategy with components of:
   (a) merchandise,
   (b) trading format,
   (c) customer service,
   (d) customer communications.
3. Support strategies, which implement the strategic direction derived by the requirements of the corporate and functional strategies. Typically these are:
   (a) marketing,
   (b) finance,
   (c) operations,
   (d) property,
   (e) human resources,
   (f) systems.

Our thesis is that *process* operates most effectively when functional strategy operates within the direction (or context) of corporate strategy and consequently the support strategies should be working within the context of both corporate and functional strategies. Clearly, the organization structures of most retailing companies do not infer this. Our observations suggest that while the organization charts show the conventional structures of business organizations (i.e. managing director/chief executive supported by a marketing, finance, operations directorate), it is the way in which the overall organization is made to work that differentiates the successful from the unsuccessful.

Some examples might help. Consider the situation in which a company identifies a problem in which its sales and profit show a declining trend. Research shows that the company's customer base is steadily ageing and visiting its outlets less frequently and spending less. The research also shows the market to be growing rapidly and competitors are increasing both turnover and profit. Clearly, the company must reconsider its market positioning (as well as its mission and objectives). It could attempt to increase its operating margins by rationalizing outlets, merchandise and operations (a *consolidation and productivity strategy*), or seek to participate in the more profitable market segment (by pursuing a *repositioning strategy*). This was very much the case for Dickens and Jones, which, after identifying the problem, undertook a major repositioning strategy by modifying the merchandise offer, store environment, customer services and customer communications (Walters 1986).

Both Sainsbury and Tesco are pursuing *growth strategies* by using economies of replication. Having rationalized their outlets (by closing small units and opening large, optimal-sized stores) they are expanding their successful formats on a geographical base; Tesco rationalized its non-food merchandise range. Here we have examples of consolidation and productivity and growth strategies.

Dixon (audio visual products and brown and white durables with Curry) pursued a *growth strategy* by expanding its merchandise offer into a range of categories which were adjacent to its mainstream merchandise offer (and therefore 'manageable' from a sales, display and distribution point of view) but also it was 'accepted' by customers who saw it as a logical extension of the merchandise range and who (until recently) expanded their range of purchases.

A retail strategy model

These case studies are examples of how the strategy model works. While we do not presume to suggest that the model outlined in Figure 3.1 was used by each of the four companies discussed, we would suggest that it can be used to *explain and describe* the process of strategy in retailing. The model in Figure 3.1 suggests that the critical success factors (and key variables) have a major part to play

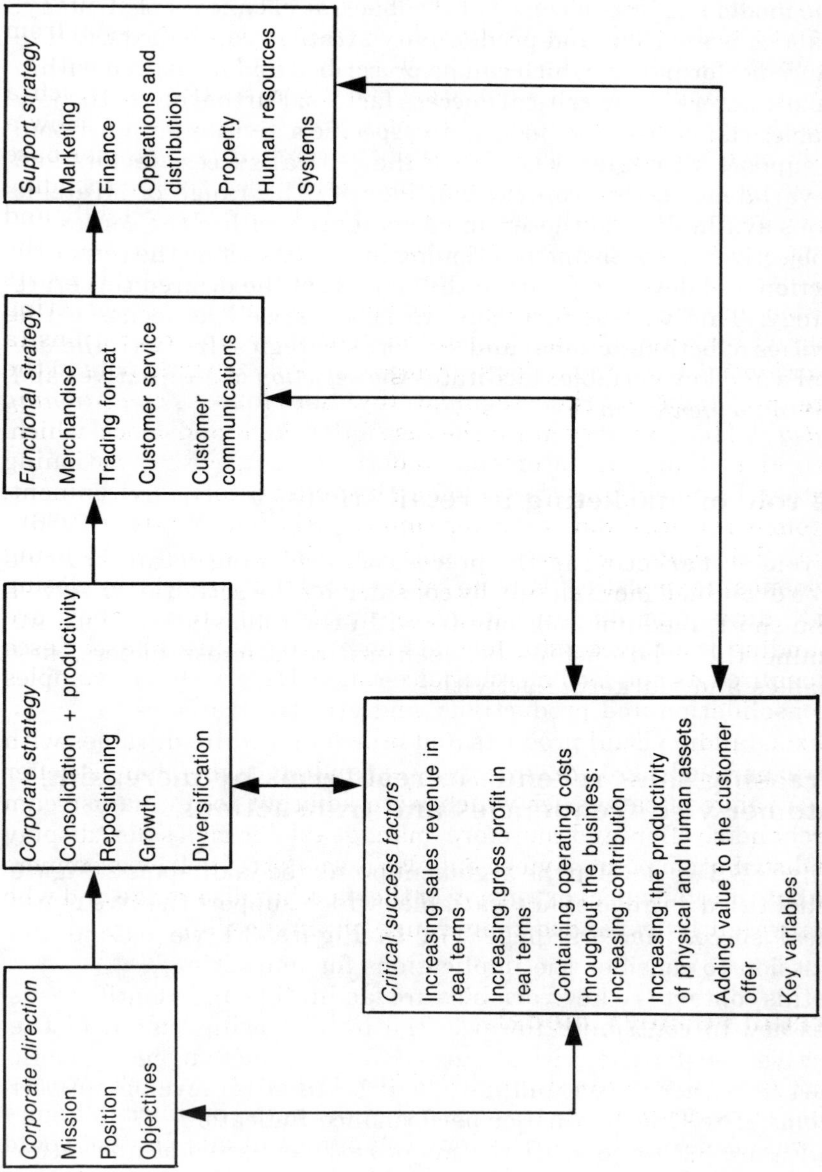

Figure 3.1 *Linking the elements of strategic decision-making*

in both *planning required performance* and providing information for the *control* of the business in order to meet objectives.

The model suggests a constant feedback at each level of strategy. Thus a consolidation and productivity strategy can be expected to produce performance, which can be prescribed and measured within the parameters of the critical success factors. Furthermore, the key variables can be useful in identifying specific activities for functional and support strategies. The use of the critical success factors and key variables in this context can identify the range of strategic options available, and these can be evaluated within the context of the objectives, mission and positioning intentions set by the corporate direction and developed within the context of the desired corporate strategy. This will in turn contain risk, as well as focusing the activities of both functional and support strategies. In short, the use of CSFs and key variables facilitates the *selection* of alternatives and their *implementation*.

The role of marketing in retail strategy

The role of marketing in the process of developing retail strategy can be examined more closely by considering the activities involved in the short, medium and long term. In the following sections we examine the relationships between critical success factors, key variables and marketing activities.

Increasing sales revenue in real terms by increasing customer visit frequencies and transactions

In Figure 3.2 we develop the argument presented in Chapter 2. Figure 2.1 identified a range of key variables which support the five major critical success factors (page 17). In Figure 3.1 we extend the discussion to consider the implications for marketing.

In this context the key variables are facilitators and identify tasks necessary to contribute towards the overall achievement of the objectives set for the critical success factor. They suggest specific issues to be addressed and may well be used to develop support systems. The CSF is a major performance indicator.

In Figure 3.2 we identify the major tasks expected of marketing in the achievement of this critical success factor. Essentially, it is to attract customers, to persuade them to purchase from the merchandise assortment and to continue to do so. These tasks can be considered in more detail. For example, customer attraction can

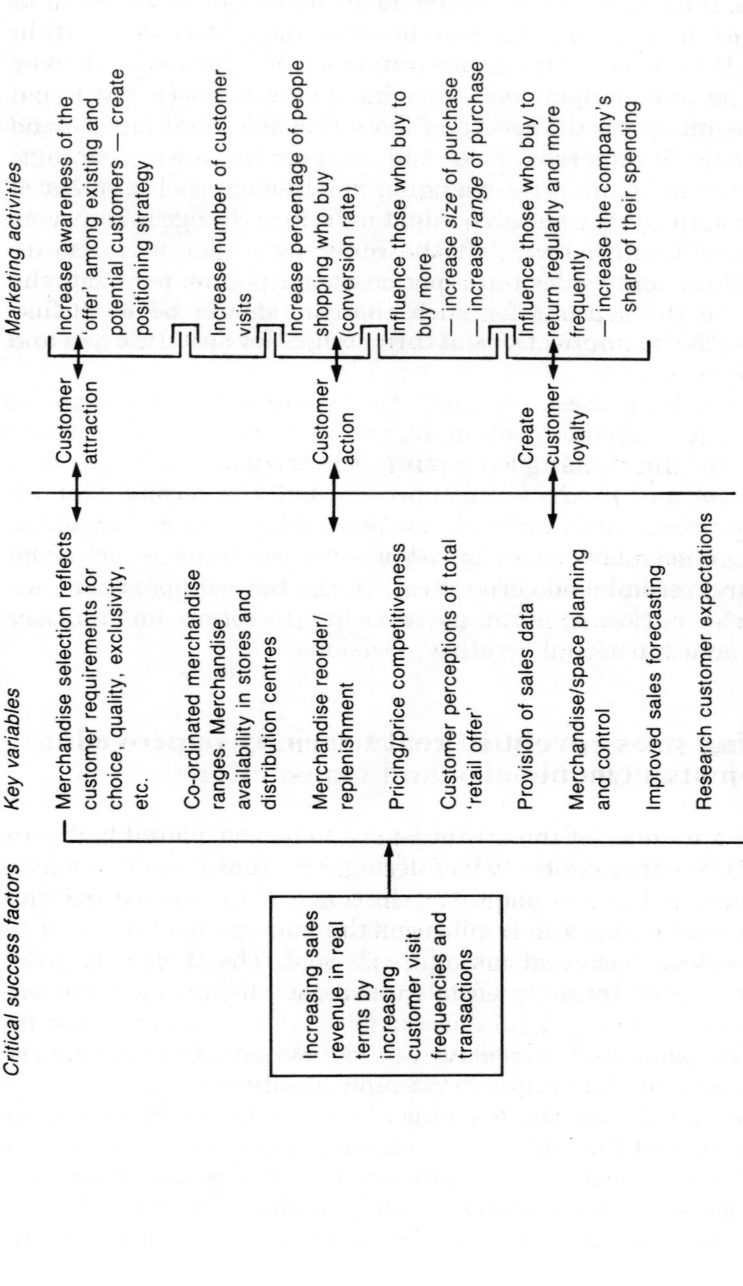

Figure 3.2 *Marketing activities identify corporate needs*

be achieved by developing an increased awareness of the company's offer among existing and potential customers. This will require research to establish the validity of the offer to both groups of customers. Subsequently, recommendations will be required as to the changes to be made to the merchandise and related issues if the offer is to have appeal. There are a number of issues arising here. One may be that competitive offers have become more attractive, and as a result of this the company should consider making changes (rationalizing its merchandise and outlets, reviewing pricing, adjusting service) to meet the changing requirements of the customer base. Alternatively, the research might indicate a change in consumer characteristics which have left the company's offer with limited appeal and reducing sales total (per customer pound, per customer items). Here the reasons for such changes should be identified, together with the implications of the changes for specific aspects of the offer.

We can see from these examples that quite different issues are involved, requiring equally different actions at the level of corporate strategy. The first example requires the company to consider a *consolidation and productivity* approach, but the second example suggests a *repositioning* strategy. The process involved is interactive. Marketing is seen here as a support or service activity, which helps identify and recommend corporate strategy but *cannot* create and lead with a marketing strategy; this has to follow on from the corporate and functional strategy decisions.

Increasing gross profit in real terms by improved margin management

There are a number of important issues to be considered here (see Figure 3.3). The first relates to identifying opportunities and problems which surround the merchandise selection and to making changes where necessary; the second concerns the management of margins between selling price and cost of goods sold. The third, and most important, is to maintain (preferably increase) customer satisfaction throughout.

Essential issues for marketing to address are: to increase the average transaction; to improve the profitability of the merchandise range; and to increase the margins of the merchandise mix. Once again, we suggest that the key variables can be seen as facilitators and can be developed as sub-systems. The role of the marketing activities is to evaluate, analyze and recommend direction.

Within the context of this critical success factor much of the

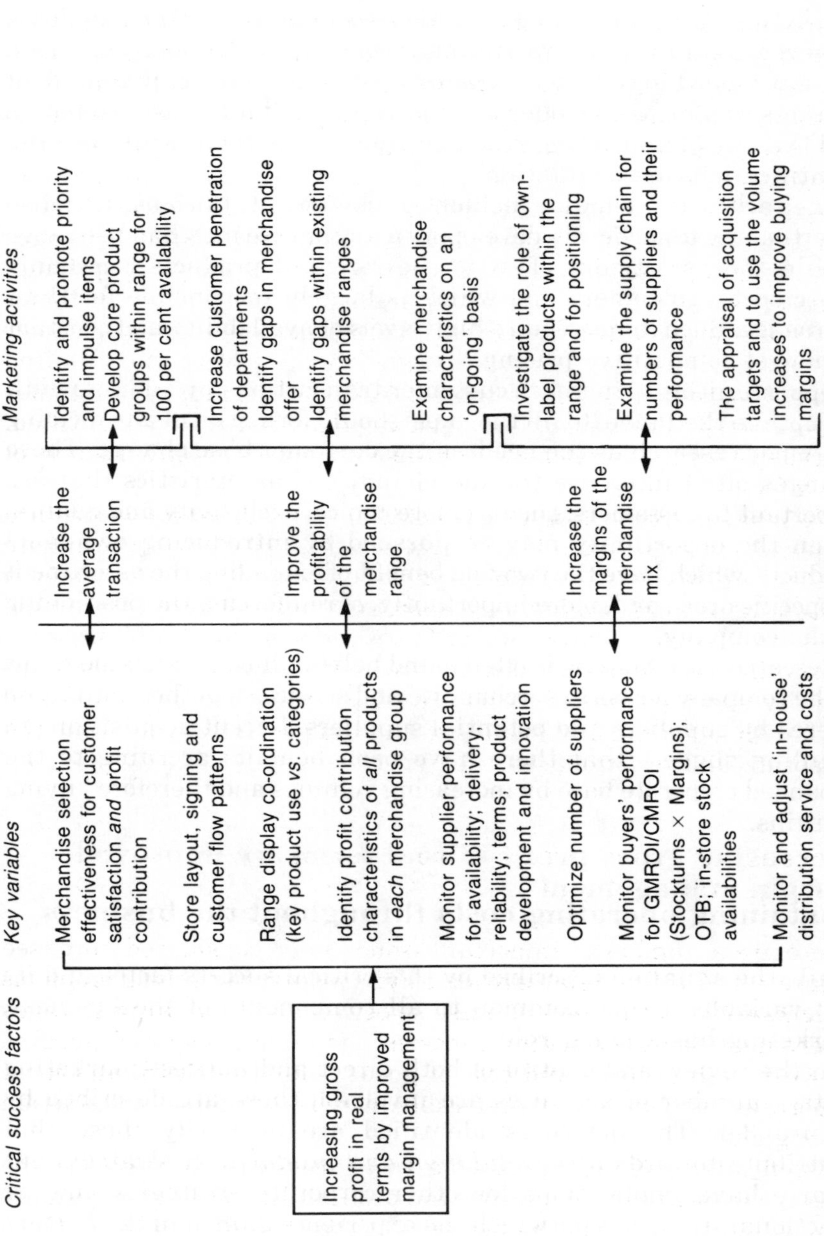

Figure 3.3 *Marketing and margin management*

marketing effort is directed towards *consolidation and productivity*; however, continued underperformance of margin management would suggest a need to consider *repositioning*. *Growth* in related product markets would possibly offer an improvement in margins, and to this end the role of marketing research would be extended into market identification and evaluation.

The activities should include a review of the merchandise assortment with a view to developing a key or core merchandise range within the assortment. This is the range of products commonly expected by customers and which is largely responsible for their patronage. Such items require high levels of availability and constant review of competitive pricing.

Opportunities to increase customer transactions by adding width or depth to the range (to fill the gaps) should form part of any ongoing customer research as the needs of the customer base change. These changes often influence the merchandise characteristics that are important to customers, such as more choice, exclusivity and quality. Often the opportunity may be pursued by introducing own-label products, which have the two-fold benefit of extending the assortment in specific areas and, more importantly, of reinforcing the positioning of the company.

Research into sourcing is often found helpful. It can match the needs of the company for both merchandise and services together with those offered by suppliers and potential suppliers. Recent acquisitions in retailing suggest that there have been benefits accruing to the expanded corporate base by increasing volumes and therefore buying margins.

Containing operating costs throughout the business

While the situation described by this critical success factor and its key variables is one common to all components of the business, marketing has a major role.

In the review and control of both direct and indirect marketing costs a number of activities are involved; these are described by Figure 3.4. The activities identified are primarily those that contribute towards a *consolidation and productivity* strategy, but clearly have implications for other corporate strategies and for functional strategies for which the experience gained in the current business could prove to be extremely useful.

The activities identified are typically those of any on-going marketing activity. However, for retailing companies there is the need to add the supply dimension. Here it is suggested that the costs

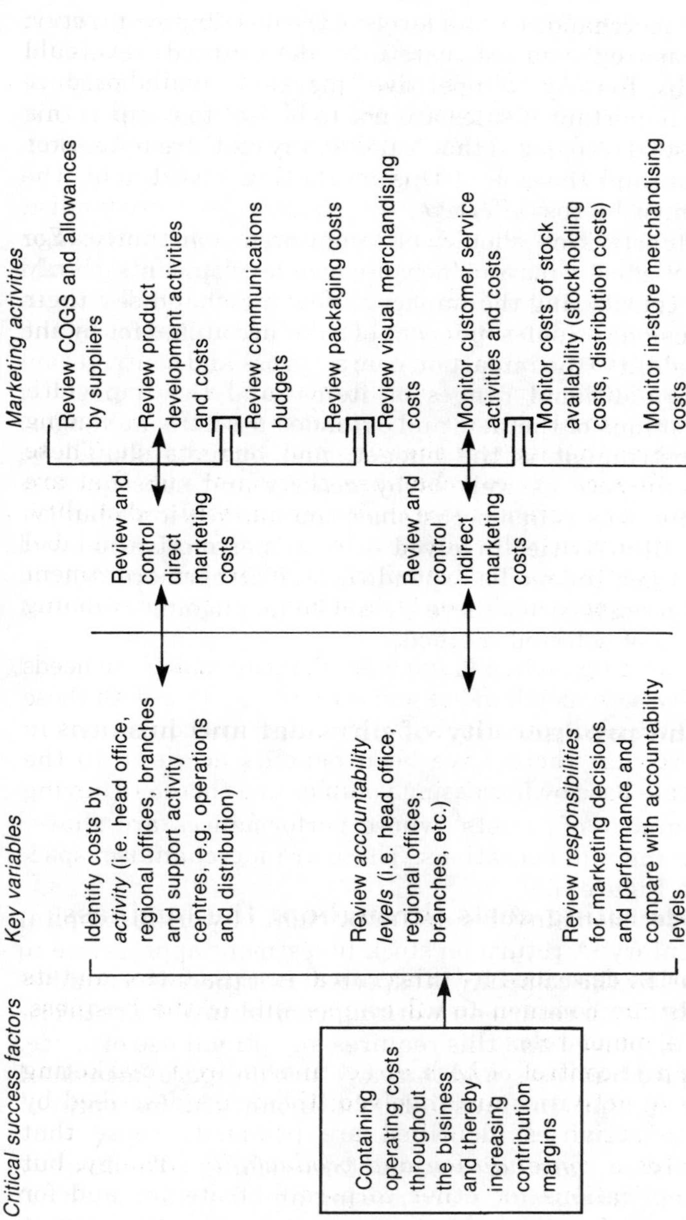
Critical success factors
Key variables
Marketing activities
Containing operating costs throughout the business and thereby increasing contribution margins
Identify costs by *activity* (i.e. head office, regional offices, branches and support activity centres, e.g. operations and distribution)
Review *accountability levels* (i.e. head office, regional offices, branches, etc.)
Review *responsibilities* for marketing decisions and performance and compare with accountability levels
Review and control direct marketing costs
Review and control indirect marketing costs
Review COGS and allowances by suppliers
Review product development activities and costs
Review communications budgets
Review packaging costs
Review visual merchandising costs
Monitor customer service activities and costs
Monitor costs of stock availability (stockholding costs, distribution costs)
Monitor in-store merchandising costs
Monitor selling costs
Review marketing overhead costs

Figure 3.4 *The involvement of marketing in budgetary control of its own and related activities*

of availability of merchandise at all levels of the distribution function should be measured against carefully determined levels of effectiveness. In fiercely competitive markets availability of merchandise is important if sales are not to be lsot to competitors. However, it must be recognized that 'sales at any cost' are not a long-term proposition and the use of this marketing investment (the merchandise) must be cost-effective.

A number of activities should be monitored constantly. For example, the cost-effectiveness of 'new product developments' should be reviewed by considering the impact of new merchandise ranges and range extensions on sales (per cent of sales accounted for by the activity), profitability (the impact on overall gross and contribution margins of the additional ranges or items) and the impact on consumer perceptions of the new and extended assortment ranges.

The major instrument is the budget, and budgets should be established by *purpose* as well as by *activity* and subsequently monitored in this way. Thus a customer communication's budget should include all activities involved in customer motivation and information, not just the media expenditures. Furthermore, within each of the budget categories there should be an ongoing review of cost-effectiveness of selected methods.

Increasing the productivity of physical and human assets

There are a number of 'assets' whose performances are shared between marketing and operations. These are merchandise, space and people (see Figure 3.5).

Merchandise decisions involve an investment of working capital in stock or inventory. A return on stock investment appropriate to the objectives set by the company is expected. But there is a number of issues in addition to return on working capital investment. The stock has to be displayed and this requires an optimal use of space. The space occupied has costs, and thus a return on space (measured in sales and contribution) must also be monitored for optimal utilization.

Productivity issues are, of course, far-reaching. The use of distribution assets (transport, warehousing and distribution staff) are important issues in this respect. The evaluation of the impact of sales and asset productivity is another very useful task, which marketing can fulfil. Again, recent developments in food retailing give examples of companies improving both sales and asset productivity (Tesco and Hillards, together with Asda's acquisition of a number of Gateway superstore outlets).

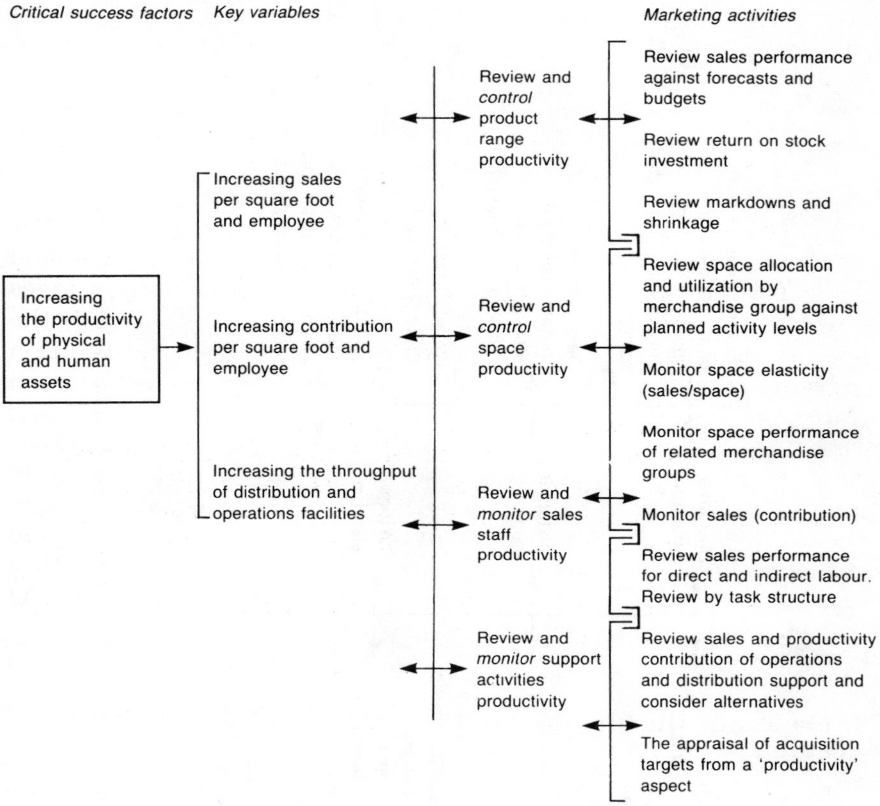
Critical success factors
Key variables
Marketing activities
Increasing the productivity of physical and human assets
Increasing sales per square foot and employee
Increasing contribution per square foot and employee
Increasing the throughput of distribution and operations facilities
Review and *control* product range productivity
Review and *control* space productivity
Review and *monitor* sales staff productivity
Review and *monitor* support activities productivity
Review sales performance against forecasts and budgets
Review return on stock investment
Review markdowns and shrinkage
Review space allocation and utilization by merchandise group against planned activity levels
Monitor space elasticity (sales/space)
Monitor space performance of related merchandise groups
Monitor sales (contribution)
Review sales performance for direct and indirect labour. Review by task structure
Review sales and productivity contribution of operations and distribution support and consider alternatives
The appraisal of acquisition targets from a 'productivity' aspect

Figure 3.5 *Marketing responsibilities for productivity extend throughout the company*

Adding value to the customer offer

The important marketing issues are: customer attraction; customer action; and customer retention. The problems of adding value to the customer offer present major benefits if they are achieved at appropriate levels and quantities (see Figure 3.6).

The primary objective of customer service is to add to the retail offer and increase the relative differentiation between the company and its competitors. In other words, it seeks to create competitive advantage by adding customer benefits at an acceptable level of costs. Clear customer service objectives follow:

1. Increasing the customers' utility of the basic product by adding support services, for example:

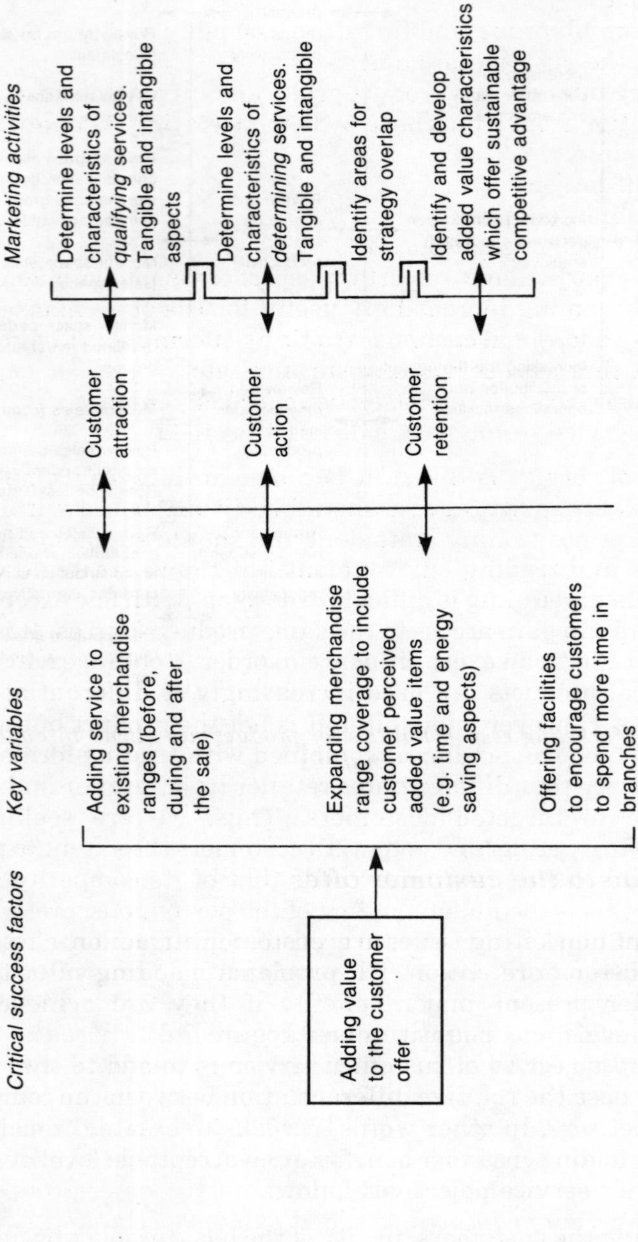
Critical success factors
Key variables
Marketing activities
Adding value to the customer offer
Adding service to existing merchandise ranges (before, during and after the sale)
Expanding merchandise range coverage to include customer perceived added value items (e.g. time and energy saving aspects)
Offering facilities to encourage customers to spend more time in branches
Customer attraction
Customer action
Customer retention
Determine levels and characteristics of *qualifying* services. Tangible and intangible aspects
Determine levels and characteristics of *determining* services. Tangible and intangible
Identify areas for strategy overlap
Identify and develop added value characteristics which offer sustainable competitive advantage

Figure 3.6 *Marketing and customer service as an input to added value to the retail offer*

   (a) notifying customers of new merchandise ranges known to be of interest to them;
   (b) offering garment services such as fur storage, cleaning and repair;
   (c) room planning and furniture assembly and arrangement in the customers' homes.
2. Creating interest in a product group and increasing customers' satisfaction from a purchase by demonstrating its application, for example:
   (a) golf lessons,
   (b) fashion advisers,
   (c) DIY demonstrations.

   (This is a particularly important aspect of visual merchandising and is becoming increasingly useful for life-style marketing.)
3. Creating additional customer traffic by offering service products such as financial services, insurance, etc.
4. Using service(s) to increase customer convenience.
5. Using service to increase sales and profit.

If this view of service is taken, it becomes an integral component of retail marketing strategy; it should be firmly based within the overall market positioning statement and should supplement both merchandise and trading environment functional strategies.

Added value in retailing is difficult to develop. With few exceptions, most retailers can gain access to the same product sources. It is true that large retailers can exert influence in order to obtain exclusivity, and own-label products are used increasingly to differentiate key product areas. However, more often it is not the product but rather the way in which the product is combined with trading format and customer service that differentiates retailer from retailer and offers added value to targeted customers. Thus, we are seeking to demonstrate to existing (and potential) customers the extent to which the offer of a selected retailer exceeds that of its competitors.

The key to this is the understanding of the perceptions, preferences and choice influences of a selected customer group and the relating of these to the resource base of the company in terms of its retail marketing mix.

The nature of the competitive advantage should be based on those elements that maximize differentiation from competitors, and these are usually based on consumers' perceptions of the added-value aspects of the retailers' overall offering. They may well be based on merchandise features, service or trading style, i.e. those features that the customers rate highly. Clearly, different customer groups will have differing views concerning added-value aspects, and it is the identification of these, and their combination into co-ordinated retail packages, that are economically viable and that distinguish the successful retailers.

Added value has both tangible and intangible characteristics. examples of tangible benefits offering added value to customers are:

- An exclusive range of merchandise.
- In-store services and service facilities.
- Price advantages.
- Extensive after-sales services.
- High-quality own-label products.
- Co-ordinated merchandise groups.

Intangible benefits may include:

- Time-saving 'wardrobe' services.
  The knowledge that problems will be resolved promptly.
- The 'peace of mind' that national multiple-outlet coverage guarantees for prices, warranties, etc.
- Identification with a 'prestige' retailer with whom the customer has much in common concerning style and taste, etc.

Summary

In this chapter we have explored the role of marketing as being an 'initiator' in identifying, evaluating, recommending and implementing overall retailing strategy.

Figure 3.7 identifies the process whereby the market positioning strategy of the company is implemented through its merchandise, customer service, trading environment and customer communications strategies. These have obvious implications for the company's critical success factors and both have issues which the marketing function analyzes, considers and participates in, in the implementation of overall strategy.

We suggest that marketing, along with finance, operations, human resource management, property and systems, are functions that all contribute to the overall retail strategy. By using a framework, or structure, that identifies customer-based opportunities, the central strategic thrust is the positioning of the company in terms of its merchandise, service and trading environment offer such that it is clearly recognizable by the customer group to which it is directed. At the same time the fundamental requirements of the company can be identified and established as performance requirements which need to be achieved if the overall long-term objectives for profitability are to be met and the critical success factors can then form a planning structure for company strategy decisions.

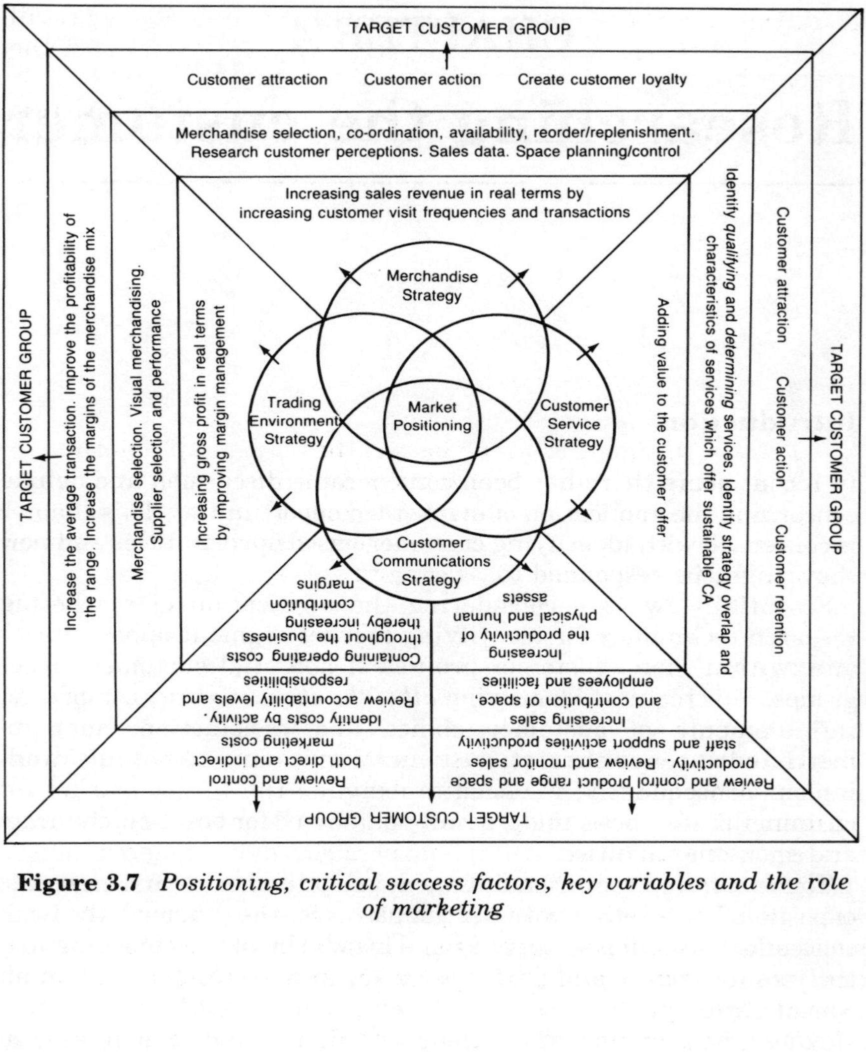

Figure 3.7 *Positioning, critical success factors, key variables and the role of marketing*

CHAPTER 4

Researching the customer

Introduction

In recent years there has been considerable discussion and debate concerning the application of market-led opportunities. This chapter is concerned with identifying customer-based opportunities and how they might be responded to.

Essentially, we are considering the application of marketing research techniques for identifying market segment opportunities and, within them, customer profiles of potential customer target groups. This requires identifying *all of the characteristics* comprising the elements of customer choice and satisfaction, such as merchandise, environment, customer service and communications issues. Consequently, we need to examine the target market for customer preferences (and current behaviour) for both merchandise and shopping facilities.

The discussion requires that we develop the issues and elements of positioning, together with the company response, through the basic concept of marketing segmentation. This will involve us in identifying the requirements and criteria of segmentation, together with consideration of the process and implementation of segmentation strategy. Research methods, their advantages and their problems, will be discussed, and some examples of segmentation exercises will be given. Finally, we will consider the problems of those retailing activities that have wide appeal to broad customer bases.

Segmentation: requirements and criteria

There is an extensive literature concerning the benefits of segmentation, and the requirements and criteria of segmentation. Here we intend to review these principles briefly and focus more on the application of recent developments.

Segmentation requirements

The concept of segmentation is as applicable to retail marketing as it is to other marketing problems. And the requirements are much the same:

1. Segments should be *identifiable* with significant response differences. These may be different responses to the same stimulus, e.g. some consumers will respond to high levels of service (by frequent visits and high spends). Another group may find the high levels of service (and other features such as price levels) unacceptable.
2. The segment must have *meaningful characteristics*. It must have features or responses that can be converted into commercial opportunity. An obvious example is sport or hobby enthusiasts whose interests make them prime spenders. Other less obvious examples concern customer responses to, say, after-sales service. Where a follow-up call after a major purchase may create a strong customer-loyal base.
3. Any segment must be *reachable*. There must be some form of medium that can be used to address the segment group members. This is becoming less of a problem. The printed media (newspapers, journals, magazines, etc.) have become sophisticated in identifying interests, attitudes and opinions, all of which can in turn be segmented and combined in ways that interest specific consumer segments and groups of suppliers. Information technology is being applied to the processes of customer information and transaction management with increasing success and application.
4. The segment should have a *viable size*. Viability is understood to be economically influenced by sales and profit potential. There are numerous ways in which a market segment may be disaggregated, and at each level of segmentation significant differences may appear. The issue is: how significant are they in commercial terms? How big is the market segment? How far spread (geographically) is it? And can it support the costs of servicing it?
5. Finally, it should be *stable over time*. This is a problem in many forms of retailing, particularly the clothing markets, where fashions can and do change over short periods of time. It is here where specific attitudes towards a *type* of fashion may be more useful than the attitudes towards a *specific* fashion at one particular moment in time.

   For example, attitudes may be reasonably constant in so far as traditional, classic, up-to-date, contemporary or innovatory classifications are concerned. However, at any one season specific items within these groups may fail to win the approval of the customers who share these fashion attitudes. To accommodate these types of problem, time should be measured on a life-cycle basis of customer interests. Research shows that customer interests do demonstrate cyclical behaviour, fashion attitudes correlate with demographic and socio-economic characteristics and thus these may be useful for planning purposes.

Segmentation characteristics and customer profiles

So far in this chapter we have discussed segmentation requirements and criteria. We need to consider the use of segmentation to produce customer profiles around which appropriate 'retail offers' may be developed.

Before discussing these in any detail we shall make a few broad points.

The first concerns the relevance of each item to any specific retailing business. There are some obvious common denominators, which are shared by all retailers, but equally there are some characteristics that have more application to specific types of retailing. Clearly, all retailers have considerable interest in demographics and socio-economics.

Demographics identify customer numbers and purchasing volume potentials while socio-economics are a strong indication of the ability of the customer group to allocate large (or small) amounts of disposable income to specific merchandise groups. Other topics such as socio-cultural characteristics often have specific application. Design and style attitudes are important characteristics to apparel and home furnishings retailers, but are of less importance to food retailers.

The purpose of segmentation is to identify a viable marketing opportunity and to address it with an appropriate offer. For retailing this implies a process of identifying specific characteristics of a group of customers. It requires the development of a *customer profile*. From this we can better define the information requirements for successfully identifying market segments. In other words, because there are numerous ways in which segments may be identified, we should commence the process by first identifying the type of information we require. Figure 4.1 suggests a number of topics comprising a customer profile.

While much of the data used to compile the customer profile format

Demographics and socio-economic characteristics

Age; sex; marital and family status; position in family life cycle.

Occupation; income; type, location and ownership status of residence.

Shopping-related life-styles

Attitudes towards family, work and leisure. Shopping as 'work' and shopping as a 'leisure pursuit'. The level of interest in shopping trends. Shopping as a symbol in customers' aspirations. Their concept of value (quantity/price; quality/price; exclusivity/price).

Shopping-related perceptions and preferences

The extent of customer knowledge concerning competitors:

who they are,
what they offer,
comparative ranking.

Preferences for:

Merchandise characteristics (choice, quality, style/design, exclusivity, availability, the role of price, brand loyalty and own brands).
Store type (location, environment, methods).
Customer service mix (proportion of services that are determining services *vs*. qualifying services). The extent to which customers are sensitive to changes in services offered.

Shopping-related behaviour

Media habits (for shopping information and advice)
Purchase behaviour:

reasons for visits,
frequency of visits,
size of purchases,
range of purchases,
store loyalties/brand loyalties,
method of purchase.

Trade-off behaviour:

price/quantity,
price/quality,
price/exclusivity,
price/availability,
price/convenience,
price/service,
price/environment (ambience — theatre, comfort, etc.).

Specific needs such as large sizes, health food ranges, etc.

Figure 4.1 *Developing customer profile characteristics*

in Figure 4.1 are typically in use and require very little explanation, some comments are helpful.

Recent developments by CACI, Pinpoint and SAMI in the field of geo-demographics have extended the usefulness of catchment area analyses by adding consumer expenditure data and retail outlet activities (number, size and location). This information, together with store and location visits, offers very useful information concerning store performance and potential. However, a caution is offered. The increasing sophistication of these packages does not negate the need for managerial decision-making: they remain information inputs.

Life-style research and marketing

The evidence of retailing developments over the recent past (the 1980s) suggests that segmentation characteristics or determinants are strongly dominated by socio-cultural aspects. The growth of clothing multiples such as Next, and the subsequent imitation that occurred, extended typical segmentation variables to consider (and include) research techniques that identify clusters of consumers who share similar values, attitudes, beliefs, behaviour, expectations and aspirations, the total of which is an expression of that group's *life-style*.

Life-style research, psychographics or, as we prefer, socio-cultural aspects of consumer research have been widely discussed (Mitchell and MacNulty 1981; Blackwell and Talarzyk 1983; Mitchell 1983; Michman 1984). It is an interesting concept when applied to retailing decisions because, as we suggest in Figure 4.2, when it is fully

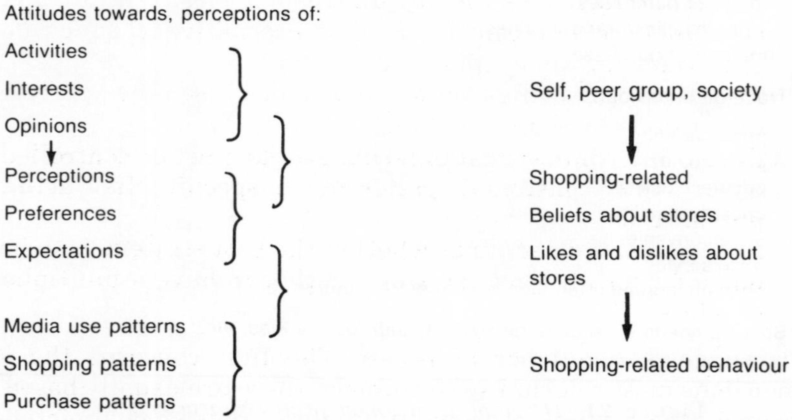

Figure 4.2 *What is 'life-style'?*

understood it permits a detailed offer to be made to the target group. A number of life-style 'kits' are available (Grafton-Small 1967; Bowring 1985; Lesser and Hughes 1986).

However, the point we make in Figure 4.2 is that the research required is not simple. It requires an extended enquiry, which first investigates broad values on which attitudes towards, and perceptions of, self-peer group and society are formed. These are then used in conjunction with perceptions, preferences and expectations that are shopping-related. Finally, when media use, shopping and purchasing behaviour are researched, the whole may then be used to explain and predict shopping-related behaviour.

Developing customer profiles and a positioning strategy

Market and product positioning

Very simply, a company's market position is its interpretation of the needs, desires and behavioural characteristics of a target customer profile. It is a co-ordinated 'statement' of merchandise, store environment, customer services and customer communications (see Chapter 2). Clearly, the more closely the customer can be 'analyzed' (and categorized) the more effective the interpretation or response can be made to be. Equally, it follows that so, too, will be the customers' response in terms of shopping frequencies, average transactions and the range of spend across the assortment.

Urban and Hauser (1980) suggest four important relevant issues:

1. *Perception* identifies the key dimensions most relevant to the consumer and how consumers view alternative offerings along each relevant dimension.
2. *Preference* identifies how consumers use the perceived dimensions to evaluate offers.
3. *Choice* determines what external events must be controlled to ensure that consumers preferring a specific offer actually purchase it.
4. *Segmentation* determines whether the best strategy is to have one offer for all consumers or whether to have a multiplicity of offers.

This suggests a number of issues. The first concerns the key dimensions most relevant to consumers; these are usually based on consumers' perceptions of competitive offers, from which preferences are developed. Also of concern to us here is the issue of segmentation and the strategic decision of whether or not to have one offer for all consumers or a range of offers, each meeting (or targeting) different opportunities. This is the decision facing many retailing companies, and we have seen, generally, a move towards favouring a range of offers, judging by the number of offers based on niche or target marketing.

There are clear benefits that accrue to a segment-based niche marketing strategy over a mass market strategy. Figure 4.3 illustrates how merchandise ranges can be 'edited' to meet the more clearly defined (identified) requirements for the target customer group. However, risk is seen to increase. This occurs because, unless the customers' precise requirements are reflected in the merchandise offer, they may prefer to *buy* elsewhere. Other benefits are available. The store environment and customer service offered can be designed more specifically, resulting in a more cost-effective use of resources (increased productivity) and more perceived added value for customers. We shall discuss this issue in more depth in Chapter 5 because it is one of considerable importance to retailing, particularly for department stores and multiple food retailers.

The response to an identified, segment-based opportunity (or for a mass-market opportunity for that matter) should be clearly seen and understood by the customer group it is targeted towards. This is the company's positioning statement. It forms a major component in the *corporate direction* of the company. Together with the *mission statement* and the *corporate objectives*, it provides a primary statement of *what* the company wishes its customers to see it as, and therefore how it should be seen.

A company's market positioning 'statement' is a response to the preferences of a target customer group. It is widely accepted that 'not all customers are the same' and, as a consequence, mass merchandisers have given way to more focused forms of retailing. The problems of retailer differentiation in a changing market-place were discussed earlier.

Thus, if the positioning matrix is to be based on customers' perceptions, a clear indication of who they are and what their preferences are must first be established. The target customer profile must identify:

- Demographic characteristics.
- Socio-economic characteristics.
- Attitudes to work and leisure.
- Leisure activities.
- Attitudes to shopping.
- Concept of value.

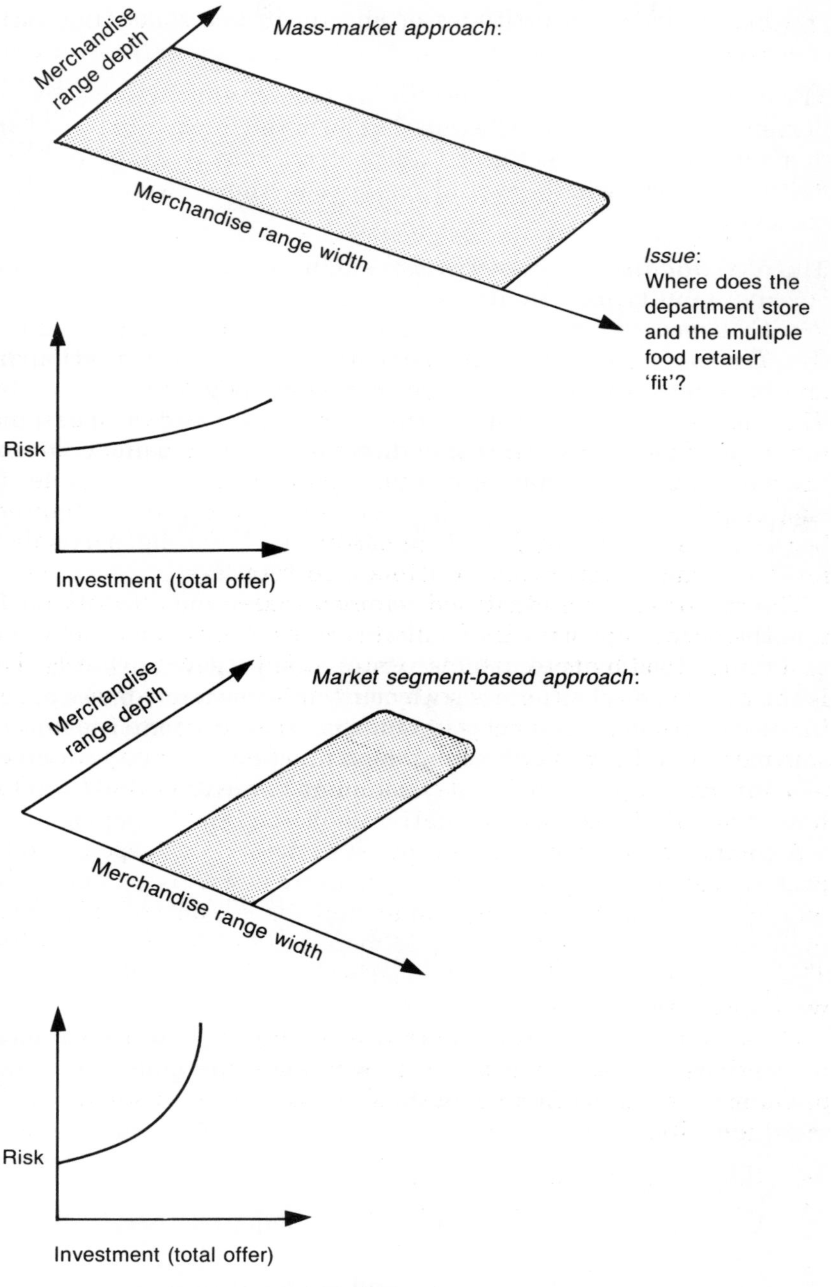

Figure 4.3 *Two broad approaches to the market: a mass-market approach and a market segment-based approach*

- Perceptions and attitudes of and towards competitive outlet types.

From the target customer profile we can obtain those issues and elements of customer satisfaction that form the important issues and elements of their expectations and perceptions. A range of likely characteristics which would comprise these would include expectations for:

1. *Merchandise characteristics*: exclusivity, quality, variety, availability, continuity, style/design and price.
2. *Customer services*: qualifying and determining characteristics.
3. *Trading format/store environment characteristics*: location and parking convenience, visual merchandising, etc.
4. *Customer communications*: personal and impersonal communications, the role of direct marketing, using customer data bases, alternative media.

With these two concepts in mind the market positioning statement should become

> A response to customer expectations involving *strategic use* of the functional strategy elements. It is based on the company's distinctive competences, its existing competitive advantage and that indicated as necessary by customer research, based on the expectations and perceptions of the target customer base. It is made manifest by combining these functional strategy elements into a unique exchange environment, relative to those specific competitors seen as alternative choices by the target customer group.

Consider a hypothetical example, that of a department store located in an exclusive area of a large city. We would expect the target customer base to comprise male and female customers who:

- Have above-average incomes from senior management occupations. Consequently, they are likely to have *high* disposal incomes and discretionary spending budgets, but *low* discretionary time budgets.
- Live in the affluent, fashionable suburbs of nearby towns.
- Be aged 35–55, married and with children who are not necessarily dependent.
- Are active socially, many having participative sporting leisure pursuits.
- Concerned with appearance and personal fitness.
- Consider themselves as individuals and dress and furnish and decorate their homes to reflect this uniqueness.

- View 'value' as a combination of exclusivity, quality and choice, together with 'convenient time-saving' characteristics of the retail environment.

Their expectations, if researched, would probably include:

- Unique merchandise.
- High quality.
- Wide choice of styles and colours.
- Comprehensive range of sizes or alterations services.
- Co-ordinated merchandise and accessory ranges.
- Merchandise continuity.
- Attentive and knowledgeable sales staff at sufficient staffing levels to provide 'service'.
- Advanced information (and 'view opportunities') on new (*but only* new) appropriate merchandise.
- Charge and credit facilities; in-store and by telephone.
- Full range of financial services.
- Free delivery service.
- Advice centres.
- Maintenance service for 'difficult' products (e.g. from furs to swimming pools).
- Easy access in-store and clear store directions.
- Co-ordinated product displays.
- Easy to reach by car with ample parking adjacent to the store.

From this perception profile, the positioning statement that might emerge may well be

> A store with appeal to discerning customers, who seek to be 'individual' in terms of their clothes, their homes and their leisure pursuits. They are likely to be in senior executive occupations with limited time available for shopping. Our offering must be both unique and extensive to ensure that their expectations for exclusivity and choice are met. We must offer an equally extensive customer service portfolio to meet the time constraints imposed by their busy work schedules.

Figure 4.4 describes how a positioning statement can be interpreted by ensuring that a coherent and co-ordinated combination of merchandise, store environment and customer service is transmitted to the target customer group by a complementing customer communication strategy.

An interesting and useful approach to positioning has been proposed by Pessemier (1980). His work followed that of Martineau (1958), who suggested that the customer base of any store is influenced by factors

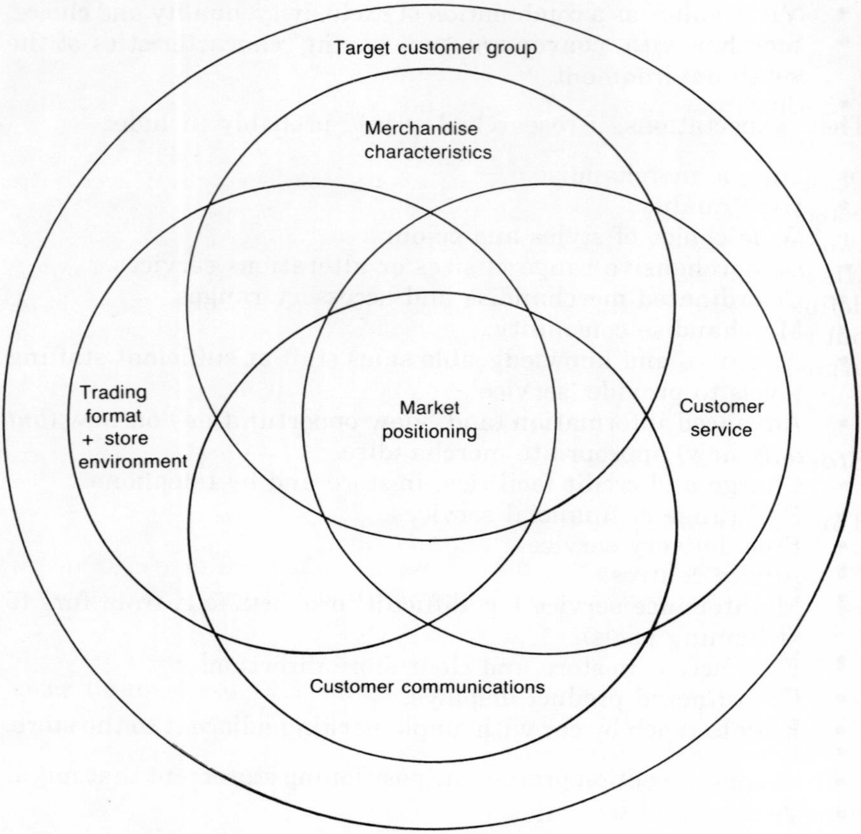

Figure 4.4 *A co-ordinated positioning statement*

other than merchandise and location characteristics: it is also 'defined in the shopper's mind'.

Much of the emphasis on demographics and socio-economics was relaxed and replaced by socio-cultural or psychographic dimensions. Pessemier (1980) saw this as emphasizing the 'dual focus of current image research on understanding shoppers and the stores in which they shop'. He saw these as shopper characteristics or customer profile characteristics and store characteristics.

Shopper characteristics

The following topics comprise shopper characteristics:

- Demographics (age, sex, life-cycle and social class).

- Shopping-related life-style (activities, interests and opinions).
- Shopping-related perceptions and preferences (beliefs about stores; likes and dislikes about stores).
- Shopping-related behaviour (media exposure patterns; shopping patterns and purchasing patterns).

Pessemier suggested that the first two types of variable describe the personal characteristics of shoppers and households, while the second two sets of variable describe the individual's relationship to the store. His argument is that demographic and life-style variables tend to define general needs and capacities of the individual and household, but rarely represent strong determinants of store choice. These, he argues, are closely linked to perceptions and preferences.

Store characteristics

This list includes the following aspects:

- Clientele mix (demographic and life-style profiles of customers).
- Life-cycle position of store type (age and maturity of store trading format).
- Merchandise (assortment dimensions, ego intensity of merchandise mix) (i.e. mix of fashion and non-fashion), price points, brand(s) profile.
- Locational convenience.
- Shopping pleasure.
- Transaction convenience.
- Promotional emphasis.
- Integrity.
- Image strength and clarity.

The increasing importance of customer service and, indeed, of service products suggests that these should be included. Essentially, Pessemier's store characteristics (with the exception of the clientele mix) represent a range of retail offer options.

These can be aggregated and the following characteristics are suggested:

- Core offer features (price, quality, exclusivity, excitement, luxury, high service).
- As *benefits, problem solutions to shopping needs* (information, convenience of location or transaction services, delivery and size options).
- For *usage occasions* (products for leisure, work, formal occasions, etc.).
- For *user category* (frequent/infrequent, regular/irregular, etc.).

Pessemier's approach offers management a means by which they can establish store characteristics by target (existing and potential) customers' groups. A number of issues arise. One is the relative importance of each of the characteristics within the product market. For some forms of retailing the shopper characteristics are dominated by *demographics and socio-economics* and the retail offer characteristics are equally dominated by *core offer features.* Many food retailers, variety chain and department stores would find this to be characteristic of their businesses. The demographic and socio-economic features, e.g. 25–44 year olds who are C1C2s, have featured prominently in the customer base of these businesses. Equally, there are examples of retailers who have focused on other characteristics for which the volume potentials have been smaller. However, in terms of the impact of their performance on the *critical success factors* they have achieved high levels of customer sales and business productivity, together with customer-determined levels of preferences and positive attitudes.

A second factor to be considered is that both shopper characteristics and retail offer characteristics are influenced by time. Both demonstrate the effects of time. Furthermore, they may be influenced by differing rates of change. For example, consumers demonstrate both demographic/socio-economic life-cycles, together with life-cycle effects for socio-cultural characteristics. The growth of Habitat during the 1960s and 1970s and that of Next during the 1980s are evidence of this. Shopping-related behaviour is also subject to change. It can be influenced by technology on the one hand (IT and home shopping), and by location changes (the OOT and off-centre development of food and DIY retailing) on the other.

Finally, there is always the competitive environment to consider. All retailing businesses will seek to differentiate themselves in order to develop competitive advantage. This may involve them attempting to be better at the existing forms of retail offer or it may involve them in innovation, developing creative new retail offer characteristics.

There is a clear link between the model proposed in Figure 4.4 and Pessemier's approach. Both seek to understand customer expectations and both propose a response. For Pessemier, the *shopper characteristics* must first be identified and the response follows as the components or *characteristics of the retail offer* are co-ordinated into a relevant and coherent response.

The model in Figure 4.4 identifies the same process, but emphasizes the need for congruence. If we combine the two, we have a strategic approach that identifies the overall positioning and the overlap areas within which competitive advantage features may be developed.

Pessemier's approach can then be used to consider planning details. It is, in fact, a means by which the strategy may be implemented.

In Figure 4.5 we propose a shopper characteristics/retail offer matrix. It offers a means by which product markets may be analyzed. *Shopper characteristics* are clearly market segmentation characteristics (customer profiles), while the *retail offer characteristics* are retail offer options (or interpretations). It is unlikely to be a symmetrical 4 × 4 matrix because the relative importance of each characteristic is likely to differ between and within product markets.

We suggested earlier that food retailers, variety chains and department stores are likely to favour demographics and socio-economics as shopper characteristics and pay limited attention to the other characteristics. The problem here is that when they offer features such as price advantages across similar ranges of merchandise the offer is often met and 'bettered'.

On the other hand, a better understanding of shopping-related perceptions and preferences, together with a knowledge of the effects of the various influences of shopping-related behaviour, can offer the means by which the retailer can move closer to the target customer group. The fact that Marks & Spencer customers have absolute confidence in the company, and express positive attitudes towards Marks & Spencer's quality service and price/value, has obvious benefits for them relative to their competitors. The principle of this argument is illustrated in Figure 4.6.

In Figure 4.6 a hypothetical segmentation/retail offer matrix for stores such as variety chains, department stores and food multiples is proposed. The dominant characteristics are demographics and socio-economics (shopper characteristics), and core offer features (usually price-based) are the primary retail offer characteristics. To generate volume traffic a *demographic/socio-economic* profile is opted for (usually a group who have average or above-average disposable income *and* the need to spend (growing families)). *Core offer features* are usually price-related at acceptable levels of quality and 'middle of the road' style or fashion (where applicable). The remaining characteristics are often ignored or given a nominal consideration due to the fact that the target customer can rarely be defined in specific socio-cultural terms. However, rapid customer handling and other convenience-based approaches are likely to elicit a positive response.

The likely customer profile for these stores will be customers (male and female) who:

- Have average incomes from supervisory/middle management occupations. They will have limited disposable income. It is

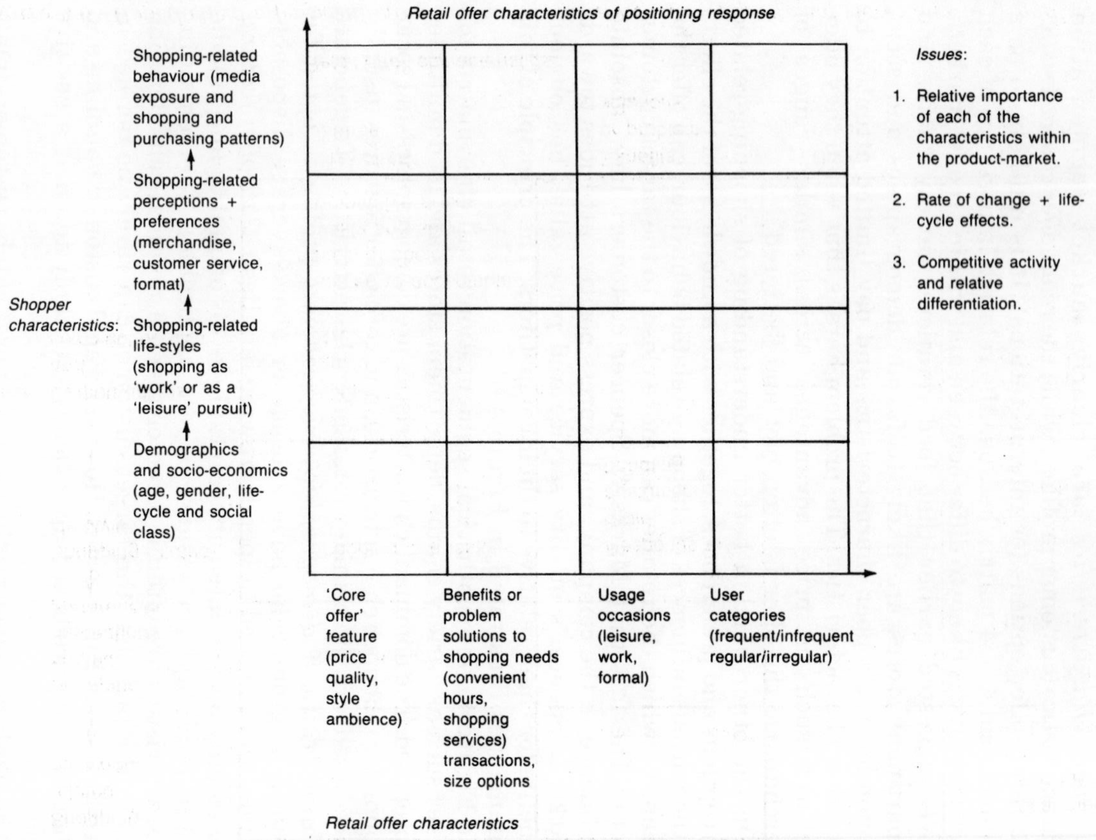

Retail offer characteristics of positioning response
Shopper characteristics:
Shopping-related behaviour (media exposure and shopping and purchasing patterns)
Shopping-related perceptions + preferences (merchandise, customer service, format)
Shopping-related life-styles (shopping as 'work' or as a 'leisure' pursuit)
Demographics and socio-economics (age, gender, life-cycle and social class)
'Core offer' feature (price quality, style ambience)
Benefits or problem solutions to shopping needs (convenient hours, shopping services) transactions, size options
Usage occasions (leisure, work, formal)
User categories (frequent/infrequent regular/irregular)
Retail offer characteristics
Issues:
1. Relative importance of each of the characteristics within the product-market.
2. Rate of change + life-cycle effects.
3. Competitive activity and relative differentiation.

Figure 4.5 *An offer/positioning matrix*

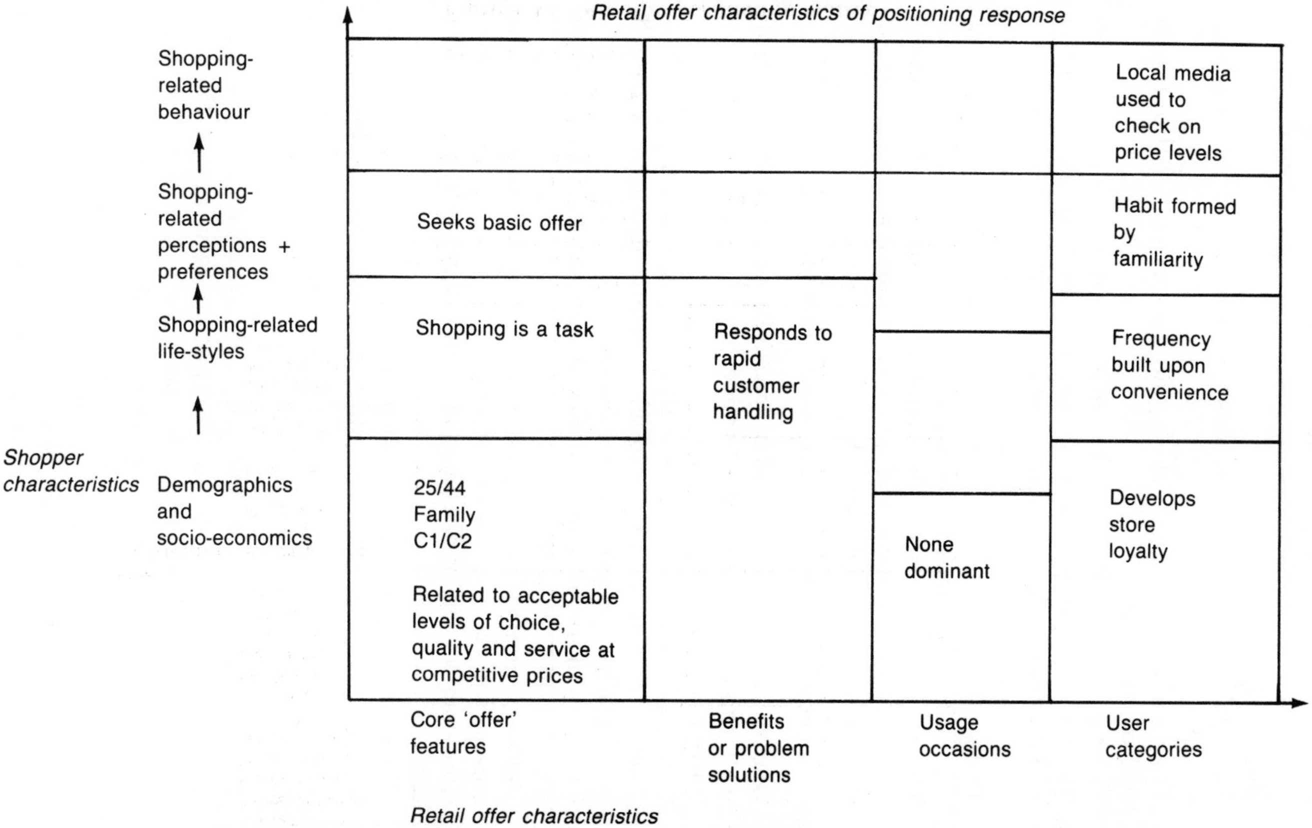

Figure 4.6 *Hypothetical offer/positioning matrix for variety chains, department stores and food multiples*

likely that if they have partners both will be working, but even then, their joint discretionary income will be limited. So, too, will be their time.

- They will live in their own home, which will be one of a large estate.
- They will be aged 25–44 with young or teenage children, who will be at school.
- Their social activities will be constrained by income; they are likely to spend much of their leisure time with their children and immediate family, and, possibly, with nearby neighbours.
- They seek long-term quality and durability from purchases. Thus, their attitudes towards style will be to favour classical/traditional styles which do not date rapidly.
- Their primary concern is to maximize the utility of their income. Value is a combination of quality, reliability, classic/durable styling at an acceptable price.

Their expectations if researched, would probably include:

- Quality, reliable merchandise, possibly store brands, certainly well-known manufacturer brands.
- Sufficient, but not extensive, choice.
- Conventional 'basic' needs with occasional 'luxury' products.
- Adequate staff to offer help when required, happy with self-service which is prompt and friendly.
- Conventional credit facilities (i.e. accept bank credit cards and possibly a store card).
- Delivery at nominal charge — but on a day and at a time convenient to them as customers.
- Customer service centre (cheque cashing (or dispensers), returns, etc.).
- Clear, unambiguous store displays.
- Easy to reach by car with ample parking close to the store.

From this profile the positioning statement that would address the customer group needs could be expressed as:

> A store for the customer who seeks quality and reliable merchandise and service at keenly competitive prices. They are likely to have preferences for both manufacturer and store-branded merchandise. They are probably working in middle management occupations; with both partners working, time is often a problem. Thus, a convenient and easy to shop, standardized store layout is available. Staff are able to offer a limited level of help. Stores are convenient to reach with freely available parking.

This contrasts markedly with the hypothetical matrix proposed as Figure 4.7. Here we see a specialist ladies' wear retailer concentrating on *usage occasions*, together with support from *benefits or problem solution*. The shopper characteristics that are targeted are the *shopping-related life-styles and perceptions and preferences*. Here the customer profile, customer expectations and positioning response are likely to be very similar to those of the hypothetical department store discussed earlier in this chapter.

Repositioning

The need to reposition an offer occurs when:

- There is a change in the target market.
- A change in the needs or benefits, etc., sought by the target market.
- Competitors' offers are perceived as better value by the target customer group.
- The addition of technology can either create greater added value or can offer the existing added value to an extended target customer base.

We have discussed the aspects of change likely to influence the matrix. Clearly, the target market may change because of demographic shifts (e.g. the declining number of teenagers and the increasing numbers of elderly people). This will require management to consider the relative importance of demographics in the shopper characteristics. Socio-economic shifts occur.

During the 1980s, a polarization in disposable income has occurred and this has resulted in an emphasis on the price/quantity aspects of retail offers for some consumers while increased disposable income has had the opposite effect for others. These have demonstrated an Engel's effect by buying less 'staple' merchandise and more 'luxury' items. This effect implies a shift of emphasis from demographics and socio-economic characteristics, as well as shopping-related life-style characteristics, towards perceptions and preferences, and shopping-related behaviour. At this point, a change is identified in the needs and benefits sought by the target market as well as a shift in the target-market itself.

There is an interesting relationship between customer perceptions and expectations. Shuch (1988) suggests that when perceptions exceed expectations the customer sees greater added value in that retailer's offer and this, he suggests, is a source of competitive advantage. A clear link with the matrix in Figure 4.5 can be seen. We can see the

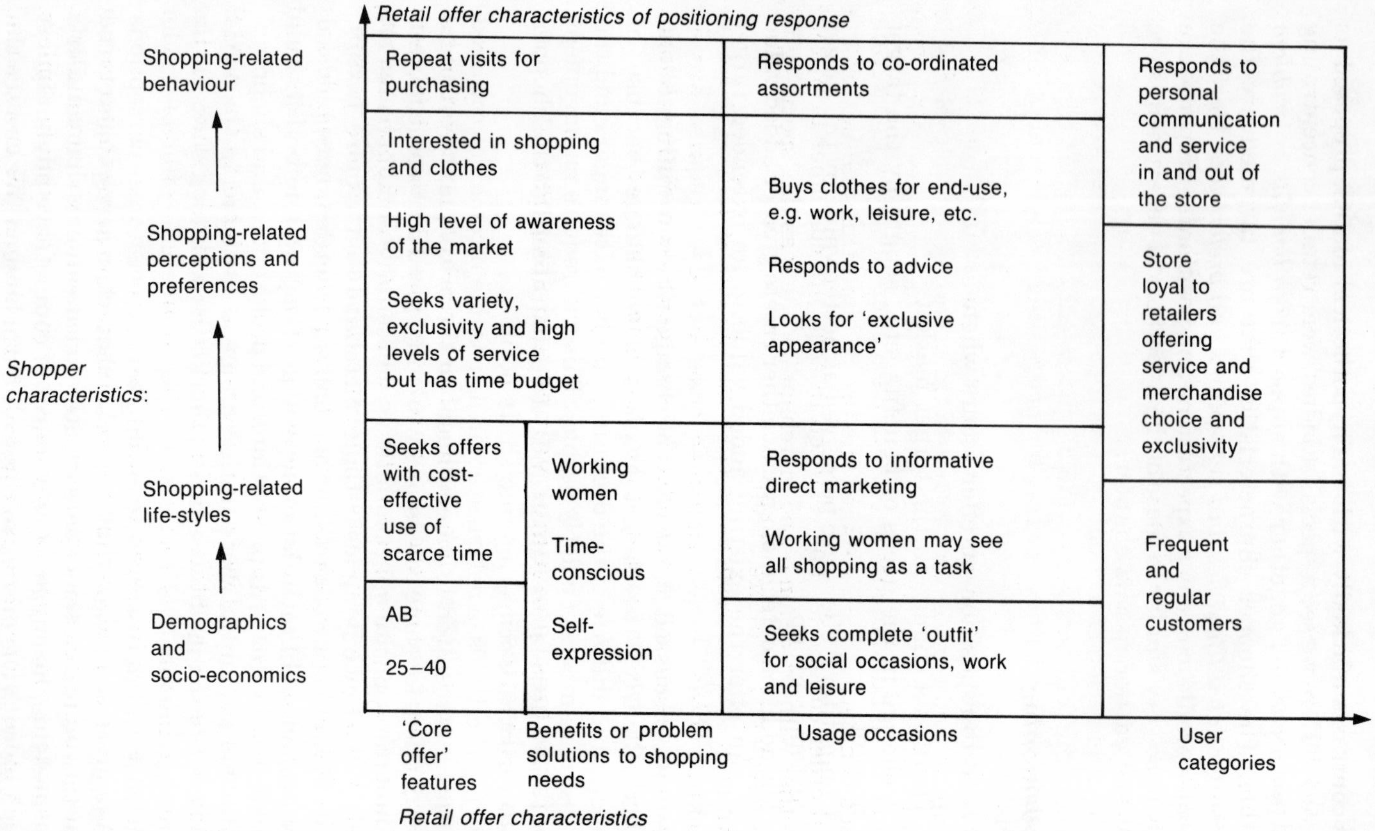
Retail offer characteristics of positioning response
Shopping-related behaviour
Shopping-related perceptions and preferences
Shopper characteristics:
Shopping-related life-styles
Demographics and socio-economics
Repeat visits for purchasing
Responds to co-ordinated assortments
Responds to personal communication and service in and out of the store
Interested in shopping and clothes
High level of awareness of the market
Seeks variety, exclusivity and high levels of service but has time budget
Buys clothes for end-use, e.g. work, leisure, etc.
Responds to advice
Looks for 'exclusive appearance'
Store loyal to retailers offering service and merchandise choice and exclusivity
Seeks offers with cost-effective use of scarce time
Working women
Time-conscious
Self-expression
Responds to informative direct marketing
Working women may see all shopping as a task
Frequent and regular customers
AB
25–40
Seeks complete 'outfit' for social occasions, work and leisure
'Core offer' features
Benefits or problem solutions to shopping needs
Usage occasions
User categories
Retail offer characteristics

Figure 4.7 *Hypothetical offer/positioning matrix for specialist ladies' wear retailing activity*

link more clearly in the hypothetical situation proposed in Figure 4.7 (the matrix for a specialist ladies' wear activity) where perceptions and preferences across usage occasions dominate the offer being made. In this situation it is likely that the essence of continued success (sustainable competitive advantage) is attributable to clearly identified consumer perceptions and preferences, together with life-style issues matched with a positioning response strongly emphasizing in-usage occasions, which are relevant to the target customer group.

The application of technology, specifically information technology, to retailing will be discussed in a subsequent chapter. At this point we should consider how it can influence positioning and repositioning decisions.

Information technology (IT) can offer the retailer benefits in planning and control and in marketing. The application of EPOS can improve productivity and sharpen the merchandise offer. The use of IT to build a customer data-base offers a major marketing-based competitive advantage. The use of IT in this manner by the mail order companies has resulted in accurate customer profiling, together with precision-based merchandise offers as the 'specialogue' has developed (Walters 1988).

An accurate and responsive customer data-base holds the key to tracking shifts in the *customer base*, but does require overall *consumer response* to make effective conclusions concerning changes in both the target market and/or target market needs.

Social values, consumer values and shopper characteristics

A basic input to life-style or socio-cultural research is the broad but basic values shared by the target group because it is these that form a foundation for all aspects of behaviour. Mitchell (1983) suggests that 'Values are defined as the entire constellation of a person's attitudes, beliefs, opinions, hopes, fears, prejudices, needs, desires and aspirations that taken together govern how one behaves and which find holistic expression in a lifestyle.'

Much of the initial work in this area was initiated by the VALS study in the United States during the 1970s. A similar study for the United Kingdom has resulted in the commercial offer of Taylor Nelson Futures Research of social value groups.

A point to be made is that it is not sufficient to know that a target market comprises self-explorers, social resisters, experimentalists, conspicuous consumers, belongers, survivors, or the simply aimless. Much more information is required. For example, the broad social

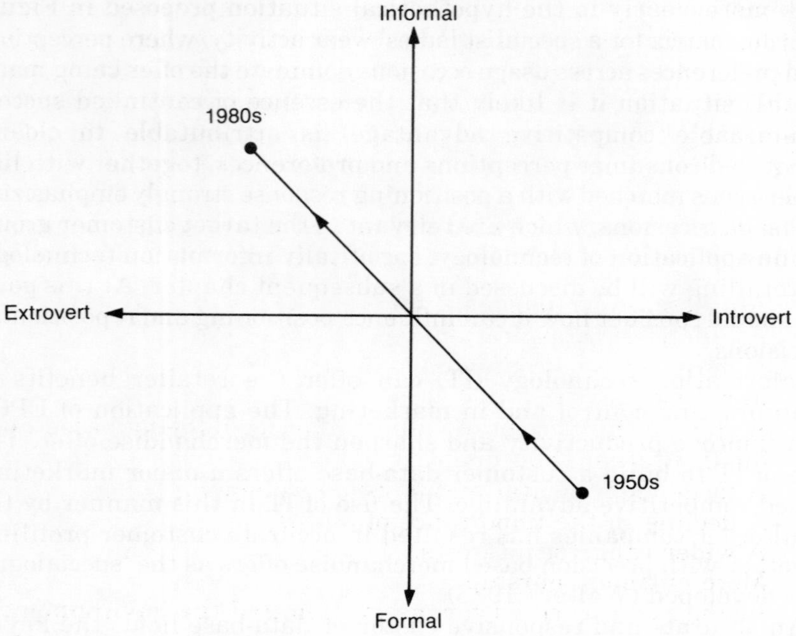

Figure 4.8 *A hypothetical social values map*

trends that have occurred, and their implications and relevance to retailing, are necessary inputs. Also vitally important is information concerning how these have developed and how they influence attitudes towards, and perceptions of, different forms of retail offers; alternatively, how social values influence the development of consumer values and, therefore, the store selection and product purchasing decision.

Consider the example suggested by Figure 4.8. Here we have a hypothetical plot of the way in which a 'society' has changed on two important dimensions. As a society it has moved away from formal attitudes, when much of its population saw itself as introvert (1950s). It is now more progressive and more extrovert (1980s).

From this broad picture we need to identify retailing specific components. These two broad issues suggest implications for apparel merchandise retailers. A move away from formal attitudes is likely to change attitudes towards views held about formal *vs.* informal situations and occasions, and what is appropriate in terms of dress.

On the other dimension we can see implications for this market with the overall shift towards being more extrovert. It could be expected that attitudes to dress would become more flamboyant as the extroverts use 'fashion' to differentiate themselves. These broad characteristics set a backcloth against which specific research can then be conducted. Furthermore, it should be noted that other macro-issues may exist and all should be considered when the research commences. Typically there is an overlap and there are usually a range of linked characteristics, some having more interest than others.

The Taylor Nelson work on the United Kingdom has suggested a number of trends that are seen. In particular they suggest:

- An increase in informality.
- An increase in aspirations.
- A move towards individualsim.
- More exclusivity.
- A shift in the concept of value with criteria being based upon quality rather than quantity.
- A focus upon mental and physical well-being.
- A decline in the importance of status.
- A wider range of interests.
- More entrepreneurship.
- Increased concern with conservation and the environment.

The important next step for the retailer is to identify clusters of indicators that are meaningful in a retailing sense, i.e. social values that influence the development of consumer values. To develop workable customer profiles, the retailer has two requirements of this approach. One is that the data generated can be used to develop a retail offer with a directly related set of strategies for merchandise, store environment, customer service and customer communication. Second, and vital to the retailer's success, is that customer clusters are very close to each other for each component of the offer. What we mean by this is simply that customers are targeted such that all aspects of the retailer's offer are equally attractive. Figures 4.9a and 4.9b illustrate this point. In Figure 4.9a customers in each of the four departments are closely clustered. This means that there can be a co-ordinated and coherent positioning statement made with specific and related offer characteristics to a target customer group whose perceptions and expectations are based on shared values.

However, in Figure 4.9b the retailer has a problem. Despite how well he has researched the customer base, the mapping suggests four quite different customer groups whose perceptions and expectations are clearly quite different.

Segment coupling is feasible with variables such as price/quality/style. The concept is illustrated in Figure 4.10. Here we see a 'trade-off' offer being made to potential customers between price, quality

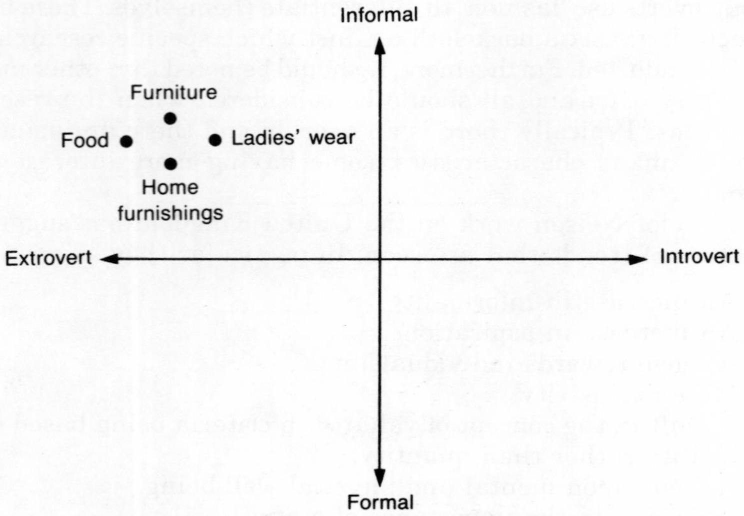

Figure 4.9a *Hypothetical plot of* ideal *customer type profile by merchandise group*

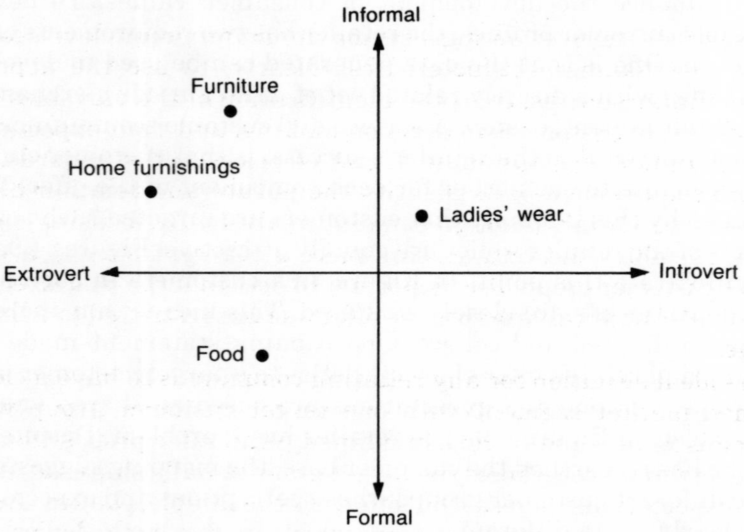

Figure 4.9b *Hypothetical plot of* less than ideal *customer type profile by merchandise group*

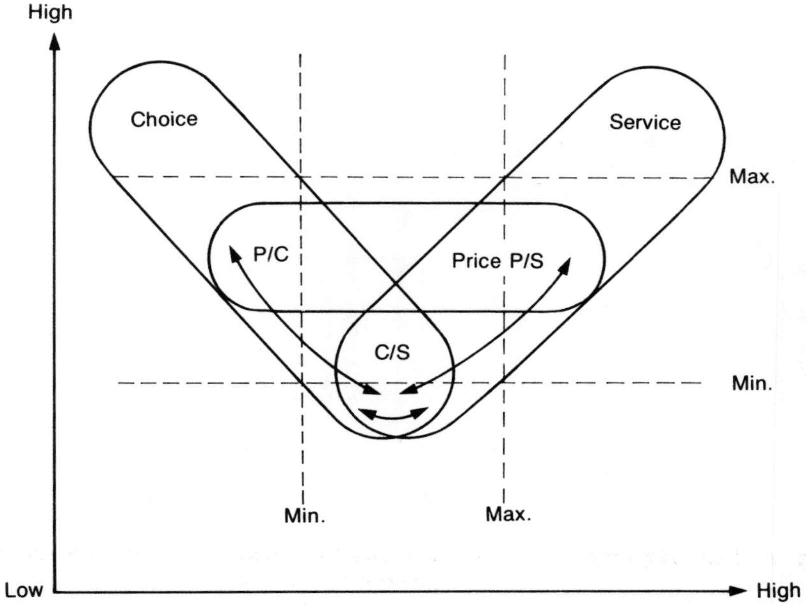

Figure 4.10 *Segment coupling: identifying common denominators or shared basic characteristics with trade-off potential*

and service. The overlap suggests maximum/minimum levels for the three merchandise characteristics. Clearly, to use the approach successfully requires, first, the identification of the variables most significant to customers in decision-making, and their expectations for maximum and minimum levels of prices and standards. The second requirement is to identify the nature and relationships of trade-off potentials through conjoint analysis. By focusing on just three variables the retailer can make a coherent offer to a wider target customer group. It is important to note that the characteristics are equally applicable *across* the offer and not restricted to a limited range.

The ideal situation for any retailing company is to have a clearly defined market segment with one target customer group which responds to an equally clearly defined retail offer proposition. For these fortunate companies the target group usually shares attitudes and expectations *across* the offer. For example, Laura Ashley customers have design expectations which are met by the ladies' wear household textiles and children's wear ranges. Next has a similar appeal.

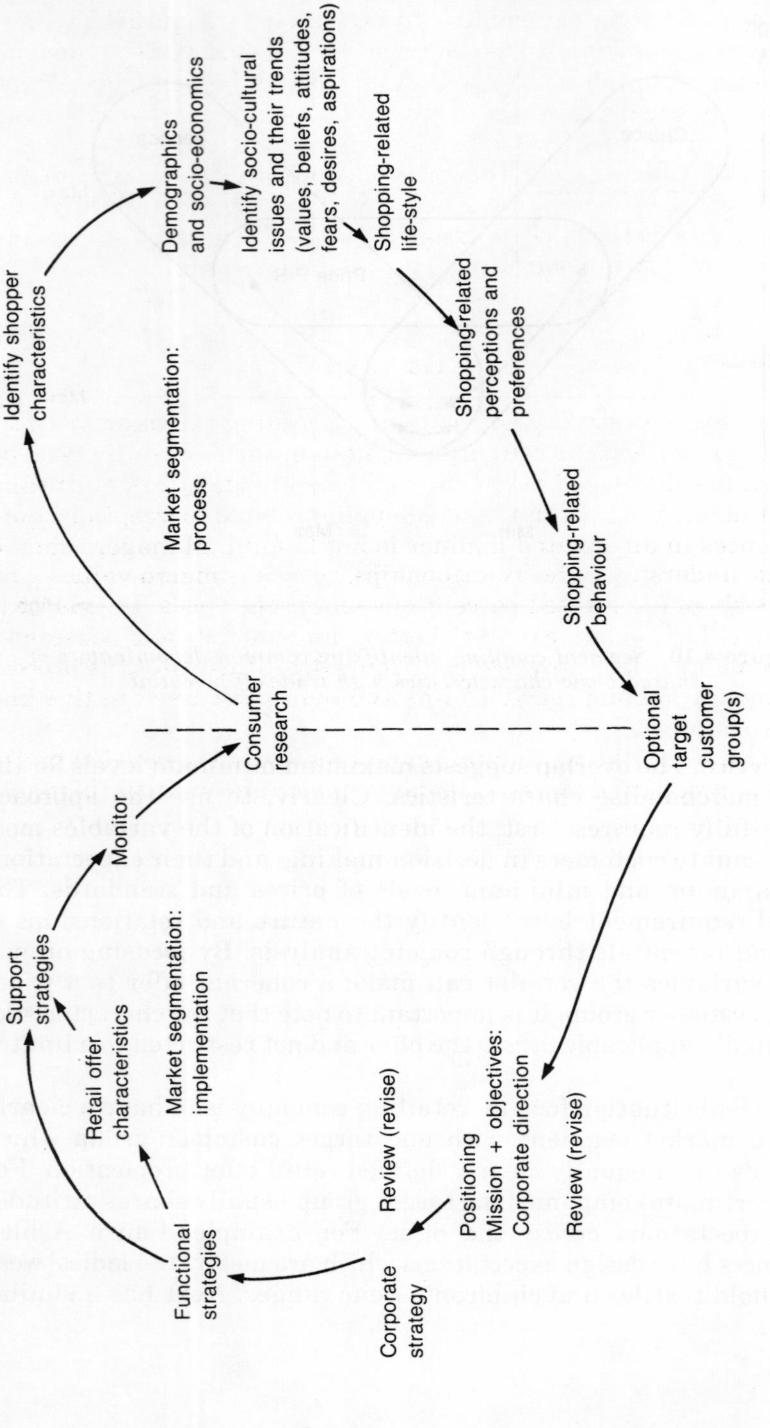

Figure 4.11 *Market segmentation process and implementation*

However, for some companies (those typified by Figure 4.9b) there are targeting problems. The solution for them may be to develop different positioning strategies around each of the customer groups, particularly where there is a high risk of presenting an overall image of confusion (especially for department stores and variety chain multiples). Alternatively, they may look for links between broader classifications of merchandise, and to couple segments into viable customer groups to which a reasonably well co-ordinated offer might be made. This, we would suggest, is segment coupling.

Summary

Market segmentation and customer profiling is now strongly influenced by socio-cultural issues. These in turn are influenced by basic values developed over time and which usually are culturally based. Identifying values and shopping-related perceptions and preferences in an isolated manner is not helpful. Managers should seek to understand the relationships between macro-values and specific shopping-related perceptions and preferences. In this way, shopping behaviour can be better understood and customer requirements better provided for. Figure 4.11 illustrates the process of segmentation and serves to link the topics discussed in this and earlier chapters.

In Figure 4.11 the segmentation process is used to develop target customer groups and serves as the major input into strategic planning decisions.

PART TWO

Creating and Implementing a Retail Positioning Strategy

Introduction

Earlier chapters have considered the role of marketing in strategy decisions and the issues of customer and consumer research. In Part Two we examine the nature of marketing-based decisions. We consider merchandise, trading format, customer service and customer communications as components of the positioning strategy, and consider each from two aspects. The first discusses the components of each activity by considering them as strategic decisions and the second considers how these decisions may be implemented.

Researching market opportunity and deriving customer profiles

Central to the discussion in Part Two is the role of customer-based market opportunity research.

The previous chapter discussed the research process at some length; here we seek to reinforce the importance of this approach. In the subsequent chapters the discussion will be based on the assumption that such an approach to market and customer definition has been undertaken.

In Figure P2.1 we suggest a model that encapsulates all of the information inputs required to reach a target of *core customers*. It will be remembered that earlier we established that core customers are those whose characteristics and expectations are known and understood, and around whom an offer can be built. The company should have confidence in the fact that meeting the needs of this target customer group will result in achieving the revenue and profitability objectives implied by the critical success factor performance parameters.

The benefits of this approach are that three essential issues are resolved. Firstly, it enables the company to make decisions concerning *core merchandise characteristics*; it also identifies the issues comprising the *key features of the retail offer*. Secondly, it identifies *major competitors*; and thirdly, it establishes the *requirements for establishing sustainable competitive advantage.*

Core merchandise characteristics reflect the basic issues of width, depth and availability, together with quality/price and exclusivity/price (or other combinations) considerations. The benefits of customer targeting are that the research identifies those factors to which the selected core customer group are responsive.

Defining *key supporting features* of the *retail offer* characteristics in this way also results in developing those elements of the business

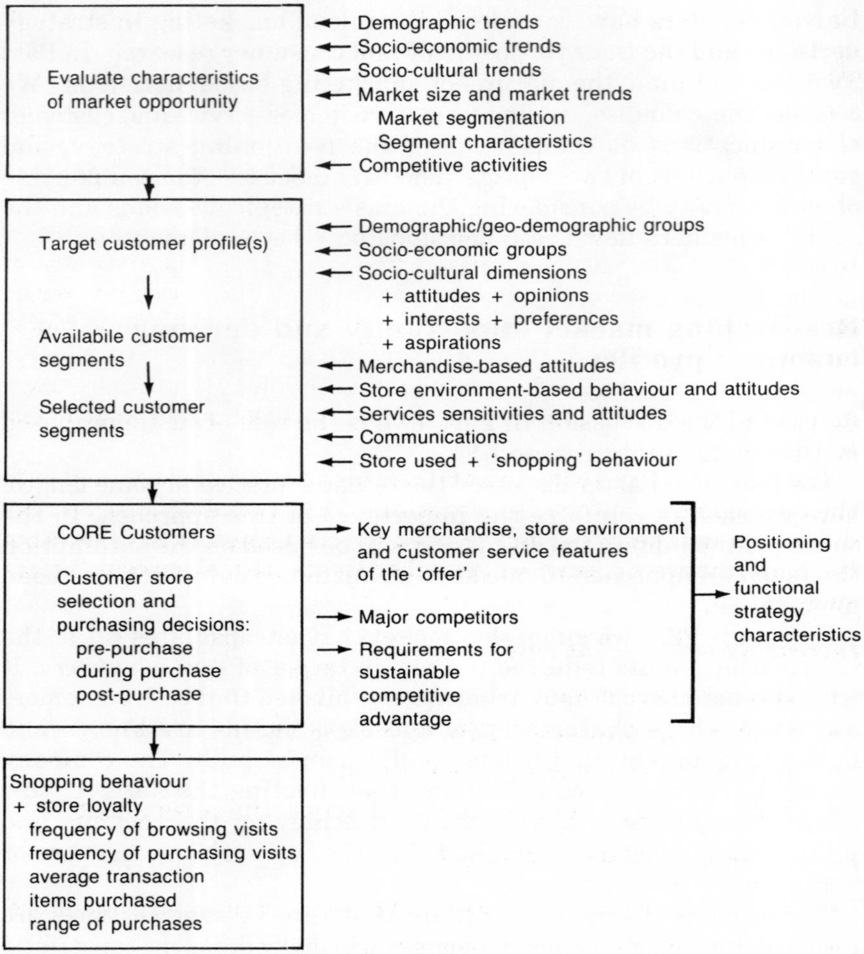

Figure P2.1 *Researching market opportunity and deriving customer profiles*

which will best satisfy the tangible and intangible aspects of the core customers' requirements. These may be service aspects, which are added to existing merchandise ranges (such as fashion advisory/consultancy services); or service products (such as financial advisory and investment services, hairdressing, etc.); or facilities such as crêche and childcare areas.

The identification of *major competitors* can be more difficult than it may at first appear. They are those whose merchandise and service offers match or are very similar. It is possible to use customer research to help here — similar attitudes and perceptions towards a group of stores is a clear indication that customers see them and their offers as similar. In addition to identifying current competitors it is a worthwhile exercise to consider market trends and segmentation characteristics with a prospective view concerning opportunities that competitors *may be able to pursue*. Clearly, *potential* competition should also be identified.

The *requirements for sustainable competitive advantage* are likely to be aspects of the business that will be specific to the target customer group. They may be merchandise, service, format or, possibly, based on a distinctive method of customer communication. Whatever form (or forms) these aspects take, they will be performed in a clearly superior fashion at predetermined delivery levels that are both acceptable (to the customer) and viable (in cost-effectiveness terms) to the company).

The following eight chapters will consider the issues concerned with the development and implementation of functional strategies. The discussion will be based on the need for the company to determine the performance parameters described by its critical success factors such as

Increasing sales revenue by:

- Increasing customer visits.
- Converting browsing visits to buying visits.
- Increasing the average transaction.
- Encouraging customers to spend across the assortment.

Increasing gross profitability by:

- Supplier selection — number and criteria; performance monitors.
- Evaluating assortment performance.
- Monitoring customer decision criteria.
- Improved margin management.

Containing operating costs and increasing contribution by:

- Evaluating cost-effectiveness of activities.
- Review accountability levels.

Increasing the productivity of human and physical assets by:

- Increasing sales and contribution per employees and selling space.
- Increasing throughput of distribution facilities.

Adding value to the customer offer by:

- Adding service(s) to existing merchandise ranges.
- Expanding merchandise ranges to include customer-perceived added-value items (time and energy savings, 'healthy' aspects, etc.).
- Offering facilities to encourage customers to spend more time in the stores (e.g. crêche and childcare facilities).

During the discussion, the importance of identifying strategy and implementation issues that have an impact on the other functional strategies will be considered. The potential for creating added value (and competitive advantage) by developing these overlap areas will also be explored.

The chapters will follow a similar format. There will be a chapter on the *development of the functional strategy* (i.e. merchandise, customer service, trading format and store environment and customer communications). This will be followed by a chapter discussing the *implementation of the strategy*.

Central to any functional strategy decision is an understanding of the customers' store selection and purchasing decisions, together with their perceptions and expectations of the 'retail offer' of both the company and its competitors; the retail offer being the explicit statement of their positioning.

In each of the chapters that follow we have made the assumption that the role of marketing is to influence the store selection and purchasing decisions activities, and to 'progress' or 'process' the customer through the search, comparison, transaction, delivery, use extension and evaluation stages of the store selection/purchasing activity and to establish them as store-loyal customers who revisit the store frequently and consider it their 'first choice' store.

Thus, each of the functional strategy chapters considers the issues implications of this task and develops a functional strategy to achieve this. The implementation chapters develop the strategy into operational plans and consider the issues and influences on supporting activities such as operations management and distribution. Each implementation chapter has a discussion on the issues of monitoring and controlling the plans and discusses the use of the performance data which are produced.

CHAPTER 5

Developing merchandise strategy

Introduction

In this chapter the issues concerning merchandise strategy are discussed. Having identified and explored these important factors, the process of implementing merchandise strategy is examined in some detail. Both models used in this discussion will use the approach offered in Figure P2.1 to identify market opportunity and develop a core customer profile.

Merchandise strategy decisions

There are two areas to be considered when making merchandise strategy decisions. These are featured in Figure 5.1 and comprise: marketing considerations and financial considerations.

This chapter considers both of these in some depth. They are not mutually exclusive and the interrelationships will be explored. Figure 5.1 suggests that a sequence exists. Our research supports this assumption, and the sequence is initiated by establishing the implications for strategy decisions of the relative customer perceptions and expectations to and of the merchandise offer.

Marketing considerations

As established in the introduction to the following chapters, we have assumed that central to any merchandise decision (or for that matter any of the other functional strategies) is an understanding of the customers' store selection and purchasing decisions, together with

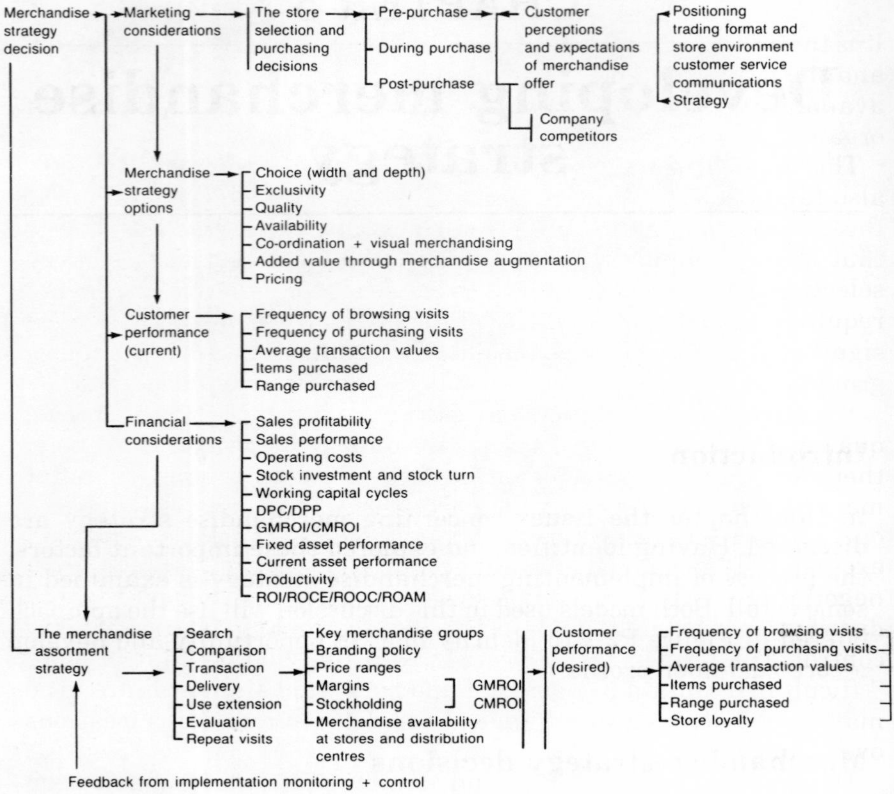

Figure 5.1 *Developing the merchandise strategy*

their perceptions and expectations of the 'merchandise offer' of both the company and its competitors.

Figure 5.1 uses this assumption to explore the *merchandise options* available to influence the store selection and purchasing decisions of the target customer group. The initial customer research will have identified the major issues (see Figure P2.1), but these options must be examined in detail if the objectives of the company are to be realized.

Merchandise strategy options

It is the customer that indicates expectations of an assortment profile and the issues of choice (width and depth), exclusivity, quality and availability have major implications for structuring the buying organization as well as funding the stockholding.

The implications for buying structures are important. They are also fundamental to the philosophy of the buying organization. If the core customer group seeks wide choice and exclusivity, it suggests that buyers should be given a brief to be creative and to be very selective in their sourcing. If high levels of *merchandise quality* are required then the cost implication of quality control will be a significant factor. The reverse obtains for a price-led core customer group, and the brief to buyers will be significantly different.

The buyers' task is to source across a narrow range, to meet specific quality standards at very competitive purchasing prices. It is likely, therefore, that the management styles in these situations will differ markedly. In the first example, the buyers will be expected to source only after extensive searching for merchandise that offers choice and exclusivity. In the second example, the emphasis will be placed on negotiation skills with suppliers who can offer volume, quality and distribution reliability. Both approaches require high levels of quality control. The former, in many ways, will find quality control more difficult to maintain if consistent and persistent standards are to be maintained across a wide range of suppliers in numerous locations over time.

The implications of width and depth requirements have been inferred in the discussion above, and are illustrated in Figure 5.2. The assortment profiles illustrated can be seen to have quite different implications for both customer offers and buying/merchandising organization structures. The financial implications will be discussed below.

Assortment profiles have other important considerations. These are availability and co-ordination. Both are closely connected with pricing decisions.

Availability (or service level) is variously defined. It simply means the level of stock required to ensure that a planned level of sales is achieved across the assortment and with product categories. This will vary as shown in Figure 5.3a: the higher the level of availability sought, the higher the level of stockholding costs.

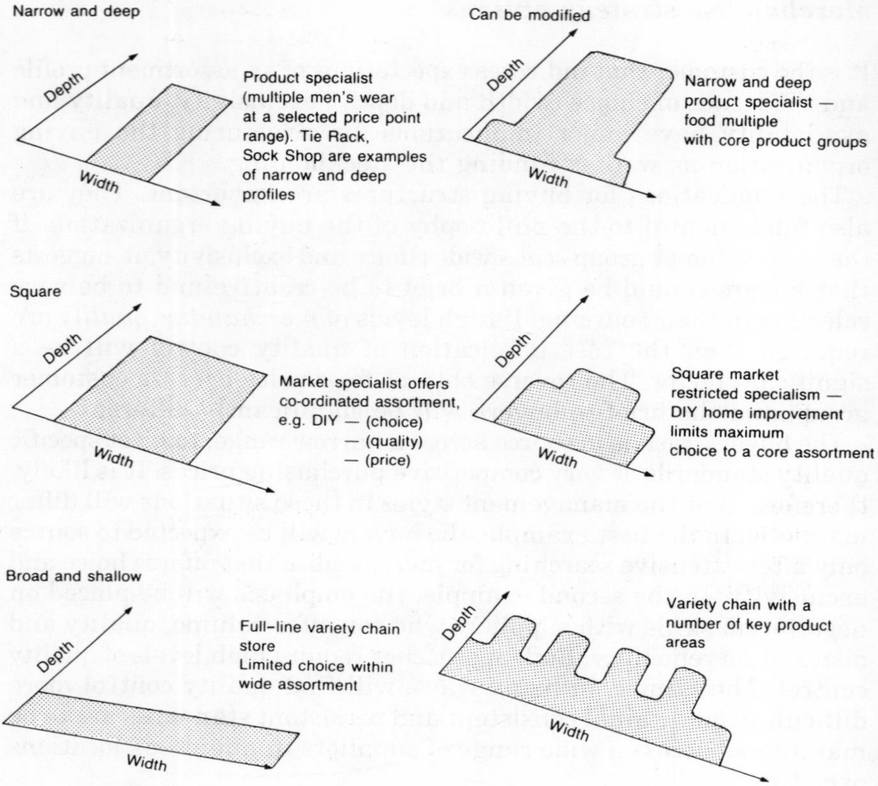

Figure 5.2 *Assortment profiles for differing merchandise strategies*

Availability is typically measured as a percentage of orders met over a specified timespan. This is necessary because it introduces the notion of reorder/replenishment cycles. Thus, an availability performance of 98 per cent implies that from a specific allocation of merchandise, 98 per cent of orders were satisfied. The suggestion made in Figure 5.3a is that very high levels of availability are accompanied by very high levels of stockholding costs. The justification of these costs can be ascertained by considering the sales response curve. If high levels of stockholding are met with an increasing level of sales, it follows that there may be an advantage to be gained by maintaining high availability. It has been found that to do so does require a large amount of working capital. An increase of just 2 per cent in availability, say from 95 per cent to 97 per cent, may involve an increase of some 15 per cent in stockholding costs.

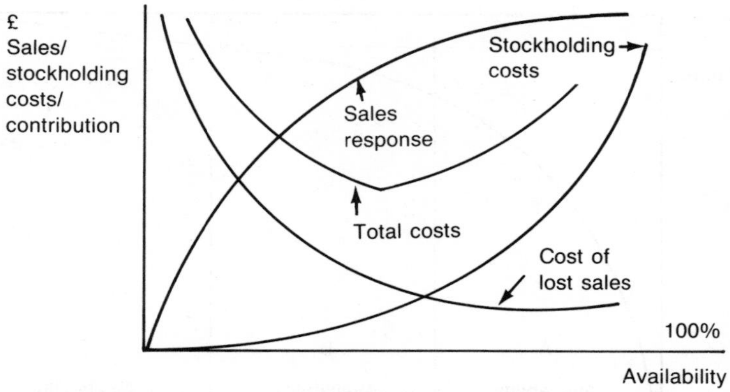

Figure 5.3a *The implications of availability on stockholding costs*

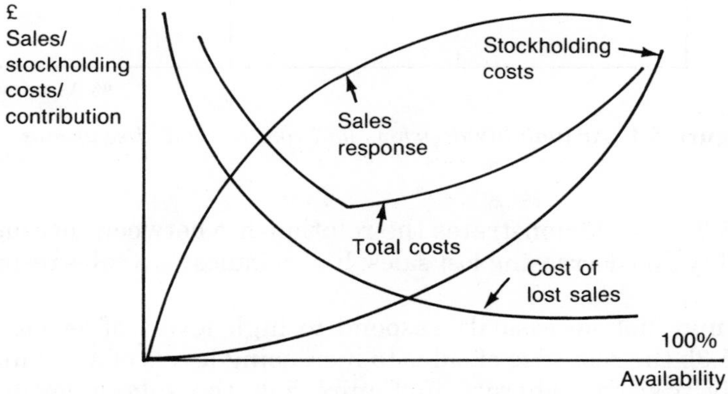

Figure 5.3b *High availability is met with increasing rate of sales*

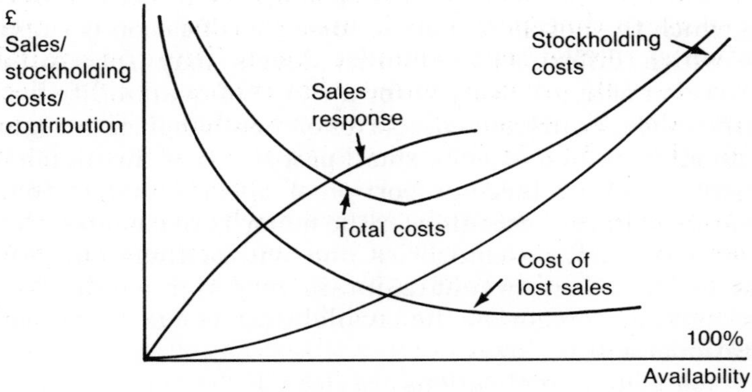

Figure 5.3c *High availability does not increase sales*

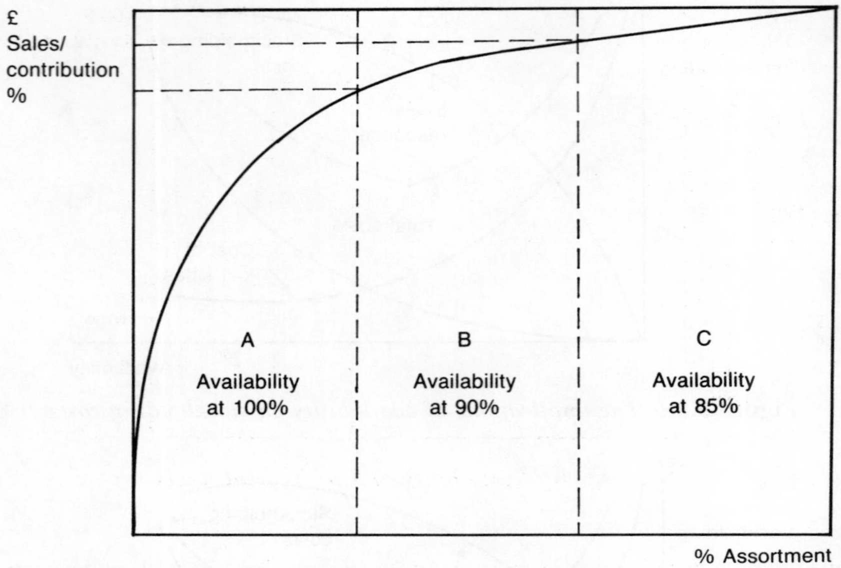

Figure 5.4 *Availability decisions and core merchandise groups*

Figure 5.3a also demonstrates the relationship between increasing availability and decreasing lost sales. It also indicates a sales response curve.

Sales may not necessarily respond to high levels of service. In Figure 5.3b the response of sales to increasing levels of availability is clearly positive, whereas in Figure 5.3c the sales response is disappointing and clearly there is no advantage to be gained by continuing to increase the level of availability.

The implications for merchandise strategy are illustrated in Figure 5.4, in which the notion of merchandise classification is suggested, across which differing availability levels may set. A further consideration of availability is for a range of availability levels to be established for different categories of merchandise. In Figure 5.4 a Pareto effect is suggested (a small proportion of the merchandise range accounts for a large proportion of sales). Thus, for that part of an assortment that accounts for the majority of customer demand (i.e. core merchandise categories and within them the effective purchasing range), we would maintain very high availability. For slower moving categories the availability levels (and customer expectations) will be lower.

The stockholding implications are clear. If the company is offering

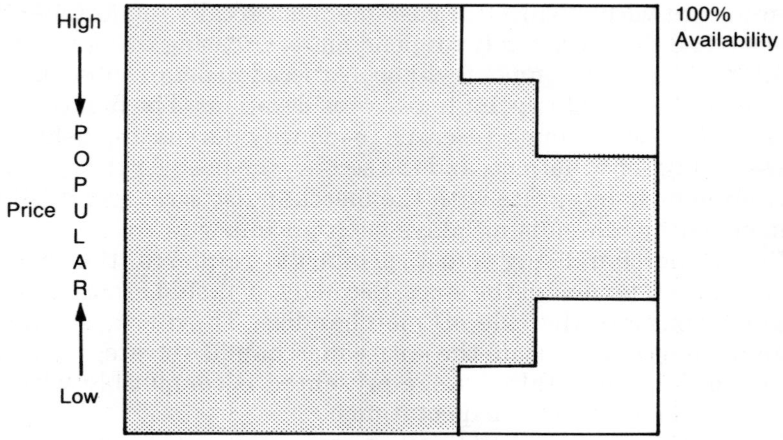

Figure 5.5 *Availability and price point levels*

choice as a major customer benefit, it is not viable to offer the same level of availability across the entire range. However, if an effective purchasing range of the target customers can be ascertained, then this may be the limit of the range carried to offer high availability. Research will identify the dimensions of the range necessary for this treatment.

There is a price/availability consideration. In Figure 5.5 the situation is illustrated whereby only merchandise in the popular price range is carried to offer high levels of availability. The same consideration can be applied to size, colour and styles. However, it is likely that it may be more difficult to develop trends for styles.

Co-ordination and visual merchandising are often seen as an aspect of customer service. Examples of successful co-ordination and visual merchandising are most frequently seen in apparel retailing. The Limited and, in the United Kingdom, Next, demonstrated the effectiveness of co-ordinated merchandise display. They provide advice to customers who have doubts concerning the matching potential of styles and colours, and they increase customer purchasing visits and transaction sizes. As discussed earlier, when combined with market segmentation, the notion of *edited retailing* is developed. One of the major benefits is a high level of choice for a specific customer group, together with a lower level of stock investment.

There is considerable overlap between merchandise decisions and those made when considering trading format and store environment. Together, the merchandise and store trading style create an environment within which the customer feels totally comfortable (and relaxed) and therefore likely to spend more. Creating the appropriate retail exchange environment will be discussed in detail subsequently.

Here it is sufficient to point to two considerations. The first concerns the need for the customer research to identify purchasing behaviour across a range of situations; and the second, the need for the exchange environment to integrate with the merchandise strategy. It is here that visual merchandising plays such an important role.

Visual merchandising must primarily reinforce the market positioning statement of the store. Secondly, it should arouse interest in (and stimulate the sale of) merchandise. Thirdly, it should co-ordinate and communicate the entire merchandise strategy, thereby ensuring that the total message presented is compatible with the target customer group's expectations.

To do this successfully often requires some changes to management's attitudes and style. To be effective the visual merchandising activity should be included in merchandise selection as well as in-store design and space allocation. Often merchandise that is inappropriate to the positioning being transmitted is featured in assortments. Invariably, the reasons for doing this are based on financial or economic motives. These may be because 'We have always sold this . . . and this . . . and this'; or because 'Our competitors stock it'. The result is usually reflected in the sales pattern: the average transaction is lower, dominated by sales of the one item. Meanwhile, the market positioning 'statement' becomes diluted and confused.

Often it is the visual merchandising activity that identifies ways and means of augmenting the merchandise assortment. This may be by identifying complementary products (such as accessories in men's wear and ladies' wear) or by combining merchandise into life-style groups which identify product applications for the customer and, in doing so, increase the value of the customer transaction by suggesting that a *range of items* is required.

Product or merchandise augmentation may extend into product-services as well as minor product differentiation. A typical example, common to many forms of retailing, is to include a service package with the product. Examples of this can be seen in motor vehicle sales. Virtually all vehicle manufacturers include AA and RAC membership for the period of the vehicle warranty. Simple product augmentation/differentiation can be the sale of electrical items with batteries and plugs; while the principle can be expanded as it has been by appliance retailers to include the installation of the purchase, ensuring that it functions and removing the replaced item. The customer service implications of merchandise augmentation will be considered in Chapter 7.

Price is another component of customer expectations. There are two aspects of pricing. One is retailer profitability, the other is concerned with optimizing customer satisfaction.

Dealing first with optimizing customer satisfaction, it is important to understand that customer satisfaction is only achieved when a number of characteristics of the retail offer are in balance.

Commercial research often reports consumers as primarily seeking value for money. We suggest this is confusing at best, misleading at worst. Customers are prepared to make trade-offs between offer characteristics, one of which is price. The other characteristics include quality, variety, exclusivity and availability, together with aspects of store environment and customer service. In this chapter our concern is with merchandise strategy and we shall therefore discuss customer satisfaction in this context, but we are clearly aware of the influence of other issues and will return to them subsequently.

The evidence for suggesting that customers optimize price and other merchandise can be seen in the range of segmentation that exists across all forms of retailing. In food there is a range of offers available from the specialist and exclusive offers made by Fortnum and Mason and by Harrods (often replicated by independents in suitable catchments). There are offers such as those made by Waitrose and Safeway, who offer customers both choice and exclusivity. There are the quality-led offers of Tesco and Sainsbury. Also, there are the price-led offers of Kwik Save; and there are the convenience-led offers of the symbol groups, who interpret availability in a temporal and location context. In each segment there exist profitable and long-established businesses.

Price also has a communications aspect. For many consumers price indicates quality, exclusivity, choice, etc. In this context, price is used by consumers to make choice decisions. they develop expectations of price/quality, price/exclusivity based on the 'messages' given by retailer pricing within overall merchandise strategies. These are compared and evaluated. At a group discussion concerning pricing in food outlets, one participant summarized this activity by saying: 'I do my shopping there [named store] because it is nearest . . . but every three or four weeks I go elsewhere to check on prices and product ranges.'

For the retailer, price decisions are fundamental. Without adequate margins the business cannot exist for very long. There is a number of objectives for which price has important influences. As a business, the retailer seeks profitability, growth and cash flow, but the business competes with other retailing companies and price is important in competitive strategy. Pricing strategy can either be proactive or reactive. It can be used to increase customer appeal (among those for whom price is a primary feature in determining choice). Conversely, price changes may be reactive. They may change only when competition in specific merchandise areas becomes focused on price offers and when sales volumes may be put in jeopardy by not meeting or beating price reductions of competitors.

Price is an integral element of merchandise strategy. It should not be considered as a separate issue. For some retailers it forms the major part of an offer, but it should always be considered as serving a supporting role for strategy. It reinforces the positioning statement and contributes to the market positioning statement made to customers, competitors and suppliers. In so doing, it makes a contribution to achieving the performance requirements prescribed by the company's critical success factors.

Customer performance

In Figure 5.1 *customer performance* characteristics are identified and used as a basis for identifying and developing merchandise strategy. The analysis suggested in Figure P2.1 will identify the core customer target, their merchandise requirements and shopping behaviour. Of particular interest here is their shopping behaviour in terms of visit frequencies, average spend per visit (transaction) and the range of items purchased.

Detailed knowledge of these items enables the merchandise planner to determine what should be stocked, its characteristics, such as branded item *vs.* own-brand (or in what proportions both should be stocked), what items are purchased together, what substitutes are acceptable and how often the merchandise should be replenished. It is important to know rates of sale because this will help plan space allocation and distribution frequencies.

The *range of purchases* made by customers is important for a number of reasons. Clearly, the 'range' purchased/'range' stocked is a key factor in determining the overall financial performance of assortment, but it is just as important when positioning is considered. If the company is positioned such that 'offering exclusive products of high quality with exceptional choice' as opposed to 'offering quality and lowest competitive prices' then the range purchased/range stocked ratio becomes a very important issue. It could also be described as the range coverage required to be seen as credible, as a significant retailer in the assortment area.

This credibility factor is clearly an issue of competitive advantage. However, it can also be seen as a measure of risk. For example, a retailer offering an extensive range across a number of product groups within an assortment has a major investment in stockholding. The

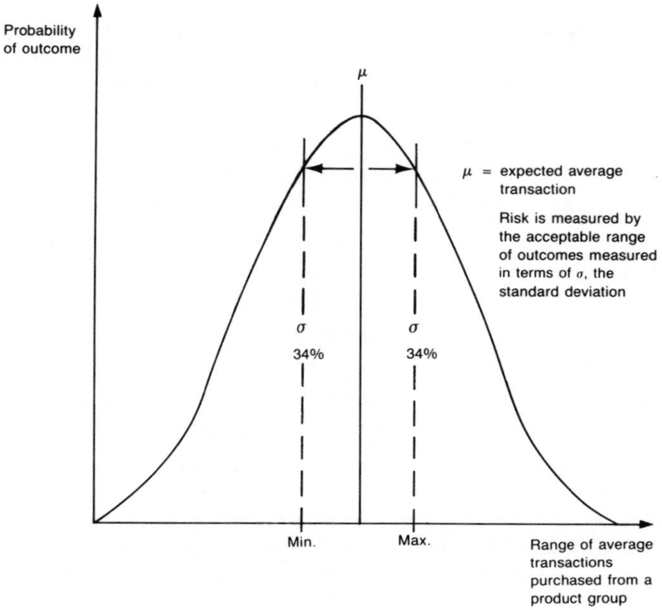

Figure 5.6 *The normal curve: mean return and standard deviation*

return on this investment may or may not be acceptable. The level of the return may be unsatisfactory, and consequently the risk involved in offering a wide choice can be very high. This point was made earlier in the discussion on availability.

It is in the interest of the retailer to maximize the range of purchases consonant with both positioning and financial objectives. To clarify: if the positioning objective is concerned with 'offering exclusive products of high quality with exceptional choice' then the risk of a low return on stock investment can be quite high. One method of appraising risk in this context is to use simple probability theory to act as an indicator of the effective range of purchase by the average size of transaction and therefore the level of risk involved in providing choice.

Risk can be measured statistically. It is a relatively simple measure to apply and relates the actual performance achieved against expected returns. The returns may be measured in terms of sales or profit achievement (for example, the average transaction per customer) and involves a measurement of standard deviation. Put simply, the standard deviation measures the distribution of performance outcomes around a *mean average transaction*. This is shown as Figure 5.6.

In Figure 5.6 the most likely average transaction (that with the

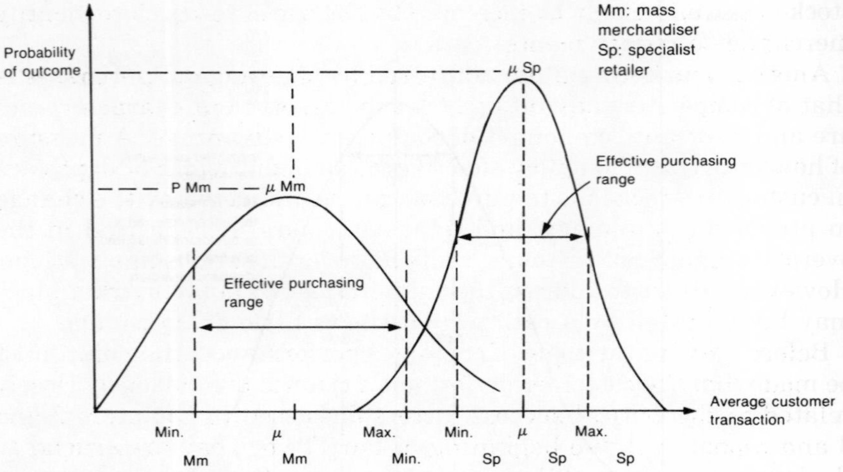

Figure 5.7 *Edited retailing can achieve higher than average transactions with greater probability and lower risk (together with lower stockholding)*

highest probability) is the mean average return, μ. Risk is represented by the measure of the standard deviation. The spread of $\pm$ one standard deviation includes 68 per cent of all results (i.e. the acceptable: effective purchasing range). Because some events (such as the rate of sale or profit returns) are more predictable, it can be expected that the distribution of returns for some products (e.g. basic, non-differentiated products such as food) will be across a narrower range of outcomes. It is also likely that a specialist retailer with a closely targeted customer group will be able to predict more closely the purchasing behaviour of customers. It follows that for this type of retailer the merchandise assortment may be more easily *edited* to eliminate any unnecessary width of merchandise, while at the same time, maintaining essential choice and variety. This will lead to the situation described by Figure 5.7.

Figure 5.7 demonstrates the fact that for a closely targeted customer group merchandise selection may be directed towards achieving an average transaction that is higher than that for a broader merchandise offer (μ Sp > μ Mm). It also suggests that the effective purchasing range will be between a smaller range of average transactions. A benefit from this will be a much more relevant assortment with lower stockholding and consequently higher stock-turn. It will also offer lower markdowns and enhances the impact of merchandise co-ordination. Thus the range purchased/range stocked can effectively be increased by the use of research to identify merchandise requirements.

Another marketing issue addressed by the range of purchases is that of competitive advantage. Clearly, assortment characteristics are an important component of competitive advantage. A measure of how important (and how effective) assortment width or depth are in customers' decisions to purchase can be indicated by the change in proportion of old/new and total customers. A reduction in the overall frequency of customer visits has overall serious implications. However, failure to address the changing needs of the market-place may be indicated by a ratio which shows little or no change.

Before leaving the topic of customer performance, the point must be made that the customer performance criteria are obviously closely related to the critical success factors discussed in Chapters 2 and 3 and repeated at the beginning of Part Two. They are crucial to the long-term success of the company and to its financial performance.

Financial considerations

Within the process of determining merchandise strategy some financial performance expectations are necessary. Before discussing what these might be, a number of broad issues should be raised.

The purpose of any performance objective or measure should be to help plan as well as control any particular activity. Furthermore, different companies have different needs; what is of specific importance to manufacturing companies is often less vitally important to distribution companies — this is particularly valid for measures such as stockturns.

Because it often involves long processes, manufacturing accepts the fact that low stockturns are unavoidable, and often protracted stockturns add value to a product, e.g. whisky. However, while the manufacturer may accept this, the retailers' view will be quite different. They will seek to stock those malt whiskies with the highest consumer appeal, together with a high stockturn.

In Table 5.1 we suggest how financial ratios may be used to indicate performance assessment across a range of activities. Some of these do not directly influence merchandise strategy, nor are they all within the range of responsibility of the merchandise manager. However, they do all have an indirect influence and are worthy of consideration.

Another approach to this issue is shown as Figure 5.8, which is an adaptation of the well-known Dupont financial ratio approach. In Figure 5.8 we have developed a series of ratios which, if used to compare trends over time (and in conjunction with the issues raised

Table 5.1 Financial analysis and resource analysis

Financial ratio		Used to assess
1 *Return on capital*		Overall measure of performance
Return on operating capital		Unit or individual performance
2 *Sales/cost structure*		
Sales profitability:		Assortment selection
Gross margin		Buying efficiency
Operating margin		Pricing policy
		Operations management efficiency, Distribution, Store operations
Sales performance:		Sales growth trends (Y/Y)
Assortment		Sales participation %
Product group		(Y/Y)
New products	%	Sales performance
Existing products	%	Assortment performance
Gross margins	%	Product group/product
Direct costs	%	profitability
Costs:		
Labour		Productivity 'Added value'
Occupancy		Productivity
3 *Asset turnover*		
Fixed assets (outlets, facilities, systems)		Capital intensity (use of assets within component parts of the business)
4 *Net current assets*		
Stockturn:		Merchandise selection
total		Opportunity cost of cash
product group		'Choice', 'Availability'
product		performance
Debtors		Credit sales effectiveness/ service. Opportunity cost of cash
Creditors		Supplier selection Opportunity cost of cash Use of negative working capital
Cash		Opportunity cost of cash resources

Table 5.1 *continued*

Financial ratio	Used to assess
	(current business development, future business development)
Working capital cycle	Efficiency in converting stocks to sales
5 *Liquidity*	
Current ratio	Short-term risk
Acid test ratio	Stockholding policy/ positioning policy
Inventory to net working Capital	'Choice' Availability
6 *Capital structure*	
Debt/equity	Long-term risk of financial structure
Debt/assets	Extent and use of financial resources to finance the firm's operations Expansion potential

by Table 5.1), offers a useful way to analyze the effectiveness of component activities; the sensitivity of changes in cost components upon operations at differing levels and upon ROI; and budget items, which are often expressed as a percentage of sales.

Considering Table 5.1 and Figure 5.8, the cost implications for merchandise decisions are given by the sales/costs structure and net current assets. A review of these may prove helpful. However, it must be remembered that no one measure should be considered in isolation. Other related items should be considered.

Sales profitability is measured by gross margin (and gross profit) if we consider volume × (selling price − cost of goods sold). As an overall measure, an increasing level of sales profitability suggests that the assortment selection is effective and is responded to positively by the target customer group. Gross margin measures the effectiveness of the buying activity. But it should be cross-checked with other measures. For example, it may be found that a high gross margin may be accompanied with increasing distribution costs/sales, suggesting that suppliers are being squeezed for additional margin but are not providing the company with an adequate level of distribution service. Gross margin is also a useful indicator of pricing

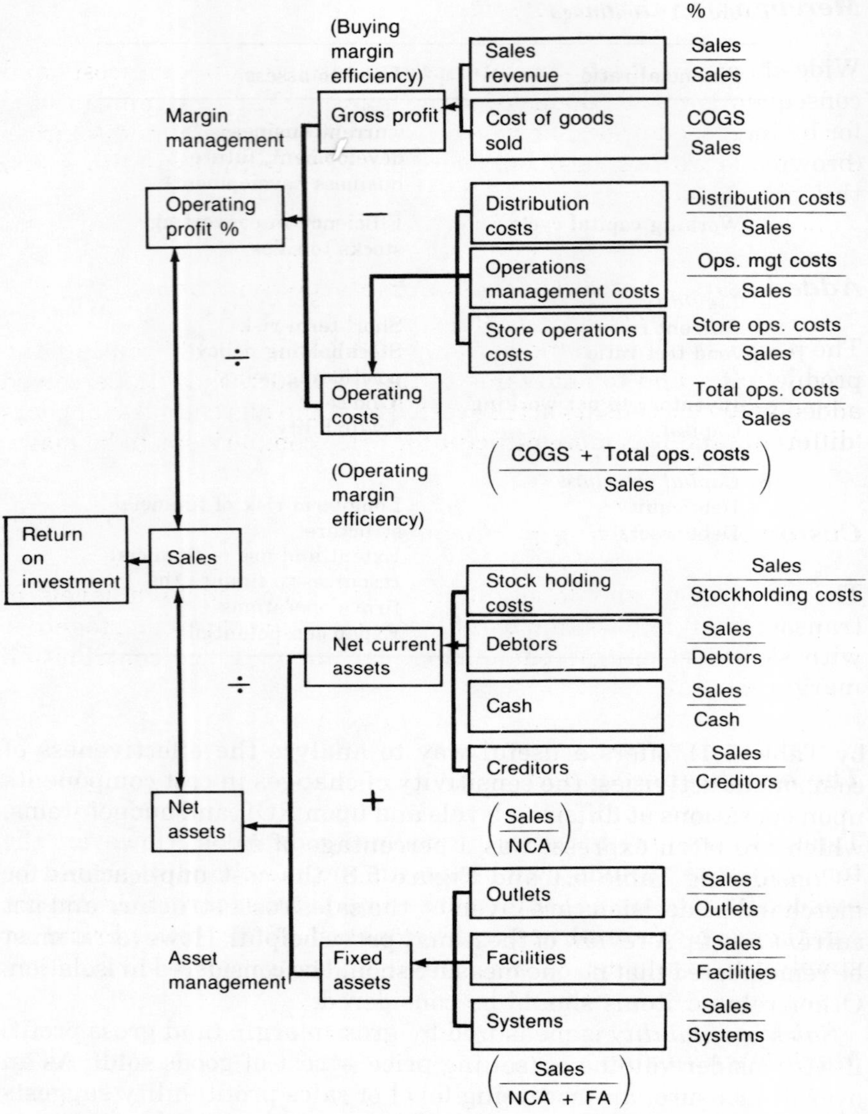

Figure 5.8 *Using ratio analysis for merchandising planning and control*

policy effectiveness. If margin is high and prices are high, but sales volume is declining, then it follows that prices may be set at levels unacceptably high in the view of some customers.

Initially, sales profitability is planned around gross and net (or operating) margin targets. These are set after consideration of the following issues:

Merchandise characteristics

Wide choice and high availability increase stockholding costs and consequently impact upon operating margins. They are compensated for by increased prices, however, in competitive merchandise areas (brown and white goods), but there is a limit to the extent to which this may be done.

Added value through merchandise augmentation

The purposes of merchandise augmentation are to differentiate the product offer and to add value to the offer such that its perceived added value exceeds its actual cost. Thus, the merchandise appears 'different' and it is more difficult for price comparisons to be made.

Customer purchasing performance

The assortment should be planned to encourage high levels of transaction. It follows that careful consideration of pricing, together with skilful visual merchandising, can increase the contribution margin per sale.

The own-brand content

Typically, own-brands offer higher gross margins. However, the temptation to include own-brands in the merchandise should be avoided if there are no sound marketing reasons for their inclusion, e.g. they are essential to the development of the 'retail brand' or simply not available.

Markdown history

Many merchandise categories (e.g. fashion) are known to have higher levels of risk than others. Fashion merchandise has a much higher probability of markdown than 'non-fashion' merchandise. They may both be apparel items. Markdown trends can be used when the margin mix for assortments is initially planned such that compensation for the eventual markdown may be made by initial pricing and merchandise assortment selection decisions. The purpose of planning a margin mix is to optimize the offer made to the customer *and* the profitability of the company.

Sales performance

By the overall assortment and by product group this can offer a useful insight into the overall performance of the effectiveness of existing and new products. The sales participation of existing and new products can demonstrate the need to make revisions to the assortment and how effective recent decisions have been.

Operating costs

These are identified for distribution, field operations and store operations. When expressed as a percentage of sales these can (over time) indicate changes that have occurred as well as measure operating efficiency. From the merchandise manager's point of view, they can provide a useful insight into the changing nature of costs that may occur with changes in the merchandise offer. For example, an increase in availability may be accompanied by an increase in store operations costs as well (as might be expected) as distribution costs. A change in the characteristics of the merchandise (e.g. a move towards chilled products away from a mostly ambient product range) will have cost implications. It is important to be able to review these in the overall context as well as separate cost items. The implications for overall ROI can also be calculated.

Stock investment

Stock investment is of major importance to merchandise strategy decisions. The marketing implications of stock investment have already been explored; the costs of that investment are clearly important. The rate of stockturn gives management both an objective and a performance measure; and these can be set within the context of the positioning of the company. For example, a company offering wide choice and/or high levels of service might well accept a slow rate of stockturn. But this must be reviewed in the context of the performance of the company's critical success factors. We would expect to see a higher than average sale per customer, accompanied by a high level of items purchased and of the range purchased. If these do not follow it would suggest that the stockholding is not a worthwhile investment.

Working capital cycle

This is closely related to stock investment. It is a measure of the company's efficiency in converting stocks into sales. Identification of the location of inventory and the number of days' cover that exists at each location reveals the time-period for which the company must finance inventory in the cycle.

An example will be useful:

	A	B
Depot stocks	28	17
Outlet stocks	7	3
Credit customers' payment	30	10
	65	30
Less credit from suppliers	42	30
Days to finance	23	0

In this hypothetical example Company A operates with a total of 65 days' stock overall. There is a store card facility, which offers customers 30 days' free credit and the company takes 42 days' credit from suppliers. It is left with 23 days' stock cover to finance. The situation described by Company B suggests the use of IT to accelerate stockturns throughout the system. Credit is extended via a third party (a credit card company is used) and outstanding credit is only 10 days. If it pays its suppliers' invoices within 31 days, it can receive an additional settlement discount. It funds none of its stockholding.

The point highlighted by this example is that by reducing stockholding levels and using a credit card operating company it can reduce the working capital cycle. Clearly, it does have some advantages. It will have made considerable IT investment and possibly does not have detailed access to the customer data-base. If Company B followed A's example concerning supplier payments, it could operate on its suppliers' working capital.

DPC/DPP

Recent developments in both IT and in improved supplier/distributor relationships have facilitated the progress made in developing direct product costing and direct product profitability. Considerable work has been conducted in this area and we would mention it within the context of merchandise strategy decisions. Current views would suggest that DPC/DPP is basically a cost accounting system applied to the warehouse and store activities of retailers. The approach allocates direct handling costs to individual products and, therefore, helps to identify product changes or handling methods that will reduce handling costs. Furthermore, it measures the profit contribution for individual products.

Retailers do want to maximize the DPP of their products, but not without considering the key merchandising objective of customer satisfaction through choice, quality, exclusivity, etc. DPP does not have an impact as such until it becomes a strategic part of the decision-making process. In other words, DPP at the individual product item level may prove to be dysfunctional in its impact on merchandise objectives, *unless* it is used *in conjunction* with the overall objective of customer satisfaction. In a straight comparison between two products, the DPP of one may be much higher, but in a consumer blind test the consumers' preference may suggest that the other would outsell it by, say, a factor of 3 to 1! Mere DPP figures are interesting, but they should only be used in conjunction with other established data (such as consumer preferences) to improve retailers' business.

When used in an integrated way, DPP can play an important role in the merchandise strategy. It can be used for:

- Measuring product group profitability, together with overall assortment profitability.
- Eliminating unnecessary costs in transportation, handling, case size, product configuration and shelf position.
- Considering bilateral promotion and advertising efforts.
- Evaluating (together with EPOS data) space allocation and merchandise location in-store. Research suggests that many products experience an increase in sales when located next to related items, thus the joint DPC and DPP data may prove more useful in this situation.

A model based on work conducted by the IGD and others to develop a 'standard model' is presented in Figure 5.9. Its major differences comprise the addition of inputs which influence merchandise strategy decisions (consumer preferences and customer performance topics). In addition, there is a requirement to consider sourcing and supply chain issues, which have an impact on downstream direct costs. Also included are space occupancy and support costs (fixtures, energy, etc.), together with direct employee costs. We would argue that both of these can be product-specific and are influenced by the choice of

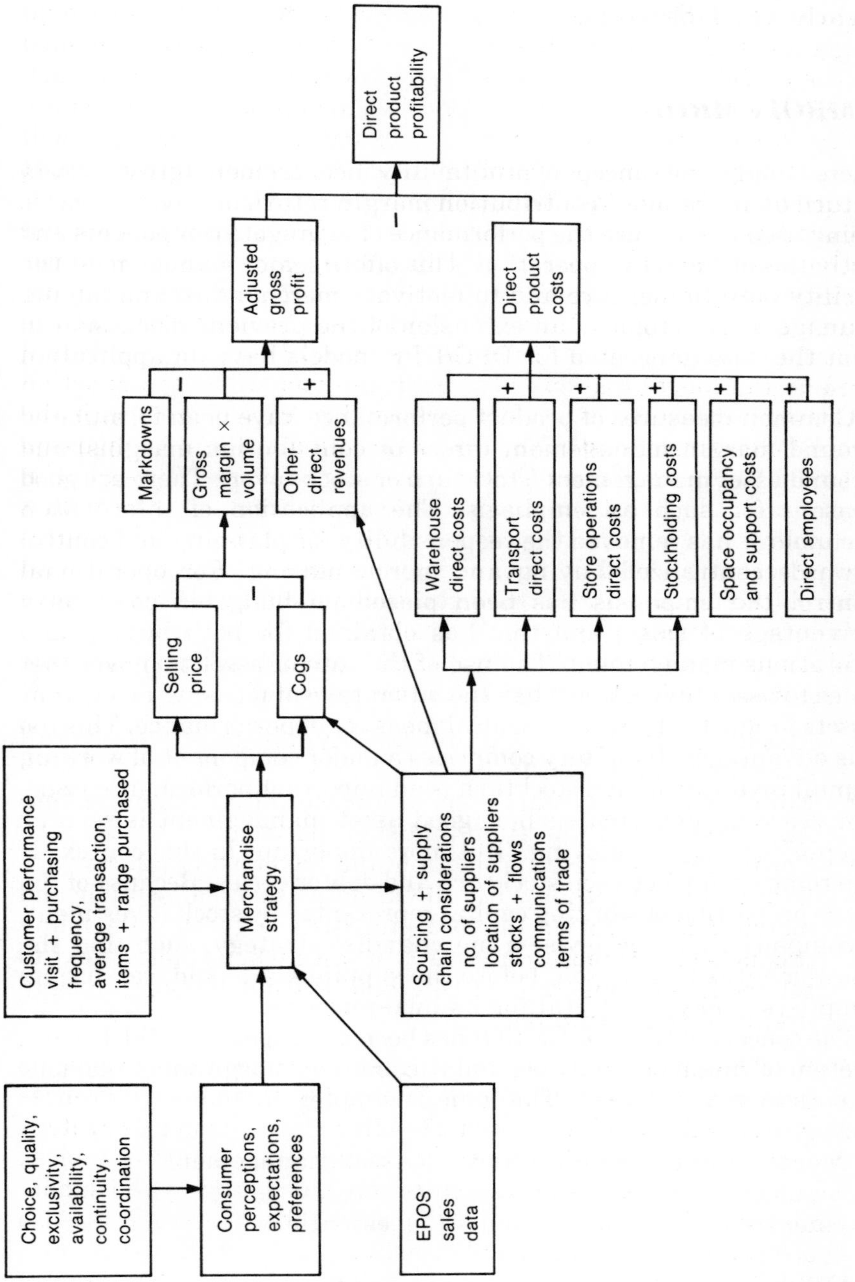

Figure 5.9 *A DPC/DPP model*

merchandise in an overall merchandise strategy. As such they are clearly avoidable costs.

GMROI/CMROI

Increasingly, the concept of profitability measurement (gross margin return on investment/contribution margin return on investment) is being used to measure the performance of aggregate components and activities of the retail operation. This offers senior management the facility both to measure and to motivate merchandise and buying managers. This topic is an extension of the previous discussion in that the data generated for DPC/DPP models have an application here.

Common measures of product performance have been formulated around margin management (gross or contribution margins) and around asset management (stockturn or stock cover). There are good reasons for such an emphasis. The application of information technology has removed the responsibility for planning and control towards centralized buying and merchandising. For operational control the emphasis has been placed on budgeted costs as a percentage of sales, and this has obtained for both buying and operations management. The use of the rate of asset turnover (net sales to asset investment) has the advantage of focusing on current assets productivity as an essential measure of performance. This too has advantages. Inventory comprises a major component of working capital investment, and stockturn is an important performance issue. For reasons suggested earlier, good asset management is seen as keeping the 'assets moving'. But more important in this context is the relationship between stockturn and debtor cycles. Because of the large proportion of working capital represented by stock investment, a company that can devise a merchandise strategy, such that the assortment is largely sold before the suppliers are paid, can use its suppliers' working capital for its own purposes.

The concept of GMROI/CMROI has been developed from the Dupont system of financial analysis, and it combines margin management and asset management. The logic is simple:

'Margin management'	and	'Asset management'
is essentially;		is essentially
$\frac{\text{Profit}}{\text{Sales}}$		$\frac{\text{Sales}}{\text{Assets}}$ (or inventory)

by simple cross multiplication:

$$\frac{\text{Profit}}{\text{Sales}} \times \frac{\text{Sales}}{\text{Assets}} = \frac{\text{Profit}}{\text{Assets}}$$

Combined, we have gross margin (or contribution margin) on inventory investment (GMROI/CMROI):

$$\text{GMROI} = \frac{\text{Gross margin (£)}}{\text{Average inventory investment}}$$

$$\text{CMROI} = \frac{\text{Contribution (or operating) margin (£)}}{\text{Average inventory investment}}$$

There is a number of advantages. Firstly, there is the facility to enable management to relate directly to the performance of buying and merchandising activities to the overall performance of the firm. Secondly, it focuses attention on the performance of inventory as an investment. Thirdly, GMROI/CMROI offers the means by which alternative assortment strategies may be evaluated. Fourthly, GMROI/CMROI calculations require *no* additional data; margins and stockturn data are used, which are usually readily available from accounting systems.

GMROI/CMROI is the product of margins and stockturn and can be represented graphically. Figure 5.10 shows that for any one value of GMROI/CMROI there is a curve that links all values of stockturn and gross/contribution margins that meet the target GMROI/CMROI, such as:

Margin (%)		Stockturn
50.0	Target	4
40.0	GMROI	5
33.3	= 200	6

Any assortment will contain merchandise for which there will be a range of margin and stockturn performance outcomes. The purpose of GMROI/CMROI is to plan the range such that the overall performance reaches a desired level of performance. This is illustrated as Figure 5.11. By setting target maxima and minima for gross margin and stockturn the merchandise strategy is reflecting merchandise characteristics – quality, style, choice, availability, exclusivity *and* price levels; and inventory levels necessary to achieve customer satisfaction and profitable sales.

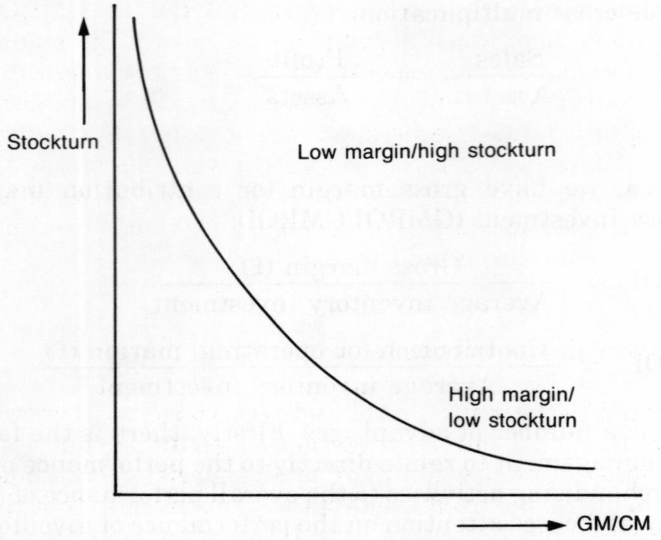

Figure 5.10 *GMROI/CMROI: the product of stockturn and margins*

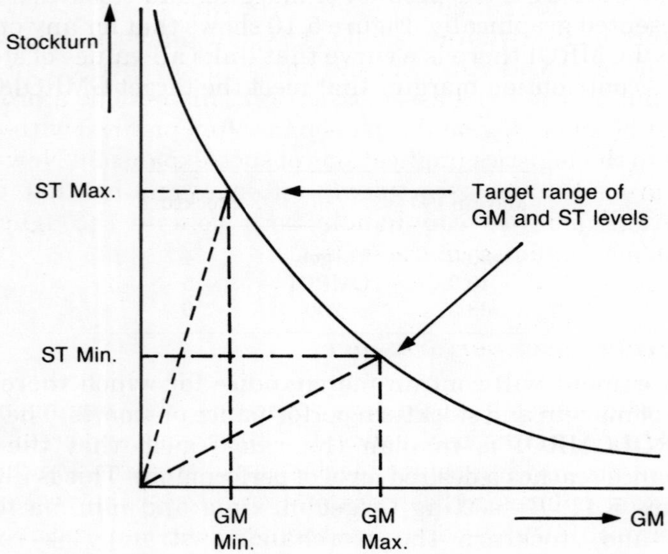

Figure 5.11 *GMROI and range planning to meet target positioning*

The issue of whether to measure GMROI or CMROI is an organizational one. Much depends on the role of the management whose performance is being measured. For example, a certain number of retailers structure selling organizations around buyerships. In such a situation it would be necessary to deduct a number of direct costs from gross margins achieved. Hence the view should be that it is a *return on assets managed* (ROAM), or the *return on operating capital* (ROOC) that is important. Here we suggest that performance can be linked to motivation and incentives.

Fixed asset performance

Fixed asset performance is of indirect concern to merchandise strategy decisions, but is nevertheless an important issue. The concern must be that when merchandise decisions are made, they attempt to utilize the fixed assets of the company such that the return on those assets meets expectations. If this is not possible it suggests that at senior levels there has been poor communications concerning corporate strategy (at the very best) or a complete lack of planning integration. Fixed assets, such as retail outlets, distribution centres and systems structures, are an integral part of the business and a decision not to use part of the fixed asset structure in support of the overall retail offer cannot be made arbitrarily.

The more usual situation is one of expansion of the sales activity without prior consideration of the impact of an increase in volume throughput on the fixed asset structure. This may be a problem in a number of ways. Regional expansion is often planned without prior thought to the logistics implications of such expansion. New product groups are added to assortments, often assuming that existing distribution facilities can handle both volume throughput *and* different merchandise characteristics.

Net current asset performance

Net current asset performance concerns the management of stockholding costs (discussed above), debtors, cash and creditors. The discussion on working capital cycles illustrated the importance of establishing policies for debtors and creditors. The research into customer profiling will determine their use of credit and give strong indications as to the likely size of average customer credit balance and payment times. This in turn can be considered when decisions concerning store cards *vs.* third party card services are made, together with the interest rate to be charged on outstanding balances. If the customer profile suggests heavy use of credit, this should be considered when the assortment profile is being decided, in order to ensure that the price levels and realized margins are sufficient to include this cost of doing business.

The use of suppliers' working capital was also discussed earlier (and will be considered again). There are both positive and negative aspects to be considered. It is sound financial management to take advantage of payment terms offered by suppliers. In monopsonistic situations, such as those enjoyed by large multiple retailers, extended payment terms may be part of the negotiated terms. However, if the extended payment results in decreasing service from suppliers the policy may eventually be counter-productive. Thus, the merchandise strategy should be planned around a mutually acceptable payment cycle.

The management of cash surplus is a treasury function. However, the merchandise/buying director should be concerned to see that no undue pressure is put on the merchandise/buying organization (to produce cash balances for use elsewhere in the business) that is dysfunctional to the merchandise strategy. Cash/cash flow is important, but it must be remembered that the purpose of the merchandise strategy is to achieve a level of performance prescribed by the critical success factors.

Productivity

Productivity of people and space is of importance to the merchandise strategy. Many retailers use the sales per square (or linear) foot as an early measure for planning purposes. Sales per employee is often used for staff level planning. Clearly, productivity is of concern for both planning and control purposes and hence these measures are of major concern to merchandise strategy decisions.

An important factor concerns the impact of assortment changes or additions on productivity levels. Repositioning has a fundamental impact. The reason for this is often not pursued by retailers, who overlook issues such as the differential merchandise densities and differing staff numbers and skills that are to be considered when changes are made. Research by the authors suggests that in ladies' wear merchandise density and staff attitudes and abilities are major issues in store selection. Many ladies' wear retailers are criticized by customers for attempting to display too much merchandise and maintaining staff levels at very low levels of both quantity and quality.

ROI/ROCE/ROAM/ROOC

These are all measures used by retailers to monitor organizational performance. There is no 'best measure' here. Rather, the measure should be selected to meet the needs of the organization and to reflect the task roles and culture of the organization. Earlier we suggested that GMROI/CMROI have merit in measuring the performance of merchandising/buying activities, *together* with productivity measures for space and employees.

Measures used should attempt to match accountability and responsibility.

Summary: the merchandise assortment strategy decision

Merchandise strategy should consider the issues raised in this chapter and develop a merchandise assortment strategy. The purpose is to give merchandise/buying management a clear and concise direction for their activities and at the same time to develop competitive advantage. The merchandise assortment strategy should provide reasoning and logic as well as specific quantified directions. Typically, it will cover:

Customer purchasing characteristics and selection expectations

This section provides the rationale for the detail that follows. It should use the customer store selection and purchasing decision model identified and relate these to both critical success factors (i.e. visit frequencies, purchasing frequencies and average transaction detail) and to key the strategy issues.

Key merchandise groups and sales forecasts

Here the profile needs to identify the merchandise groups that are to be sold. It should break these down into demand centres, classes and categories. For each a proposed sales forecast will be given.

A typical merchandise classification for an apparel retailer would comprise:

Merchandise *group*:	men's wear
Merchandise *demand centres*:	suits jackets casual wear accessories
Merchandise *classes*:	formal occasion suits business suits casual suits and co-ordinates leisure co-ordinates
Merchandise *categories*:	styles sizes and length options materials colours

Branding policy

The customer research should have identified customer preferences for brands. These may be national or international (particularly for men's and ladies' wear) and should consider where feasible the development of both 'pseudo-brands' (specifically targeted merchandise with exclusive characteristics) or a store brand (merchandise ranges reflecting the primary offers of the store, e.g. quality and choice at competitive prices).

Price ranges

These should be set within the merchandise strategy and should reflect:

- Perceived customer price point requirements.
- The relationship between price and other merchandise characteristics (e.g. quality, choice, exclusivity, etc.).
- The stock profiles at price point intervals in order that maximum availability can be given at the important price levels.

Margins

Both gross and contribution margins should be established. This guide is necessary for range planning (width, depth) and supplier selection (numbers, capacities, capabilities).

Stockholding

Overall stock level, together with merchandise group stock levels, will also be determined in the profile document. Buyers will need this information to plan purchasing and open-to-buy targets.

Performance measures such as GMROI or CMROI can be suggested by using the margins and stockholding objectives. These may be set for merchandise groups, demand centres, classes or for categories.

Availability levels at stores and depots

Stockholding has both marketing and financial implications. It is important that the merchandise strategy considers the interrelationships of both issues and makes an explicit statement concerning levels of availability that are to be maintained. Again, these may become quite detailed in terms of the levels of the business to which they obtain.

The purpose of any strategy is to allocate resources such that objectives are achieved. We suggest that the measure of this achievement can be judged by changes in customer performance across the range of factors which influence corporate success, that is:

- Frequency of browsing visits.
- Frequency of purchasing visits.
- Average transaction values.
- Items purchased.
- Range purchased.
- Store loyalty.

The merchandise assortment strategy becomes a major input to the next stage of the activity — merchandise management. It provides both rationale and direction to merchandisers and buyers and, if it has been developed jointly with them, becomes an effective means by which the merchandise strategy may be implemented.

CHAPTER 6

Implementing merchandise strategy

Introduction

In Chapter 5 we discussed the issues facing decision-makers when deciding on merchandise strategy. In this chapter we move on to identify and discuss the tasks involved in making merchandise strategy explicit. There are a number of issues and these are outlined in Figure 6.1.

Clearly, there is an overlap in the activities. Precisely where deciding on strategy ends and implementary strategy commences will differ from company to company. Figure 6.1 assumes that the *merchandise assortment strategy* will have been developed by considering the issues discussed in the previous chapter. This provides the directional input required for implementing merchandise strategy.

There are nine components to be considered during the process of implementing a merchandise strategy:

1. The merchandise assortment strategy: review.
2. Factors that influence the merchandise plan.
3. Developing the merchandise plan.
4. Range planning and merchandise allocation.
5. Developing the merchandise sales plan for company and branches.
6. Review: consideration of the implications of the merchandise plan for company critical success factors.
7. Sourcing the merchandise plan.
8. Distribution planning and control.
9. Monitoring and control issues.

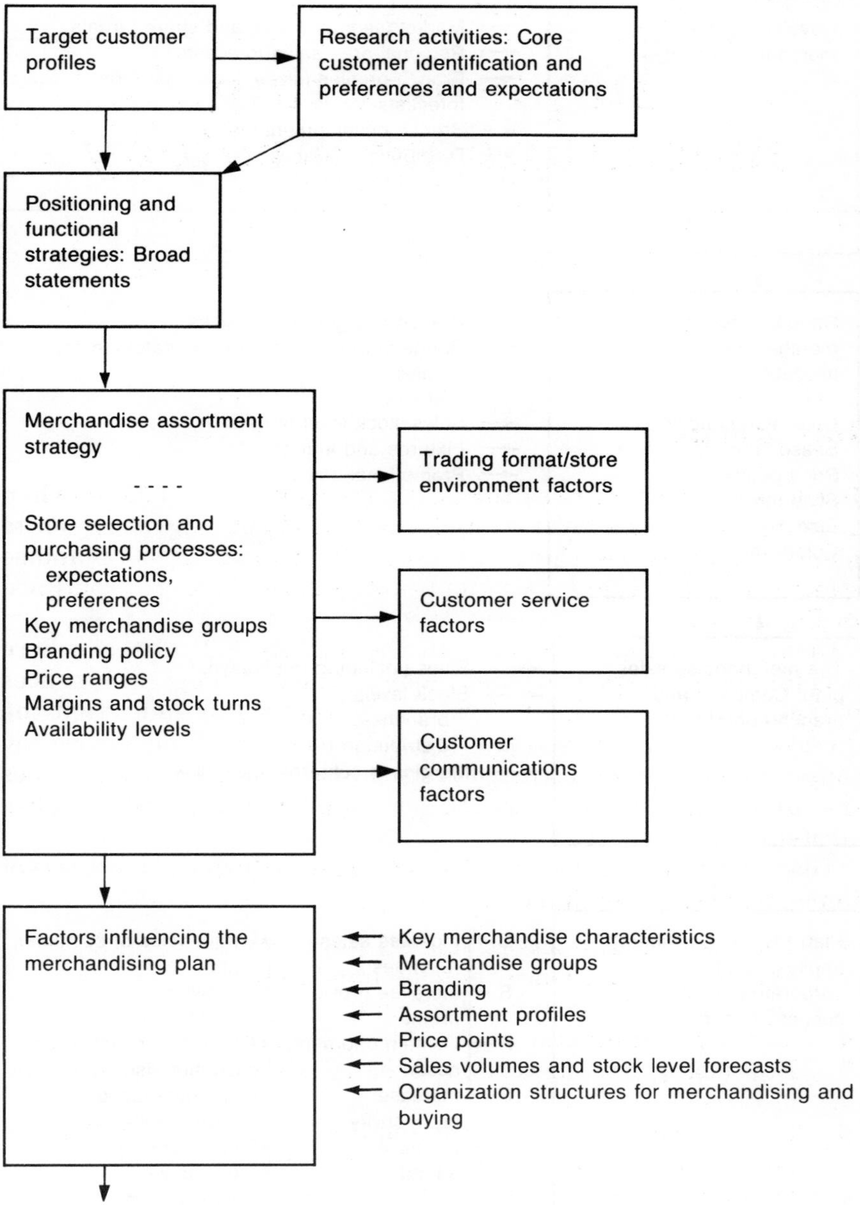

Figure 6.1 *Implementing merchandise strategy*

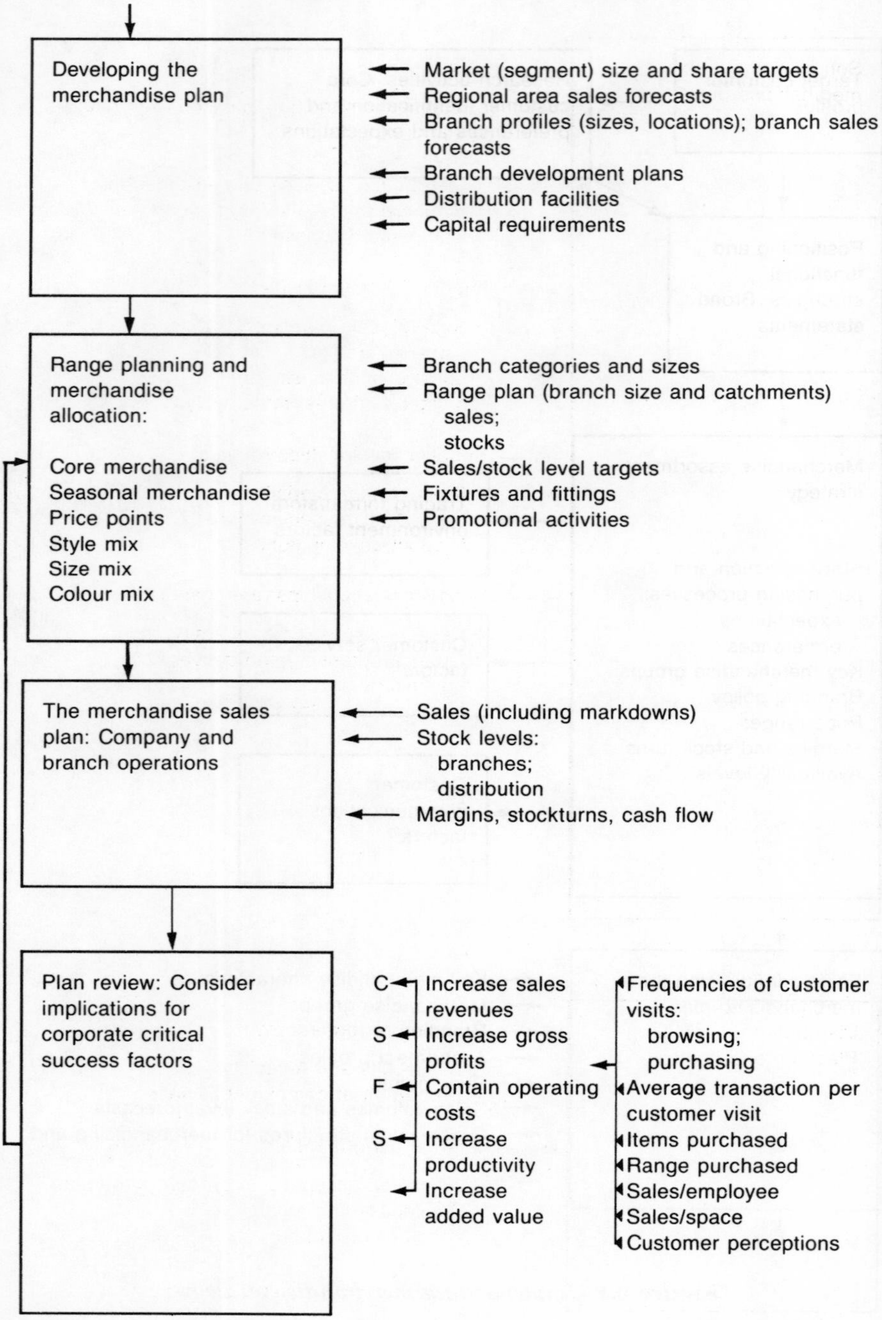

Figure 6.1 *continued*

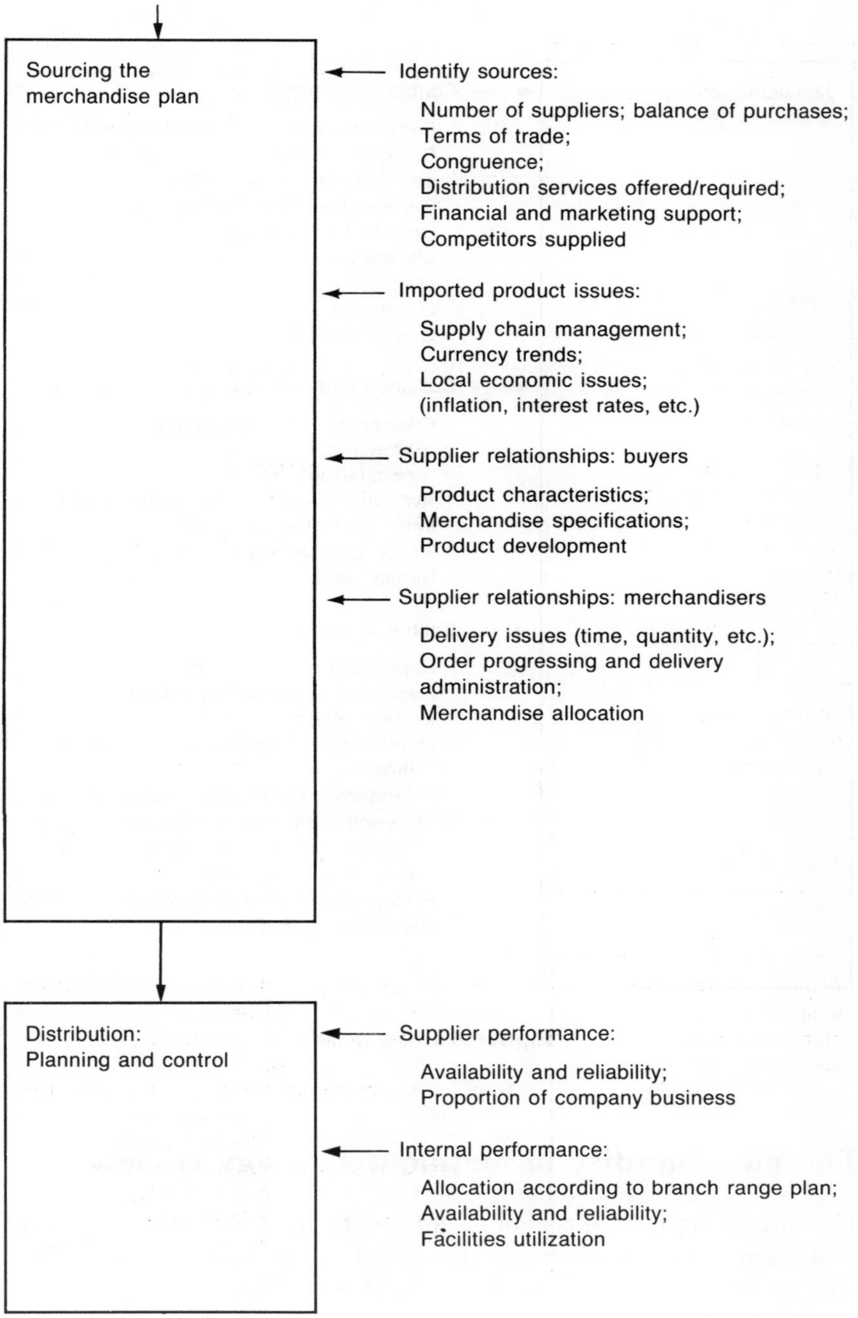

Figure 6.1 *continued*

Monitoring and control issues

← Control instruments:

- Forecast/actual: sales and margins;
- Stock levels and availability at depots and branches (stock cover);
- Stock replenishment levels;
- Open-to-buy/open-to-order;
- Markdowns;
- Margins;
- Direct costs;
- GMROI/CMROI

← Customer performance:

- Frequencies of customer visits:
  - browsing;
  - purchasing
- Average transaction per customer visit;
- Items purchased per visit;
- Range purchased per visit;
- Repeat visits

← Central decisions:

- Repeat purchases/intake;
- Rescheduling/cancelling deliveries;
- Price changes;
- Identification of additional opportunities:
  - promotions;
  - expanding merchandise categories;
  - consolidating merchandise categories;
  - rationalizing merchandise categories;
  - extending the assortment;
- Regrading branches to reflect performance;
- Repositioning decisions

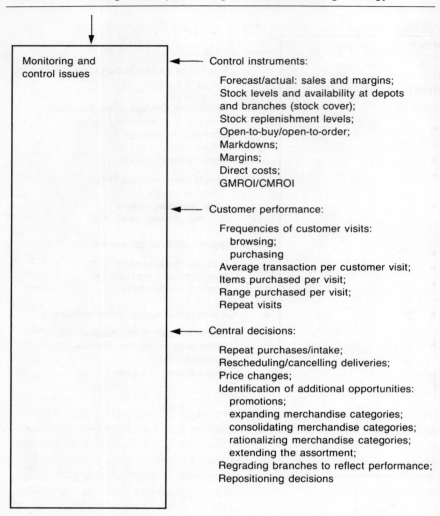

Figure 6.1 *continued*

The merchandise assortment strategy review

The broad topics that should form the basis of this important document were introduced at the end of the previous chapter. They will be dealt with in more detail in this section.

Customer store selection and purchasing decision processes: expectations and preferences

It is essential that buyers know as much as can be obtained about target customers. Consider the following customer profile of a department store's target customer group:

- Customers are 70 per cent female, 30 per cent male.
- Their age group is 35–55 years.
- They own houses in expensive locations.
- Typically, they both work in well-salaried senior managerial occupations.
- They have children in their late teens or who have left home and are at university; thus they have considerable disposable income.
- They have two cars.
- They have *all* major consumer durables.
- They work long hours and value leisure highly.
- They are concerned about health and fitness.
- Shopping is seen either as a chore (food and household items) or as marginally pleasurable (clothes and leisure purchases).
- Preferences are for exclusivity and choice in all product purchases – style is conservative and high quality is assumed.
- They are store-loyal if their requirements for merchandise and service can be met.

A number of conclusions can be drawn. Apart from the obvious implications for merchandise selection, such as exclusivity (which requires extensive searching for appropriate sources) and variety (which will have implications for stock investment as well as space, usual merchandising and distribution issues), there are also important considerations for quality, availability and co-ordination. It is also very likely that services will be important; menu suggestions, home delivery and even catering services (within the food hall) and 'wardrobe' facilities in ladies' wear. The furniture sales department would benefit from a design consultancy service.

Future location decisions could consider the preference for keeping shopping activities to a minimum as well as the fact that the target customers live in well-defined catchment areas. Store environment design should be based on product usage rather than any other theme, but merchandise groups (and subsequent classifications) should seek to offer strong co-ordination among each other.

Customer services could consider offering a wide range of leisure, interest-based facilities. These could range from a ticket agency for sport and theatre to sports coaching and other leisure-based topics.

Communicating frequently with the target customer group is essential. News of new merchandise of specific interest would undoubtedly generate a response. In time, a catalogue or telephone ordering service could be used effectively.

Key merchandise groups

The strategy will identify those key merchandise groups that are essential if the store is to be considered as a main or first choice store for the target group. Furthermore, the essential merchandise characteristics for each merchandise group should be considered at this particular point because range width and depth are important aspects of any sales forecast. It is also important to consider the dimensions of the demand centres, classes and categories for forecasting purposes.

Branding policy

There is a number of facets to branding decisions. Possibly the most important issue concerns the strength of the customer franchise enjoyed by the retailing company. Companies such as Marks & Spencer have shown that such is the consumer confidence in their merchandise they can operate exclusively with own-brands. However, this may be exceptional and other issues to be considered may well influence the decision. One obvious factor is the preferences that consumers express for manufacturer brand *vs.* store brands. There is research evidence to show that in canned and packaged food products there is an expression of greater confidence in manufacturers' brands by C2, D and E consumers. They see these brands as having an offer of a guarantee of quality, more so than store brands.

Another aspect of store brands concerns the use made of them to reinforce their own *retail brands*. Own-brands have undergone interesting changes. In the 1960s they were used as low-price alternatives to manufacturer brands. While price was lower (and margins higher) the specification was often markedly lower than the manufacturer brand. The emphasis shifted towards *bench-marking*, a process by which product quality and performance remained on a par with manufacturer brands. Price and margin benefits were obtained from volume sales. More recently own-brands have been used to enhance the positioning of the retail brand. It may be that the retailer's strategy is to create or reinforce a perception of exclusivity, or of choice, or perhaps innovativeness. This can be done with retailer own-brands. It is questionable whether all retailers could do so; research will be necessary prior to undertaking such programmes.

To combat the strength of national (often international) brands and labels, many department stores develop and brand specific ranges of ladies' and men's wear. Based on extensive research they develop and position these ranges to attract a carefully researched and targeted customer group. The Galeries Lafayette have introduced three brands — Avant Premier, Jodhpur and Briefing — which sell alongside the store brand. In this particular instance the store brand is used across the entire assortment, the offer it makes is one of a company guarantee of quality, style and choice at competitive prices compared with manufacturer/supplier labels and, of course, competitor stores.

The branding question has a number of issues. The major issue concerns the strength of the customer franchise and what the customers see as the company's capabilities. If a retailer attempts to introduce an own-brand into a merchandise range for which it lacks credibility, the likelihood of success is quite low. These issues will be developed in the buyers' specification brief.

Price ranges

The merchandise assortment strategy should indicate pricing policy aspects of:

1. *Market positioning*: the relationship between price and other merchandise characteristics, together with price and its relationship to customer services and store environment.
2. *Price points together with stock allocation* (store profiles): at each price point for each merchandise group and where practical for demand centres, classes and categories within each merchandise group.
3. *Price breaks* within the overall price point structure. For example:

Prices between £1 and £5	Prices between £5 and £10	Prices between £10 and £200 and above
0.25	0.49	0.49
0.49	0.75	0.99
0.75	0.99	
0.99		

Finally, a clear indication should be given concerning competitive pricing. For example:

- Competitor pricing below company price levels for:
  - promotions,
  - short term,
  - long term.
- Competitor pricing below company at cost price (at which point the competitor should become a supplier).
- Competitor pricing consistently above company price levels and for which there appears to be no consumer resistance (which would suggest that a price increase should be considered).

Margins and stockturns

Management should indicate their expectations for margins by merchandise group. Any variations across the group should be identified. For example, margin reductions for promotional purposes or for acknowledged price sensitive merchandise groups should be acknowledged when preparing the merchandise assortment strategy.

In Chapter 5 we discussed the overall implications of stock levels for working capital investment. The merchandise assortment strategy should determine overall stockholding levels for merchandise groups (and where feasible, down to more disaggregated levels). Factors to be considered by buying are:

- The marketing and financial implications of stockholding.
- Seasonal variations for sales.
- Seasonal variations for procurement.
- Customer-determined preferences for variety and availability.
- General guidelines for *open to buy* (the amount of merchandise that may be bought for delivery during the balance of a 'control period' if a planned closing stock is to be achieved) or for *open to order* (the amount of merchandise buyers should order each month, regardless of delivery, thereby establishing a planned total of outstanding orders each month).

  Note: For many products orders need to be placed well ahead of a sales season to assure accurate and timely deliveries. Often buyers are making capacity commitments with suppliers rather than actually purchasing product.

Availability levels at stores and depots

There are two important considerations for management. The first concerns the achievement of marketing objectives; clearly, the availability of merchandise is a key issue here. The second concerns the achievement of financial objectives. This is a little more complicated because it involves not only achieving a satisfactory return on inventory investment but also a return on the investments in stores and distribution facilities. It is, therefore, essential that parameters are set for availability levels that do achieve optimal utilization of all *facilities*. For example, if planned availability levels are too low, and this results in persistent stock-out situations followed by either an increase in the frequency of deliveries to stores or unplanned reordering on suppliers (or both), a situation may occur in which sub-optimization operates. Stock levels have been maintained at low levels (with high return on inventory investment) but the cost to productivity within the system as a whole may prove unacceptable, particularly so if additional resources are bought in to relieve the problem.

Factors influencing the merchandise plan

The purpose of the merchandise assortment strategy is to give direction to the buyers for assortment range building and procurement.

Key merchandise characteristics

The merchandise assortment strategy will have detailed those customer purchasing characteristics which are seen as important for merchandise decisions. It will also have specified the merchandise groups to be included in the assortment. Within these the demand centres, classes and categories will have been determined as will their formats.

Another requirement is for the merchandise characteristics to be both qualified and quantified for each merchandise group.

The hypothetical customer profile introduced earlier clearly has implications for buying decisions. These were:

- Exclusivity.
- Quality.

- Style/design.
- Continuity.
- Convenience, suggesting:
  — co-ordinated displays (to assist choice across items), and
  — merchandise continuity (to facilitate re-purchasing of styles).

The *exclusivity* requirement suggests high search costs in order to locate merchandise that can only be obtained in the company's stores. Quite often this will imply sole agency arrangements with well-known suppliers, who may be in a situation where they can select from a number of retailers seeking to become sole franchisees. If the competition is intense, the supplier may also seek exclusive terms. It is not unknown for suppliers in this situation to insist that competitive suppliers are excluded from the assortment or to insist on privileged in-store location!

Quality has two cost elements. Materials and labour specifications will require that input costs will necessarily be high, but so too are the costs of quality control. These latter costs have obvious benefits. Marks & Spencer, Sainsbury and Tesco maintain high levels of activity in suppliers' manufacturing facilities. Quality control of own-label ranges is extremely important, particularly when they are major components within an overall retail branding strategy.

Style/design has cost implications. Again, a number of factors must be considered. Exclusive design is expensive. Designers of both products and store environments have a scarcity value (quite often for a period of time only) and respond to excessive demand in a similar way to that for all scarce resources. Style and exclusivity have close links and any attempt to amortize high design fees across a high level of production clearly has an adverse effect on exclusivity. Further consideration must include the increasing requirement for compatibility between product and store environment. The redesigned store interiors introduced by British Home Stores in the late 1970s and early 1980s was not accompanied (initially) by product changes and this incompatibility was soon detected by consumers. In 1986/7 the repositioning exercise undertaken by Dickins & Jones *was* achieved by co-ordinating both store environment and product design issues. Finally, there is the risk factor. It is usual for high levels of risk to accompany avant garde or 'innovator' design. This is not to suggest that low or no risk is attached to 'classic' styles; these too may have problems in being accepted.

Continuity has cost implications. One aspect of the cost of continuity concerns the issues referred to in the previous paragraphs: that is, the cost of implementing a style/design theme across both product *and* store environment. A further aspect concerns the need for designers to consider the time issue. A successful design theme must be planned so that it may be extended over time as well as over other product (and store) groups. Often this is difficult because tastes can change unpredictably and competition can influence consumer preferences. For some product groups there is also the consideration of product availability over time. For example, porcelain and glass are product groups for which time availability assurances are usually sought by customers. Whatever way this may be achieved – by extensive stockholding, low-capacity production, one-off production runs – there is an obvious cost implication to be considered.

Convenience has two aspects. The first is closely linked with earlier topics of style/design and continuity. For many customers co-ordinated displays facilitate purchasing. The co-ordinated themes offered by Next were considered helpful in this way. They were also seen as an element of convenience because related items were displayed together and customers responded by spending more and visiting more frequently. There is also the aspect of risk. It has been found that co-ordinated merchandise displays present a fashion view, a view of compatibility between styles and colours, etc. This is often appreciated by those customers who may be unsure of their own ability to make these decisions. One other view of convenience is that of merchandise continuity. Here we are concerned with the service offered to customers by offering continuity of styles, colours, etc., such that customers know that they can 'always find' a particular style or brand in the retailer's outlet. Examples of such attention to detail were common to one-off specialist stores, where details of shoe and hat sizes and styles were kept on file. This has been replaced by the data-base file and forms a small part of such facilities at wardrobe services operated by large department stores. It also offers a facility to extend the offer into a mail order service.

Merchandise groups

Earlier we identified the basic issues of concern if the objective is to become first choice of store among a target customer group. The classification suggested (i.e. merchandise group, demand centres, classes and categories) is an initial stage in defining the structure of merchandise within the store. However, other factors should be taken into account. For example, a view should be taken concerning the expansion of the merchandise offer in the medium and long term. Questions that should be asked in this respect are:

- What is the current role of a specific merchandise group?

- What does it contribute to the marketing (positioning) and financial objectives?
- What is its life-cycle position?
- What is the role of the merchandise type in customer purchasing and usage patterns?
- Do these suggest:
  — stable usage?
  — developing usage?
  — declining usage?
- How is the merchandise purchased? For example, what is the customer buying process? How is selection made? Are comparisons made? Is it a complementary purchase? Is it substitutable? Is it a repeat order? What information does the customer seek? Are there particular features or characteristics of the merchandise that customers use to select items for purchase such as end-use, style, colour and size.
- Is it a merchandise group that may have development potential into:
  — a specialist range of outlets?
  — a major product group within the existing store group?
  — a supporting merchandise offer?

Answers to such questions give a lead for the formation of merchandise groups and emphasis to be placed by buyers. The issues raised in the discussion on segmentation will be useful in this respect.

Branding, own-brands and concessions

Given that the merchandise strategy has been developed around a positioning strategy, the role of the retail brand in its support of the positioning strategy will be explicit. However, the role of own-brands and concessions will require detailed discussion.

Clear directions for the development of own-brands should be given to the buyers. These should consider:

1. The role of manufacturer brands in the merchandise strategy:
   (a) Are they important to customer choice of store?
   (b) Are they congruent with the positioning strategy?
   (c) Are current suppliers (and potential alternatives) sufficiently innovative to make a contribution towards product development?
2. Are there gaps in the current merchandise range?
3. Can margins be improved by an own-brand addition? If so, what impact will it have on existing sales?

4. What are the technical and administrative issues that need to be considered if own-brand products are introduced? Does a supplier base exist?
5. Is the customer franchise strong enough?
6. Does the opportunity exist to transfer merchandise concepts and ideas between product groups?
7. Can the own-brand be used to extend properties over other markets?
8. Is there an opportunity to develop sustainable competitive advantage?

The answers to these questions should resolve the marketing issues arising between manufacturers' brands, own-brands and concessions. For example, if customer loyalty is very strong (such as enjoyed by Marks & Spencer), then an own-brand policy for product development must be advisable. However, if the company is considering an entry into a new range of merchandise for which they have no recognized expertise, it may best be achieved by developing recognition and credibility through manufacturer brands or possibly concessions.

Other important issues concern the ability to transfer ideas between product groups or to extend favourable customer perceptions into related areas of merchandise. An example of this can be seen with Tesco non-food activities in children's products.

The important issue is that it is the retail brand and positioning strategy that must be used as a basis for decisions. The positioning strategy is an interpretation of and response to customer preferences. Any product decision that does not support this is likely to be dysfunctional.

Assortment profiles

These are an interpretation of customer expectations for both variety and availability. Because of the obvious implication for costs of a high offer of variety and/or availability it is helpful to quantify both.

In Chapter 5 we discussed the cost components of availability. Usually, availability is measured by the 'first-time satisfaction' of orders, expressed as a percentage of total orders. For example, if the company sees high availability as a competitive necessity, it will set itself a target to reflect this, say, 97 per cent, 98 per cent or, for key products, even 100 per cent. Figure 6.2 gives some indication of the relationship between stockholding costs and availability. Clearly, high levels of availability are expensive to maintain and should only be established (and maintained) when research has established the

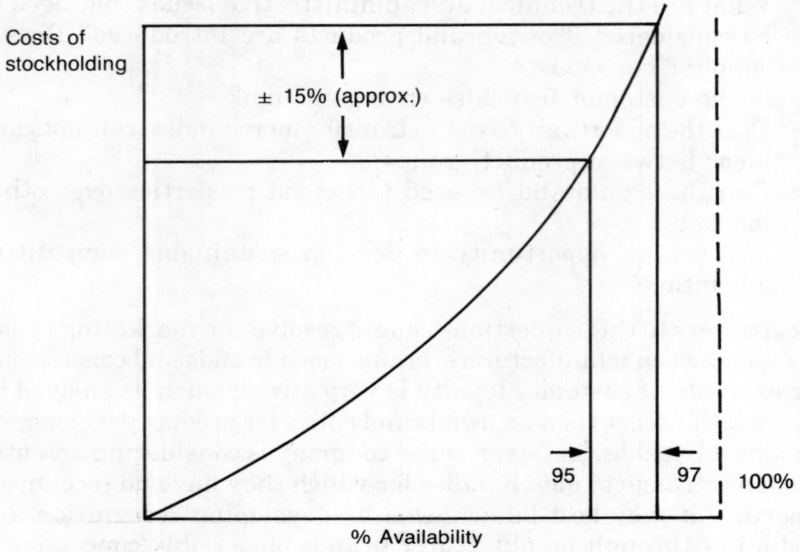

Figure 6.2 *The relationship between availability and stockholding costs*

importance of so doing. Often specific products (designated core products) are maintained at 100 per cent availability, the basis being that they are products that customers expect always to be in stock.

The high costs of variety are intuitively apparent and it is possible to contain them by close targeting of merchandise. Again if, from a competitive standpoint, wide choice is essential, some control is required. A balance is necessary between wide variety and excessive costs and narrow choice which restricts customer appeal but contains inventory investment.

Ideally, we should quantify variety and one helpful analytical method is the application of the Pareto principle (often known as the 80/20 rule; implying that 80 per cent of sales are generated by 20 per cent of product items) to inventory management problems. In Figure 6.2 three possible situations are portrayed (although there is, potentially, an infinite number available). The main feature of the Pareto principle is that, typically, product sales (and profit) are seldom in balance. That is to say that it is hardly likely to find the situation where all products sell at the same level or rate of sales and, consequently, contribute the same level of profit. It is much more likely that one or two product groups (and products within product groups) will account for a majority of the total sales achieved.

This is illustrated in Figure 6.3. PG_2 suggests that something like

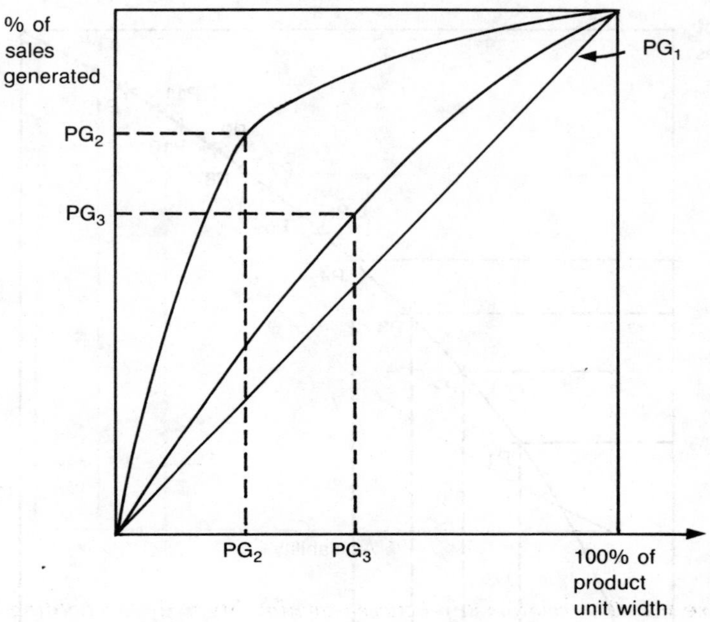

Figure 6.3 *A perspective on sales contribution across a product range*

80 per cent of sales are generated from 20 per cent of the products within a particular product group, whereas PG_3 suggests that 40 per cent of the products account for 60 per cent of sales in its product group. PG_1 illustrates a situation where all products contribute equally across the product group.

It is more helpful to consider the cumulative distribution percentage of sales *vs.* percentage of items (shown as Figure 6.4), for each merchandise group and for divisions within each group. In Figure 6.4 we can see the profile of sales such that two products, P1 and P2, together account for some 60 per cent of sales; with P3 and P4 adding a further 20 per cent. Thus, the product group as such has a profile which very few products account for sales activity and the remaining nine products, with 20 per cent of sales, offer choice.

The relationship between gross profit and inventory investment is shown in Figure 6.5. In this example, sales and gross profit are shown together with the inventory investment required. It can be seen that 25 per cent of the items produce 80 per cent of gross profit and they account for 50 per cent of inventory investment. It suggests that inventory investment should consider the extent to which both *choice* and *availability* be offered across the product range. The implications

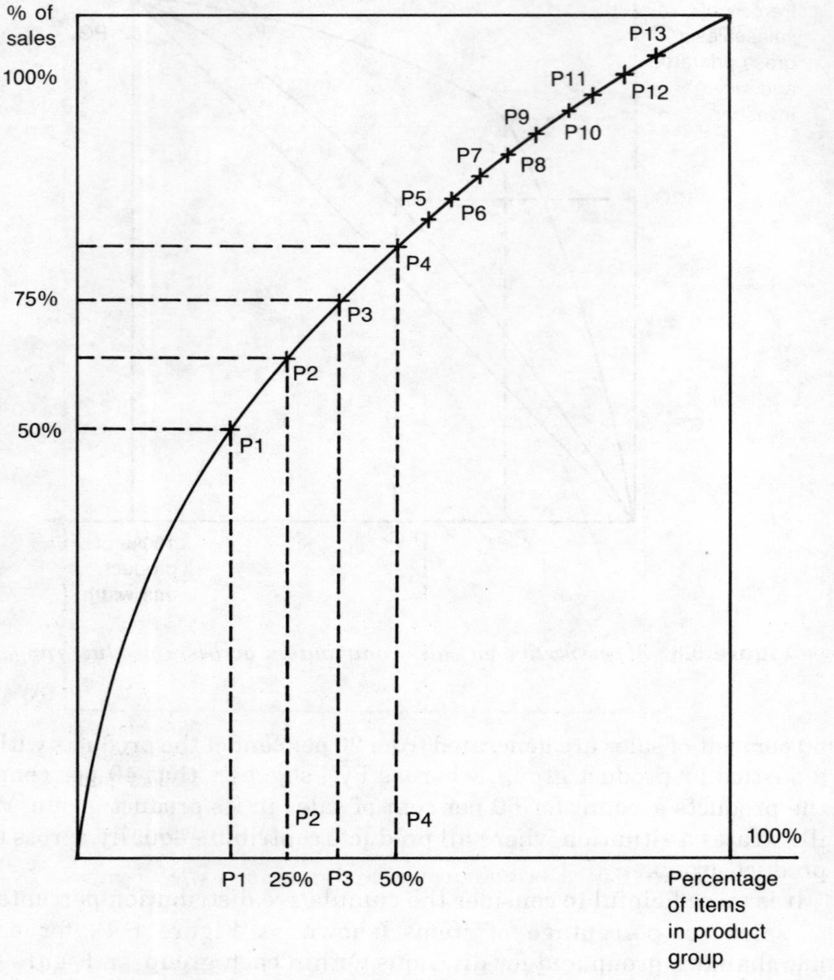

Figure 6.4 *Cumulative distribution percentage of sales versus percentage of items*

of Figure 6.5 are that *choice* and *availability* should be offered selectively, such that high levels for both should be restricted to those product groups within an assortment (and to products within product groups) that are essential to the implementation of the merchandise positioning statement.

The implications for offering high levels of choice and/or availability are shown in Figure 6.6. The inventory investment profile is now much closer to both the sales and gross profit curves, suggesting that such

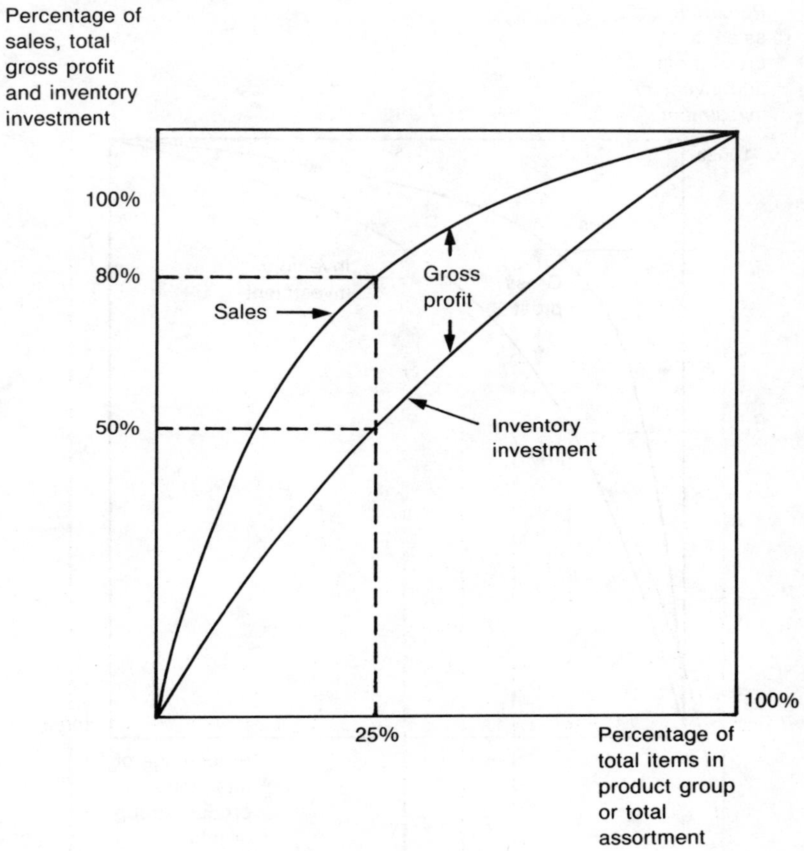

Figure 6.5 *A perspective on profit/inventory effectiveness*

a policy would reduce overall profitability. There are other factors to consider. Stock obsolescence would or could be very high, requiring a high level of markdowns. Distribution costs in the form of warehouse space (for storage) and transportation costs (to maintain availability) would also reduce profitability.

A solution is offered by the ABC analysis favoured by materials management. The sales pattern is analyzed to identify those products (product groups) which contribute to both marketing and financial objectives and classify them as A, B or C 'category' items. For each, choice and availability profiles are assigned. Thus, in Figure 6.7 the important products are assigned higher levels of choice and availability depending on the level of *sales and profit* each are required to produce. Choice can be indicated by indices for both width and depth, with 100

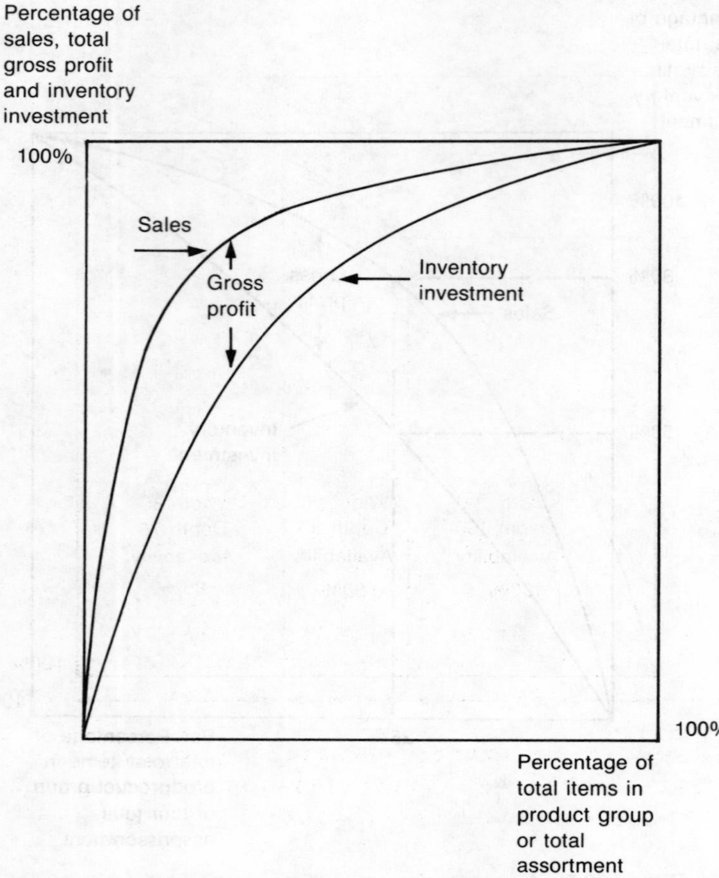

Figure 6.6 *A perspective on profit/inventory effectiveness: the problems of high levels of choice and availability*

being set on the basis of major labels or brands available within the product classification. Accordingly, indices of 95 and 80 would reflect lower levels of choice. Availability may be measured in the usual way, by service level targets. Again, these would be established by first considering the implications of high service for achieving customer response and then the impact on inventory investment and profitability.

The actual product mix may be described by allocating products to each category, i.e. A, B or C, and the dimensions of each group by defining the dimensions of A, B and C in terms of percentages as shown in Figure 6.7.

In Figure 6.8 we illustrate alternative sales/profit mix profiles.

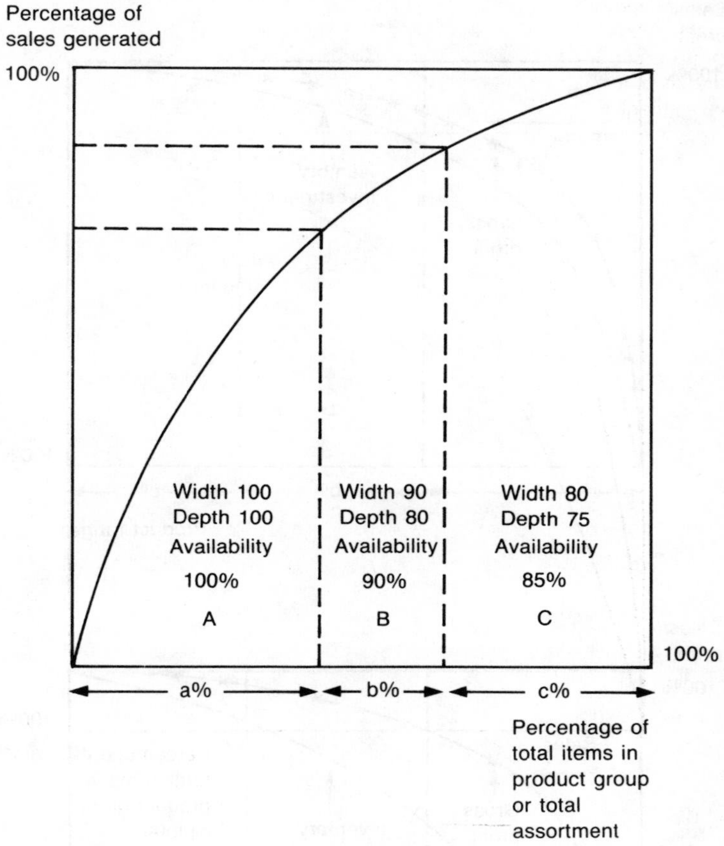

Figure 6.7 *ABC analysis prescribing choice and availability across the range*

Figure 6.8a is the profile that may be expected if the market positioning is a wide choice/high availability offer. Alternatively, a limited range discounter may opt for the profile shown in Figure 6.8b.

In Figure 6.8a we have ten product groups in category A, five in category B and four in category C. Clearly if, in addition to choice, a high level of availability is offered, the inventory investment will be high and contribution margins lower than for the limited range diameter. The situation illustrated in Figure 6.8b is one in which four product groups are responsible for most of the activity (in Group A), three product groups comprise Group B and only two Group C. Consequently, the inventory investment required to support this

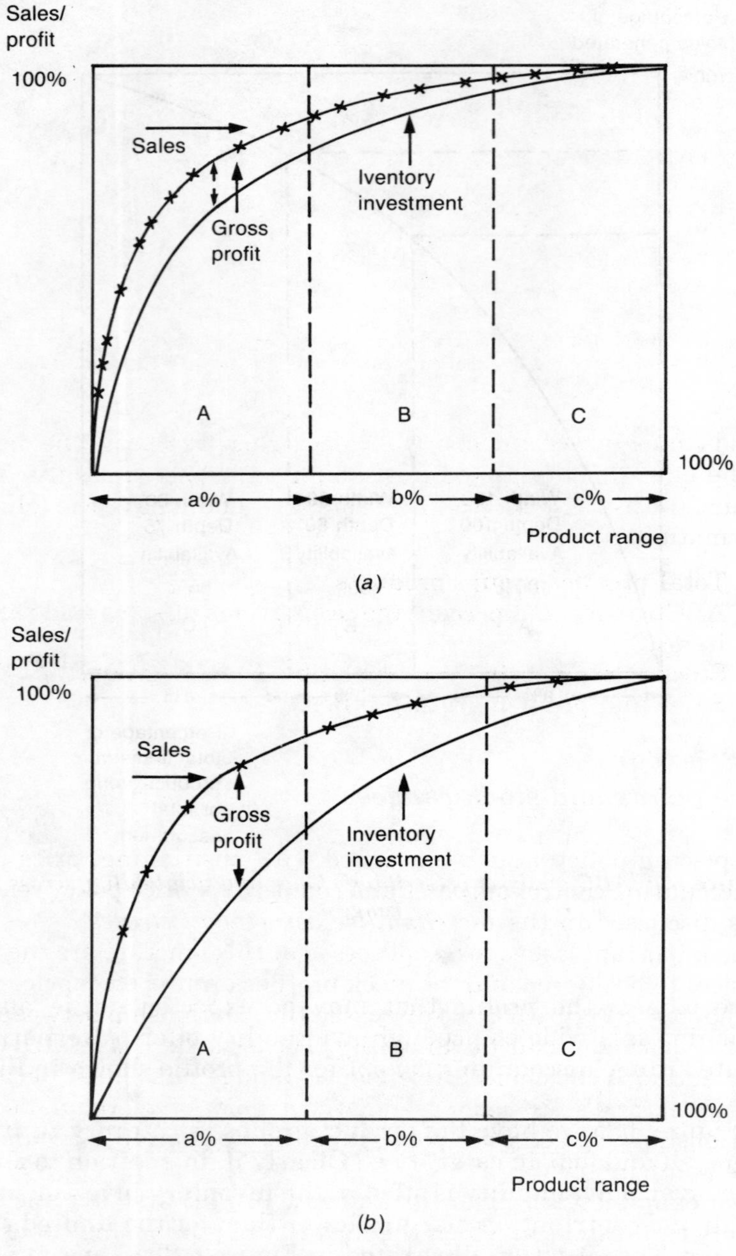

Figure 6.8 *Planning the sales profit matrix*
(a) Specialist: offering wide ranges and high availability;
(b) Discounter: offering limited choice but low prices

Table 6.1 The assortment profile

	A	B	C	Gross profit	
No. of product groups	10	5	4	19 items	£
Proportion of sales	75%	20%	5%	100	£
Proportion of profit	70%	20%	10%	100	£
Proportion of stock	60%	30%	10%	100	£
Width index[a]	100	90	80		
Depth index[b]	100	80	75		
Availability %	100	90	85		

a Percentage of labels, brands, etc., 'expected' by customers.
b Percentage of style, colour, size options 'expected' by customers.

offer is much lower and contribution higher. For both, the decision on the offer must be made in the light of expected results.

Thus, the assortment profile (Table 6.1) should have the following information:

1. Total product groups/products.
2. ABC ranges and percentage proportions of sales and range of items.
3. Stockholding costs – total and by A, B, C group.
4. Sales and profit margin profiles.

Price points and stock ranges

The pricing policy issues concerned with positioning, price points for accounting control purposes and competitive price policy reactions were discussed in the *merchandise assortment strategy*.

The important issues to be addressed at this juncture are the range of prices to be offered and the stock profiles around each price point. In Chapter 5 (Figure 5.6) we discussed the relationship between price point levels and product availability. The issue here is related to this topic but adds the choice dimension. Management must decide on: the price range for each relevant category of merchandise; the relationship between price points; and the stock profiles around each price point interval.

Two examples are given in Figure 6.9. The first is typical of a variety chain store in which the majority of purchasing takes place in medium-range price brackets. The second example is of a targeted specialist ladies' wear outlet for which the price sensitivity is low but for which wide choice is essential.

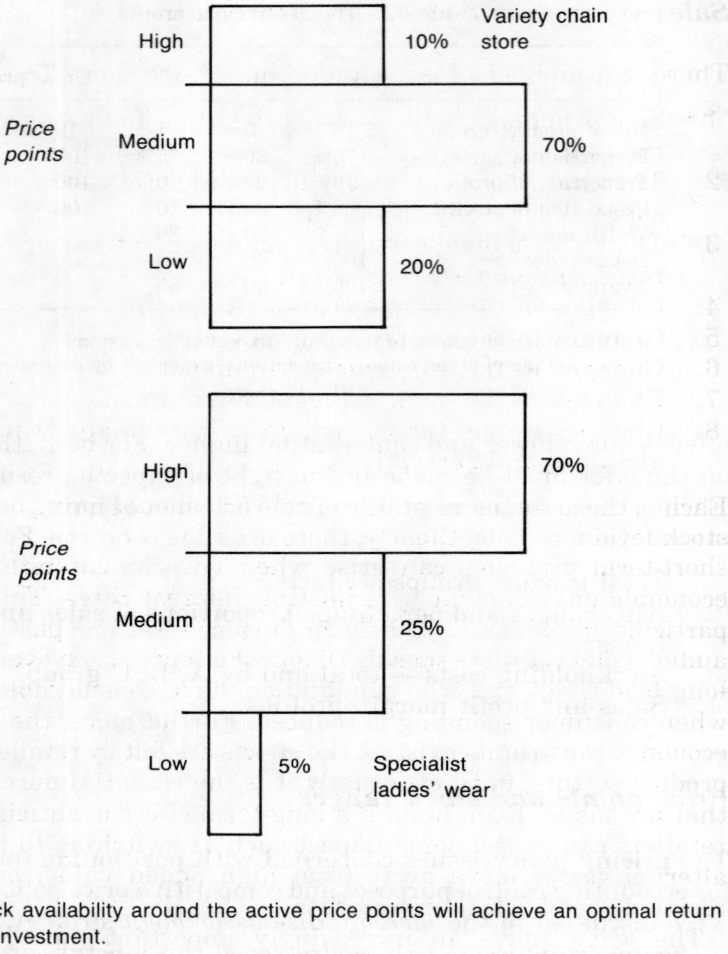

Figure 6.9 *Price points and stock allocation (a) An example of a variety chain store; (b) A specialist ladies' wear outlet*

As we have seen earlier, the costs of holding stock are high and therefore any unnecessary stockholding should be avoided. By linking stock allocation to the price points that are most popular and have been prescribed as such in the positioning strategy, non-essential stockholding can be reduced. Clearly, this is not the only economy. Unnecessary stock occupies storage and space in the distribution system. It also has an opportunity cost because it occupies expensive sales area and also accounts for working capital that could be used effectively elsewhere.

Sales volumes and stock level forecasts

There is a number of issues to be considered here. These include:

1. Senior management's view of the sales and profit potential of the company.
2. The level of sales necessary to produce profits acceptable to the shareholders (and to the City!).
3. The views of middle and store management who are ultimately responsible for success or failure.
4. Changes in the competitive environment.
5. Changes in the supply environment.
6. Changes in the economic environment.
7. Changes in the 'political-legal' environment.
8. Changes in the target customers' 'needs and wants' and in attitudes and perceptions.

Each of these issues must be considered when deciding on sales and stock-level forecasts. Clearly, there are time concerns. For example, short-term problems can arise when government influences the economic environment by adjusting interest rates. This presents particular problems for consumer durable retailing, particularly for audio/visual retailers such as Dixon who source from overseas, have long lead-times and who can (and do) have considerable problems when consumer spending is reduced. Furthermore, the longer the economic constraints exist, so the effects are felt by retailers in other product sectors, until eventually it is the essential purchases only that are made. Even here, if a long-term effect is anticipated, food retailers can expect some impact such as switching to lower-price alternatives, a move away from high added value, or prepared recipe dishes back to ingredients.

The 'City' plays an increasingly important role. For quoted companies there is considerable activity by stockbroker analysts whose views and opinions can and do influence management's prediction of sales and profits. Often, the 'required' performance is unrealistic and leads to difficulties in achieving what is expected.

Changes in the competitive environment are usually predictable. Any market-aware company should be monitoring the market-place and be ready to counter a challenge. It is not very often that a new offer appears without those companies most likely to be affected not knowing. What is important is to be ready to adjust to competition. For example, the expansion by the food multiples in the south and south-east of the United Kingdom has offered both threats and opportunities to regional operators. Some have resigned themselves to the 'inevitable'. Others have identified aspects of service or some other feature with which to reinforce their positioning. Changes in supply markets can present difficulties for retailers with a large imported proportion of merchandise. Local inflation and labour and materials shortages can result in large gaps in merchandise ranges or possibly merchandise low in competitive appeal. Because of very long lead-times this issue can be a serious problem. Indeed, the problems of long supply lead-times present problems generally. This can be an ongoing issue for retailers whose access to suppliers is distant geographically as well as temporally. For example, retailers in Australia who target in AB apparel markets find it essential to seek exclusivity with international brands. Travel budgets and buyers' time spent travelling are costly, particularly when competitors equally concerned are just as active. Furthermore, it adds some strength to suppliers' negotiating abilities, often with an adverse impact on retailer margins.

Changes in target customer 'needs and wants' should be monitored. The company that finds itself surprised by sudden changes ignores the dynamics of the market-place. Often change occurs because of the impact of competitive influence, but tracking studies and other research techniques identify trends. Argos (a catalogue-based retailer) monitors very closely the changing nature of demand, being particularly sensitive to a decline in price appeal and an increase in customer service at the point of sale.

These are some of the factors to be considered when developing the merchandise budget. Typically there are six basic activities:

1. Forecast sales.
2. Plan inventory levels.
3. Plan reductions.
4. Plan purchases and the open-to-buy.
5. Plan initial margins.
6. Plan cash flows.

Sales forecasts can be developed in three ways. A *top-down* approach calls for an overall company forecast of sales (and profit) and is then broken down into components (merchandise groups and store/regions). A *bottom-up* approach works in reverse. Store management and merchandise/buying groups review past performance (and future opportunities) and produce forecasts which are aggregated at appropriate levels to produce a company forecast. Each method has both benefits and weaknesses. The top-down approach may ignore regional and local issues, and the bottom-up approach may be too local. The third approach — to use both approaches independently and investigate and resolve discrepancies — is favoured by many retailers. Some guidelines are necessary and for both methods the procedure should be:

1. Begin with previous year's sales.
2. Analyze sales trends.
3. Analyze industry or sector factors.
4. Review competitive activities then project likely activities.
5. Identify and analyze company specific factors.

Step 1 will produce a basic forecast. This is modified by the analysis of steps 2, 3, 4 and 5 to produce:

6. A company/merchandise group/outlet forecast.
7. An annual/monthly forecast for each area (i.e. company, merchandise group, outlet).

Inventory levels for each month should focus on three objectives:

1. Satisfying customer demand.
2. Adjusting inventory levels to meet variations in seasonal sales.
3. Controlling inventory investment such that both the margins achieved and the stockturn meets profit objectives.

Methods used to achieve these objectives vary from judgement based on experience to much more sophisticated methods. The method used should reflect the nature of the business. For example, a business with relatively low turnover and stable monthly sales could use the *safety stock method.* The beginning-of-month inventory (BOMI) total is calculated by adding a level of stock which will act as a cushion against unforecasted sales fluctuations.

For those businesses with high stockturns a *percentage variation method* is suggested:

$$\text{BOMI} = \text{Average inventory} \times 1 + \frac{\text{forecast month's sales}}{\text{average monthly sales}}$$

where average inventory is the product of sales divided by turnover.

In businesses where it is essential to plan sales on a weekly basis the *week's supply method* offers a suitable alternative. It is simply calculated by dividing 52 by the desired or achieved stockturn. It is *not* very helpful for retailers with large fluctuations in sales.

Finally, the stock-to-sales ratio (SSR) assumes that it is necessary for the retailer to maintain a fixed proportion of inventory to sales:

$$\text{BOMI} = \text{SSR} \times \text{forecast month's sales}$$

This method is easy to use and is best adopted when monthly

planning is operated. The SSR is an average figure derived from experience and observation of trade information and practices.

Clearly, POS data-capture facilitates planning inventory levels. EPOS information, together with one of these methods, will provide a useful management tool. However, these are only tools and the need for managerial judgement is always necessary.

There are a number of views concerning what comprises a *reduced price*. It is unrealistic to assume that full margins will be realized. At best, the objective should be to minimize the reasons for this not occurring. There is a school of thought that favours the view that there are markdowns and planned reductions. Markdowns occur when a decision is made to reduce prices to alleviate excess stock created through buying errors (such as wrong sizes, colours, styles), or to reduce stock levels that have arisen due to poor forecasting or possibly due to reduced demand levels.

Planned reductions are the result of decisions taken to meet competition, to create multiple-unit prices or due to obsolescent stock.

Promotional discounts can be forecast around programmed sales activities. Other forms of discounts, which can also be projected, are those allowed to the staff and possibly to community concerns.

Finally, shrinkage dilutes margins. Again, this can be estimated and accounted for.

Planning purchases and the open-to-buy is the fourth step. The open-to-buy (OTB) is the amount of merchandise a buyer is responsible for buying during a specific planning period if a planned closing stock (opening stock for the next period (BOM)) is to be achieved. The two most important elements are planned period sales and planned stock levels, e.g.:

End of month (period) planned stock		280,000
Plus	planned sales for period	150,000
Total		430,000
Minus stock on hand		30,000
=	planned purchases	400,000
Minus	outstanding orders for delivery (during period)	50,000
=	open-to-buy (OTB)	350,000

It has been found that the OTB does not control the timing of orders. Accordingly, an open-to-order (OTO) plan may be preferred (for example, merchandise sourced from overseas suppliers). The OTO indicates how much should be ordered each month, regardless of time of delivery.

Both require strict discipline and monitoring. If sales exceed expectations then they should be increased, but if sales fall short of forecast then steps should be taken immediately to reduce them.

The purpose of planning an *initial mark-up* is to identify the relationships between volumes and selling price and with expenses. This information identifies potential problems before they happen. For example, a consumer durables retailer can identify the impact of cost inflation on his business. To this end it is very worthwhile for this stage of the planning to consider some form of sensitivity analysis. By forecasting labour rates, interest charges and supply market inflation the impact of increases in any of these on eventual profitability can be assessed. The benefits of the analysis are that stockholding and labour use may be planned such that the impact of the changes on customer service and the subsequent impact on sales as well as on margins can be assessed.

Finally, the *buying plan* is prepared. Increasingly, retailers are

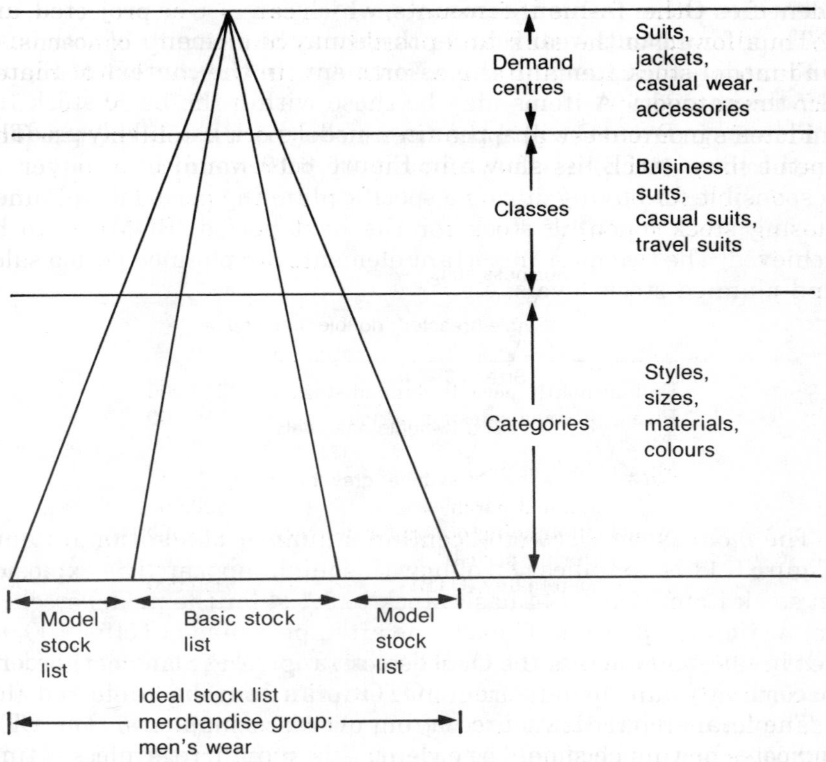

Figure 6.10 *The ideal stock list*

using buying plans. A moment's thought concerning the rapid expansion in consumer choice in recent years will provide an obvious answer as to why this should be so. By this time, issues concerning positioning and the investment consequences have been resolved, what remains concerns the actual assortment and its depth. The buying plan quantifies those issues discussed in this and the previous chapter and seeks to satisfy the demand requirements of the target customer profile (their store selection and purchasing decision processes — a hypothetical set of these cases was outlined at the beginning of this chapter).

Many retailers find it useful to operate with an ideal stock list which comprises a basic stock list and a model stock list. The principle of this approach is shown in Figure 6.10. The *basic stock list* is often used to identify these items which form the 'staple' component of demand within the merchandise group. Quite often this is used only by retailers offering non-fashion merchandise, such as food. However, the food multiples' assortments have expanded rapidly such that they, too, have a fashion element to their offers. The *model stock list* identifies these fashion items.

Thus, for a men's wear retailer there may be elements of both basic and model stock items in the assortment. In the context of Figure 6.7 the category A items may be those within the basic stock list and items in B and C will appear in a model stock list. Likely products in the basic stock list shown in Figure 6.10 would be:

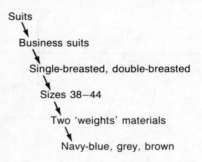

Suits
↓
Business suits
↓
Single-breasted, double-breasted
↓
Sizes 38–44
↓
Two 'weights' materials
↓
Navy-blue, grey, brown

The *model stock list* would contain a number of additional items. Figure 6.11 is an indication of how this might appear. The explosion in stock items (from 144 basic stock to 5,184 for the model stock) is immediately apparent. Clearly, no attempt is made to offer 100 per cent availability across the model stock range, and many of the items become available to meet customer orders and are not held in stock.

The final step creating the buying plan is to *plan cash flows*. The purpose for this becomes very clear. When the pattern of sales for most retailing companies is considered, some 25–30 per cent of sales

Basic stock list		*Model stock list*
Demand centres:	Suits	Suits
Classes:	Business suits (1)	Casual suits; Travel suits (2)
Categories: *Styles*:	Single- + Double-breasted (2)	Traditional; City; Country; Classic (4)
Sizes:	38, 40, 42, 44 (12); medium, short, long	36, 38, 40, 42, 44, 46 (18); medium, short, long (plus in-store alterations)
Materials:	Two 'weights' (2)	Three 'weights' (3)
Colours:	Navy-blue, grey, brown (3)	Navy-blue: plain + stripe; Grey: two shades, two checks, two patterns; Brown: two shades, two checks (12)
Items:	1 × 2 × 12 × 2 × 3	*Items*: 1 × 2 × 4 × 18 × 3 × 12
	= 144	= 5,184

Figure 6.11 *A detailed ideal stock list*

can occur in December. Cash flow planning to meet an uneven sales pattern is even more essential when the sourcing lead-times can extend to twelve months or more. Unfulfilled cash needs cause obvious problems such as high interest charges on overdrafts. Cash excesses create opportunity costs.

Cash flow planning differs from business to business in terms of specific problems, but essentially it involves projecting cash inflows and cash outflows. A food retailer has a different set of planning concerns from those facing a furniture retailer. The food retailer can use suppliers' funds (the concept of negative working capital) by reducing the time-period for which it finances inventory in the working capital cycle (see Chapter 5). Typically, food retailers operate on very rapid stockturns for much of their inventory and some products (perishables such as milk and bread) are sold many times before being paid for.

A simplified cash flow model is shown in Figure 6.12. The diagram contrasts the cash flow situations for a food retailer and for a furniture retailer. If we assume their sales volumes to be similar (but ignore

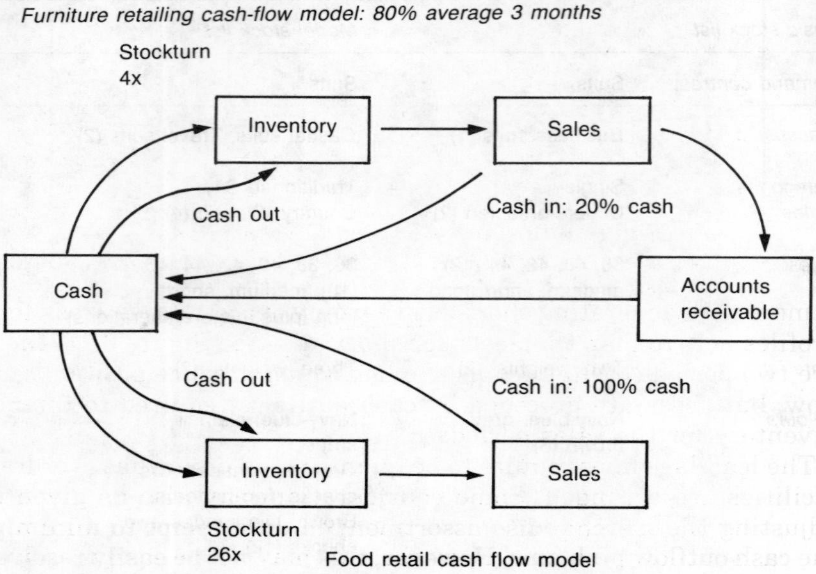

Figure 6.12 *Simplified cash flow models*

margins, etc.) we can see some of the cash flow planning issues that occur:

Sales £100 million	
Furniture retailer	*Food retailer*
Stockholding £25 million	Stockholding 2 weeks; approx. £2 million
Accounts receivable £80 million	Accounts receivable nil
Stockholding costs @ 15 per cent p.a. £375 million	Negative working capital benefit factor 50/26 = 1.8
	Therefore £45 million approx. in the business
Accounts receivable (A/R) funding 80/4 £20 million	£45 million at 15%
@ 15% per annum £3 million	
Stockholding and customer credit costs £6.75 million	Cash flow benefit £6.75 million

It can be seen from this example that the furniture retailer requires to plan to meet cash flow outpeaks if sales are unevenly distributed throughout a trading period. However, the food retailer's concern

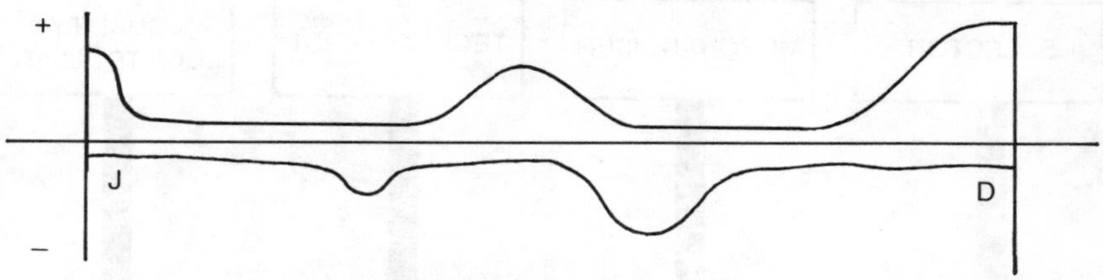

Figure 6.13 *Cash flow profiles for planning*

is more with generating short-term earning opportunities. Cash flow profiles help to plan the needs for shortfalls. See Figure 6.13. there are two periods of high levels of sales which produce positive cash flow, but these are preceded by cash outflows required to finance inventory for the sales periods.

The lead/lag-times require to be quantified in order that overdraft facilities are arranged. Some consideration may also be given to adjusting the merchandise assortment in an attempt to minimize the cash outflow problems. However, this may not be easily resolved due to the cyclical nature of most retailing businesses.

Organization structures for merchandising and buying

Marketing as a strategic concept and process has arrived late in retailing. Consequently, there are many companies where merchandising and buying are activities quite independent of any marketing influence; equally there are examples of companies where there is no merchandising and within which 'the buyer buys and the seller sells'.

Ideally the merchandise function is 'marketing-directed' and follows a process, described earlier and simplified here as:

Defining market segments

↓

Develop target customer group(s)

↓

Identifying the groups' store selection and purchasing processes: its expectations, preferences

↓

Developing a market positioning response to the opportunity and co-ordinated functional strategies

↓

Developing a merchandise strategy and plan

↓

Implementing the merchandise plan

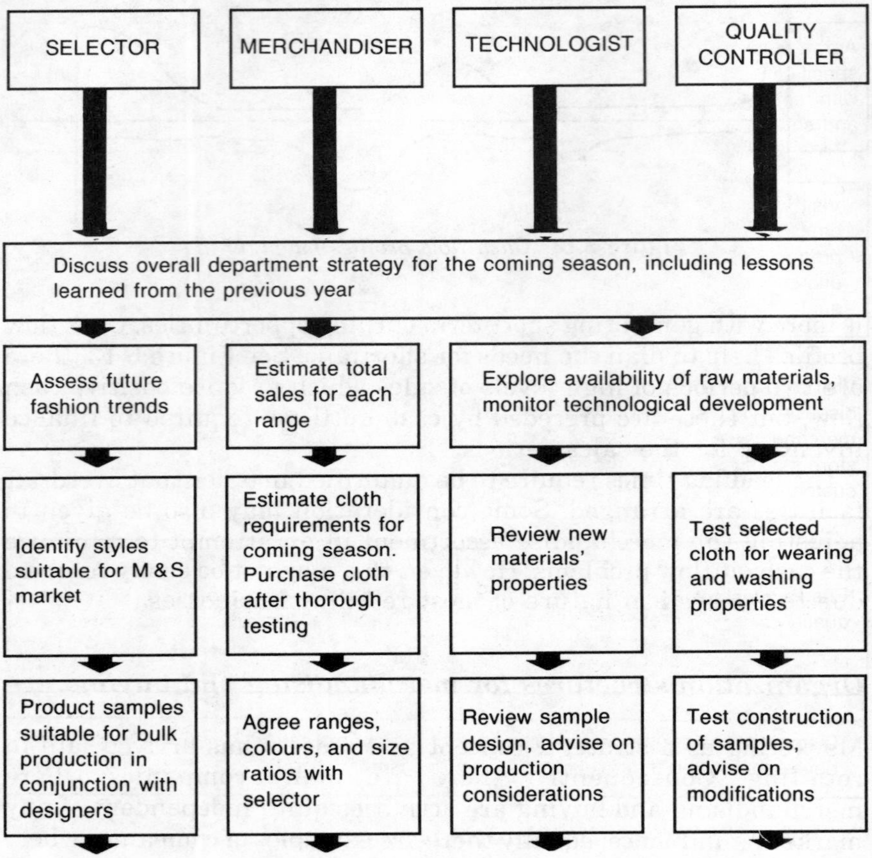

Figure 6.14 *A typical merchandise/buying organization structure*

Source: *International Trends in Retailing*, vol. 6, no. 2, Tse

Within the two extremes there is a differential marketing influence, and to a large extent the model adopted by retailers is a function of history, culture and power relationships within the organization and a function of its entrepreneurial attitudes.

Numerous models exist. Possibly the most common is that of a buying department which selects merchandise with little or no direction, and which intuitively decides on its assortment. There are many examples of 'buyer-led' stores. This was typical of Woolworth prior to the acquisition of the company by Paternoster. Similar approaches exist elsewhere.

Other companies exist on the basis of 'what has sold traditionally will continue to do so'. For these companies buying is essentially a replacement function reacting to a stock central department.

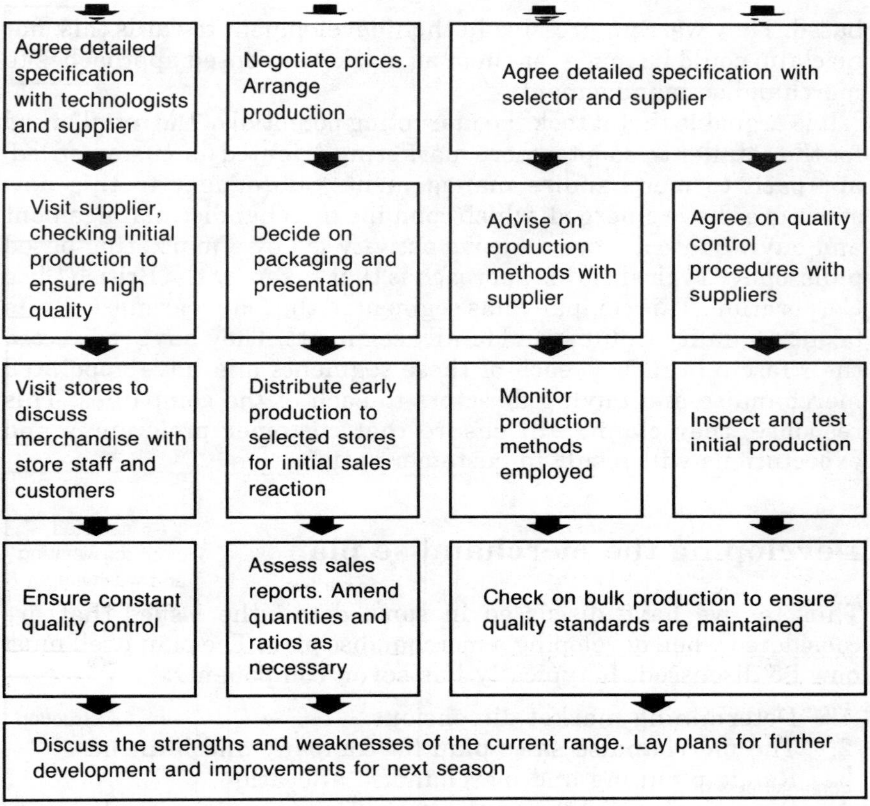

Figure 6.14 *continued*

The more enlightened companies in the 1970s and 1980s combined the talents of the buyers who produced the merchandise, merchandisers who allocated merchandise to branches based on the sales forecasts they developed and technicians who specified its quality and content. This too was a reactive approach, but more recently it has been modified by Marks & Spencer (see Figure 6.14) where an overall strategy for a department is developed and within which a quality controller is added to the merchandise decision group (Tse 1989).

Other companies developed buying structures in which replacement orders were delegated to a stock control function whereby basic stock items (core merchandise groups) were reordered automatically to predetermined levels set to maintain stock availability. This released buyers to investigate new or alternative lines.

None of these approaches, however, could be said to be marketing-based. They were progressive in their development towards this, but no claim could be made for them as marketing-based approaches to merchandise management.

It is arguable that it took the marketing potential of the retail brand for the retailer to adopt a more marketing-oriented (or customer-led) approach to merchandise management. Subsequent to this new structures have emerged, which combine merchandise management and buying into a more cohesive activity led by a marketing-based philosophy. Typical of this approach is that taken by the British Shoe Corporation. This company has segmented the footwear market into fashion, quality, volume and family segments. They have redirected their fascia brands to each of these segments and have appointed merchandise and buying directors to each of the companies. This response, they claim, will ensure that customer preferences and expectations will result in customer satisfaction.

Developing the merchandise plan

Thus far we have discussed in some detail the issues that are considered when developing a merchandise plan. The plan itself must now be discussed. It typically has seven components:

1. Determining market dimensions.
2. The merchandise sales plan for company and branches.
3. Range planning and merchandise allocation.
4. Review: consider the implications for company critical success factors.
5. Sourcing.
6. Distribution: planning and control.
7. Monitoring and control issues.

Having derived a sales forecast and stockholding plan within the buying plan, the next activity looks at detailed area and store forecasts, i.e. *determining the market dimensions*. If the sales forecast has been developed using a combination of *top-down* and *bottom-up* approaches, a considerable amount of this work has already been completed. What is required at this juncture is to develop some detailed information concerning:

1. Targets for market/market segment shares overall.
2. Regional area sales forecasts.
3. Branch profiles (size, locations) and branch sales forecasts.
4. Branch development plans.
5. Distribution facilities.
6. Capital requirements.

Targets for market/market segment shares

This is essential, unless the company considers itself to be a mass merchandise retailer. It requires a clear understanding of the nature and distribution of demographic, socio-economic structures of the market as well as, where possible, its various views concerning merchandise and outlet perceptions and expectations. With this information it becomes a little easier to forecast sales by merchandise and store type. This is particularly important for retailers whose offer is very specialist. Any misreading or misunderstanding of the nature (and size) of the market may lead to very poor performance. This broad approach enables the merchandise manager to consider the initial allocation and distribution of merchandise. Thus, where applicable, macro-market/market segment forecasts should be made for the individual fascia brands and merchandise groups within the brands.

Regional area sales forecasts

The company's sales forecasts will have been developed using top-down and bottom-up approaches, both of which will have input to the regional area's sales forecast. The purpose of this step is to develop a profile of merchandise flows (by group, demand centre, etc., and by volume) in order that distribution facilities can be planned. This is important because, for stores (and merchandise in them) offering wide choice and high levels of availability, the distribution service requirements are not as stringent as for those whose offer may be based on price and limited choice.

Branch profiles and branch sales forecasts

The location, size and shape of a store is fixed in the short term. Any or a combination of all of these factors may limit the type of merchandise sold and the sales volumes. These constraints will have been considered during the bottom-up stage of the sales forecast. At this juncture the detailed issues should be considered. For example, a small store located in a well-defined catchment should be ranged with a carefully chosen selection from within the ideal stock list ensuring that both basic and model items are selected in a manner such that customers' demand satisfaction is maximized and profit optimized within the constraints imposed. The purpose of this activity is to refine the sales forecasts of individual branches in order that distribution service to the branches can be planned and to give management an initial indication on staff needs.

Branch development plans

There are two aspects to be considered — possible change of size and possible change of format or environment. If either of these developments is likely to occur during a forecast period, there may be significant changes in both sales volume and volume mix. Obviously, these changes will be planned activities, but if the plans themselves are not clearly communicated to operations management then the merchandise in the stores may be inappropriate and be in incorrect amounts.

There is also the need to consider how the branch might be developed to provide a greater contribution to both sales and profits. It is not unusual for the trading area of a store to change and with it, the needs and requirements of catchment customers. This may occur when major residential development takes place, thereby changing the demographics and socio-economic profile of the trading area. It may also occur when commercial development takes place. A number of examples can be quoted of major changes to the nature and size of catchments as a result of recent shopping centre developments such as the Metro Centre, the Glasgow redevelopments, and others. Catchments expand to include wide areas of territory and consumer expectations.

For both these reasons the merchandise plan should consider current and potential branch development plans. Where necessary, *branch profiles and branch sales forecasts* should be adjusted.

Distribution facilities

The detailed forecast of sales by volume and product category will identify 'product stocks and flows' throughout the company. Furthermore, the product category forecasts, if accompanied by distribution service requirements, will provide the distribution planning team with an indication of the *quality of service* expected by each store type. For example, if the company operates in a range of market segments it can be expected that customers in a high quality/choice segment will be much more demanding of high levels of availability in-store than the customers of limited range, price-led stores. It follows that quite different distribution service requirements are likely and that these will require considerable planning skills.

Capital requirements

It follows that to achieve a sales plan, particularly if growth is forecast, some capital expenditure may be required for store and distribution facilities expansion and possibly for systems development. As retailing becomes more specialist and merchandise more targeted, risk increases. This implies the need for appropriately selected stock in equally appropriate amounts. It also requires timely and relevant information flows to ensure that the investment in the merchandise selection is maximized. For these reasons the capital requirements should be evaluated from the aspect of what additional profits may be available if the effectiveness of the system is improved.

Range planning and merchandise allocation

Figure 6.1 suggests two areas for consideration. The first concerns those elements or decisions which will reflect the positioning strategy and the other is concerned much more with the allocation of merchandise with time and branch space constraints in mind.

The positioning requirements of range planning have been discussed earlier. The decisions to be taken at this stage of planning concern determining core elements of the range, seasonal elements, price points, style mix, size mix and colour mix. It is where the earlier discussions concerning the *merchandise assortment strategy* become useful because they enable the planner to consider the financial implications of these decisions. The range plan should comprise explicit statements, as illustrated in Table 6.2.

Using this range plan the next step comprises allocation decisions. The usual approach is first to consider *branch categories and branch sizes*. The portfolio of sales outlets is analyzed on the basis of size and location and adjacency to other company outlets and the competition. The analysis will provide management with a rank ordering of stores on the basis of:

- Size and sales potential.
- Location and sales potential.
- Company presence and sales saturation.
- Company monopoly within a catchment.

From this listing an overall sales potential for each branch can be determined and a *branch range plan* devised. Size is an important constraint. Stores usually are too small; however, for merchandise which is high value, low density and compact, too much space may be a problem. In these situations the temptation to relax the criteria set in the merchandise assortment strategy should be avoided. Any

Table 6.2 Range planning

	The ideal stock listing	
Core elements of the range	Basic stock items	Model stock items
	(Demand centres)	
Seasonal elements	Basic stock items	Model stock items
	(Demand centres)	
	The ideal stock listing	
Price points and stock allocation	Basic stock items	Model stock items
	(Classes)	
Price points and availability	basic stock items	Model stock items
	(Classes)	
Choice and availability	Basic stock items	Model stock items
	(Categories)	
Styles, sizes, finishes (materials), colours	Basic stock items	Model stock items

attempt to expand price points, relax quality or exclusivity parameters will result in an overall dilution of the positioning statement. Typically, companies in this situation have expanded their range offer with complementary merchandise; for example, footwear retailers have added accessories (e.g. handbags and belts) to their ranges. However, care should be taken *not* to dilute the offer with a confusing merchandise offer. Often, additional customer research will identify these merchandise items customers would consider to be compatible within the overall offer and equally would consider purchasing.

The branch range plan, then, should not simply consider size as *the* criterion for merchandise allocation. Rather, it should consider the demographic and socio-economic structure of its catchment and their purchasing preferences and expectations. The temptation to include representation from all elements of the range should be resisted. Often research (based on simple observation) will identify merchandise groups that should be enforced because of competitive oversight. Conversely, there may be parts of the range that should not be presented at all, because of competitor superiority or due to a lack of local demand.

The detail of the range plan at branch level should include *sales forecast* by demand centre, class and categories together with *stockholding requirements* to offer availability but, at the same time, a return on investment. In many businesses there are guidelines, built on experience. For most stores the sales performance (typically in sales per square foot, p.a.) can be forecast with accuracy based on size, location, shape characteristics, etc. Furthermore, the same expertise can determine merchandise density and sales floor stockholding requirements to meet predicted sales and customer service levels. An example of this is the method used in ladies' wear retailing where the garment numbers per linear foot can be used for stock and space planning purposes. This is a necessary input for planning *sales/stock level targets*. It also influences, and is influenced by, *fixtures and fittings*. Depending on the intentions of the business (based on the 'life expectations' of the equipment), it may consider the fixtures and fittings as a constraint on sales/stock levels. Often, space can be increased. Recently, Owen Owen reviewed the use of wall-space for display and found that in many departments considerable 'extra' space was created, which they have used to widen choice offers in some merchandise areas.

Finally, the range plan should consider *promotional activity*. There are a number of issues to be included. For example, promotions often need additional merchandise. There is a number of issues:

1. The lead-times required to obtain the merchandise.
2. The working capital commitment.
3. The additional distribution facilities for storage and transportation.
4. The opportunity cost of working capital and indirect costs involved in the promotion.

When all of the identifiable costs and revenues of a specific promotion are examined in terms of contribution and cash flows it is often revealing and raises questions concerning their costs and benefits. Figure 6.15 suggests a hypothetical profile of a promotion.

One other issue to be considered concerns co-ordination. Research by the authors established that merchandise specifically procured for promotions invariably resulted in higher stock levels subsequent to the promotion. This effect is shown as Figure 6.16. It is obvious that the additional stockholding costs are just one element of the overall increase in costs. The issue clearly is: Does the long-term increase in sales have any benefits? Or is the effect only a series of short-term profit increases accompanied by increasing longer-term

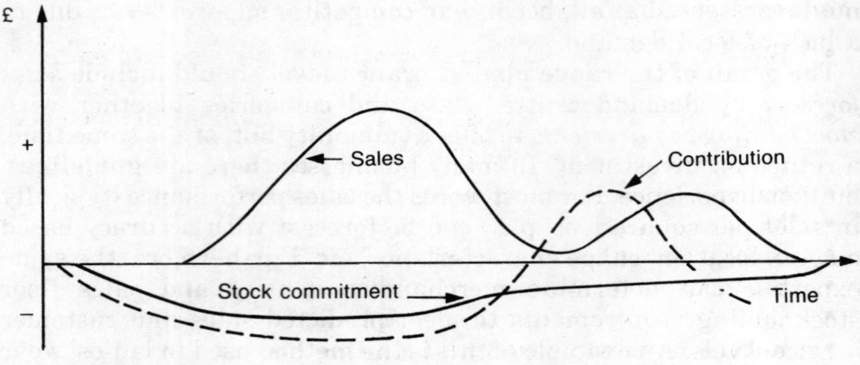

Figure 6.15 *Hypothetical cost/benefit profile of a promotion*

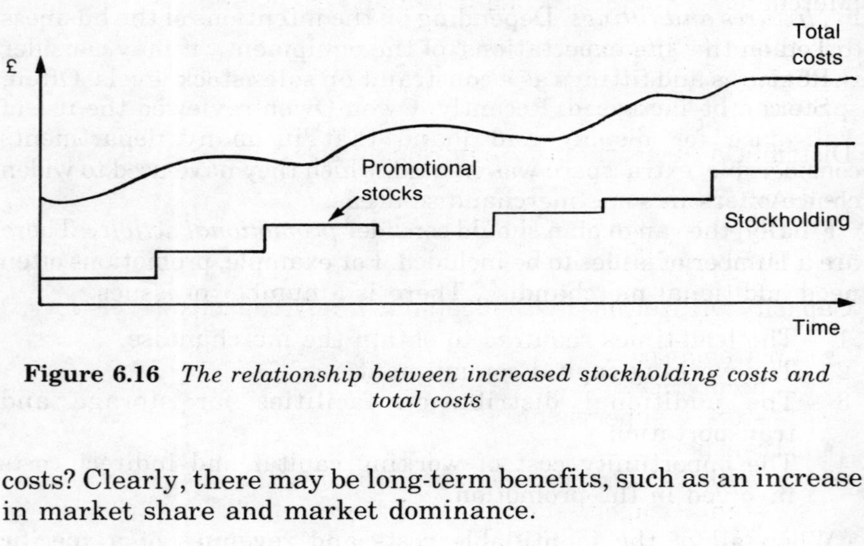

Figure 6.16 *The relationship between increased stockholding costs and total costs*

costs? Clearly, there may be long-term benefits, such as an increase in market share and market dominance.

The merchandise sales plan for company and branches

This element of the plan identifies the *sales to be realized and stock levels* to be held in the stores and distribution facilities throughout the company. Where appropriate, performance expectations should be detailed.

Details to be included are:

For stores (and regions):

• Basic stock list • Model stock list	Demand centres Classes Categories	Price points and stock profiles Availability targets

- Sales (including markdowns) expectations.
- Margins.
- Stockholding.
- Stockturn expectations.
- Cash flow expectations.
- Return on assets managed.

For distribution facilities:

Merchandise volume throughput and stockholding:

Total Region Store	Demand centres Classes Categories

Distribution performance requirements:

- Availability.
- Delivery frequency.
- Delivery reliability.

Capacity utilization and budgets for likely capacity levels for:

- Warehouse:
  occupancy,
  staff + supervision.
- Transport:
  vehicles (depreciation, operations)
  staff + supervision.

The purpose of the sales plan is five-fold:

1. It details merchandise requirements for the buyers by:

Sales season Region Store	Demand centres Classes Categories	Price points and Stock Allocation	Availability

2. It details financial requirements by identifying lead-times and consequently shortfalls and surpluses in the cash flow situation.
3. It can be used to establish the capacity requirements necessary

to produce the distribution service performance levels at branches.

4. It can be used to plan space allocation in the branches.
5. It can be used for manpower planning in branches and distribution centres.

Review: consider implications for company critical success factors

In Chapters 2 and 3 we introduced the concept of critical success factors (and key variables). Their relatonship to both marketing and financial objectives was discussed in some detail. It will be remembered that the critical success factors for any retailing business were suggested to be:

1. Increasing sales revenue.
2. Increasing gross profitability.
3. Containing operating costs.
4. Increasing the productivity of human and physical assets.
5. Adding value to the customer offer.

There is a number of ways by which each of these may be achieved. These were considered and are repeated here:

1. *Increasing sales revenue* by:
   (a) increasing customer visits,
   (b) converting browsing visits to buying visits,
   (c) increasing the average transaction,
   (d) encouraging customers to spend across the assortment.
2. *Increasing gross profitability* by:
   (a) supplier selection:
      (i) number and criteria
      (ii) performance monitors,
   (b) evaluating assortment performance,
   (c) monitoring customer decision criteria,
   (d) improved margin management.
3. *Containing operating costs* by:
   (a) evaluating cost-effectiveness of activities,
   (b) review accountability levels.
4. *Increasing the productivity of human and physical assets* by:
   (a) increasing sales and contribution per employees and selling space,
   (b) increasing throughput of distribution facilities.

5. *Adding value to the customer offer* by:
   (a) adding service(s) to existing merchandise ranges,
   (b) expanding merchandise ranges to include customer perceived added-value items (time and energy savings, 'healthy' aspects, etc.),
   (c) offering facilities to encourage customers to spend more time in the stores (e.g. crêche and childcare facilities).

It is essential that the merchandise strategy and its implementation meet the targets set for the critical success factors. These may be quantitative (as in the case of sales, margins, costs and productivity) or qualitative (as for the customers' perceptions of added value which, of course, may be quantified using a scaling technique). Should the forecast sales, stock levels and other activities not meet the CSF objectives, a review of the merchandise sales plan will be required. It will also be necessary if the CSF targets are wildly exceeded!

Sourcing the merchandise plan

By now volumes of sales and stock levels are known in detail. It follows that the merchandise procurement can be commenced by the buying activity. Prior to orders being placed some consideration must be given to three factors:

1. Identification of merchandise sources.
2. Imported product issues.
3. Supplier relationships.

Identifying merchandise sources

Within this topic there is a number of smaller issues. The first concerns *the number of suppliers* to be used and the balance of purchases among them. Almost all of the considerations here relate to risk. For example:

- Continuity of supply.
- Quality control.
- Flexibility of volume.
- Exclusivity of merchandise.
- Convenience of order administration and progressing.
- Availability of merchandise.

Another important consideration is the *terms of trade* offered by suppliers. These will include payment cycles as well as discount structures. Often, an extended payment period is more beneficial than additional discount for early payment. The reason for this is that the negative working capital effect will enable the retailer to retain suppliers' funds in the business and earn a return from them.

Considerable amounts of research would have been conducted by this time into customer merchandise preferences. One task of the buyer is to ensure that suppliers can meet these requirements. Therefore, part of the buying activity is to source from suppliers whose offer is *congruent* with the company's philosophy. This is important because the market positioning strategy will be firmly based on perceived views of customer preferences; consequently, the buyer should seek to match these preferences when reviewing sourcing alternatives.

An earlier activity in developing the merchandise plan was to identify the requirements for *distributing services* to branches. It is equally important to establish the distribution service requirements to be met by suppliers. This may include service to distribution centres, direct to stores, or possibly a combination of both. It is essential that this is clearly identified early during supplier negotiations as it has a major influence on the terms of trade.

Financial and marketing support facilities

These are usually available from suppliers, and may include stock financing plans for expensive products (e.g. cars and consumer durables) and promotional support (additional discounts, co-operative advertising, etc.). Marketing support may comprise promotional assistance, in-store merchandising services, advertising features, etc. There are numerous alternatives, and the issue for the retailer is first to identify the suppliers' role within the retailers' marketing plan and *then* to negotiate around specific support facilities *and* terms. Caution should be exercised concerning advertising allowances. Often, the manufacturer uses them to influence retailers' advertising. Moreover, advertising departments begin to rely on them.

It is also useful to know which of your competitors are also the suppliers' customers. Using previous experience of the suppliers' competitive activities with the retailers' competitors provides useful insight into what future activities may emerge. It also provides a useful view of capacity utilization of suppliers. If they appear to be operating at very high levels, then additional volume-based discounts are unlikely to be obtained and supply problems may be more likely if production problems occur.

Imported product issues

For many retailing companies overseas suppliers comprise a large proportion of their merchandise requirements. Invariably this is because labour rates are lower than those of domestic suppliers, thereby enabling quality levels to be achieved at lower overall costs. It may be that exclusivity is important and is only possible through overseas sourcing. There are numerous other reasons for sourcing off-shore. However, it is important that certain criteria, usually common to all situations of this type, are considered.These are:

1. Production lead-times; often the quoted delivery time is not met.
2. Merchandise quality can vary; the sample and the delivered order may differ considerably.
3. Merchandise continuity is difficult to manage and reordering often impossible.
4. Local inflation (or interest rate increases) may increase costs to a level at which local domestic supply is more attractive.
5. Currency fluctuations may have similar effects.

Managing the supply chain is difficult enough when suppliers are nationally based, the further they are located from the market-place the greater the difficulties become.

Supplier relationships: buyers

There has been a marked shift in the nature of supplier/distributor relationships in recent years. Typically, these changes have reflected the increasing power of retailing multiples, many of whom are considerably larger than their suppliers. This has often resulted in conflict rather than co-operation in relationships. However, a degree of sophistication now accompanies supplier/distributor negotiations and co-operation rather than conflict has resulted in closer planning activities. This has resulted in buyers working with suppliers on confidential *product specifications and product development*. These have been retailer or manufacturer brands. The co-operation and mutual confidence required has been difficult to develop, but can be seen to be mutually profitable.

Establishing (and maintaining) *merchandise specifications* is another feature of the buyers' role. It requires suppliers to be identified and contracted on the basis of production capabilities as well as capacities. Once the contract has been awarded, volume and quality objectives need to be monitored to ensure continuity of standards. Often (as is the case for food retailing) rigid inspection standards are imposed and maintained by physical presence at the point of manufacture.

Active product development is often delegated to buyers. This may take the form of searching for new product ideas from the supplier base or active involvement in innovation with potential suppliers. To be totally effective product development should be directed by the merchandise strategy. In this way a structured approach may be taken which is:

1. Based on the company's positioning strategy.
2. Based on current and emerging preferences among the customer base.
3. Integrated into existing areas of the assortment on the basis of assuming the characteristics of the merchandise group within which it will be allocated.
4. Offer similar price/value characteristics and therefore enjoy similar margins.
5. Developed as an own-label/manufacturer brand as determined by research as well as financial requirements.

Supplier relationships: merchandisers

Merchandise management is concerned with the logistics of merchandise stocks and flows. Thus the concern is with ensuring that suppliers maintain delivery quantities, times and quality schedules.

Often, merchandise management is tasked with administering the order progressing and delivery system. This ensures the availability of merchandise to meet forecast demand levels over specific periods of time. Increasingly, sales data (such as EPOS) are being used to identify which merchandise, the levels of availability and the critical times for display.

Merchandise management is also responsible for ensuring that merchandise range plans are implemented and maintained. Thus, having participated in determining merchandise allocation specifications, they are also responsible for managing implementation.

Distribution: planning and control

The tasks specified here are to plan and implement a distribution activity that will offer specified levels of service. two activities are important: the specification of *supplier distribution service* requirements and a means by which they may be monitored and similar measures of service to the branch outlets by internal company distribution services. For both, targets should be agreed and monitored for the following topics:

Suppliers		*Internal distribution*	
To distribution centre and to branches		From distribution centres to branches	
Availability Delivery reliability Delivery frequency	Basic stock items Model stock	Demand centres Classes Categories	ABC groups Price points

In addition to measuring the performance achievements of the internal distribution activity, the utilization of the components of the distribution system should also be measured. The measures seen as most useful were considered under the merchandise sales plan for the company and the business, where distribution facilities and capacity utilization and budgeting were discussed.

Monitoring and control issues

The purpose of planning any activity is to achieve a set of prescribed results or objectives. Hence the plan should set its performance measurement requirements as it evolves. For the purposes of merchandise management the measurements should be considered to be *control instruments* and these should be used by management for specific purposes. Obvious control instruments are:

Sales and margins achievements against forecast

Clearly, this is a basic control on which many other issues depend — cash flow, profit, asset utilization, etc. It also acts as a measure of planning accuracy and any over/underachievement should be investigated. The purposes of the investigation are simply to identify any influences in the business environment that may have been overlooked or have had more influence than was estimated.

Stock levels and availability at depots and stores

Sales are lost if merchandise is not available. And if availability becomes a major problem, eventually customers are lost. Hence availability achievements are essential control instruments.

Stock replenishment levels

This control is closely linked with availability in that, if these are set accurately, the availability targets will be met. At the same time, care must be taken to ensure that overstocking does not occur. Excess stocks are a poor use of working capital and in perishable and fashion merchandise sectors lead to markdowns.

Open-to-buy/open-to-order controls

The OTB control, when used effectively, limits total stock investment as well as disciplines the buying activity into relating sales, stock levels and return on investment. Controlling OTB in large retailing companies is not an easy task. However, if it is maintained with accuracy, it can return the cost involved.

Markdowns

A useful measure of buying effectiveness. By monitoring markdowns and investigating the reasons for their occurrence, management can identify sources of poor merchandise selection, excessive ordering, poor forecasting or external influences (such as increased competitive activity).

Margins

An indication of buying efficiency is given by the performance of buyers in achieving margins targets. However, simply to focus on margin achievement may result in poor performance elsewhere. For example, a wider range, different merchandise, etc., may result in higher sales and, of course, gross profit. A more effective measure is in fact gross profit and this considers the effect of volume.

Direct costs

Close control of direct costs is essential in any business, but more so in retailing where net margins are very low for many forms of retailing. The issue here is the old one of accountability and responsibility. Budgeting activities should identify and locate responsibility for direct costs. This way they can be accurately controlled.

GMROI/CMROI

These controls (discussed at pages 98–101) have the benefits of encouraging merchandise management to view stock as investment and to maximize (or optimize) return on that investment. It is not widely used, which is surprising when it is considered that the data exist in most control systems.

Customer performance

These controls have been discussed earlier. The purpose of their inclusion here is to identify the impact of the merchandise strategy in achieving greater customer penetration.

Control decisions

Control instruments must have a purpose. We suggest that those described above facilitate the merchandise management task.

In the *short term* they offer the manager the ability to:

- Control repeat intake (distribution centre/branch).
- Control repeat purchases.
- Reschedule/cancel deliveries.
- Adjust prices.

In the *medium term* they enable the:

- Identification of additional opportunities through (or by):
  — promotions.

  - expanding merchandise categories,
  - consolidating merchandise categories,
  - extending the assortment.
- Regrading of branches to reflect performance.

In the *long term* they offer:

- The facility to decide upon branch extension, closure or opening.
- Repositioning decisions.

Summary

In this chapter we have identified the topics and activities comprising the merchandise plan. Planning is part of the process of implementing strategy. We would argue that for a strategy to be effective, the planning activities and its implementation are an integral part of the strategy.

For this reason we concluded the strategy process by developing a merchandise profile which itself is based on the thesis that understanding the market and its customers is fundamental in the process of developing a merchandise strategy.

Merchandise planning has four requirements. Firstly, the positioning strategy of the company must be understood. In fact, it is more fundamental than that: it is the market and customer philosophy of the company that must be understood. This may be a chief executive's *vision* or a *consensus view* of a board of directors and senior management. Whatever it is, it is basic to deciding upon the merchandise offer. As one chief executive said to his buying team: 'Your negotiating skills should be aimed at increasing quality at a price point, not to reduce the cost and therefore the price, that is not what this company is about.'

Secondly, the merchandise plan should consider the roles and functions of support activities. It is pointless deciding on a level of activity or a range of merchandise if there is very little probability that the distribution function and operations management will be able to cope with it.

Thirdly, the plan must indicate clearly the level of activities in buying and selling. It should consider the size, location and catchment characteristics of branches, and plan to optimize their sales and profits with these in mind.

Fourthly, it must be a communication vehicle. It should make very clear to those involved the nature of their function and the performance expected of them if the plan is to be achieved. Their involvement in its preparation and in the objectives it seeks to achieve should be significant to this end.

CHAPTER 7

Developing customer service strategy

Introduction

In this chapter the issues concerning customer service strategy are discussed. As with the chapters dealing with merchandise strategy and its implementation, so too with customer service we work with the assumption that the role of customer service within retail marketing is to influence the store selection and purchasing activities and to 'progress' or 'process' the customer through the search, comparison, transaction, delivery, use extension and evaluation stages of the store selection/purchasing activity and to estabish them as store-loyal customers who revisit the store frequently and consider it their 'first choice' store.

Customer service strategy decisions

There are two areas to be considered when making customer service strategy decisions. These are featured in Figure 7.1 and comprise: marketing considerations and financial considerations. This chapter considers each of these in some depth. They are not mutually exclusive and the interrelationships will be explored. Figure 7.1 suggests that a sequence exists. Our research again suggests this to be the case, and the sequence is initiated by establishing the implications for strategy decisions of the relative customer perceptions and expectations to, and of, the customer service offer.

Marketing considerations

As established in the introduction to Part Two and developed in Chapter 5, we have assumed that central to any customer service decision is an understanding of the customers' store selection and

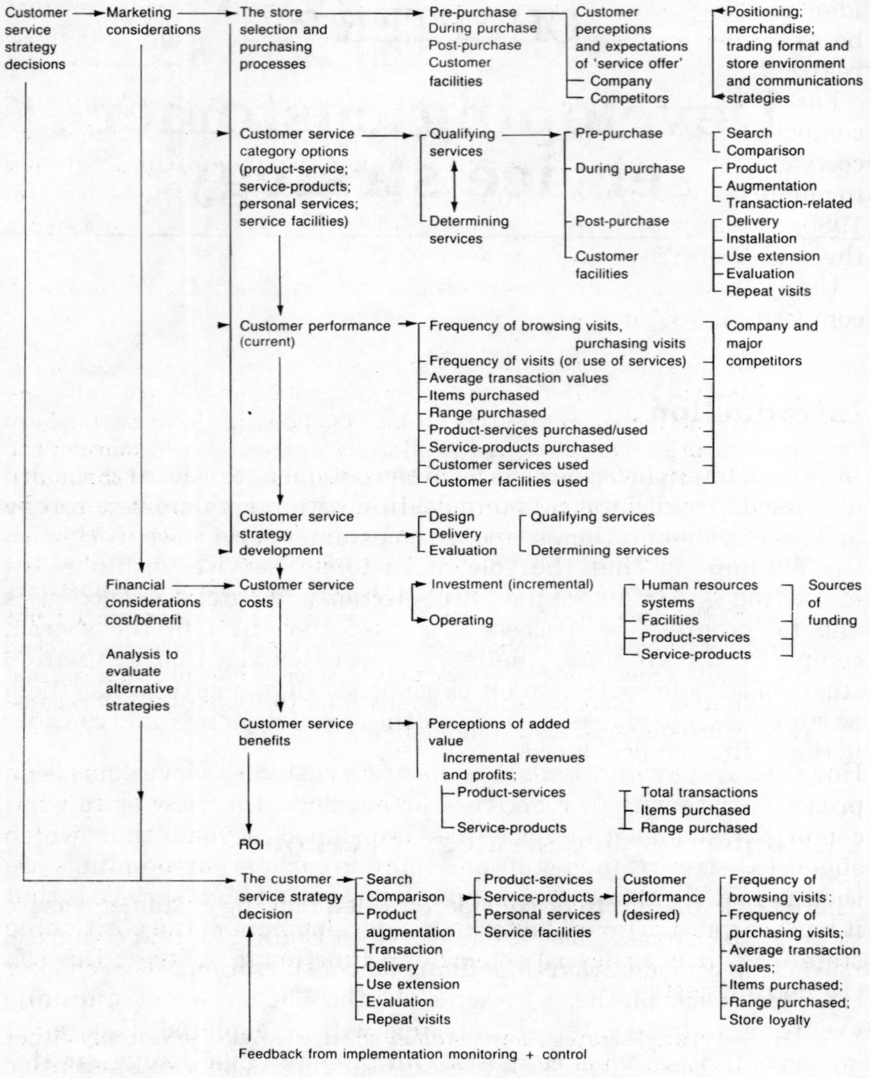

Figure 7.1 *Developing the customer service strategy*

purchasing decisions, together with their perceptions and expectations of the customer service offer of both the company and its competitors.

Figure 7.1 uses this assumption to explore *customer service* options which can influence the store selection and purchasing decisions of the target customer group. The initial customer research will have identified the major issues (see Figure P2.1), but these options must be examined in detail if the objectives of the company are to be realized.

For a considerable time during the 1960s and 1970s price dominated competition in retailing. Pressures on buying margins, high fixed costs of entry into new locations and increased operating costs led to non-price alternatives being explored by retailers. The 1970s and 1980s saw an emphasis on assortment width, on produce and, from the mid-1980s, on customer service.

Using customer service to create relative differentiation and competitive advantage is not a recent concept:

> An emphasis on price alone means easy comparison by the shopper and the vulnerability of any one retailer to unilateral action by any other. The fear of retaliation in an oligopolistic situation tends to prevent price competition, and efforts to increase one's share of the trade are therefore directed into better service. In view of the multi-dimensional and non-quantitative character of service it cannot be exactly matched, as a price-cut can be matched, and those taking the initiative often have confidence that their assessment of what the customer wants will be more accurate than that of their competitors . . . . Not only can improvement in service not be exactly matched, but it cannot be immediately matched. Whereas a price cut can be matched overnight, months or even years may be needed for the designing and installation of more luxurious fittings or for the building up of capable and courteous staff. (McLelland 1966)

However, more recently the emphasis on customer service has been proactive rather than reactive. Furthermore, the view as to what comprises customer service has broadened beyond that which suggests better-trained staff and more luxurious surroundings are the limits to its extent. The current view of customer service is that it has become a primary factor in the development of the positioning statement. It is as described earlier a functional strategy; Dawson (1989a) suggests:

> An integrated strategy for customer service can be seen simply either as a responsive approach to escape the rigours of price competition or as a more creative approach to improve retail environments, to increase sales volumes and profit margins and even as a mechanism for corporate diversification. . . . The provision of customer service . . . represents a philosophy of operation, even a corporate culture, not just a two week course on complaints handling. This philosophy of operation often is associated with an overt marketing based or customer driven strategy.

Dawson points out that many retailers develop a service offer in a way reminiscent of patterns of product range management prior to the development of more analytical approaches of recent years. He suggests that both assortment and pricing decisions are now taken subsequent to extensive research, often using modelling techniques, based on and related to specifically targeted customer groups. This, he says, seldom appears to be the case with customer services. Except for a few notable and successful examples they have been introduced in an apparently relatively haphazard and unco-ordinated way:

> One of the aims of customer service is to provide the environment in which the customer is encouraged to make purchases. There are many alternative possible environments which may be chosen by the retailer as the desired one, but having decided on an environment, then the customer services require to be co-ordinated to support the desired environment. (*ibid*.)

This view is, in our opinion, very helpful. It does identify the need to consider the role of customer service in the creation of a retail exchange environment when planning specific elements of customer service. What it also does is to remind retailing managers of the need to identify those areas of overlap between the functional strategies, where there are opportunities to create added value.

If a customer service strategy is to be developed, it should have a structured basis. Figure 7.1 suggests an approach whereby the store selection and purchasing processes are used as a framework around which a strategy may be developed. As with the merchandise strategy, it follows that to achieve the objectives of: increased browsing and purchasing visit frequencies, increased average transactions, increases in both items purchased and range systems purchased and to create customer loyalty, the store selection and purchasing process should be understood and supported by service activities.

Customer service category options

An essential step is to classify the assortment offer into three broad product areas using their service content as a basis for differentiation. In Figure 7.1 we suggest:

1. *Product services*, i.e. services that add value to the product, such as advice on how to use the product, its 'after use' care and maintenance, or possibly garment alterations to improve the fit of clothes products.
2. *Service products*, i.e. products that are service-based, such as financial services (investment, insurance, banking, etc.).
3. *Personal services*, i.e. health and fitness-based products, such as opticians, health checks, pharmacies.

A fourth category concerns the support activities of the business which enhance the overall offer and can be offered as *internal or external facilities*. These include:

1. *Internal facilities*: crêches, cloakrooms, cash points, post office, dry cleaning, waiting areas.
2. *External facilities*: bus services to and from the store, stock availability information, home shopping and delivery.

Customer service strategy decisions, unlike merchandise strategy, are intangible, and it follows that a useful aid to the development of a customer service strategy is to establish clearly in the minds of all levels of management what the primary objective of customer service is. We suggest it is to add value to the retail offer and to increase or to create competitive advantage by adding relevant customer benefits at an acceptable level of costs. Clear customer service objectives would be:

1. To increase the customers' utility of the basic product by adding support services.
2. To create interest in a product group and to increase customers' satisfaction from a purchase by demonstrating its application and other potential uses.
3. To create additional customer traffic.
4. To increase the range and value of customer purchases.
5. To use services to increase customer convenience.
6. To use service to increase sales and profits.

If this view of service is taken it becomes an integral component of the positioning strategy and should supplement both merchandise and trading format/store environment functional strategies.

If customer services are added to the retail package, without prior consideration of customers' actual requirements or of their management within the context of the overall business, high costs may result, together with difficult management tasks, with no major impact being made on customer purchases.

It is obviously very important that the services offered are those important to the targeted customer group. Arnold *et al.* (1983) have suggested that there are two aspects of service to be considered. A *qualifying service* is a service that a retailer must offer simply in order to qualify for customers' consideration. This may be because it is extremely important to customers or because most competititors offer the service and customers consider it to be the norm. A *determining service* is a service that actually determines customers' store preferences and choice. It is at this point that the issue of competitive advantage through the added value of service in the retailer offer arises. Retailers often find it difficult to attract more

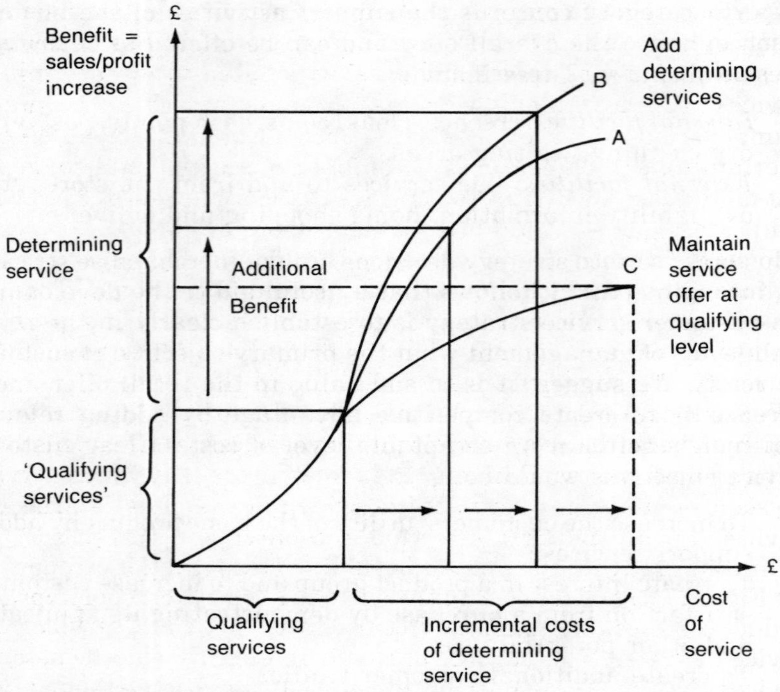

Figure 7.2 *A cost/benefit approach to customer service decisions*

customers if they attempt to increase their offer in terms of basic qualifying services, instead of seeking to identify additional determining service features that would add value.

The relationship between *qualifying services* and *determining services* can be demonstrated in cost/benefit terms. Figure 7.2 demonstrates the difference between qualifying services and determining services. Situation A is one in which an additional benefit can be obtained by increasing the *type* of service made available to the customer; the benefits, in incremental terms, exceed the costs involved. In C the situation is different, and the incremental benefits are such that they would not cover the required increase in the customer service budget.

However, B is quite another proposition. Here we can see considerable additional benefits available for quite a modest increase in the service budget over and above the qualifying level.

Research recently conducted in the ladies' wear market showed dissatisfaction with a number of facilities offered in-store. In this particular example there was considerable dissatisfaction with changing-room facilities. It was clear that some retailers should simply increase the number of changing rooms (qualifying service) to satisfy existing customers, while others would need to increase the size of changing-rooms and possibly add features (determining services to see any benefit). From the same research came another example of how additional service aspects would, if added, become determining service features. A number of respondents suggested that more space — possibly seating areas and somewhere to put coats and possessions — would attract them more often.

However, it must be stressed that the indiscriminate addition of service to the retail offer may prove to be dysfunctional. This can occur if the service offer is inappropriate to customer needs or, more importantly, inappropriate or incongruent with other elements of the retail offer, or with its positioning.

We shall deal with the problems of deciding on the point at which qualifying services become determining services later. At this stage in the process the essential requirement is to identify which services are seen as qualifying services and which are seen as determining services during the store selection and purchasing processes.

This requires that the process be detailed into smaller components (see Figure 7.1) and for each of the customer service category options: product-services, services, service-products, personal services and service facilities. The purpose of this is to identify where customer services may make a contribution to that specific element of the decision process. Two purposes may be served. One will be to help the customer pass quickly on to the next stage of the process and the other is to identify for the customer the particular advantages that the company has to offer. If these can be identified and the service inputs co-ordinated, the customer passes through the process quickly, but, more importantly, concludes that the company making this statement is most suited to them.

Customer performance (current)

As with any strategy some evidence of changes brought about by the application of resources is required. For customer service we need to know customer performance at present on a number of issues:

- Frequency of browsing visits.
- Frequency of purchasing visits.
- Average transaction per visit.
- Items purchased.
- Range purchased.
- Product-services purchased/used.

- Service-products purchased.
- Customer services/facilities used.

The measurement of current customer performance characteristics gives a bench-mark from which it is possible to calculate the revenue and profit generated by the existing level of customer service offered. It also enables management to determine the improvements they should attempt to achieve and to relate these to increases in revenue and profits. Concurrently, they should also consider the role to be taken by improved levels of customer service, together with the costs of developing and implementing a new customer service package.

It is essential that current customer performance (for the same topics) within competitors' stores and outlets be measured. Clearly, the level of service in competitors' outlets will influence the store selection and purchasing process and for this reason the level of visits and purchasing activities by customers in competitive outlets should be ascertained. This information, together with the data gathered on customer perceptions and expectations of service offers (see above), is useful in assessing the sensitivity of customers to customer service. If the customer performance of a group of customers who are loyal to a competitor (whose service offer is perceived as better than that of other retailers) is higher than that with the company, or any other competitor, then clearly customers' service is an important issue for positioning strategy decisions.

Customer service development

Thus far, we have identified a number of important issues. We have identified the aspects of service seen as important to customers as either qualifying services or determining services. We have information on customer perceptions of company and competitor service offers. And we have quantitative measures of important revenue and profit generating aspects of customer performance. This information offers:

1. An indication of the rank ordering of the importance of a range of customer service issues.
2. The relative perceptions of customers of company and competitive customer service offers.
3. The visiting and purchasing behaviour of customers in both company and competitive stores.
4. A measure of customer service sensitivity of customers.

It follows that this information set can be used to develop a customer service portfolio. Figure 7.1 indicates three steps to be taken: design, delivery and evaluation.

Design activities should commence with a review of the existing service offer, its objectives and the extent to which they have been achieved, customers' perceptions of the company and competitor service offers.

Delivery involves the examination of existing organization structures and systems necessary to provide the range of services and the level of services under consideration.

Evaluation of the customer service portfolio is essential. In this context the discussion on customer performance (current and required) comes into context. These, when used as input to a cost/benefit analysis and/or an investment appraisal model, can give an indication of effectiveness of the service offer. This will be discussed below.

This design process also concerns the extent to which competitive advantage can be developed. Figure 7.3 suggests an approach whereby having identified *the store selection and purchasing processes* the *key components of customer service* which reinforce them can be identified and their *relative importance to the core customer group be established*. At this point the company is well situated to identify its strengths in respect of customer services currently offered (its *distinctive competence(s)*) and to *establish the criteria for creating sustainable competitive advantage*. The following steps require an evaluation of the *relevance and sensitivities of service aspects for the target customer group*. During this activity the issues concerning *delivery* should be considered. There are a number of points to consider. The most important is the organizational structure necessary to implement the service strategy. Issues concerning the need to create a customer service management team, recruit and train staff must be considered. So, too, should any capital requirements and this would require investment appraisal. Closely allied to this are decisions as to whether or not all or part of the service function can be 'bought in'. This, in turn, raises the issue of the potential revenue that might be generated from the sale of excess capacity to other retailing companies.

This exercise leads to the evaluation of *costs and benefits* and the impact of various customer service strategy options on the eventual level of *customer performance*. Some rethinking and re-examination may be required at this point. This may be to reconsider *relevance and sensitivity issues* or possibly a review of the *relative importance of the service components* to the target customer group. Once established, the effectiveness of the strategy must be monitored. This

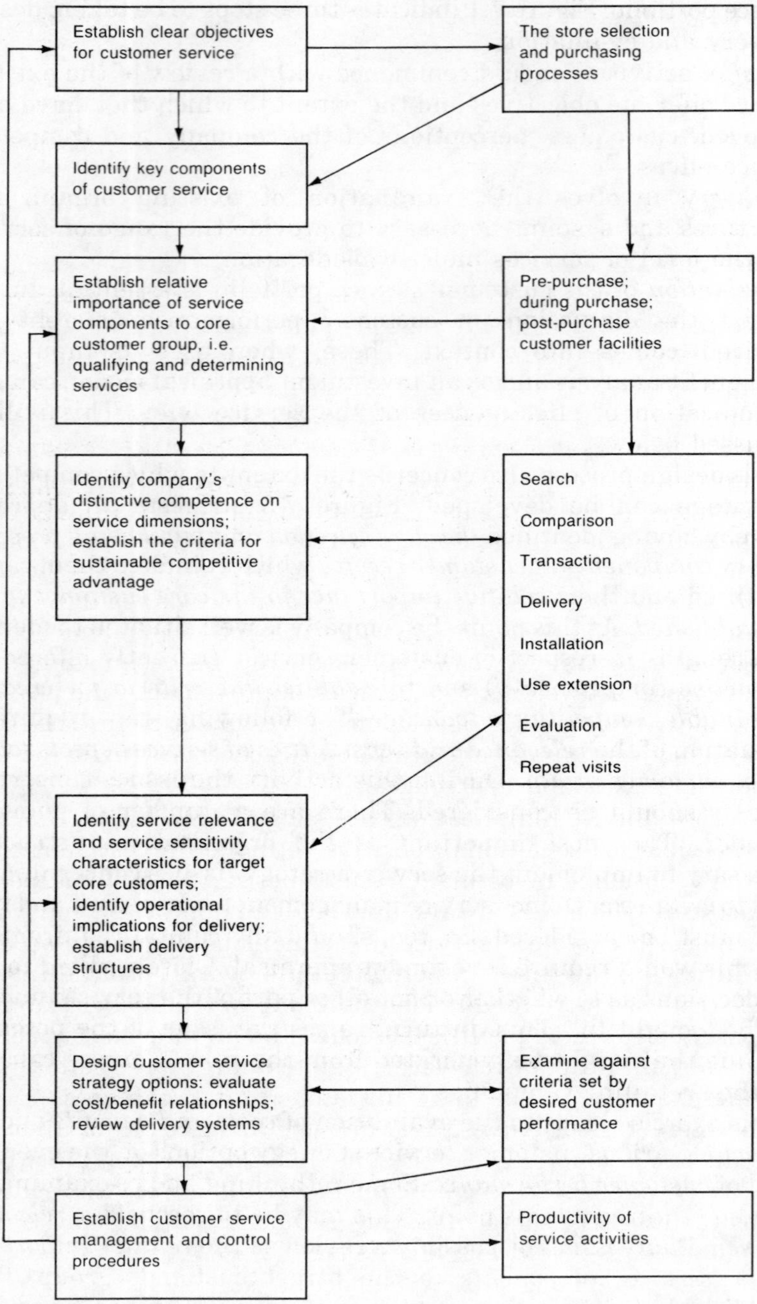

Figure 7.3 *An approach to developing customer service strategy*

is part of the implementation of the customer service strategy to which we will return in the next chapter.

Financial considerations

Customer service costs

It is useful to consider the advantages that a cost/benefit study offers, together with an investment appraisal of any proposed customer service portfolio. One of our reasons for suggesting that customer performance be monitored is that the benefits that accrue can be measured in increased sales and sales related activities. The main problem likely to be encountered is the matching of costs and benefits over time. For this reason a conventional DCF or IRR (discounted cash flow or internal rate of return) investment appraisal method may be more difficult to apply. The nature of the cash flows (costs and benefits) are illustrated in Figure 7.4. The situation (a hypothetical one) shows a ten-year period over which performance (critical success factors and customer performance) is declining while operating costs and depreciation are increasing. A customer service investment programme was initiated during which investment in human resources, systems and facilities improvements and product-service and service-product developments was undertaken. The result shows an increase in sales and profitability, together with an increase in operating costs and depreciation.

The profit and ROI implications are suggested in Figure 7.5. It is quite possible for a 'notional' positive return on investment to be made on a 'notional' investment in customer service systems, people and facilities. The issues always are: Can it be improved? And would an increase in customer service investment be accompanied by a substantial improvement in both ROI and overall profitability?

Some costs are more readily identifiable than others. For example, the costs of cloakroom facilities, crêches and an information centre are not difficult to define. However, staff training covers both service and merchandise needs and this and similar examples occur. Furthermore, for both investment and operating costs (for all of the elements of customer service) there is the issue of opportunity cost. This can be particularly significant for customer service facilities which occupy selling space. Here the argument is often that the costs of such facilities should include the contribution from sales which would have to be made from the space.

While it may not be possible to identify individual elements of cost, it may be more useful to consider *incremental increases* in costs. In

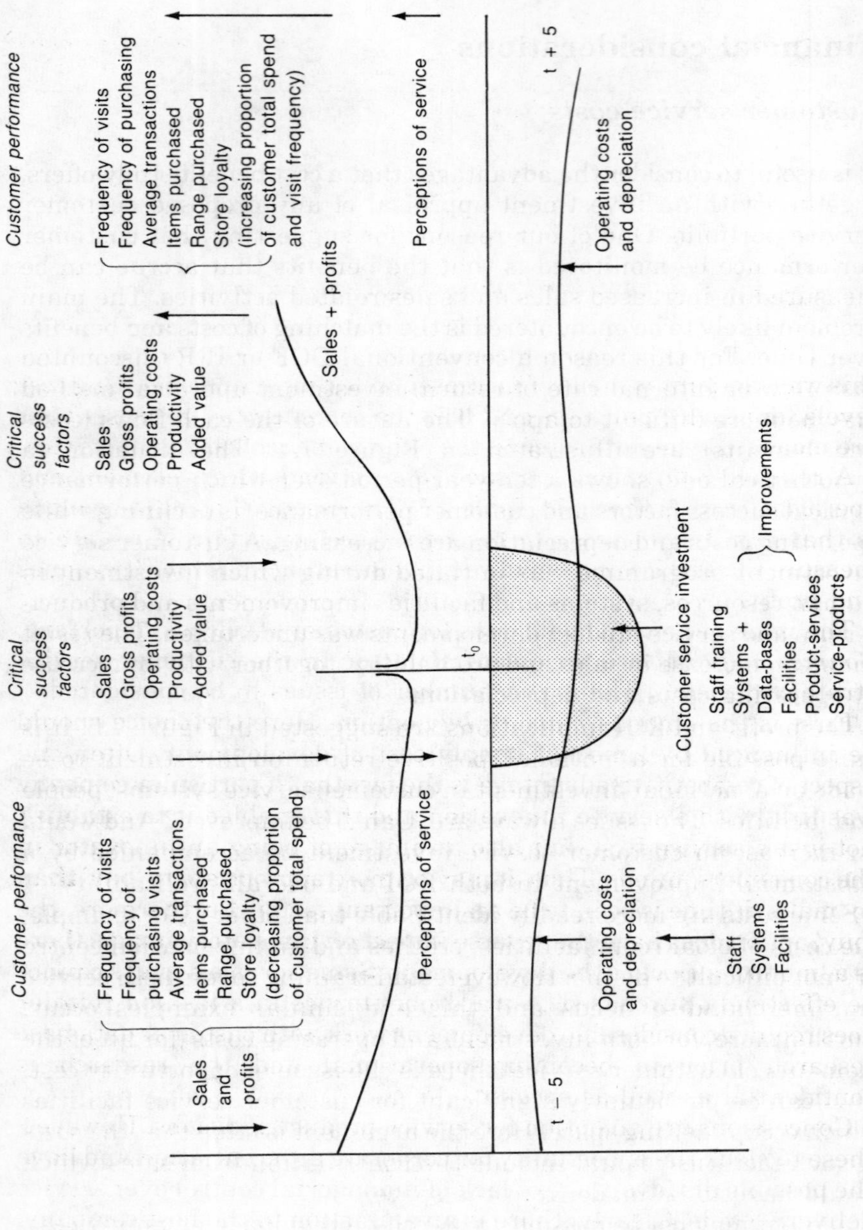

Figure 7.4 *Costs/benefits and cash flows in customer service*

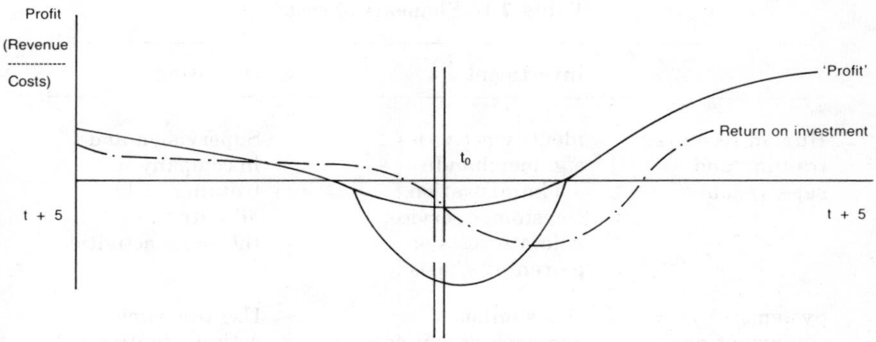

Figure 7.5 *Profit and ROI implications*

this way, account is made of increased investment and operating cost levels for service purposes and it is the incremental increases that are measured when measuring the effectiveness of customer service.

A relatively practical approach to deriving both investment and operating costs is shown in Table 7.1. The essential point to be made is that it is the *increase in costs* that are important if we are to measure the service costs involved in generating *additional* revenues and profit.

The issue of how and who pays for customer service is important. *Sources of funds* are an essential factor in the customer service strategy decision. There is a number of issues to be considered.

First is the obvious *make or buy* option. Here the choice should be influenced by time not simply cost of development. Often one aspect of competitive advantage is the fact that a particular company was first with a service innovation and this enabled it to establish not just a service first, but also an image of being an innovator in the consumers' minds. Thus, it may be more appropriate to 'buy' than to 'make' if time is seen to be an important factor. Furthermore, the 'buy' option does have the reverse impact on innovatory image: there is a 'me too' aspect to the development. Some service aspects cannot be effectively purchased. A wardrobe service in a fashion retailer does require considerable development work with customer data-base research prior to becoming operational and the research is confidential as well as specific.

Concessions are an option for service-product additions. However, these too lack the opportunity for corporate differentiation and have the possible disadvantage of lack of managerial control over service delivery levels. Clearly, there is an attraction to the host company. First of all, there is the fact that there is little or no lead-time for

Table 7.1 Elements of cost

	Investment	Operating
Human resources: training and supervision	Identify activities, e.g. merchandise administration customer service; Allocate costs on percentage basis	Supervision and in-company training costs allocated to the same activities
Systems: equipment and personnel	Use similar approach activities likely to be: accounting control operations management merchandise control administration customer service; Identify equipment-related costs and staff training costs	Use the same activity centres but do not assume the proportions will be necessarily similar
Facilities	Equipment and installation costs; major additions and development costs of existing installations	Maintenance costs; 'lost contribution'
Product-services	Specific equipment related to existing merchandise that 'augments' the product/ product range by adding value to the overall offer, e.g. after-sales servicing; installation services; new product information; delivery services (*Note*: merchandise characteristics, e.g. availability, choice, etc., are included in stockholding as a merchandise cost)	'Dedicated staff' costs and related supervision costs; maintenance costs
Service-products	The development and 'delivery' costs associated with the introduction of the service product	'Dedicated staff' costs and related supervision; maintenance costs

development and installation. Secondly, there is the benefit of complete or partial funding which lowers the risk.

Supplier co-operation is another alternative. Many suppliers consider customer service support proposals favourably, because being covert they do not expose the extent of their support for individual retailers. Furthermore, there is an opportunity for the supplier to influence the customer service strategy and in so doing influence it in his or her favour.

Customer service benefits

Similar problems exist for the measurement of benefits. While it is difficult accurately to allocate costs, benefits not only have the problems of timing but also of matching and quantification. However, some suggestions can be made. Figure 7.4 identified customer increases in performance as quantitative benefits, but as they stand they are overall measures and ideally require to be identified with specific customer service 'products' or activities. The suggestions in Table 7.2 have proven useful for some companies.

Measurement of both qualitative and quantitative issues requires a certain amount of customer research. Attitude surveys can be conducted on a questionnaire basis across a specified sample of customers provided the data-base is adequate for these needs (which, if it does not exist, can comprise a major element of both investment and operating costs of the customer service system).

Acquiring data is another problem. Store cards offer one method of collecting the information required. The application blank can be designed to obtain demographic, socio-economic and shopping behaviour data; subsequent expenditure patterns can be tracked. However, not all customers request store cards, often being satisfied with bank and other cards; furthermore, the interest charges made on store cards can be severe in times of high general interest rates and this possibility can act as a disincentive to the acquisition of many store cards. An increasingly popular alternative is the 'premier user' or 'favoured customer' approach. Frequent or 'heavy users' of a company offer are offered free membership of a 'club' or 'organization'. They are issued with a membership card (with readable magnetic strip code) and are encouraged to register visits to the company's premises or use of its services by 'wiping' the card through a card reader. Airlines are among the largest users of this system. Most offer incentives based on travel frequency together with privileges such as car hire and hotel rate discounts.

Table 7.2 Incremental changes in qualitative and quantitative data

	Qualitative	Quantitative
Relative perceptions of customer service	Increase in positive attitudes towards aspects of the service offer	.
Store loyalty	Increase in positive attitudes towards the company	Increases in visiting frequencies for browsing and purchasing; increased amount of total expenditure spent in company outlets; increases in items and ranges purchased; increase in average transactions
Product-services and Service-products	Acknowledged leadership among competitors; positive relative attitudes, i.e. 'better than' all major competitors —	Increase in item and range sales; increases in number of *new* customers attracted by offer; Increases in average transactions
Facilities	Increased awareness of facility availability; high 'relative quality' measure of facility over and above that of competitive offer	Increase in numbers of customers using the facility; increased frequency of use by individual customers; increase in average transactions, items and ranges purchased by customers using facilities

Similar uses are being made by retailing companies. The card can be used to register visits to stores, to departments and to register purchases. Each visit or purchase qualifies the cardholder for 'points' which at various levels of aggregation can be used to obtain discounts on purchases. Cardholders are often given advance notice of sale events and other similar occasions. Other applications include discounted prices for products and services.

The measurement of *return on investment* is just as difficult. Figure 7.5 indicates the likely 'profile' of a return on investment curve. The point to be made is that the time over which the investment is recovered depends upon the size of the investment made. Clearly, there is risk involved in any investment decision and management should research this when developing a customer service project.

The customer service strategy decision

Customer service strategy should be based on a corporate philosophy, which defines the customer as the central feature in any planning activity within the company. In this chapter we have identified the processes and issues to be considered. However, they are unlikely to be effective unless there is an overall corporate recognition of the need to be customer oriented. A customer service strategy should reflect this attitude and should provide reasoning and logic, as well as explicit directions, to the management group tasked with its implementation.

Some companies find it helpful to publish mission, philosophy and/or policy statements to assist operating management with the implementation of the service strategy. For example, one large food multiple has identified a range of customer service policy and philosophy issues for the activities involved in delivering service. Thus for store operations we have:

Philosophy: Customer service is going to be the next big breakthrough, affecting the company as a whole, e.g. the store becomes the customer of the distribution depot.

Target: Aim for levels of customer service and staff caring or attitudes higher than those of (competitor A) and at least equal to those of (competitor B).

Policy: For a general, friendly and helpful attitude of staff towards customers, but most importantly, courtesy towards the customer.

While it is possible to debate the content of such statements, the point made is that they are a reflection of intention and provide guidance for planning. They can also be used to define the role of the elements of the customer service options in developing competitive advantage. Arnold *et al.* (1983) suggest that customer service should be seen as a competitive tool and that some elements of service are therefore defensive and others offensive. The offensive elements of service they suggest are those around which competitive advantage may be developed. They suggest four basic purposes for customer service:

1. *To increase the form utility of merchandise*, e.g. clothing alterations, carpet installations, menu services, etc.
2. *To expand the market for merchandise*, e.g. classes for sewing, golf, fashion selection, 'colour co-ordination'.
3. *To provide comfort and convenience for customers*, e.g. rest rooms, restaurants, meeting areas.
4. *To generate additional traffic*, e.g. service facilities such as post offices, dental clinics, community exhibits.

To these we could add:

5. *To add value to the overall offer by considering time budgets of customers and offering product-services which enable them to complete aspects of the store selection and purchasing process quickly and effectively*, e.g. wardrobe services, anniversary reminders (birthdays, weddings, etc.).
6. *To increase customer repeat business traffic*, e.g. by maintaining customer purchasing and satisfaction data, by maintaining customer contact through company magazines and carefully targeted direct marketing.

The customer service strategy should be constructed around the store selection and purchasing decision process and meet customer perceptions and expectations for customer service. It should also integrate with the positioning and other functional strategies. We would suggest the following components form the basis of the customer service strategy model described by Figure 7.6.

In Figure 7.6 we propose a model by which this may be achieved. The basis of the model is described by *shopper characteristics*. It will be remembered that in Chapter 4 we proposed a segmentation approach which included *shopping-related perceptions and preferences and shopping-related behaviour*. We suggested that a number of characteristics could occur, for example: exclusivity, choice, convenience, continuity, quality, availability and merchandise co-ordination. The thesis of the model offered in Figure 7.6 assumes that many of the perceptions and preferences actually become overt behaviour characteristics as customer expectations are formed by experience with the company, its competitors and other retail offers. The model proposes that these rank-ordered characteristics form the basis for developing a customer service strategy by matching activities in the store selection and purchasing processes with a service package that reflects the perceptions and behaviour characteristics. Therefore, if the rank ordering of these issues identifies a very strong convenience motive, then both qualifying and determining services should be designed with an emphasis on convenience with other service aspects reflecting the other important characteristics.

Customer store selection, purchasing processes and service expectations

The customer service strategy should identify the process by which the target customer group selects both the store(s) to be visited and merchandise to be purchased during these visits. Each of the stages should be analyzed in detail. An essential input into this analysis is an examination of shopper characteristics which will identify and rank-order shopping-related behaviour issues and shopping-related perceptions and preferences. These are used as the basis of the customer service strategy development process described by the model in Figure 7.6.

Service offers

Service offers should be detailed at the qualifying service and determining service levels. It will be remembered that *qualifying services* are those services seen by customers as a norm, minimum services which are expected to exist and do exist in all competitive outlets. *Determining services* are those that can be used to influence customer choice and build competitive advantage. In the context of Porter's (1985) argument they are among the major elements of focus or differentiation strategies. The issues to be dealt with here are:

1. *What distinguishes a qualifying service from a determining service*? For example, changing-rooms are an essential feature for ladies' wear retailing. With notable exceptions all ladies' wear retailers offer this facility. As such, they are seen as qualifying services. However, discriminating customers respond to larger changing-rooms, with mirrors and 'make-up' facilities, chairs, etc. These then become determining services. The point at which this occurs is important to establish because it is a major issue for both costs (and opportunity costs) and benefits (increased revenues and for creating store loyalty).
2. *At what point does a determining service become a qualifying service*? This is an extremely important issue, because the

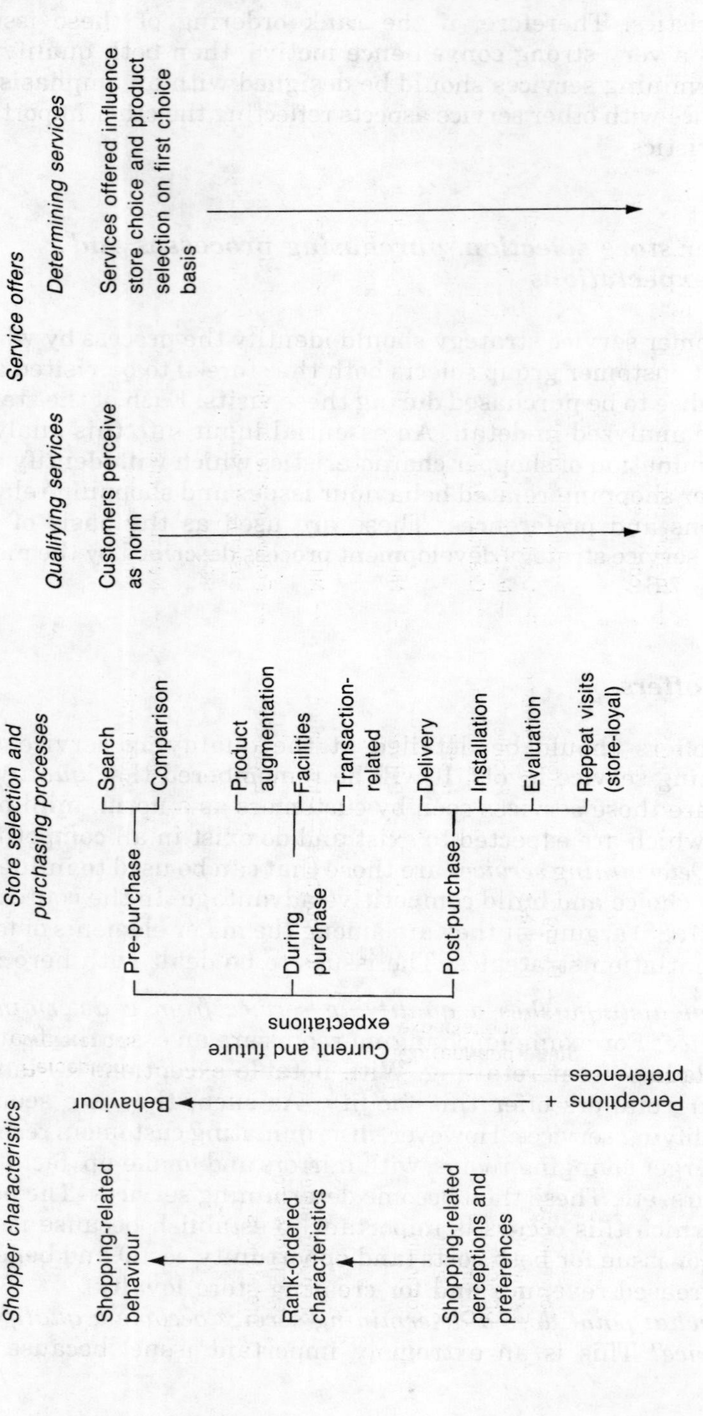

Figure 7.6a *Developing customer service strategy: a basic model*

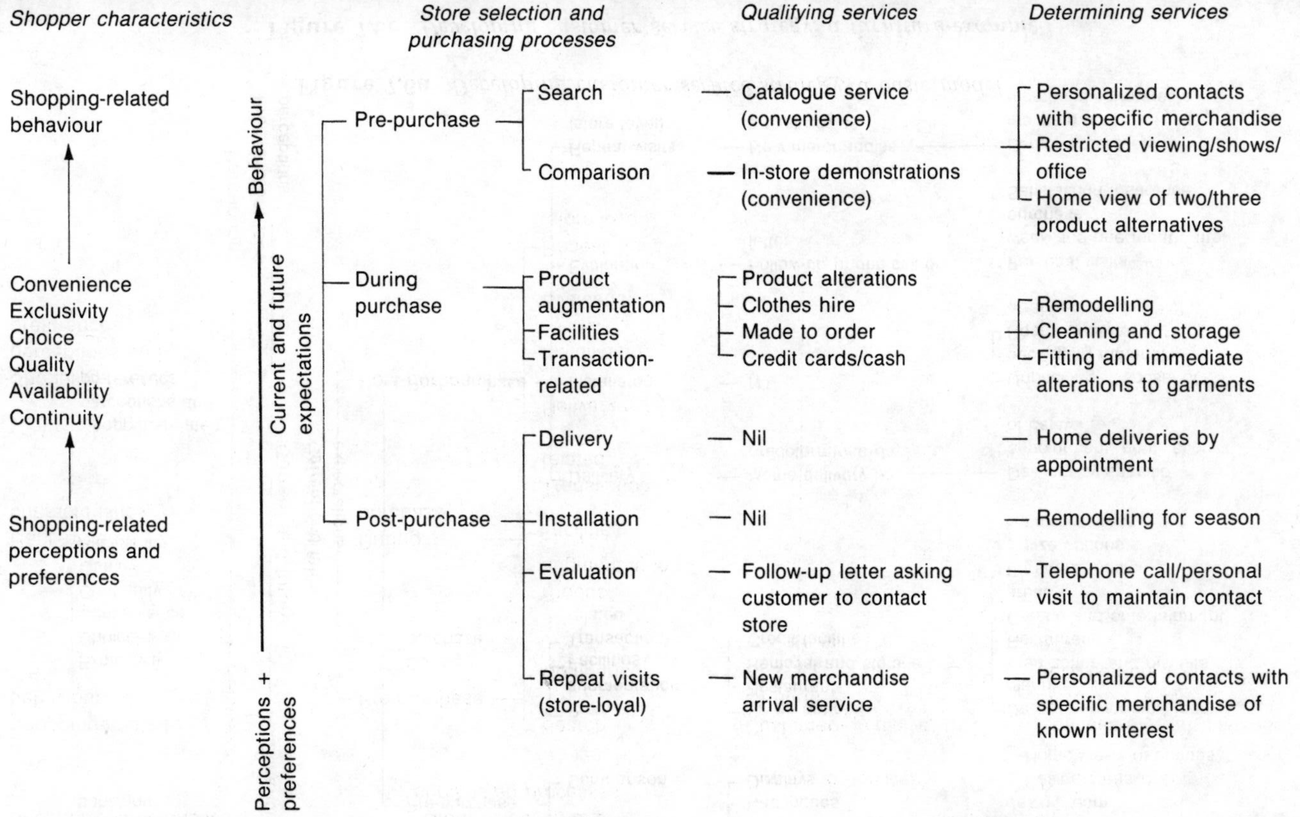

Figure 7.6b *Developing customer service strategy: a ladies' wear example*

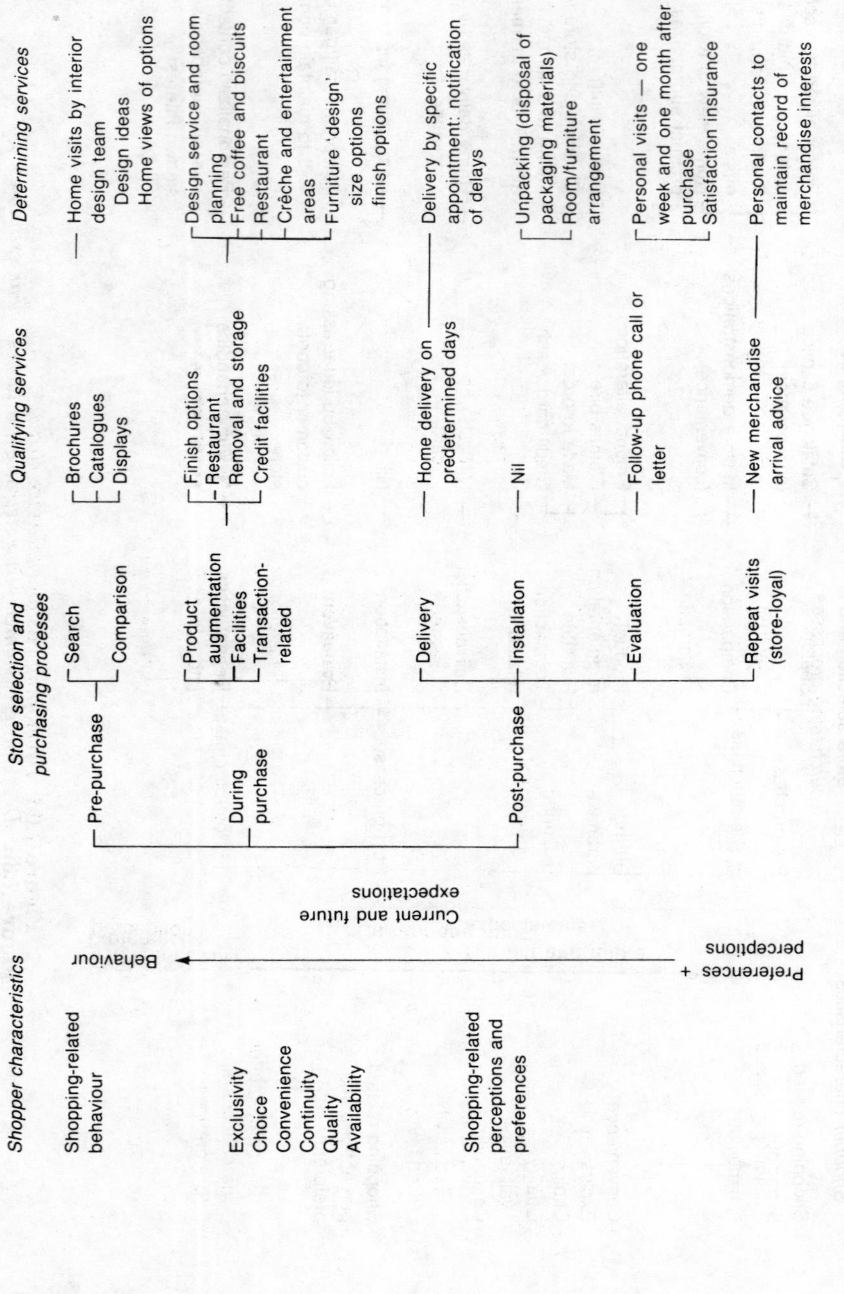

Figure 7.6c *Developing customer service strategy: a furniture example*

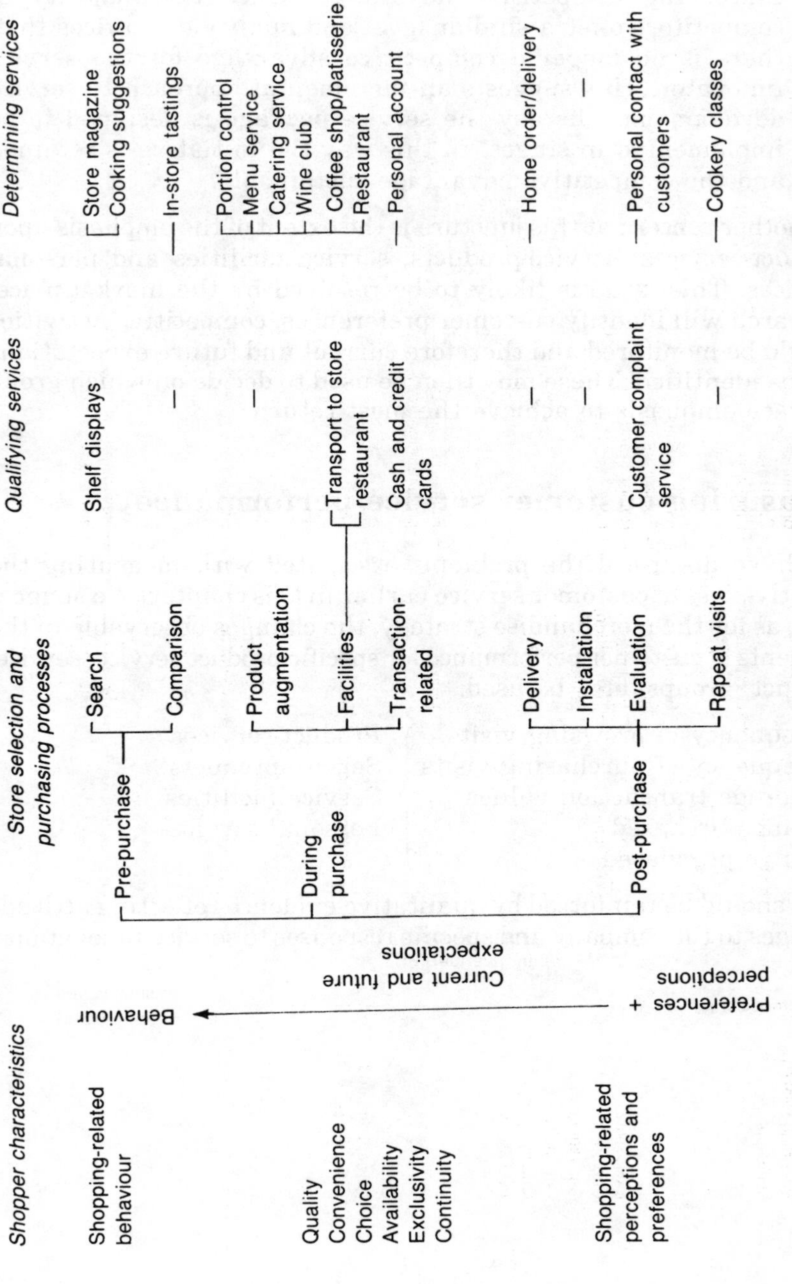

Figure 7.6d *Developing customer service strategy: a food example*

answer to this question identifies an equally important issue concerning competitive advantage. Once the majority of competitors offer a similar level and quality of services then there is no longer a competitive advantage for the service innovator. This suggests an incremental approach to service development whereby the service package is designed to be implemented in stages. In this way the initiative is retained and the competitive advantage sustainable.

Another concern at this juncture is the extent of the emphasis upon product-services, service-products, service facilities and personal services. This issue is likely to be resolved by the market-place. Research will identify customer preferences, competitive activities should be monitored and therefore current and future expectations can be identified. These may then be used to decide on which group to place emphasis to achieve the most return.

Measuring customer service performance

We have discussed the problems associated with measuring the effectiveness of customer service earlier in this chapter. We suggest that, as for the merchandise strategy, the changes observable in the elements of customer performance for specific product-service, service-product, groups, etc., be used:

Frequency of browsing visits	Product-services
Frequency of purchasing visits	Service-products
Average transaction values	Service facilities
Items purchased	Personal services
Range purchased	

This should be reinforced by qualitative evidence reflecting attitude changes to the company and specific responses to service innovations.

CHAPTER 8

Implementing customer service strategy

Introduction

In Chapter 7 we discussed the issues concerning management when deciding on a customer service strategy. In this chapter we move on to the tasks involved in implementing customer service strategy. The process is described by Figure 8.1.

As with merchandise strategy there is an overlap in the activities. The point at which strategy ends and its implementation commences will differ from company to company. In Figure 8.1 the overlap area includes the customer research, customer profiling, positioning decisions and developing functional strategies. Specific customer service strategy decisions taken to this point would have been to identify the competitive advantage to be developed by specifying the levels of the customer service offer (qualifying or determining) across a range of product-services, service-products, personal services and service facilities. The strategy statement will be based on broad intent. It is the role of operating managers to add detail and develop the strategy into operational activity.

There are six components in the process:

1. The customer service strategy.
2. Factors influencing the customer service plan.
3. Developing the customer service plan.
4. The customer service plan and budgets.
5. Review and consideration of implications for company critical success factors.
6. Monitoring and control issues.

The customer service strategy

The customer service strategy will have identified the activities seen by the board as essential to the development of sustainable

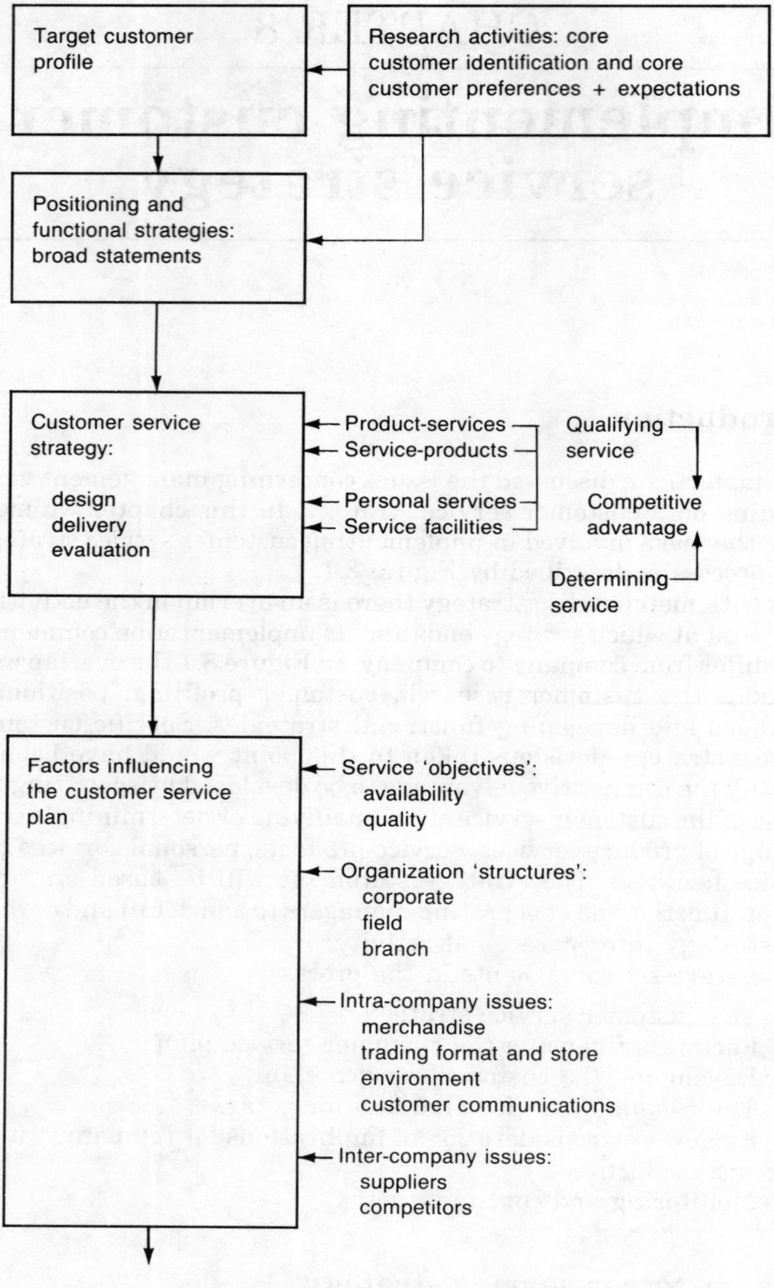

Figure 8.1 *Implementing customer service strategy*

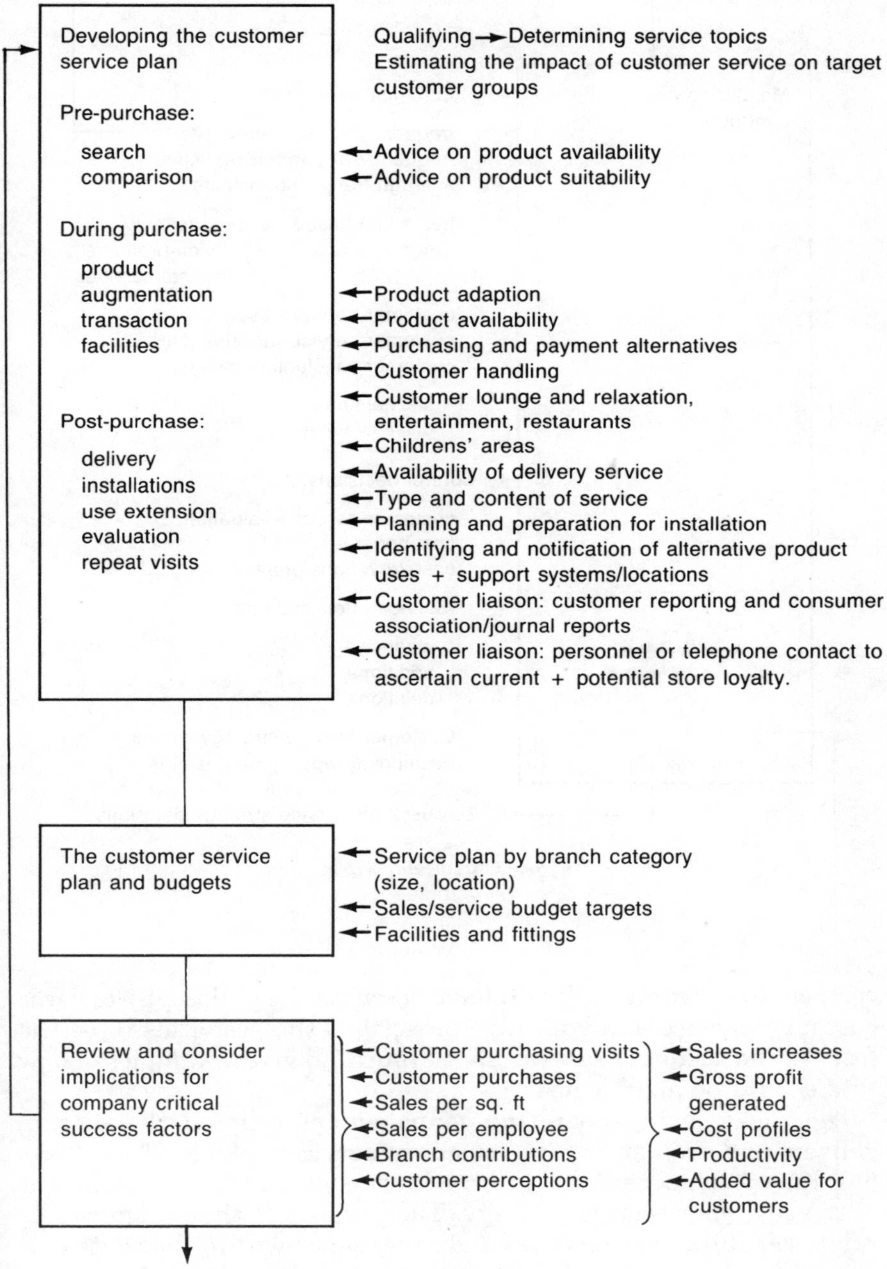

Figure 8.1 *continued overleaf*

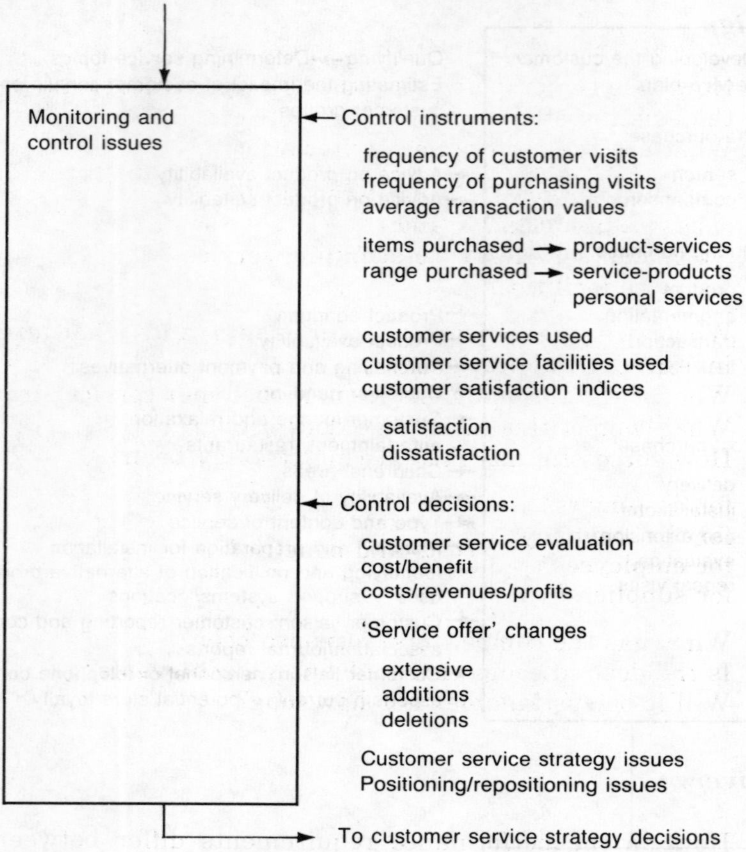

Figure 8.1 *continued*

competitive advantage. It will have described its philosophy towards customer service and will have prescribed the activities to be the focus of the customer service offer. Figure 7.6 gives examples of how this should be approached.

The tasks facing operating management concern the design, delivery and evaluation of the customer service package. These tasks will have been considered in broad terms during the development of the customer service strategy. The purpose at that stage was to relate capabilities, capacities and congruence within the context of corporate and functional strategies. At this stage the task becomes detailed and operating management should consider the following issues.

Design

- How does the proposed customer service strategy differ from the existing offer?
- What are the performance criteria for:

  product-services? service-products? personal services? service facilities? } qualifying services? and determining services?

- What are the resource requirements and what are the investment implications?
- What is the rationale for the new customer service strategy?
- What competitive advantage does it offer?
- How successful has the existing strategy been:

  for customers? for the company? for employees? for suppliers? } costs and benefits?

- What has the competitors' response been?
- Is the desired competitive advantage achievable?
- Will it be sustainable? For how long?

Delivery

- How do the performance requirements differ between the existing service strategy and the new strategy?
- What existing structures and systems are there?
- What are their performance limitations in terms of:
  - — level of outputs?
  - — range of outputs?
  - — quality of outputs?
  - — reliability?
  - — time taken to meet performance criteria?
- What *additional* structures and systems are necessary to provide the range of services and the quality of services under consideration?

Evaluation

- What measures are to be used to evaluate the customer service portfolio?

availability quality reliability	qualifying services determining services	competitive advantage

- How can we evaluate the structures and systems?
- To whom should performance evaluation be reported? Over what time-period?
- How is the evaluation to be used to modify structures and systems.

The purpose of this series of questions is to obtain a greater understanding of the performance requirements of the proposed customer service strategy and the implications of these for resource allocation and costs. Clearly, the approach taken in the model developed in Figure 7.6 requires detailed analysis before it can be considered for implementation. The analysis comprises the design, delivery and evaluation 'audit' described above. With these issues answered it is possible to move towards the planning process.

Factors influencing the customer service plan

Service objectives

In Chapter 7 we referred to six basic objectives for customer service. These were:

1. To generate additional traffic.
2. To increase customer repeat business traffic.
3. To expand the market for merchandise.
4. To increase the form utility of merchandise.
5. To add value to the overall offer.
6. To provide comfort and convenience for customers.

Cost constraints apply. It is unlikely that maximum levels of service should be applied across the offer arbitrarily, and equally unlikely that such a decision could be afforded. Therefore, before deciding on the 'breadth and depth' or the extent of the customer service offer two factors should be considered: availability and quality.

Availability

Availability has two connotations. The first relates to stock levels and this has been discussed in Chapters 6 and 7. While we do not wish to repeat this discussion here, the point should be made that merchandise availability is seen as an important element of customer service by retailers and customers. However, our interest here is more concerned with the level of availability of customer service to be offered. There are broadly two ways in which service availability may be considered in this context: the level of service to be added to the merchandise in the form of product-service or the addition of service-products, and the level of service to be offered to the customer in the form of personal services and service facilities.

The level of service availability is influenced by the need to create competitive advantage, and therefore the decision as to what level of service constitutes a *qualifying service* and the incremental increase required to develop it into a *determining service.*

Consider first the level of service to be added to merchandise. Factors that influence this decision are:

1. *Life-cycle positioning of product-services and service-products*: A recently introduced product or service may have sufficient attraction initially without diluting the margins by adding service. However, as the product (service-product) matures, service may be used to differentiate it.
2. *Cost/benefit effect*: The addition of service to the product (product-service) may have a strong impact on customer perceptions and subsequent behaviour. Consequently, the addition of service may have an advantageous effect for both revenues and profitability.
3. *Customer expectations*: Customer expectations of service availability set bench-marks for the service offer. Often these expectations set a very clear demarcation between qualifying and determining levels of service.
4. *Competitive activities*: There is a very clear link between competitive activities and customer expectations, such that competitors' service offers are used (together with that of the company) to create a *base level* of service expectations which becomes the *qualifying service* offer. To create competitive advantage, the service offer must extend beyond this base level.
5. *Core merchandise groups' profitability*: As was discussed in Chapters 5 and 6, the core merchandise groups are likely to contribute considerably more in terms of contribution than the remainder of the assortment (see Figure 6.3). If the margins generated by this range of the assortment are well managed they may permit a greater expenditure on aspects of customer service. Often this opportunity can be overlooked if management's focus is too concentrated on gross and net contribution from merchandise.

The level of service availability to customers is also influenced by the extent and the nature of the competitive advantage required. Again, there are factors influencing this decision. The decision is influenced by *customer expectations*, competitive activities and *core merchandise groups' profitability*. However, additional factors to be considered include:

1. *Target customer group profitability*: The nature of customer spending influences the extent and level of customer services. Frequent, high-spending customers are likely to respond to extensive service; furthermore, the level of their purchases (and frequency) is likely to support the cost of providing customer service.
2. *The frequency of customer sales visits*: Many products are purchased infrequently, are often of high value and require maintenance services. While the obvious product groups in this category are consumer durable items, there are others. For example, jewellery, furs, holidays, gourmet food and wine are all high-value, infrequently purchased items. There are a number of opportunities to provide service to these products. For example, jewellery appreciates and a potential service is an annual valuation for insurance purposes; furs require cleaning and summer storage; holidays can be both successful and unsuccessful, follow-up to identify customer satisfaction and to offer assistance to obtain redress (where necessary) and to suggest alternatives for the next vacation are aspects of service to be considered. Advice on the purchasing and preparation of gourmet food is usually appreciated, so too is advice on accompanying wines.
3. *Customer life-styles*: Many customers have larger disposable incomes and extensive *personal expenditure budgets*, but have minimal *time-budgets* due to pressure of work and domestic commitments. Research has found that these customers respond to the convenience aspects of service, for example, wardrobe services, gift suggestion services, theatre and travel ticketing. Recent developments in information technology now offer cost effective means by which data-bases suitable to track this customer information can be installed.

Each of these factors has an impact on customer response and on costs. Clearly, the level of availability of customer services is the product of these factors. The approach prescribed in Figure 7.2 is useful in deciding levels of service availability across the assortment and by customer group. In Figure 8.2 we use the principles described in Figure 7.2 to provide an example of service availability decision options. We have used a furniture retailing example.

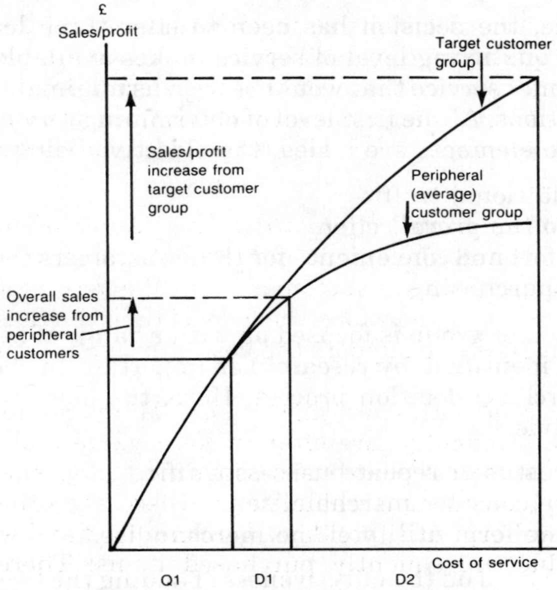

Q1 Qualifying Services

Brochures, catalogues, displays
Finish options
Credit facilities
Delivery — no choice
Follow-up contact: phone/letter
Information on new merchandise
Restaurant
Removal and storage services

D1 Determining Services 1

Design service and room planning (in-store)
Design studio; coffee, biscuits, newspapers, etc.
Crêche and entertainment areas

D2 Determining Services 2

Home visits by design team
Design service and room planning
Furniture 'design'; size and finish options
Customer specified deliveries
Merchandise unpacked and furniture arranged according to design/plan
Sales/design team visits for follow-up
'Satisfaction' insurance
Sales visits for liaison and to advise on new products
Free coffee and biscuits in design studio
Restaurant
Crêche and entertainment areas

Figure 8.2 *Customer service availability decisions: a furniture retailing example*

In this example, the decision has been to offer three levels of availability. The qualifying level of service makes available those elements of customer service that would be seen as minimal to meet customer expectations. At the first level of determining service a few additional service elements are added, the objective being to:

- Generate additional traffic.
- Add value to the overall offer.
- Provide comfort and convenience for those customers seriously considering purchasing.

The target customer group is focused on with a range of services, which have been identified (by research) as important in the store selection and purchase decision process. Here, the objectives are expanded to include:

- Increasing customer repeat business traffic.
- Expanding market for merchandise.
- Increasing the form utility of the merchandise.

The decisions are based on the effectiveness of adding the two levels of determining service in expanding sales and profitability, particularly from the target customer group. Their response in the hypothetical example shown in Figure 8.2 suggests that the service availability differentiation decisions have been profitable.

Quality

Quality is a difficult concept to define. The reason for this is possibly because it has universal usage. It is applied to both tangible and intangible products. Often it is applied to aspects of the company's offer rather than for all of it. Rank Xerox found that cost reductions and productivity increases were not the answer to competitive pressures (Hornby 1989). Their problem was not a manufacturing one but rather a service problem: it was found that while the product quality was excellent, the lack of understanding by sales people of customer requirements, or indifferent after-sales service, or poor response to telephone enquiries were major issues. From a project-based exercise a 'leadership-through-quality' process was developed. The interesting point about all this is the definition of quality:

> Quality was defined simply as conforming to customer requirements, giving the customer no less and no more than is required. Customer was defined as anyone for whom one provides a service and so includes people inside or outside the organisation. (*ibid.*)

There were many other aspects to Rank Xerox's change of corporate philosophy. However, the significant factors are the focus on the

Quantitative measures	*In-store*	*Depot*
Availability of products	X	X
Availability of product-services	X	
Waiting time at check-outs/counters	X	
Telephone response time	X	
Information accuracy		
Product performance	X	
Product availability	X	X
Product locations		

Qualitative measures	*In-store*	*Depot*
Customer complaints	X	
Customer compliments	X	
Supplier complaints	X	X
Supplier compliments	X	X
Internal conflict	X	X
Internal co-operation	X	X

Figure 8.3 *Customer satisfaction indices*

customer and customer requirements, and the quality of product and service required to ensure customer satisfaction. It is interesting to note that among measures of corporate performance, customer satisfaction indices are seen as important.

Quality of customer services for retailing is concerned with *maintaining* the levels of service decided upon. This requires motivation and incentives. A number of retailing companies have introduced customer service programmes, but few are completely satisfied with the results. There is a requirement for constant monitoring of standards and often the standards are difficult to set and almost impossible to monitor.

The levels of product knowledge, availability and locations are more easily monitored than are staff attitudes towards difficult customers. However, it is often by the latter that customer service is judged by the consumer.

A number of measures can be introduced as customer satisfaction indices; these are featured in Figure 8.3.

These measures provide management with two useful tools. One helps manage the business; regular monitoring of performance ensures that essential aspects of customer requirements are continually met. Measurements can be made on a regular basis across a sample of customers. For retailing companies with a clearly identified customer profile it may be more useful to focus on a sample comprising the target customer profile because this may prove to be much more cost-effective. The other benefit that the indices offer is a means by which incentives for the staff may be developed. Many of the customer service programmes introduced recently have offered employees a means by which their salaries can be enhanced. The indices suggested enable staff knowledge and efficiency to be monitored and abilities to be linked to performance payments.

The indices also offer a means of monitoring intra-company service achievements. In many ways this is just as important as measuring the performance of the company against the customer performance criteria because it is necessary for operations within the company to work together effectively to produce the overall offer to the customer. For this reason many retailers promote the idea that each activity within the company provides a service for another, and is, in that respect, a 'customer'. Often this is made clear in corporate policy statements. Frequent monitoring of performance ensures a measure of quality control. Service just as much as product quality requires constant auditing to ensure that consistent standards of customer service are offered to the customer and are maintained at the determined levels.

Figure 8.3 suggests the performance criteria that most management organizations would devise. However, it has been found that many aspects of service (and, therefore, performance measures) are derived by customers themselves. Consumer or customer panels which meet on a regular basis (every two or four weeks) can be responsible for introducing ideas that management may not have considered. In an interesting article on an Irish retailer, Feargal Quinn, a number of worthwhile service ideas are discussed (St Pierre 1989). For example, Quinn uses fortnightly consumer panels to solicit service ideas. He also talks to customers and makes a note of their comments and suggestions. These meetings resulted in confectionery being taken away from check-outs to remove the temptation for children and the irritation for their parents. Children shopping for parents often found themselves at a disadvantage to adults, who would push in front of them. They now have special 'I am shopping for my mum', lollipop-shaped poles, which attract the attention of sales staff and make sure the children are properly cared for.

Organization structure

There are many ways in which customer service activities can be organized. These vary from formal functions in which clear objectives and strategies are delineated, to far less formal arrangements where often the chief executive assumes a policy-making/implementation role.

Often the structure to evolve is that which suits the company's culture and style. In the example of Quinn Supermarkets, the chief executive, Feargal Quinn, started the business in 1960. From the one unit of 5,000 sq. ft, the business has expanded to 300,000 sq. ft in 12 units and the employees have increased from 6 to over 2,000 people. Having been very close to the business and being largely responsible for its development, it is not surprising that Quinn spends a considerable amount of time on the shopfloor. His involvement in customer service is a very direct one.

Size does not necessarily imply a hierarchical structure for the management of customer service. There are many examples of close control of customer service in quite large companies. For example, the managing director of an Australian department store group did at one time follow up customer complaints with customers and within the company. In this way he reassured customers that their problems were being taken care of.

However, for those companies that do build on organization structure to manage customer service the format most often followed suggests that at the *corporate level* management involvement is directed towards consideration of the role of service within the positioning strategy and how best it might be used to develop sustainable competitive advantage. This would involve a view of customer service 'objectives' and the strategy options. They are also likely to address the issues of qualifying and determining services across both the product/services offer and/or customer service segments. At this level the parameters for budget expenditures and performance expectations will be made in broad terms. See Figure 8.4.

Functional management have the responsibility of developing and communicating the customer service strategy. Theirs is the task of detailing design, delivery and evaluation. In so doing, they will be cognisant of achieving customer service objectives within the budget constraints set within the strategy guidelines. The result will be the customer service plan.

Field management are responsible for operational implementation of the customer service plan. Their task is to determine the required resources, such that performance levels are achieved at budgeted costs. *Branch management* manage the allocated resources to achieve the customer service performance. It is at store level where customer service satisfaction indices are measured.

Intra-company issues

It must be remembered that functional strategies have been established (or are being established) for merchandise, trading format and store environment and customer communications. It is usual

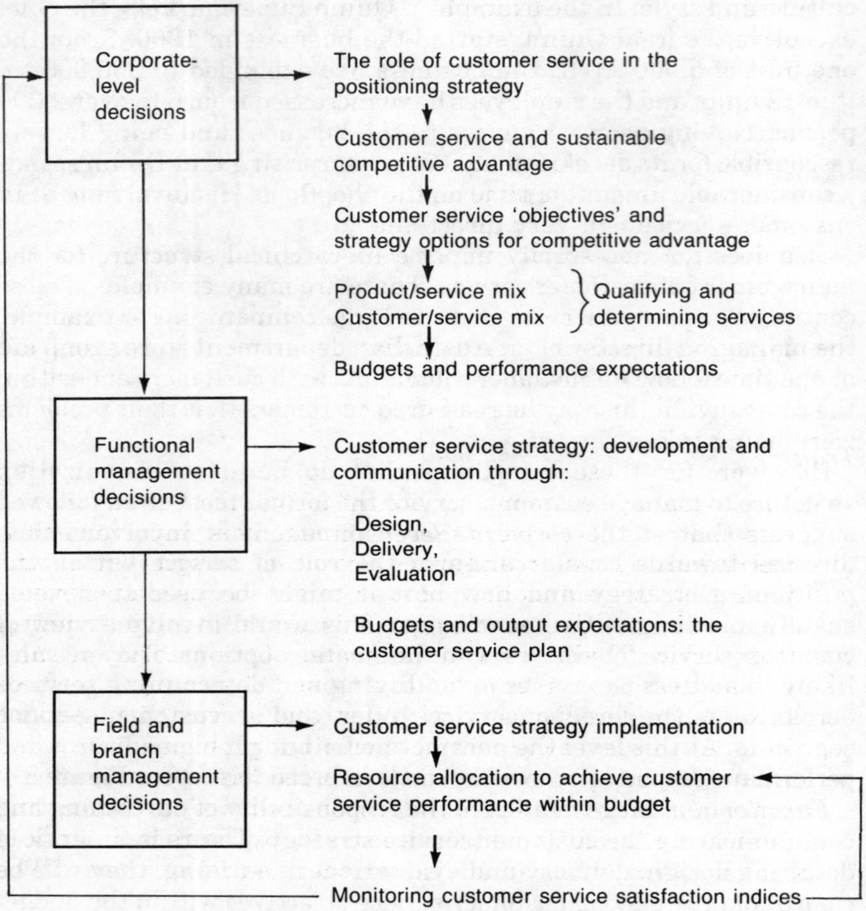

Figure 8.4 *Organizational decisions and responsibilities for customer service*

for major decisions made in one area to be communicated to each of the others. Some of the issues affecting customer service that are made in each of the other functional areas include:

Merchandise

- *Complexity* of the product range and of some products raises issues for staff 'technical' ability to advise on installation and use. This aspect covers a wide range of products from food to consumer durables. Not only staff abilities are concerned but so too is staff quantity.

- *Flexibility* of product availability or the ability to modify/alter standard products for use in non-standard situations or by non-standard sizes.
- *Availability*: despite planned levels of availability, there are often occasions when specific items are not in stock. Fall-back systems, or simply referring to other branches, can rectify lapses in service. Availability also concerns new ranges of merchandise where prior notice of new merchandise can be used as a service to potentially interested customers and information which, if in the salesperson's hands, may prevent the customer from purchasing from a competitor.

Trading format/store environment

- *Visual merchandising*: in many ways this is a shared responsibility. However, shared or not, it is important that merchandise location and space allocation, design themes and promotions are communicated to customer service management. This will ensure that adequate product knowledge training (together with where various elements of the assortment may be found) can be given to salespersons. Any changes to store layout should be discussed with customer service management in order to identify potential operations problems.
- *Facilities* (changing-rooms, rest areas, crêches) are increasingly important in the retail offer. Additions or changes to the existing facilities offered should be approved by customer services management, who can advise on location and customer flows to obtain maximum effectiveness.

Customer communications

Delivery (expectations and realization): probably the most important consideration in retailing is actually delivering the 'offer'. This comment obtains for all aspects of the offer, not simply service. However, care must be taken to ensure that the service promise made is that which is delivered.

Inter-company issues

There are two inter-company considerations that affect service decisions. These are the support facilities that can be obtained from suppliers and the competitive reaction of major competitors to customer service initiatives.

Suppliers

There are a number of areas of support that may be available. Among them are:

- *Financial support*: suppliers are always interested in ways and means by which their sales and profits can be expanded. Often promotional assistance can be obtained, but invariably the end-result is an increase in sales of *all* retailers stocking the specific merchandise. A more effective form of co-operation is to seek support for less obvious (to competitors) initiatives such as customer service. Appliance and furniture retailers have begun to develop delivery services to customers, which operate on a basis of effecting deliveries when it is convenient to the customer rather than when it is convenient to the haulier or distribution company. These are supported by suppliers' funding.
- *Customer advice centres*: these may take the form of supplier personnel located in-store (or available for home visits) to give specialist advice on applications, colour schemes, etc. Increasingly, IT is applied to the problem and can be in the form of simple video displays or complex customer integrated applications, which print out advice and answers to specific questions.

Competitors

The objective of any innovation within the retail offer is to create competitive advantage. This raises the issue concerning the type and level of a customer service offer. It will be remembered that *qualifying* services are those expected by customers and are likely to be available from all retailers. However, *determining* services are those that are likely to influence customers to make the store a 'first choice' when seeking to purchase a particular item. Issues that should be considered include:

- *Innovate or imitate*: many retailing companies prefer to be first. This attitude includes service innovations as well as merchandise. However, unlike merchandise, no exclusivity can be guaranteed and any successful service innovation may be imitated. Clearly, the more covert the service, the longer it will offer an advantage and furthermore the more reliable and effective it might be the more difficult it becomes to imitate with effectiveness.

- *The service sensitivity of customers*: for many customer groups the response to service is much greater than it is for others. Hence it follows that the service decision should be to favour *determining* levels of service rather than *qualifying* levels. In this way, there is a much more likely response from customers to service than to other aspects of the retail offer.

Developing the customer service plan

In Figure 8.1 we suggest that the customer service plan should be designed around the store selection and purchasing process. The previous chapter discussed a model (see Figure 7.6) that uses shopping perceptions and preferences, and considers how these are modified and influenced by shopping experiences to become assimilated into shopping behaviour and used in the store selection and purchasing process.

In Figures 8.5a, b and c examples of customer service plans for ladies' wear, furniture and food retailing are given. It will be seen that the service offer is based on the two levels of service discussed earlier (qualifying and determining levels). However, more importantly, the determining level of the offer is based on the *shopper characteristics*. These should be established by customer research and the data generated by the segmentation research are a primary input.

The topics identified in Figure 8.1 suggest a wide range of options, again referring to Figure 7.6 (page 176) where we suggest that the customer service offer is designed by establishing the relative importance of the options. The implications of this are that there should be a clear differentiation between qualifying and determining services such that they are closely directed towards the target customer group. If the customer service offer forms part of an integrated total retail offer, the 'trade-off issues' between price and exclusivity and price and service, etc., are planned and, accordingly, the problems of targeting a customer service offer are less.

If we refer back to Figure 7.2, it suggests that an incremental increase in the costs of customer service (i.e. to add determining services) can be very profitable, provided that the targeting of the additional service is done discriminately. A hypothetical situation is illustrated by Figure 8.6. The example suggests that by increasing the customer service budget by a factor of 4 and directing the

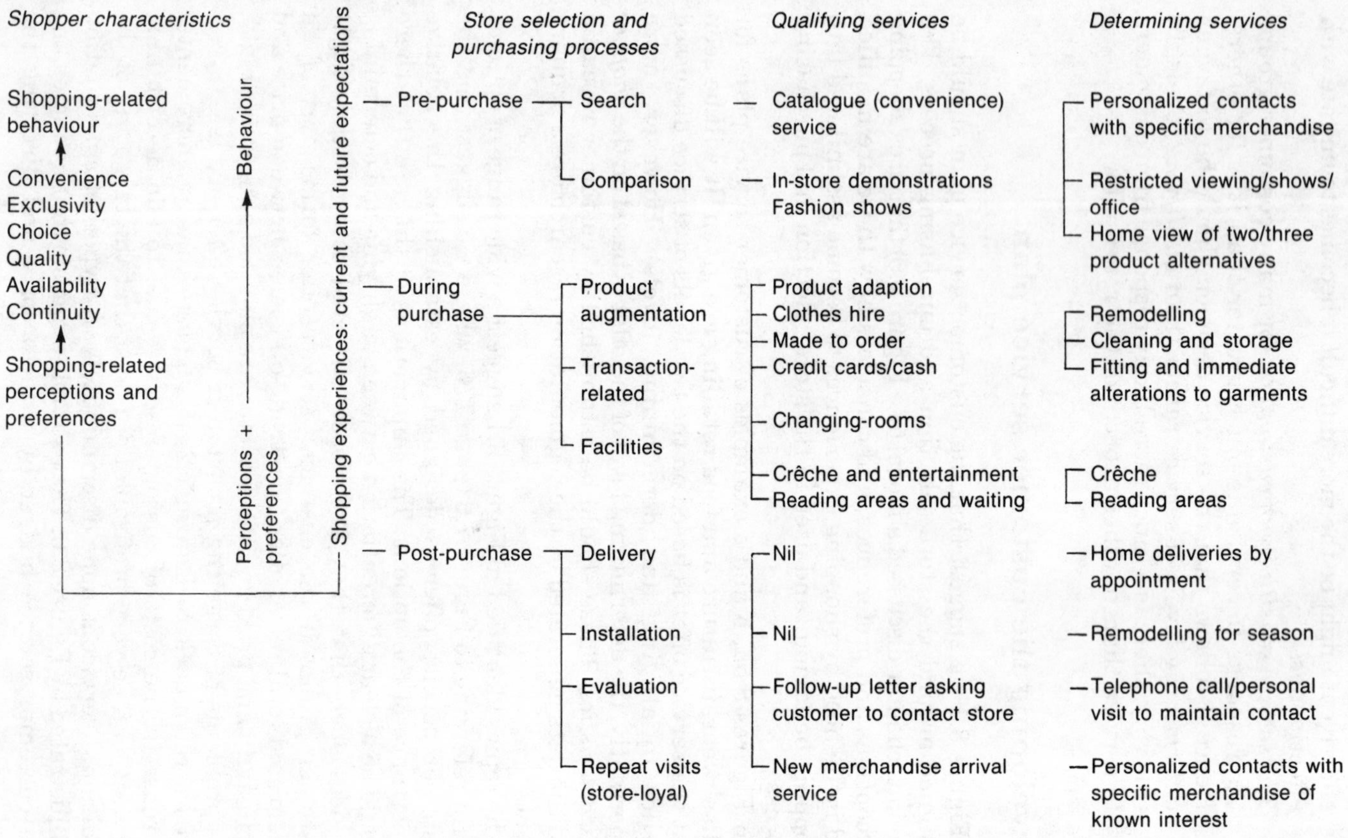

Figure 8.5a *Developing customer service strategy: a ladies' wear example*

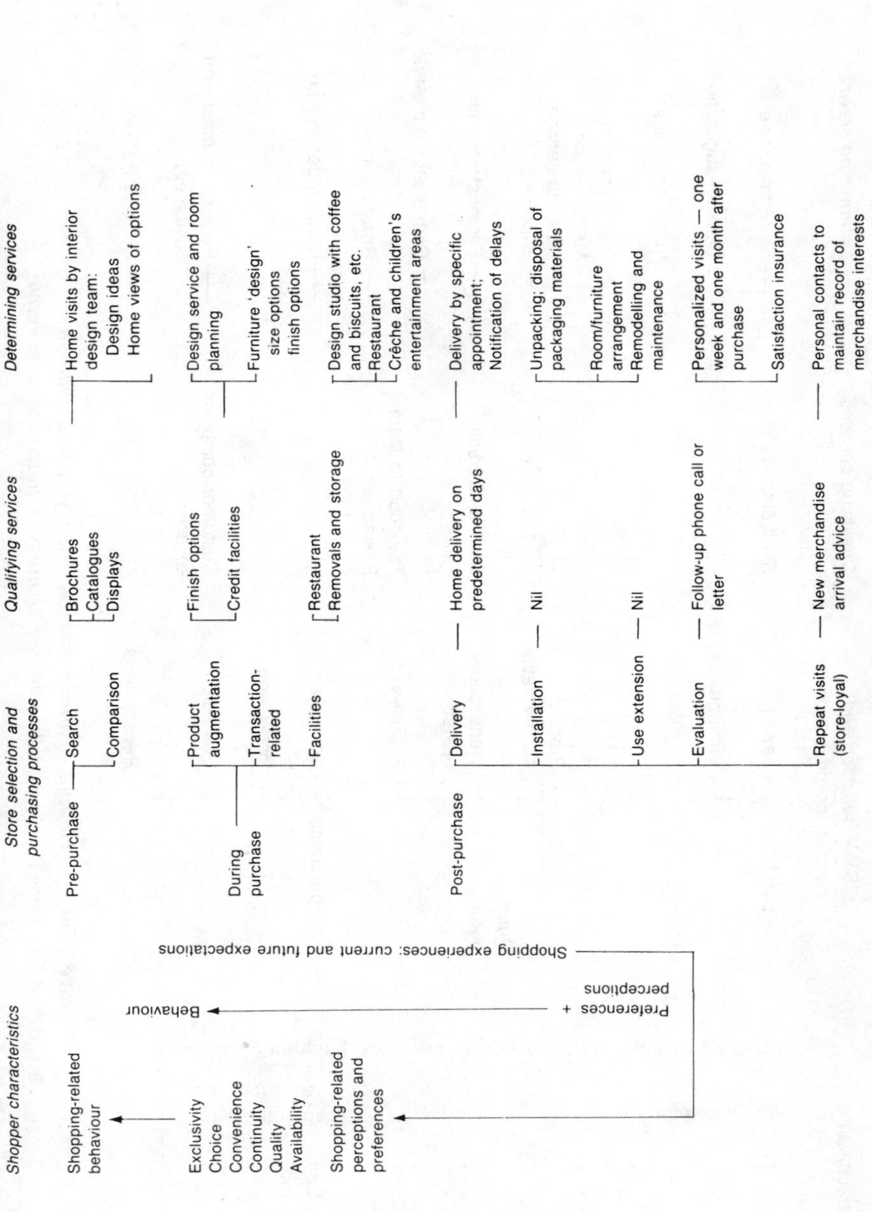

Figure 8.5b *Developing customer service strategy: a furniture example*

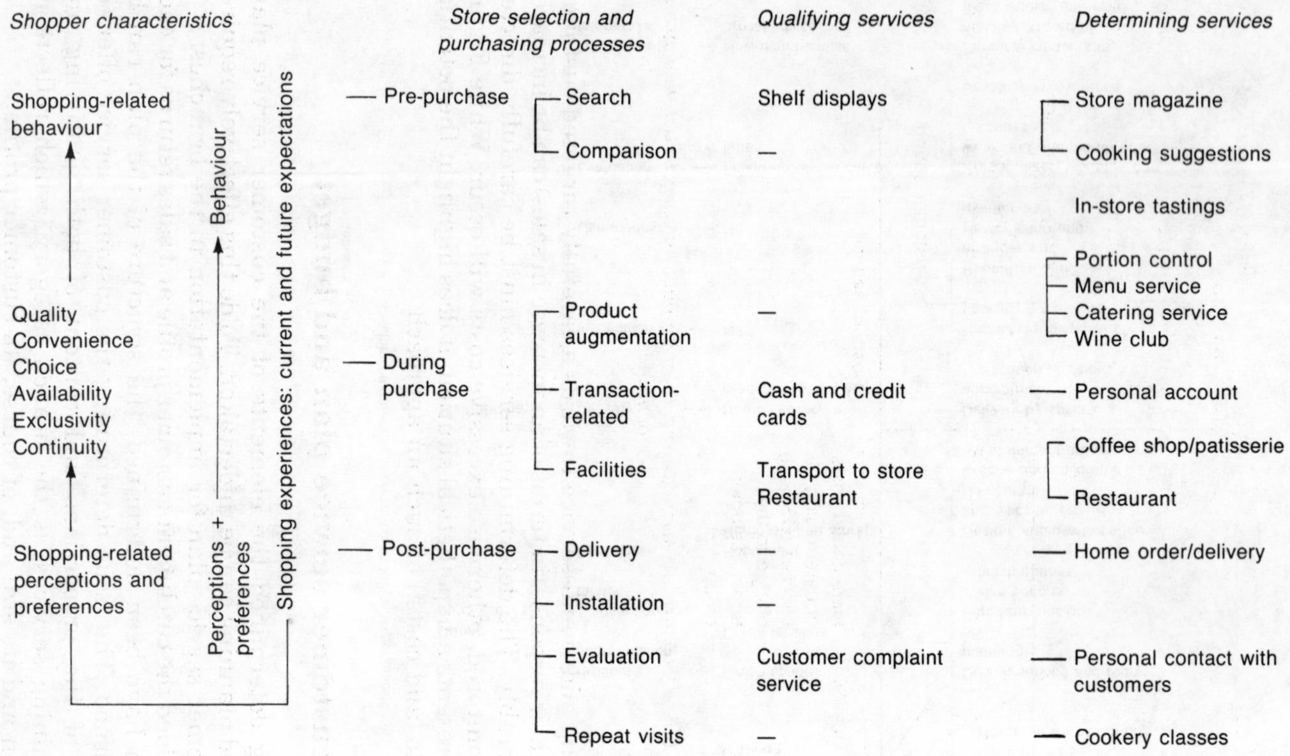

Figure 8.5c *Developing customer service strategy: a food example*

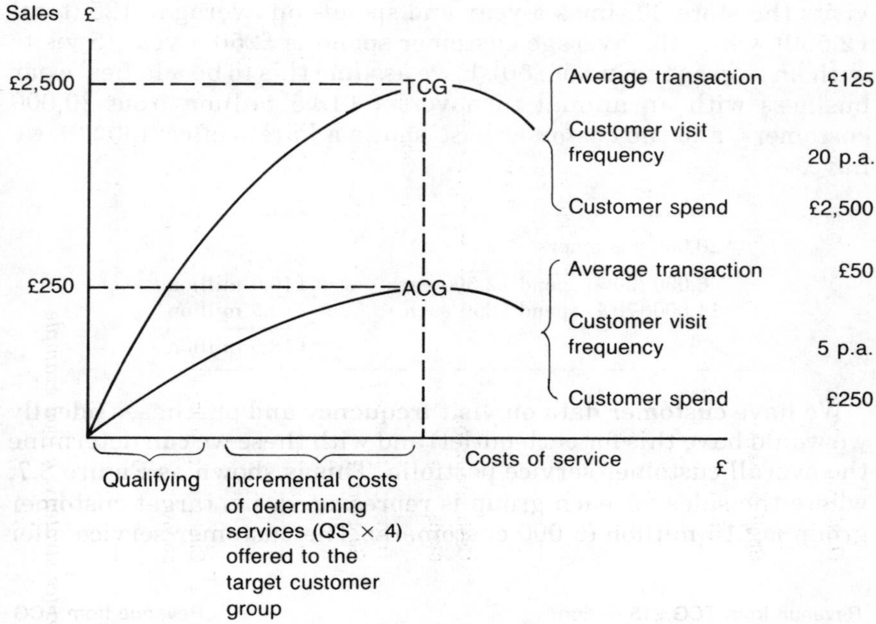

Figure 8.6 *Determining services and their impact on target customer group performance*

resulting additional service towards a carefully targeted customer group their response (in terms of an increase in sales) can be increased considerably. The determining services must be carefully directed and monitored, otherwise excessive costs will occur. While Figure 8.6 represents a hypothetical sitution, it does highlight the potential benefits (and costs!) of such an approach.

The customer service plan and budget

Having determined the elements of the customer service plan, detailed planning can be undertaken. To do this effectively requires a customer service plan for implementation in the branches.

Provided the catchment customer profile and sales returns for each branch have been determined, the structure of the plan can be established. The issue determining the customer service offer (in terms of the proportions and content of both qualifying and determining services) is the branch category, which reflects its location and its size and, of course, its customer profile.

If we return to Figure 8.6, we see that the target customer group visits the store 20 times a year and spends on average £125 (total £2,500), while the average customer spend is £250 a year (5 visits with an average spend of £50). If we assume this to be a ladies' wear business with an annual turnover of £18.5 million from 20,000 customers, and the customer base shows a Pareto effect (80/20), we have:

20,000 customers:		
6,000 (30%) spend £2,500 each	=	£15.0 million
14,000 (70%) spend £250 each	=	£3.5 million
		£18.5 million

We have customer data on visit frequency and purchases (ideally we would have this for each outlet) and with these we can determine the overall customer service portfolio. This is shown as Figure 8.7, where the sales for each group is represented, i.e. target customer group is £15 million (6,000 customers). The customer service offer

Revenue from TCG £15 million (6,000 customers)

Revenue from ACG £3.5 million (14,000 customers)

Customer service portfolio

Qualifying services

Catalogue service,
In-store fashion shows,
Product adaption (alterations),
Clothes hire,
Made to order; credit facilities,
New merchandise advice,
Changing rooms

Determining services

Personal contact for specific merchandise needs,
Personal viewing and fashion shows for TCG,
Home/office visits by sales consultants,
Garment remodelling, cleaning and storage,
Fitting and alterations in store,
Home deliveries,
Personal visits on regular call cycle,
Customer data-base,
Crêche, waiting rooms, coffee lounge and reading rooms

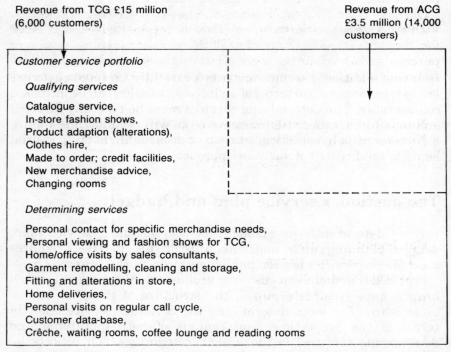

Figure 8.7 *Designing for customer service portfolio around customer spend and customer flow*

is based on making the specified qualifying services available to all customers, but focusing on the target customer group to offer the additional services (the determining services).

The plan for each branch can now be developed. It will be based on the number of customers in each category (target customer group and average customer group, as determined by spend and/or visit frequency) together with the branch managers' estimate of the number of potential customers, who may move into the target customer group. This can be estimated with reasonable accuracy by comparing the actual customer profile against the catchment profile, as described by a CACI or Pinpoint estimate.

Detailed costings are required before accurate budgets can be established. These should consider the possibility of the company providing some elements of the service package from a centrally-based source and thereby create economies of scale. Brochure and catalogue services and data-base design may possibly be developed and managed centrally but other elements included in the example in Figures 8.5a and 8.7 are more likely to be much more effective if managed locally. The responsibility for maintaining desired performance is both a field and branch task.

Once the costs are established these should be considered, together with branch sales forecasts and a customer service budget established for the branch. The more detail there is concerning customer purchasing behaviour the more accurate the service budget will be. In broad terms the information required (last period/forecast period) is:

Number of target group customers (TCG) Number of potential target group customers	Purchases + visits
Number of average customers (ACG)	Purchases + visits
Total (TCG + ACG)	Purchases + visits

Catchment potential:
  Target customer group
  Average customers

Branch penetration TCG%
  ACG%

Last year sales
Last year customer service budget
Service as percent sales

A capital budget may be required for facilities and fittings. The forecast of sales by customer type is helpful here. If the potential to attract the high-spending (TCG) customer type is high it may be necessary to allocate capital to improve these facilities.

Review and consider implications for company critical success factors

It is important to consider the impact on critical success factors of the proposed customer service plan. The way in which this can be measured is to consider the desired changes in quantitative terms and to review their impact on the critical success factors (see Figure 8.1). This can be extended for planning purposes and can be seen in Figure 8.8.

Figure 8.8 suggests the process by which the impact of increases in both qualifying and determining services will influence customer performance and, through these, impact upon critical success factors. As suggested by Figure 8.8, the values of the critical success factors have been established by the corporate marketing and financial objectives. The benefits of this approach are that it helps quantify the relationship between the service offer and customer response. It also offers an iterative facility whereby aspects of service may be increased, decreased or eliminated from the offer altogether.

Clearly, any adjustments considered necessary can be evaluated by returning to *developing the customer service plan* and reviewing first the *availability levels* and reviewing changes within the process of Figure 8.8 and, if those do not produce the desired results, consideration must be given to an alternative format with which to implement the customer service strategy.

Monitoring and control issues

As with the merchandise strategy, the purpose of planning any activity is to achieve a set of prescribed results of objectives. With this in mind, the plan should set its performance measurement requirements as it evolves. Again, we suggest the use of *control instruments*, which relate to decisions taken to manage the activity within the context of the business.

Control instruments

The primary methods of measuring customer service achievement have been discussed. The customer performance criteria established

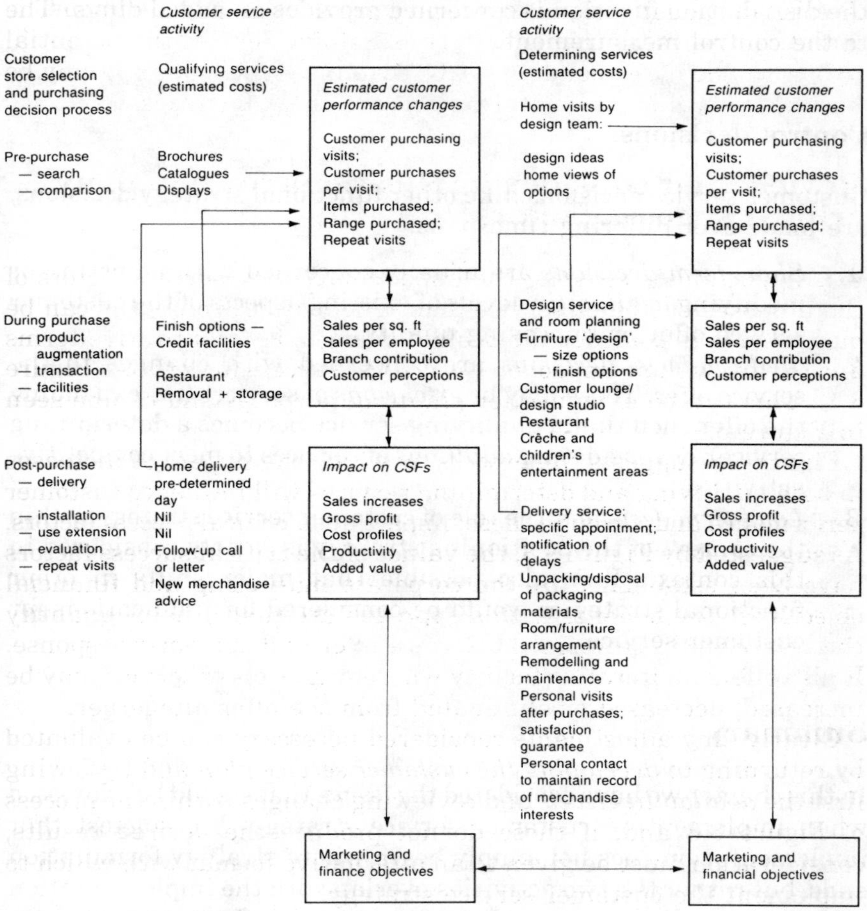

Figure 8.8 *Reviewing the impact of the customer service plan on critical success factors and corporate objectives (furniture retailing example)*

during this chapter are ideal measures, together with the usage rates of customer services and service facilities.

Detailed information on the volume and range of purchases of product-services, service-products and of personal services should be monitored closely and significant changes (particularly decreases) recorded. The reason for this is quite obvious: customer service and service support is an expensive aspect of retailing operations and should be operated cost-effectively.

The use of customer satisfaction indices (Figure 8.3) offers a means by which feedback can be obtained as a response to the service offer. The adoption of the view that the stores are 'customers' as far as the distribution function is concerned provides an added dimension to the control measurement.

Control decisions

Customer service decisions, like other functional strategy decisions, are made over differing timespans:

1. *Short-term decisions* are usually concerned with adjusting or modifying *availability* levels of existing aspects of the customer service offer or improving quality.
2. *Medium-term decisions* are concerned with changes to the service offer. These may be *extensions* of services (i.e. expanding the offer such that a qualifying service becomes a determining service); or considering *additions* of services to meet competitive activities.
3. *Long-term decisions*: the role of customer service strategy within the context of the positioning strategy is clearly considered in this context. It is also possible that major shifts in other functional strategies would be considered for implications for customer service.

Summary

In this chapter we have considered the issues that should be addressed when implementing customer service strategy. We suggest that implementation does not simply begin where strategy formulation ends, but rather the two activities overlap with the implementation activity formalizing many of the issues and influences that arise during the development of a customer service strategy.

The emphasis followed attempts to give customer service strategy and implementation a facilitating role whereby it supports the other functional strategies in the objective of moving the customer effortlessly through the store choice and purchase decision process.

Within the implementation process there must be a monitoring activity. Unless the effectiveness of customer service decisions and offers are measured, no sensible decisions can be made concerning resource deployment.

CHAPTER 9

Developing trading format and store environment strategy

Introduction

As with the previous chapters, we first discuss the strategy issues and process when considering trading format and store environment. The issues concerning implementation are discussed in the following chapter. We use the model developed in Figure P2.1 on which to base the discussion, and this in turn will be based on the issues of matching strategy with customer perceptions and expectations. We shall consider the implications of these for catchment analysis, but will not be dealing with property development issues.

Trading format and store environment decisions

Two areas should be considered when making format and environment decisions. These are developed in Figure 9.1 and comprise marketing considerations and financial considerations.

As with the earlier discussions, we have developed a framework to explore each of these topics, together with the areas in which marketing and financial considerations overlap.

Marketing considerations

As with the discussion on merchandise and customer service strategies, the store selection and purchasing decision process forms a central issue. The type of shopping visit and its frequency of occurrence, together with the transaction size, has an influence on store selection. For example, a weekly shopping visit for food will have quite different consumer criteria from a shopping expedition for furniture or for ladies' wear. Research shows that for many women

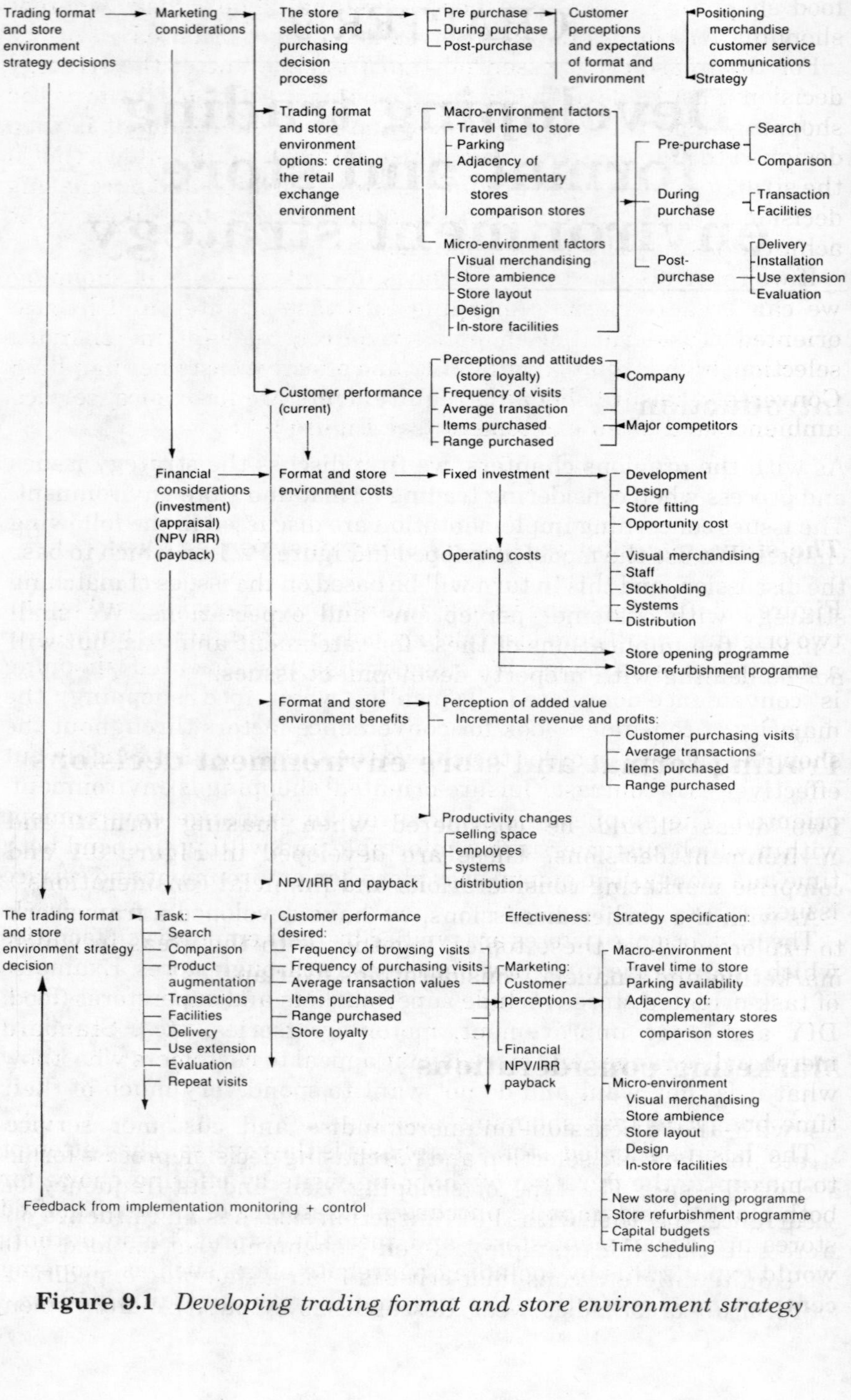

Figure 9.1 *Developing trading format and store environment strategy*

food shopping is seen as a necessary (and odious) task, whereas shopping for clothes for themselves is pleasure-oriented.

For this reason it is essential that from the outset the strategy decision must be developed around customer attitudes towards the shopping task; the trading format and store environment is then designed to help customers maximize satisfaction. It follows that if the strategy is developed around the store selection and purchasing decision process, customer satisfaction is much more likely to be achieved than if the process is ignored.

If we return to consumer attitudes towards the type of shopping, we can broadly classify shopping into task-oriented and leisure-oriented. Task-oriented shopping requires relevant merchandise selection, high levels of availability and effective customer handling. Conversely, leisure shopping requirements are for choice, service, ambience and often excitement (see Figure 9.1).

The store selection and purchasing decision process

Figure 9.2 illustrates the issues that require to be addressed by the two orientations. There is no clearly polarized situation, but rather a continuum of attitudes. We suggest that 'task-oriented' shopping is convenience-dominated. Typically, when food shopping, the majority of consumers look for convenience factors throughout the shopping activity in order to achieve the shopping visit quickly but effectively. By contrast, 'leisure-oriented' shopping is environment-oriented. The emphasis is on creating an exchange environment within which customers are comfortable and willing to spend both time and money. The emphasis is placed on environment and service issues.

The 'task-oriented' stores are typified by their emphasis on facilities which progress the rapid flow of customers through stores. Examples of task-oriented stores include supermarkets and superstores (food, DIY and home improvement, motor accessories, etc.). Standard merchandise ranges and store layout appeal to customers who know what it is they want and do not want to spend very much of their time budget in task shopping.

The 'leisure-oriented' stores' emphasis is the reverse. They attempt to maximize the duration of shopping visits by offering choice for both planned and impulse purchases. Examples of leisure-oriented stores are department stores and specialist stores. Some authors would expand this by including aggregate offers such as shopping centres and classify these by size and variety of retailing offers.

Store selection and purchasing decision process	*Shopping attitudes*	
	Task-oriented (convenience-dominated) ⟷	Pleasure-oriented (environment-dominated)
Pre-purchase		
Search	Convenient location	Exclusive store merchandise
	Ample parking	Wide choice
Comparison	Close to other 'task-oriented' stores	Prestigious image
	Relevant merchandise selection	
During purchase		
Product augmentation	High availability	Ambience and excitement
		Visual merchandising
Transactions	Competitive prices	In-store facilities
Facilities	Rapid cash handling	Product-services centres
		Credit facilities
Post-purchase		
Delivery		
Installation	Product displays }	Theme displays }
Use extension	Customer advice areas }	Customer advice areas }
Evaluation		
Repeat visits		

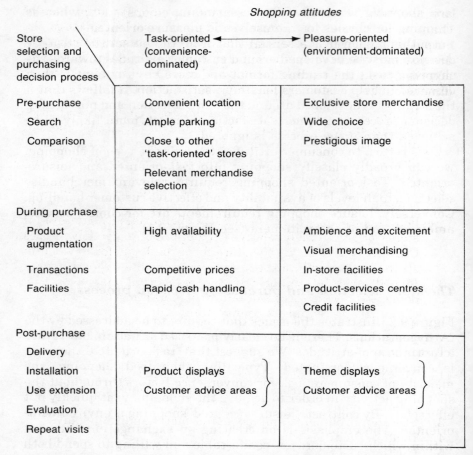

Figure 9.2 *Attitudes towards shopping influence trading format and store environment strategy decisions*

Customer perceptions and expectations of format and environment

Strategy decisions should be based on customer (and potential customer) research. There are a number of techniques available to determine these (see Chapter 4 for a discussion concerning customer research).

A frequently used method is perception mapping based on multi-dimensional scaling. One of the authors, together with Hooley, explains this technique and its use in mapping customer perceptions of store groups (Hooley and Cook 1984). While a number of methods are available, each of differing complexity, their fundamental characteristic is that, although input data are ordinal rankings, the output is a map showing relative positions of the stimuli. Input data are usually collected in the form of rankings of pairs of stimuli according to their similarity. As a research technique multidimensional scaling can offer a number of benefits:

1. It can help uncover the features of the stores under investigation that are important to both existing and potential customers by differentiating between them. The dimensions of the perceptual map show clearly the attributes considered by consumers when making store choice decisions.
2. The position of stores on the perceptual map shows clearly the consumers' perception of the positioning statement, i.e. the beliefs of the existing customers and potential customers of the stores' offer and their relative perceptions of competitive stores. Current beliefs about the store form the basis for developing strategies that will meet unsatisfied consumer requirements.
3. Identification of changes in the perceptual map over time demonstrates the success or failure of marketing strategies, both of the company and its competitors.

A hypothetical map is shown as Figure 9.3. Here the attributes cluster into:

1. Merchandise quality, choice and exclusivity.
2. Convenience of access, parking, transaction processing and opening hours.
3. Store environment, ambience and merchandise displays.
4. In-store facilities.
5. Customer service.
6. Price levels.

Our interest in this chapter concerns the trading format and store environment characteristics. However, if we are to consider the entire exchange environment, we must of necessity consider format characteristics within the context of the other issues. This follows if we accept that the market positioning is a co-ordinated response of the functional strategies which responds to the expectations of a targeted group of customers by creating an exclusive exchange environment, relative to defined competitors, and to which the customer group responds with frequent purchasing visits with high spends.

Thus, Figure 9.3 identifies a number of characteristics which define the exchange environment. It shows a number of positions. *A* is strong in merchandise selection, while *B* is favoured for service. Stores *C*

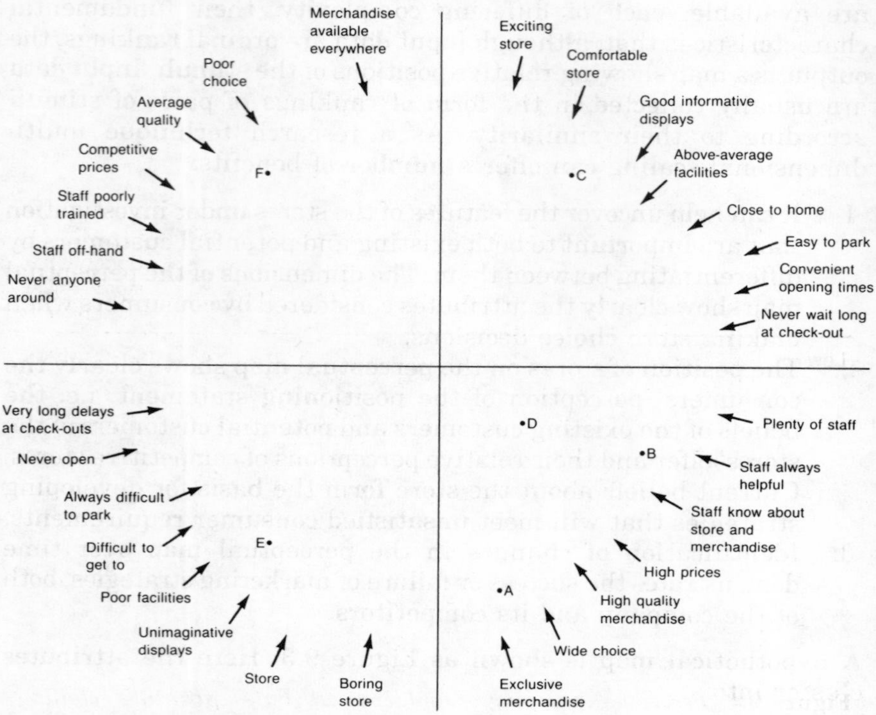

Figure 9.3 *Hypothetical perceptual mapping of retail offer*

and *D* have perceived strengths in service and store environment, *C* being stronger on store environment characteristics. Stores *E* and *F* have limited appeal and do not score highly on any aspects.

These and similar studies are useful in comparing customer relative perceptions. If stores *A*, *B*, *C* and *D* are assuming they are targeting similar customers, the customers themselves have quite different views of specific corporate strengths, with only *C* being seen as having major strengths in format and store environment characteristics. Furthermore, if it is found that format and store environment issues are important in the store selection and purchasing decision process (perhaps as supporting features in furniture retailing), then it is important that customer expectations are met and, if possible, exceeded. In some situatioins it may be worthwhile mapping customer perceptions of critical format and store environment features.

In Figure 9.4 two aspects of store ambience are mapped: the exciting store and the comfortable store. This situation is an interesting example of how two attributes, which may seem to be similar, can

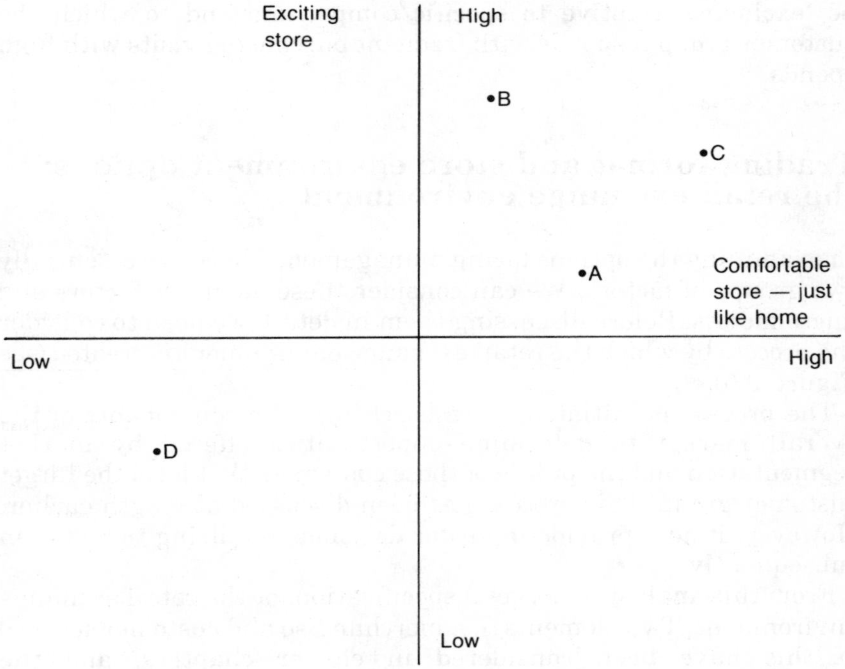

Figure 9.4 *Perceptual mapping of ambience attributes: furniture retailing*

be quite different in specific retailing situations. One such study among furniture consumers found marked differences in the perceptions of a selected range of stores. Store A, which proved to be the most profitable, had interpreted the consumers' needs more accurately than had the competitors. The consumers' needs were for an environment with which they had some familiarity and in which they could visualize the merchandise as if it were in their own homes. Competitor B had misread the research and had assumed that the customer was looking for something new, different and exciting. Competitor C attempted to be both exciting and comfortable, was seen as such by two quite different customer segments, but created confusion; whereas D appeared not to have considered the research conclusions at all seriously.

It is important that two factors receive consideration. The first concerns the overall combination of merchandise, format and service into a congruent statement. Each activity supports the other, and the positioning statement thereby creates an integrated exchange environment. The second consideration concerns competitive differentiation. The exchange environment, to be successful, should be 'exclusive' relative to specific competitors and to which the customer group responds with frequent purchasing visits with high spends.

Trading format and store environment options: the retail exchange environment

In examining the options facing management, there are essentially two groups of factors. We can consider these as macro-factors and micro-factors. Before discussing them in detail, we need to consider the process by which the retail exchange environment is created (see Figure 9.5).

The process is initiated by research into the components of the overall market to determine opportunities offered by market segmentation and the profile of those customers that form the target customer group. This process has been discussed at length earlier. However, it does provide input for decisions requiring to be taken subsequently.

From this analysis emerges a specification for the retail exchange environment. Two elements (i.e. merchandise and customer service) of this have been considered in earlier chapters, and the communications strategy will be discussed subsequently. The environment issues concern us here, but clearly (as Figure 9.5 demonstrates) the process is both integrated and sequential.

The macro-environment is concerned with location, size and situation of the retail store. The micro-environment is concerned with the in-store characteristics of ambience and design, visual merchandising, personnel and in-store facilities.

The macro-environment

Driving or travel time: The reason for this is based on research into consumer behaviour and shopping travel expectations. Travel times vary. Typically, consumers will travel further/longer for specialist offers. The important issue here is volume potential from the prescribed catchment.

Parking is required, particularly for bulk shopping and out-of-town locations. For most forms of retailing, parking is an essential convenience factor, for some it is imperative (food retailers, DIY), where not only the quantity of parking spaces is important but so too is the ease of access to parking.

The adjacency of *complementary stores* is an additional incentive to attract consumers. They may be stores of a general nature but

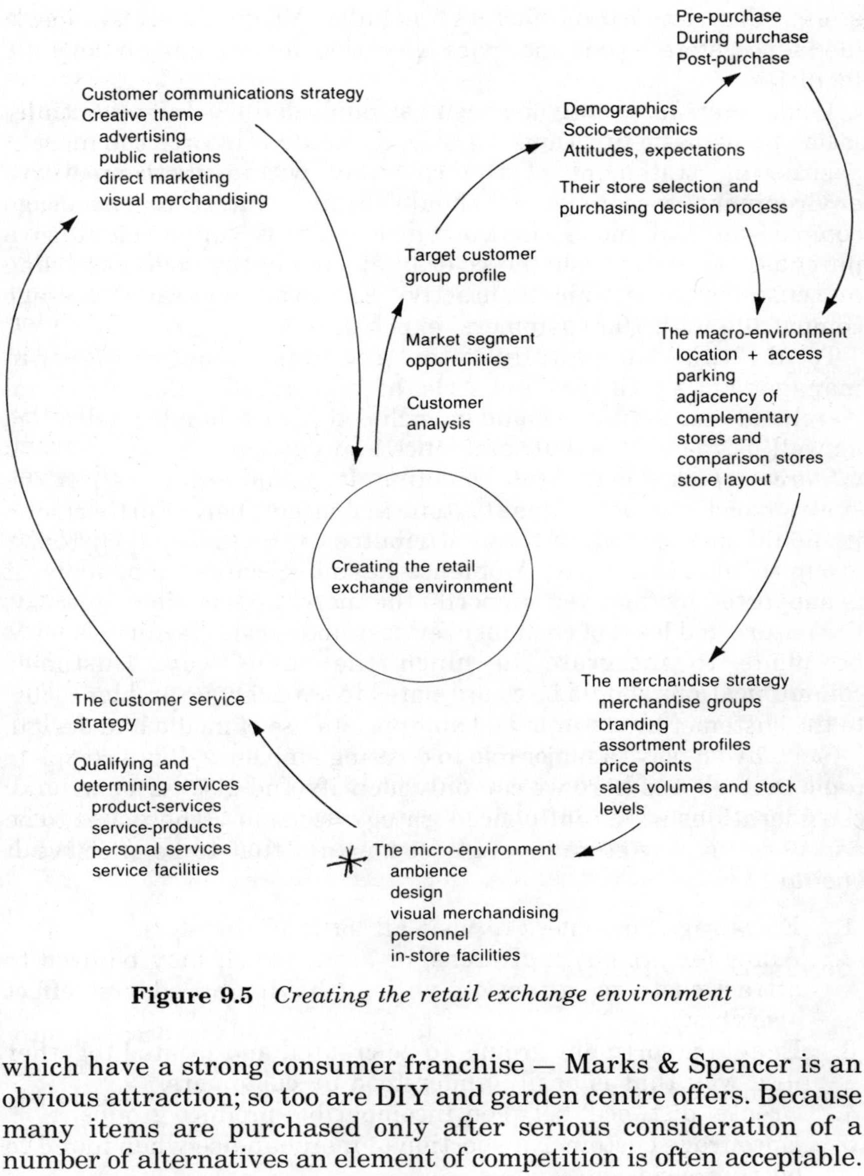

Figure 9.5 *Creating the retail exchange environment*

which have a strong consumer franchise – Marks & Spencer is an obvious attraction; so too are DIY and garden centre offers. Because many items are purchased only after serious consideration of a number of alternatives an element of competition is often acceptable. Thus *comparison stores* can also be an added attraction.

The micro-environment

A number of factors are concerned when considering the issues of motivating customer purchasing behaviour when they are in the store. The important factors include: Visual merchandising (ambience, store layout and space allocation, and design) and in-store facilities.

Visual merchandising has been variously defined, but essentially it has three basic functions. Firstly, it should reinforce the market positioning statement of the company within its competitive environment. Secondly, it should arouse interest, encourage comparison and move the customer towards commitment to a purchase. Thirdly, it should co-ordinate the entire merchandising and customer communications activities into an integrated message compatible with the customers' expectations.

To do this successfully often requires some changes in management's attitudes and style, because totally effective visual merchandising activity should be included in merchandise selection, as well as in-store layout, ambience and design.

Store ambience is difficult to define. It should aim to reflect the store's mood, character, quality, tone and atmosphere. Furthermore, it should spell out all of these attributes to the targeted customer group it aims to attract. Ambience has no specific components; it is supported by (and yet supports) the merchandise offer. Equally, the nature and level of customer services and service facilities should be made to integrate in much the same way. Customer communications should be co-ordinated to transfer the ambience feel to the customer by a subtle and appropriate use of media and design.

Store layout plays a major role in creating ambience. It is a complete topic in itself and here we can only identify and discuss some basic considerations which influence strategy decisions. The issues to be addressed by any store layout decisions are that to be effective it should:

1. Encourage customers to visit all parts of the store.
2. Allow for promotional areas, or areas which may be used to attract customer attention, without having an adverse effect elsewhere.
3. Enable assortment groups to be created and located together in a way that is easily understood by customers.
4. Create 'distance' between incompatible product groups.
5. Encourage customer inspection of merchandise when found to be appropriate.
6. Offer flexibility if required for seasonal changes or for more fundamental re-merchandising.

The general factors can be distilled further. Store layout planning has a number of aspects:

1. Classifying merchandise into related groups or departments that

respond to customer shopping and purchasing decision processes, such as:

(a) *generic classes for price or quality comparison* (e.g. all sweaters, sofas),

(b) *appeal to target customer groups* (e.g. parents concerned with children's development, health food fans),

(c) *purchasing purpose* (e.g. school clothing, gifts), storage or re-merchandising requirements (e.g. produce and fresh foods),

(d) *to indicate price offers* (e.g. bargain basements).

2. Departmental space requirements and determining department locations are closely related. Locations are often determined before space requirements are decided, indeed some locations (e.g. men's wear in department stores) are located by tradition. Furthermore, both depend very much on the positioning statement that to some extent is repeated in the approach to merchandise classification.

One often favoured method of calculating departmental space requirements is to consider the merchandise needs of customers and use the merchandise plan as an input for space allocation. Having adopted an approach for the merchandise classification which meets the positioning requirements a *model stock plan* is used to reflect the characteristics of choice, exclusivity, co-ordination across styles, colours, sizes, materials, price points or other relevant factors. There is a considerable number of computer-based techniques which can be used to evaluate the profitability of assortment selections, some will make assortment proposals and allow the merchandise manager to fine-tune the selection to meet particular market or customer needs. Once decided upon the programme will calculate:

1. The sales and profit expectations of the assortment compared with departmental goals.
2. The stockholding requirements for display and for reserve stocks.
3. Fixture and fittings; suitability for display and costs.
4. Detail re-merchandising of fixtures and identify costs of storage and transfer of reserve stock to fixtures (a number of issues for concern, such as security of valuable merchandise, transfer problems of bulky items during store opening hours, etc.).
5. Determine service requirements for each merchandise group and ascertain space requirements for service facilities and for staff.

If each of the core merchandise groups is considered by this method, an overall view of the ideal space requirement is reached. If it equals (or is less than) the space available, the plan can be confirmed and implemented. Typically, the requirements exceed the space available and revisions are necessary.

Clearly, the *productivity of space* is important and should be seen as a major influence on departmental space allocation and location. The ratio of sales per square foot or linear foot is used for planning and controlling department size and location. The sales per square foot ratio will differ by merchandise type and with the level of stock held on display and the value.

The *value of space* is an important consideration. It is a well-researched fact that sales per square foot vary considerably in multi-floor stores because of the difficulties of encouraging customers to shop the second, third and fourth floors. In order that some realistic view of profitability is reached, 'rental values' are reduced progressively for upper floors. For large stores each floor may be zoned, with the rental being varied according to its distance from the vertical transportation. Zones or areas close to floor entry points may be charged 'rentals' that are two or three times the floor rate, while distant points of the floor would be charged at one half or one quarter of the floor rate. Customer traffic flow counts can be used to determine the weights.

However, apart from the difficulty in arriving at rental values there is the advantage that this space can be used to display furniture and other large pieces to its advantage. The low customer traffic allows those interested in purchasing more room to do so.

Sales productivity and the cost of space are, therefore, two important factors in determining the location of selling departments. Other considerations exist. The nature of the merchandise is clearly one. For example, impulse merchandise *vs.* demand merchandise is one factor. Whilst almost all products may be bought on impulse at some time or other, there is a clear difference between items frequently purchased on an unplanned basis. Assortment groups comprising a number of impulse items benefit from being located in areas of high customer traffic flows. Demand items are planned purchases and customers will visit such locations without concern. Often the store layout is designed so that customers pass through the impulse ranges when accessing demand-type merchandise.

Departmental adjacencies are important in stores with large assortments. By locating those departments shopped for specific purchases (e.g. ladies' wear and accessories; food and wine; furniture, floor coverings and curtains) customer convenience is increased, and usually so too is the transaction.

Seasonal merchandise requires flexibility in its space needs. It requires large areas for short periods and should be located so that it does not disrupt the overall theme of the store. Toys and garden furniture are typical of this type of merchandise.

Design is another concept that is difficult to define. Dawson (1989b) explores the issues concerning design as a concept and as a process. He suggests that a central theme emerges from the literature and that design is a process:

> Design adds value. This value may accrue to the seller or the buyer, or both. Value may be added in a variety of ways. Some examples are:
> improving aesthetic quality;
> improving ergonomic acceptability;
> solving a consumer need;
> increasing supplier profit through more efficient use of materials or production processes;
> reducing disutilities such as the danger element;
> making products accessible to new market groups;
> simplifying product usage;
> increasing hygiene standards;
> improving comfort. (*ibid*).

And he suggests a very useful working definition of design:

> design is a process;
> design seeks to optimise profit and consumer satisfaction;
> design involves creativity;
> design is ubiquitous in a corporate environment;
> design comprises elements of performance, quality, durability, appearance and costs. (*ibid*).

It is interesting to consider how retailers use design. Some have appointed a design co-ordinator whose responsibility is to oversee all aspects of corporate design. This is the case for W.H. Smith, whose design manager is responsible to the board for all aspects of W.H. Smith design activity. This includes internal and external stationery, own-brand product packaging and store design. The corporate view is that design is an important element in store image and market positioning such that it requires to be co-ordinated centrally in order that an overall design style is established and presented to employees, suppliers and, of course, the customer.

While *in-store facilities* are very much concerned with customer service they do form part of the exchange environment for the store. Depending on the nature of the business the need for product-services such as changing-rooms to try on garments or design studios for furniture retailing will vary. There are three considerations with an impact on the micro-environment. First, the use of product-services and their impact on sales is important. Virtually all ladies' wear retailers offer a changing-room facility. Some do not offer sufficient numbers and for them the issue concerns productivity of selling space.

Often it is overlooked that allocation of additional space to this and other service activities can create extra sales because of the customer convenience that is created, and this adds value to the overall offer. The second consideration concerns location of these service facilities. An opportunity cost is involved in providing service facilities. For this reason it is usual to locate merchandise that is subject to an extended buying decision process in areas of lower-density traffic rather than in the high-value merchandising areas.

A third consideration concerns the integration of franchised service facilities. This issue also concerns the integration of concessions. If a uniform approach to visual merchandising is to be maintained, it follows that service and merchandise concessions should be integrated into the overall theme of the store. Usually, the purpose of these concessions is to broaden the merchandise and service offers to the customer: typically, the responsibility for quality control is with the retailer. It follows that concessions should be persuaded to adopt design themes established by the host company.

The purpose of both the macro- and micro-environments is to take the customer through the store selection and purchasing decision process effectively. This requires not inconsiderable research to identify the critical issues of concern to the customer, which are accommodated in the design of the retail exchange environment.

The success of the design will be seen by monitoring *customer performance characteristics*. If these are measured prior to modification or re-design of the exchange environment and then monitored on an ongoing basis, together with identifying why customers are behaving the way they are, then progress can be evaluated. However, before firm decisions can be taken concerning the design of the exchange environment, two important questions must be addressed: What is the cost of the proposed environment? And what increases in customer performance are required to make the investment worthwhile?

Financial considerations

Additional investment in fixed and working capital in any business requires justification. So too does the investment in format and store environment. In this section we consider methods for making investments appraisal and discuss the problems of identifying costs.

It is quite clear that retailers approach the investment in format and store environment with a degree of financial sophistication. David Stewart, of Addison Design (interviewed Dawson (1989b)), discusses this issue. He contrasts two approaches – one of which uses the environment of the shop to make a statement about the offer and market positioning. In this approach the design is changed frequently and capital expenditure is written down over a much shorter time-period than most other retailers. The frequent changes are seen to be an important part of the offer, with product influencing store design. The alternative approach is to opt for a classic design in which the store makes a neutral statement and the merchandise, through its colours, design and fabric together with skilful visual merchandising, is responsibile for a large input in the overall offer message. Stewart suggests that the classic approach using good materials has major advantages. If the original investment in natural materials is taken over a five- or ten-year period, the benefit of low-cost maintenance and eventual replacement is lower. This raises the issue of investment appraisal.

The financial management literature offers a range of investment appraisal methods. A detailed but very readable discussion is available in Myddleton (1988).

Myddleton discusses a number of problems associated with investment decisions. One, which is clearly important to this discussion, is the difficulty in estimating accurately the future net benefits from a project. The forecasting of future sales of tangible goods and services is difficult, but the impact of a store environment on customer purchasing is even more so. We shall return to this topic.

Appraisal methods essentially fall into two categories. The difference is that one group of methods considers the influence of time and uses the fact that future income has a lower value than current income. The other methods, which are far simpler to operate, *ignore* the *timing* of the returns. Within the context of format and store environment development, both methods are used and have good reasons for this. First consider the options.

Payback is a simple, widely used method of appraisal, and shows how many years it will take before the original amount invested in a project is 'paid back', i.e. before the cumulative returns exceed the initial investment. Clearly, the shorter the payback period the better. It follows that retailers who opt for frequent environment changes would use payback as an appraisal method. However, payback has three disadvantages:

1. While it measures and identifies the shortest payback period (assuming more than one alternative), in itself it does not have the ability to identify the maximum payback that would be acceptable.
2. More important is the fact that the payback method ignores cash receipts expected after payback. This is essential: there can be

no profit unless we receive back more than the original investment.
3. Payback measures risk (the sooner the payback occurs the lower the risk), but it does not measure profitability.

In the context of format and environment decisions we can estimate what income is required to recover an original investment by calculating either what we should expect as revenues (note we are considering *cash* receipts not accounting *profits*, therefore, we do *not* deduct depreciation from the cash inflows) over a *specified* period or consider the likely payback periods from careful forecasting of cash flows.

The other approach outlined by David Stewart suggests that time and the time value of money become significant. There are two ways in which time can be accommodated in the appraisal analysis. The *present value* concept is based on the fact that a given amount of money now is worth more than the same amount in the future. The reasoning is quite simple: it can be invested today to yield a return over the same period. Thus, given an interest rate, which reflects the cost of capital to the company, we can use it to calculate the value of a capital sum at any future date (compound interest tables). Discount factor tables can tell us the *present values* of future money amounts. The rate of interest used is often referred to as the 'opportunity cost of capital'. This varies with the capital structure of the company, but a simpler view is to consider bank deposit rates. If the bank will pay 15 per cent on deposited funds, any company investment should seek to exceed this if an investment is to be worthwhile. It is variously known as the *criterion rate* or *hurdle rate*.

There are two *discounted cash flow* methods available. Both involve forecasting the *amount* and *timing* of incremental cash flows expected to result from a project. To use the net present values method to determine profitability, we simply see whether or not the present value of the project's discounted cash inflows exceeds that of the cash investment involved. If it is equal to or exceeds the investment, then the project is worth consideration.

The alternative method (the internal rate of return, or IRR method) also uses discounted cash flows. Whereas the NPV method considers amount and timing of all expected cash flows and applies a *pre-selected* discount rate to establish whether the NPV is positive (acceptable) or negative (reject or reconsider cash flow forecasts), the IRR method *determines* the discount rate at which the cash flows produce a net present value of exactly zero. The rate of interest that produces this result is the internal rate of return of the project, which must be compared with the criterion or hurdle rate to determine the viability of the project.

While this description is necessarily simplified, it does offer ways and means of evaluating both alternative positioning strategies and within them alternative format and store environment options.

Most businesspeople prefer IRR to NPV, probably because the result is expressed as an annual percentage rate of return, readily comparable with market interest rates. A number of refinements can be made to improve the accuracy of both methods. These include different ways of allowing for risk and uncertainty, as well as the influence of inflation on revenues and costs (important for retailers in price sensitive market segments).

Readers wishing to consider this topic in detail are recommended to read the relevant chapter in Myddleton (1988).

An examination of costs suggests two areas of costs to be considered: fixed and operating costs. These will be common to both store opening and store refurbishment programmes.

Among the *fixed costs* are development and design, which will be amortized across the number of stores opened or refurbished. The amount of expenditure for both of these items, together with store fitting costs, depends on some of the basic decisions concerning store positioning. The more luxurious or theatrical the environment the greater these costs will be. An opportunity cost exists concerning the alternative use of capital resources; and the investment appraisal should consider these by using as the criterion rate the rate of return likely to be earned by employing the capital elsewhere.

The *operating costs* will vary with the level of activity eventually decided upon. Some will be variable costs in the sense that they will only occur as stores are opened. Others are more likely to be incremental and will occur either if adjustments are made to staff or stockholding levels or if refurbishment results in larger stores requiring more staff, etc. Systems and distribution may also be considered as incremental in that the increase in sales volume will put an increased load on systems and distribution capacities and therefore costs.

The benefits will be *soft and hard*. The *soft* benefits will be seen as shifts in customer perceptions of the company and of the increase in added value attributable to the new store or a refurbished store. It is possible to evaluate these ahead of implementing the expansion/refurbishment programme by using concept tests through focus groups, etc. The *hard* benefits will be the incremental increases in sales and profits derived from the new and/or refurbished stores. These will be due to increased customer flows; average transactions (and therefore total transactions); items purchased and range of purchases. These should be monitored together with the *productivity changes* which occur in sales area, employees and in increased utilization. Together, the costs and benefits offer sufficient information to calculate both a DCF-based evaluation and payback. The benefit of this approach is that, by using the investment appraisal methods, together with the qualitative measures, the options available can be identified.

The trading format and store environment strategy selection

The financial considerations of the format and environment options will have produced cost and revenue profiles of each of them. At this point, the decision has to be made concerning which strategy option would be most successful in reaching the company's objectives. A number of questions should be asked:

1. Which option is seen by the target customer group as being closest to the company's positioning?
2. Which option is likely to be most effective in helping the customer to move rapidly through the store selection and purchasing decision process?
3. What is (or will be) the impact on customer performance:
   - (a) frequency of browsing visits?
   - (b) frequency of purchasing visits?
   - (c) average transaction values?
   - (d) items purchased?
   - (e) range purchased?
   - (f) store loyalty (repeat visits)?
4. What are the revenue and profit implications?
5. What are the NPV/IRR and payback performances?

Given satisfactory answers to these questions, management has sufficient information to be able to select an option and to issue a specification for the format and environment strategy.

CHAPTER 10

Implementing trading format and store environment strategy

Introduction

As with earlier functional strategies, subsequent to discussing them within the context of strategy development and reviewing conceptual issues that arise, this chapter considers the implementation of the format and environment strategy.

It is likely that aspects of previous format and environment strategies are continuing to exert an influence. This is particularly so where store development is occurring. Typically, large multiple retailers will have an ongoing store development activity which attempts to roll out an existing format and environment specification. This may well be for ten or twenty stores a year. We can assume that the implementation of a format and environment strategy will follow this pattern. Changes will be made to the strategy, but unless there is a major repositioning strategy, it is likely that such changes will be small, minor modifications.

For the implementation task we suggest there are five areas to be considered:

1. A review of the trading and store environment strategy.
2. Factors influencing the trading format and store environment plan.
3. Developing a trading format and store environment plan.
4. Project planning and management.
5. Monitoring and control issues.

Figure 10.1 identifies these topics and their sequence.

The trading format and store environment strategy specification

The implementation of a format and environment strategy will be required to take consideration of both the merchandise and customer

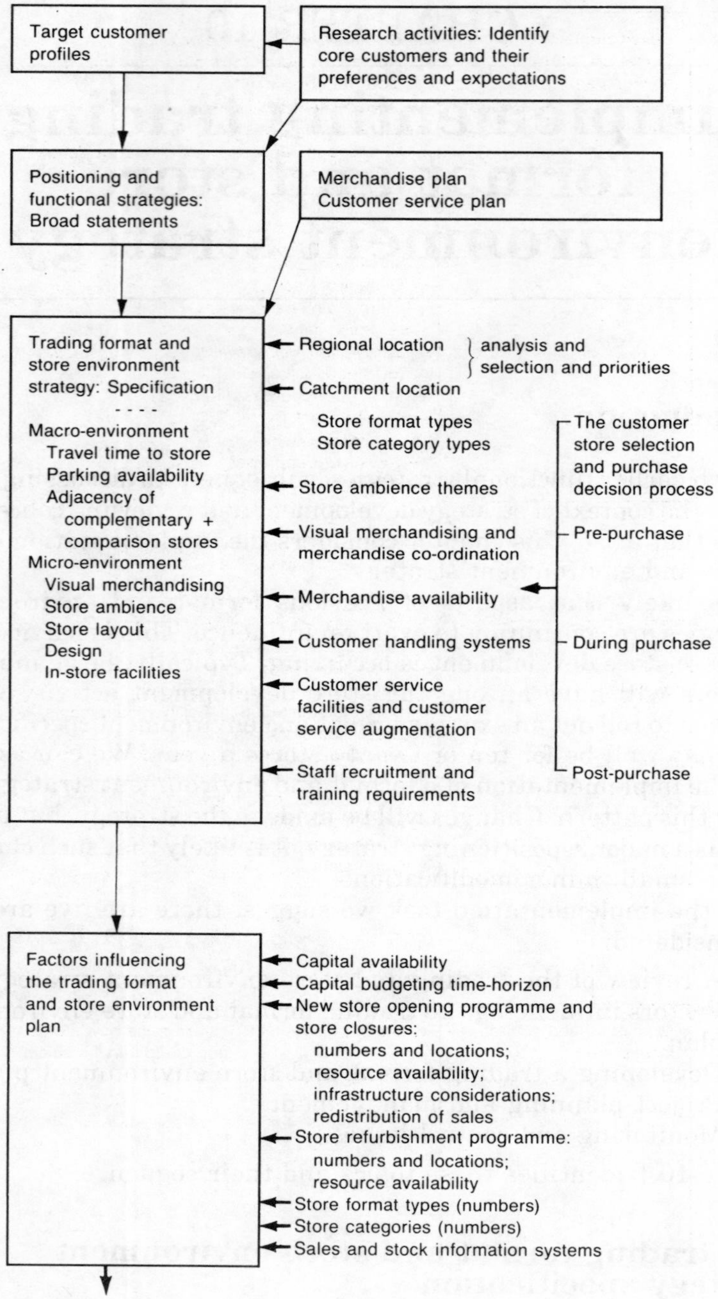

Figure 10.1 *Trading format and store environment: planning and control*

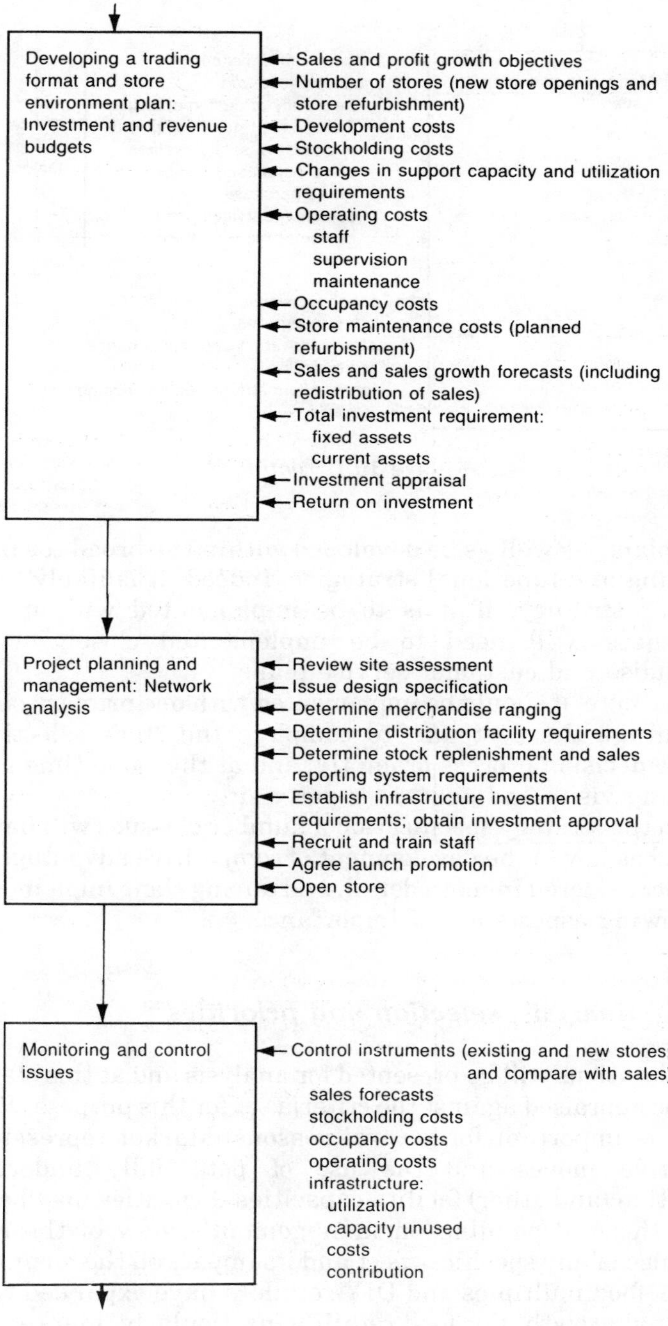

Figure 10.1 *continued overleaf*

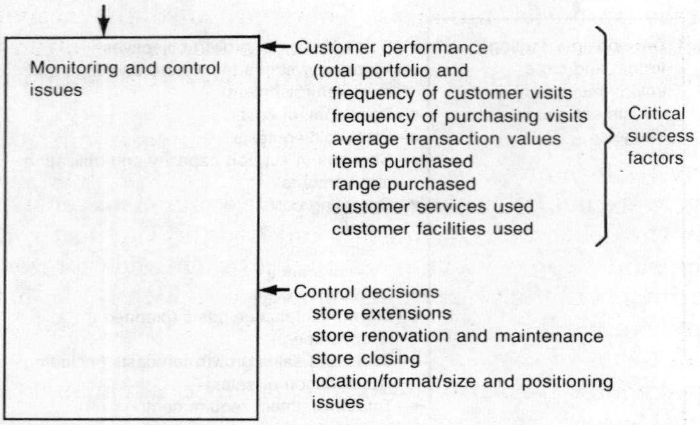

Figure 10.1 *continued*

service plans, as well as be developed within the broad terms of the positioning and functional strategies. Indeed, it is likely that this particular strategy, if it is to be implemented with maximum effectiveness, will need to be implemented closely with the merchandise and customer service plans.

Furthermore, it should be implemented with one primary objective: to encourage the customer to complete the store selection and purchase decision process promptly, and at the same time increase purchasing visits and purchases per visit.

Within the strategy specification a number of issues will have been identified as key to the development of competitive advantage. These are now considered in more detail, and during their implementation the following aspects are of importance.

Location analysis, selection and priorities

Specific locations will be presented for analysis and at this stage they should be appraised against the criteria set for this purpose. *Regional* location is important for several reasons. Market representation, competitive moves and the use of potentially underutilized distribution (and other) facility capacities. Priorities may be set for each of these, depending on management's view of the relative importance of any specific aspect and its impact on the business. For example, food multiples and DIY retailers have expanded recently by regional growth. For food retailing particularly, market growth rate has been minimal and volume growth has only been achieved by increasing outlet numbers. There are also the activities of competitors to consider. Furthermore, locations are often taken, developed and operated in an attempt to create regional barriers to entry.

Market representation is also sought for competitive reasons. In the early 1970s many of the food multiples that now have national coverage were in fact only strong in specific regions: Sainsbury and Tesco in the south and south-east, and Asda in the north. Each of these companies can now claim national coverage and representation. This is important for a number of reasons. Firstly, a 'national' company can achieve much more cost-effective use of advertising media in terms of cost per 1,000 exposure. Secondly, the volumes developed enable innovative own-label product development to take place and the wide geographic and volume coverage facilitates their rapid 'roll out' and evaluation. Thirdly, the overall volumes generated offer larger buying margins, together with increased influence in negotiations. Increases in volume throughput enable economies of scale in operations and distribution to be developed.

An expansion in the number of outlets is also considered when distribution and operations systems are underutilized. It is possible that this motive may have featured to some degree in Asda's recent (1989) decision to acquire a number of Gateway superstore locations. Quite often the decision to close branch outlets is taken *without* considering the impact of such action on infrastructure utilization.

Catchment location analysis of new and potential sites is conducted routinely. The approach of Tesco has been described elsewhere (Penny and Brown 1988). Their system incorporates:

1. *1981 Census of Population* provides household structures, economic conditions, mobility and tenure. When combined with measures of household expenditure on different product groups from various national surveys (e.g. Family Expenditure Survey), it provides direct measures of purchasing power and hence consumer demand.
2. *Customer origin surveys*: Some 8–10 per cent of Tesco superstore customers are interviewed once a year. These provide for the definition of catchment areas and the calculation of expenditure by population zones.
3. *Branch data-bases*: Store data (in-store measurement, merchandise ranges, sales history, life-cycle stage), combined with customer survey data, produce a comprehensive set of store profiles. (EPOS data are increasingly useful at this stage.)
4. *Competitors' data-base*: Data collected during visits to competitors' outlets.

5. *Information network*: Data collected from links with local authorities, local press and from local store management.
6. *Digitized road network*: Interfaces with other data-bases allow for the computation of travel time between any two geographic points. The data are used as input to a spatial interaction model, the basic concept of which is that the interaction between two cities varies directly with some function of their population size and inversely with some formula of the distance between them. Consequently, retail sales will be influenced by these factors.

Catchment analysis is offered as a commercial service – CACI, Pinpoint, Mosaic, etc. – and these are very useful inputs for both initial location analyses and for identifying changes to the customer profile base. Considerable residential property development has taken place in recent years and these changes have resulted in extending catchment areas and altering their customer profiles. Clearly, these changes can have a significant impact on the business and may require changes to assortment, shopping hours or possibly store size. Once again, priorities should be considered and set to enable the most effective use of capital expenditure allocation.

Store format and category types are also influenced by this type of analysis. Both regional and catchment locations should influence store format type, while the business potential will influence the size category of the store. Catchment analysis and customer profiling will assist in deciding on an optimal store size and its assortment ranging. Prior to using such approaches many retailers would attempt to offer 'scaled down' versions of their assortments in *each* of their stores. This often resulted in a complete lack of focus, together with a failure to take advantage of competitive weaknesses. It also resulted in lower profit margins in stores where a weak attempt at competing with a strong competitor was attempted.

Store ambience themes

The analysis discussed in the previous paragraphs provides valuable input for implementing strategy in this respect. In operational terms there are often very good reasons why ambience themes cannot be easily implemented. One such reason is that to do so would 'move' the store away from its existing customer base, particularly if the store has been a recent acquisition. There were many examples of this problem during the 'growth by acquisition' move of the early 1970s. The department store groups of Debenham and the House of Fraser expanded very rapidly during this period by acquiring independents or small, regional department store chains. Subsequent to the acquisition, they imposed some dramatic changes on the newly acquired stores which included not simply merchandise changes (range expansion and contraction, shifting pricing emphasis, quality, style and exclusivity) but also store ambience. Thus we saw themes that had worked in the south imposed on stores in the north; self-service and cash points in stores that had for many years been strongly oriented towards personal service.

Another operational aspect of this topic, which occurs quite often, concerns the physical characteristics of stores. Many ambience themes require (or are most effective in) specific space dimensions and shapes. Often, centrally designed ambience themes ignore the fact that the branch property portfolio varies markedly in shape and size. Hence a theme that works well in an outlet with wide frontage may not do so when implemented in those with very narrow fascias. The application of CAD (computer aided design) techniques to this problem often suggests design modifications which enable the ambience design to work more effectively. CAD software packages are becoming increasingly sophisticated. They have an extensive colour palette and offer 'texture finishes' in addition to offering the facility whereby store dimensions may be adjusted to enable the designer to consider different fascia dimensions.

Space allocation and space performance (sales and profitability per linear or square foot) can be incorporated into recent CAD packages. This facility is very useful because it can use EPOS data to suggest space allocation and calculate store performance. If this is unsatisfactory the design team can adjust the space allocation (either by reallocating footage or by increasing the selling space by adding to it vertically) and then assessing the visual effect. Retailers using CAD find the facility to 'file' each store invaluable when performance characteristics are compared or individuality investigated.

Visual merchandising and merchandise co-ordination

This topic follows logically. Once the format and category issues have been resolved and the ranging determined across the outlet portfolio, the visual merchandising issues can be addressed.

It will be remembered that visual merchandising has three basic functions:

1. It should reinforce the market positioning statement.
2. It should arouse interest, encourage comparison and move the customer towards commitment.
3. It should communicate a co-ordinated offer to the target customer group.

To do so visual merchandising should understand the store selection and purchase decision process intimately. If the customers' mood can be sensed, if the buying process is understood, then the store exchange environment can match that mood and the merchandise selection and its presentation be co-ordinated with maximum effect.

It will be remembered that we discussed the structure of buying responsibilities in Chapters 5 and 6. The argument made there was for the structure of the merchandise selection and of buying to reflect the customers' demand patterns. This obtains equally, if not more so, for visual merchandising. The merchandise should be presented to reflect both life-style and merchandise characteristics, together with a co-ordinated approach which combines merchandise groups in a manner the customer perceives as logical. This is not always an easy task. Often the customers' 'logical perceptions' vary from one purchase situation to another. For example, food shopping is seen as a task purchasing situation, and therefore the visual merchandise department should not experiment a great deal, but rather stay with store layout patterns with which the customer has become familiar and which do at least respond to the need for convenience and a rapid shopping visit. Conversely, ladies' wear shopping is seen as leisure shopping and enjoyed. It follows that visual merchandising can be creative in this situation. There is an opportunity to develop on the themes which are seen as 'logical', e.g. clothes for casual wear, clothes for the executive lady, clothes for formal entertaining, etc. Within these themes there is the potential to suggest experimentation because the customer is not only purchasing clothing (assuming the merchandise offer is appropriate), but also sees the visit to the store as part-leisure. In these situations the visual merchandiser should consider how the store offer might enhance the performance of the critical success factors by:

1. Increasing sales revenue by:
   (a) increasing the range of items purchased,
   (b) increasing purchasing visits.
   (Both due, in part, to the interest developed by merchandise display.)
2. Increasing gross margin by:
   (a) directing purchasing intentions towards higher margin merchandise ranges:
3. Containing costs by:
   (a) using visual merchandising to move the customer through the purchasing process rapidly (possibly without excessive presence of sales staff).
4. Improving productivity by:
   (a) increasing the size of the sales transaction, converting

browsing visits to purchasing visits (thereby increasing both sales per square foot and sales per employee, etc.).

5. Adding value to the customers' purchases by:
   (a) offering advice on style and colour co-ordination through visual merchandising.

Clearly, visual merchandising can be very influential in the store selection and purchasing decision process. To be fully effective the visual merchandise team should co-ordinate its work with the decisions on customer service and in particular on the characteristics suggested by research and shown in Figure 8.1.

Merchandise availability

The issues surrounding merchandise availability were discussed in Chapters 5 and 6. What is of interest here are the additional issues that arise due to visual merchandising decisions.

An obvious implication of visual merchandising decisions concerns the themes developed and the merchandise featured in them. If the impact of visual merchandising is to be beneficial, it follows that the availability of the featured merchandise should be sufficient to respond to any demand patterns that result. Sizes, styles and colour choices should be considered when planning availability levels.

At the same time the availability level considered within the context of the merchandise strategy should be used to establish a bench-mark. It would be confusing for customers to find excessive differences between merchandise groups.

Concern for space productivity is another important issue. If availability is maintained at very high levels (and it may be both necessary and justifiable in marketing terms), there is an in-store storage problem to be considered. The way in which this problem is addressed is clearly an issue for the visual merchandising team. Often it is possible to use the stock merchandise to create display impact with colour (as is done by Benetton with knitwear), choice (furniture and floor coverings) or even application.

Customer handling systems

Operations management is concerned with achieving sales and profitability objectives from a prescribed merchandise mix and optimal space and human resource inputs. Given a positioning strategy to work towards, it is not always possible to maximize profits by containing costs. Quite possibly the ratio of wages and salaries to sales (in-store) may well be high for formats majoring heavily on service, and often the most cost-effective methods of customer handling are precluded by the marketing requirements for customer care.

The location of customer handling systems is an important store environment consideration. If the format is one for which service features as a dominant part of the overall offer, the facility should be located and designed (and staffed) to reflect the service theme. Recent developments in footwear retailing are interesting in this respect. To continue the 'customer care' approach that is necessary at the point of selection and purchase, *customers are accompanied* to a cash-and-wrap facility. It is often overlooked by retailers (who claim to be customer service aware) that an impression of service developed between sales assistant and customer during purchase selection may be damaged (possibly completely destroyed) by mass handling at overcrowded cash points.

Customer service facilities and customer service augmentation

The type of service offered and its differentiation (qualifying or determining) was discussed in Chapters 7 and 8. Here the concern is with their integration into the store environment.

There are some facilities that are of necessity located within the merchandise sales areas. Changing-rooms are essential features of both ladies' and men's wear offers. Their location and size is important, and once again should reflect the offer made by the positioning statement. For example, an exclusive ladies' wear retailer should consider the need for the 'exclusivity' theme to be continued and reinforced by the inclusion of mirrors, clothes hanging facilities, seating and possibly vanity units in changing-rooms. The theme could also include seating and refreshment facilities for customers' partners, etc. This becomes a design issue because not only should the facilities blend with the overall store environment design, but they also utilize selling space and where at all possible no opportunities for increasing average transactions should be missed. In this particular example sample menus for the restaurant or relevant offers available elsewhere in the store could be displayed prominently.

Customer service augmentation (and for that matter service-product sales) may be located in less productive selling areas. For example, customers' export administration problems may be located on third or fourth floor areas where the allocation of space for business and comfort may be more generous. The thesis here is that the customer would prefer to be dealt with in more comfortable and confidential surroundings. However, the requirements for aesthetic surroundings and compatible ambience remain. The design requirements for customer service areas should be integrated with those of the remainder of the store offer.

Staff recruitment and training requirements

It is often overlooked, but staff who reflect the purpose of the business and can reflect and communicate the company's positioning represent a major asset. To this end staff recruitment should be made with this in mind. A store environment reflecting avant garde fashion should be staffed with people who have an interest in such an approach and whose appearance reinforces the design of the store environment.

Staff training should include sessions explaining the rationale of the environment theme, together with instruction on how the staff can complement the store environment and how the customer facilities are to be used.

Factors influencing the trading format and store environment plan

Among the issues influencing the format and environment plan the most important concerns the role of the store development programme in maintaining the sales and profit flow of the company. Thus it is with this in mind that the plan should be developed.

There are three further issues, and these are derived from the primary one of sales and profit-generation. The first concerns the availability of capital to implement the plan; the second concerns the deployment of the capital available in order that the sales and profit objectives are met; and the third concerns the programming of the plan.

Capital availability

The amount of capital to be made available for store development is clearly a board decision. In reaching the decision the directors will have considered:

1. The overall required return on capital employed by the business.

2. The sources of capital availability.
3. The cost of capital.
4. The opportunity cost of capital allocated to store development.

It becomes the responsibility of management tasked with implementing the store development programme to work towards achieving the objectives set by the board. In addition to sales and profit contribution, cash generation is important. Often the cycling and recycling of cash generated from store development is a major feature of a store expansion programme. Thus the capital made available should be allocated to new store opening, store refurbishment and the development of infrastructure such that sales, profits *and* cash generation are optimized.

Capital budgeting time-horizon

Again, this is a board decision but the time-horizons specified for investment appraisal provides an indication of the board's views. The use of payback as an investment appraisal method, together with a relatively short payback period, probably implies that the cash flow generated from store opening is expected to be recycled.

At this stage of the store development programme the emphasis should be placed on revenue and cost forecasts and developing a rank order of store opening activities. This is extremely useful if there are more opportunities than there is capital available. It can be achieved quite simply. The investment appraisal method is adjusted by applying probabilities to both revenue and cost forecasts and developing expected values (i.e. £ revenue (cost) × probability = expected value of the revenue (cost)). This will provide a means by which the options may be evaluated. Clearly, those with the higher expected values of total cash flow will be preferred.

New store opening programme and store closures

The rank ordering of store opening options identifies those that are most attractive. There are two important factors to be considered at this point:

1. The *availability of human resources* is an important issue. Typically, the appraisal is conducted using standard labour rates. However, in many areas (usually those with the greatest potential) the local demand for labour far exceeds supply, and consequently there is a shortage or the rates that are offered

have to be increased, often significantly above those used in the feasibility study.

2. This has major consequences. It may result in a reappraisal of the ranking of potential store opening opportunities; or it may result in not opening the site at all, particularly if there is likely to be a long-term shortage of labour. The marketing implications of poor service, low availability, etc., should be an important consideration, as poor performance initially may well inhibit the eventual long-term profitability of the location. Clearly, store closures raise issues of redundancies. Where possible, staff are relocated, but for those who cannot be offered employment the costs of redundancies should be set against the store development programme.

Infrastructure considerations concern the extent to which support systems (primarily distribution) can service the new stores. Distribution systems cannot operate at extended capacity levels for very long. Therefore, the impact of the projected volume increases on such facilities should be considered prior to the expansion. Store closures will have the reverse effect. There is inevitably a reduction in the productivity of infrastructure systems when the branch network is reduced. Care should be taken then, when branch closures are considered, to ensure that system throughput continues to be sufficient to maintain the overhead recovery on this element of the company's investment.

The *redistribution of sales* that may occur between branches as new outlets are opened should be considered. Initially, this may not be significant, particularly if the new locations are well beyond the travel distances of customers of existing stores. However, as penetration increases, the impact of additional stores (company-owned and those of competitors) may become an important consideration in terms of marginal revenue increases only and large increases in costs.

Store refurbishment programme

A continual review of the existing store portfolio should be undertaken. Trading formats and store environments become outdated. Of particular importance in this regard are the features affecting customer service and convenience. Inadequate car parking facilities, limited check-out numbers, dated fixtures and fittings, and dull store layout and design all contribute to dating stores. This often occurs because management loses sight of the fact that as new stores are opened the 'generation gap' extends rapidly and, if ignored, the company is left with a major reinvestment programme such as Asda found in the late 1970s/early 1980s (Walters 1988).

The implications of this problem in competitive terms becomes obvious as competitors open new stores in adjacent areas. Not so obvious are the promotional implications, particularly for large multiple groups who feature their 'latest and best' stores in advertising programmes. Often the local store for many is of an older generation and, if a potential customer is encouraged to make a trial visit on the basis of seeing a 'state of the art' store featured in the advertising, the disappointment can be long-lasting.

The impact on incremental revenues should not be overlooked. For many retailers the incremental revenue/incremental investment ratio can be very attractive. Often in competitive terms much can be achieved by refurbishment programmes. It avoids the problems outlined in the previous paragraph and is usually well received by loyal customers whose average spends increase.

A refurbishment programme requires some thought. It should be subject to research which identifies the most cost-effective use of refurbishment funds. Furthermore, the overall capital budget should be evaluated within the context of maximizing its effectiveness. This suggests that an overall review of expenditure on *both* new stores and refurbishments should be undertaken. The analysis includes estimates of the opportunity costs of not opening new stores and the impact of refurbishing existing stores on local competition.

Store format types and store categories

This issue follows on from the previous discussion. The fact is that formats require to be reviewed due to the changing patterns of consumer perceptions and expectations, together with increasing competitive pressures.

Often store refurbishment programmes present the opportunity to increase sales area and this in turn presents the opportunity to increase the merchandise range offered. It does, of course, raise issues concerning the positioning of the store in as much that it may well be saying something very different to the customer base within the catchment. The result might well be a completely different format from that previously offered.

Another consideration that should be made concerns the category of the store. For many multiples a store category is an important classification which determines a number of operations and distribution activities. Thus an upgrading of a store category may well increase the level of these activities to a point at which the infrastructure systems have difficulty in coping.

There are also marketing implications. A range of store formats requires that each is dealt with separately and therefore dilutes the promotional budget. Furthermore, it also requires additional management to co-ordinate the activities of a multi-brand operation. It also requires an increase in stockholding to support the availability targets set for each format. Store categories can present problems for local management, particularly for multiple groups operating a large range of store sizes/categories. Typically, national promotions feature large, recent stores in the multiples' chains. Problems arise when customer expectations of the implied wide ranges of merchandise and services cannot be met. Quite often a compromise offer of elements of each range results in a higher level of customer confusion and dissatisfaction.

Sales and stock information systems

We have discussed the need to consider the extent to which distribution systems are able to cope cost-effectively with changes in volume throughput. Another consideration concerns the requirements for different systems to service the merchandise requirements of differing formats and store categories. It is very unlikely that the merchandise assortment strategies of two different formats will be the same and clearly the systems requirements will also differ. The investment costs and subsequent operating costs of two quite different systems may well cause management to reconsider any decision to develop alternative formats.

The store category issue can be seen as a different problem. Here, because the assortment range is likely to be narrower and overall throughput lower, the consideration should be concerned with flexibility of the system. Ideally, the design of a sales and stock information system should be able to deal with wide ranges of both volume and frequency of data input. Thus, despite the fact that the stores themselves reflect the overall positioning strategy of the company (with similar merchandise and customer service functional strategies), there is a need to ensure that the systems responsible for stock replenishment and providing sales information are capable of doing so cost-effectively.

Developing a trading format and store environment plan

A number of issues and components comprise the format and environment plan. Essentially, they are financial in their nature and

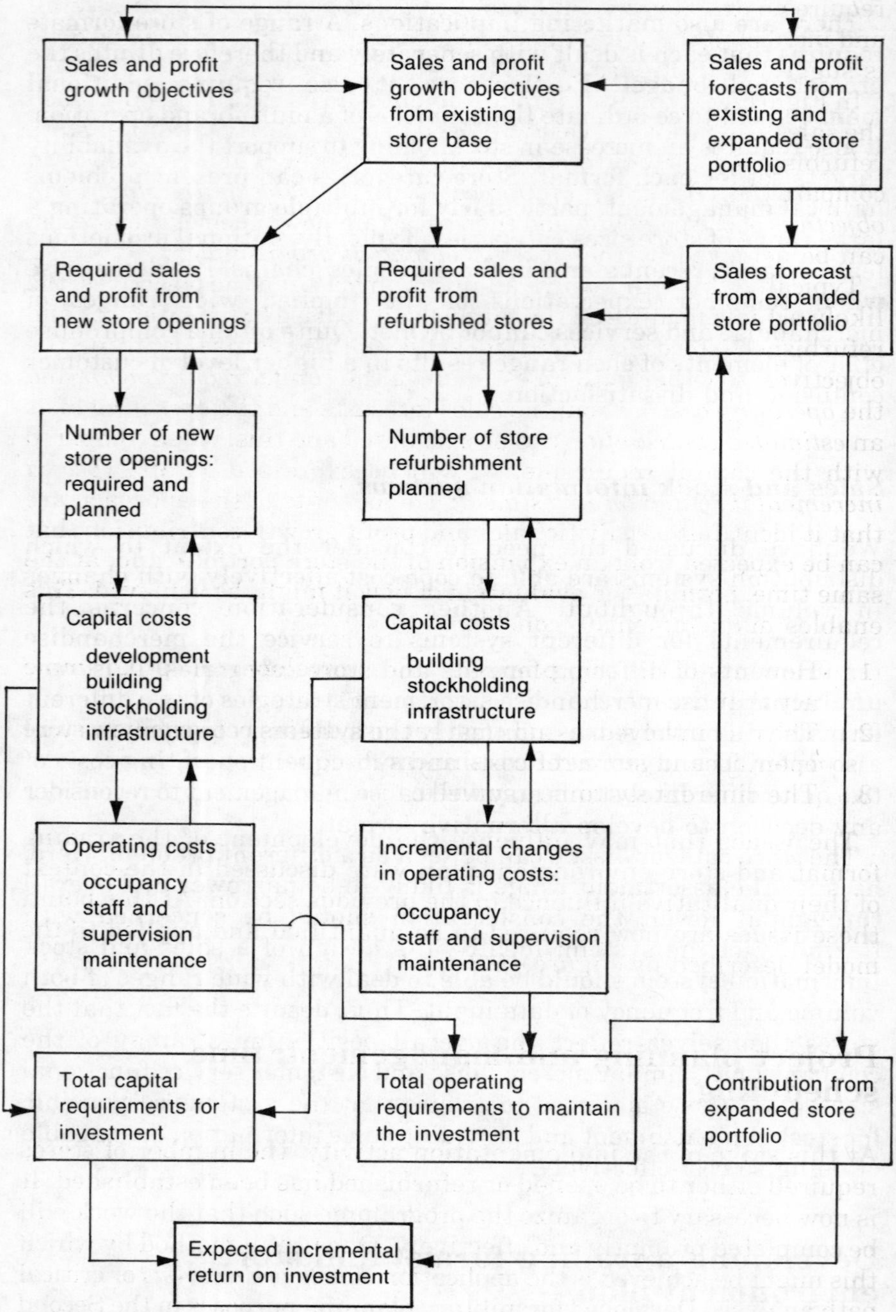

Figure 10.2 *Evaluating the impact of store development and return on investment*

require an examination in the context of their influence on the overall and incremental profitability. The process by which this may be done is suggested in Figure 10.2.

In Figure 10.2 the initial requirement is to ascertain by how much the sales and profit forecast will need to be reinforced by either store refurbishment or new store openings (or both). The first step is to compare the *sales and profit forecast* with the *sales and profit growth objectives* of the company and then ascertain how much of the forecast can be achieved by the *store development programme.*

Typically, this will involve an iteration between the objectives, the likely achievements and the methods to be used (i.e. new stores and refurbished stores required to achieve the requirements of the objectives, together with an estimate of the *capital requirements* and the *operating costs*). From the sales forecasts and the *operating costs* an *estimated contribution* can be calculated and this, when compared with the capital requirements, will be expressed as an *expected incremental return on investment.* The benefits of the approach are that it identifies a realistic sales and profit growth contribution that can be expected from an expansion of the store portfolio and, at the same time, permits the evaluation of how it might be achieved. This enables management to consider:

1. How realistic the planned store development programme actually is.
2. The risk involved (assuming that risk differs between new store opening and store refurbishment).
3. The time likely to be required.

The issues that may influence the development of the trading format and store environment plan were discussed in the context of their qualitative influence in the previous section. At this point, these issues are now required to be quantified and applied to the model described by Figure 10.2.

Project planning and management: time scheduling

At this stage of the implementation activity, the number of stores required either to be opened or refurbished has been established. It is now necessary to organize the programme such that the work will be completed promptly and effectively. One useful method by which this might be achieved is the application of *network analysis* or critical path analysis. Developed for military planning purposes in the Second World War, it has been adapted for management use subsequently.

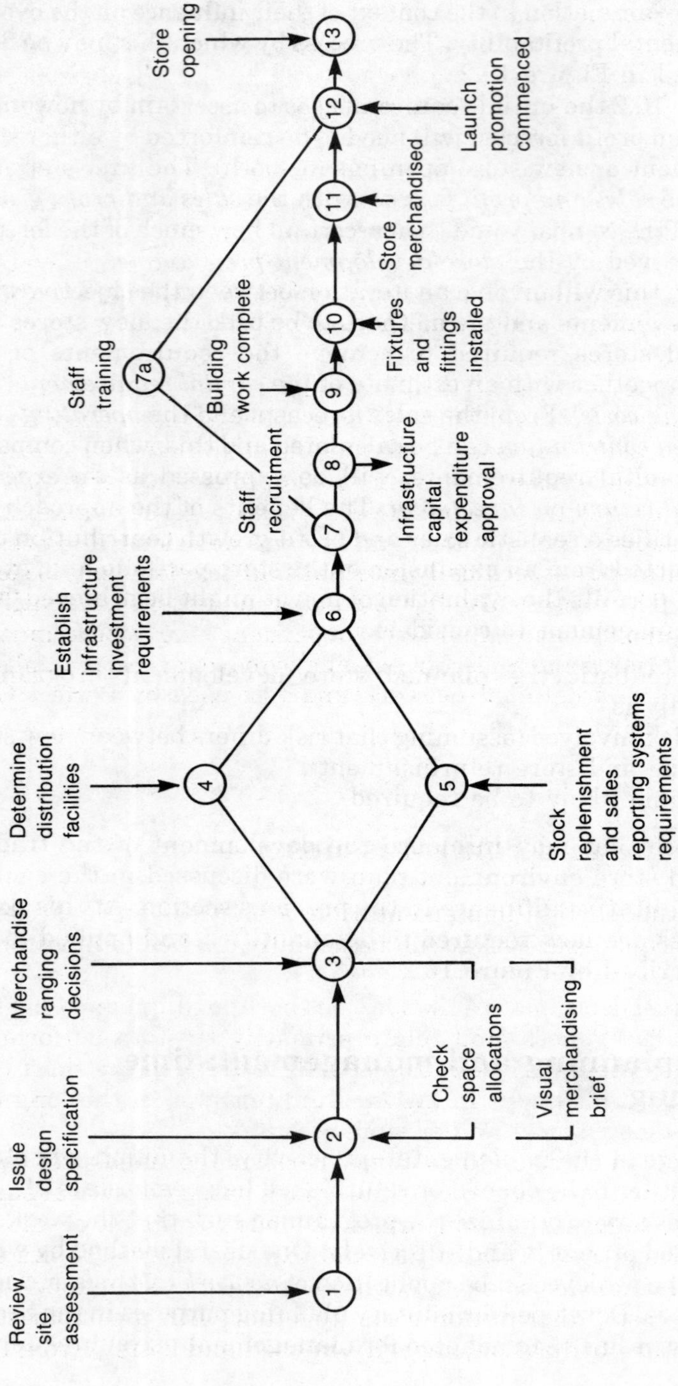

Figure 10.3 *A simplified network analysis of a store opening project*

The technique approaches project planning by breaking the project into component activities and showing these activities and their interrelationships in the form of a network. By considering the times and resources required to complete each of the activities, it is possible to locate the critical path of activities which determines the minimum time for the project. The programme can also be used to schedule resources into the project and to consider the impact of changes in one area of the project on others. Network analysis is particularly useful for projects that have reasonably well-defined start and finish dates and for which it is important to consider not only the interrelationships between activities within the project but *also* between activities across projects.

Figure 10.3 is a simplified example of the network analysis activities across a range of store opening and refurbishment activities. The benefits of the approach can be appreciated when it is considered that large companies may have 20 or 30 projects underway at any one time. The facility to be able to 'bulk' together some of the activities such as merchandise and systems decisions (and possibly staff recruitment — specifically internal staff development) is clearly beneficial. The process also has the major advantage of identifying activities upon which others are dependent and which must be completed prior to the project being able to move towards completion. Figure 10.4 is a detailed network analysis used by Perfect Glass (Walters 1988).

Monitoring and control issues

As with the earlier implementation activities, there are some performance measures that can be usefully applied to monitor and control the activity.

The control decisions are likely to be short, medium and long term in their effectiveness, and relate primarily to store performance indications. These may be to adjust selling areas in the short term; to plan a refurbishment in the medium term, or in the long term to consider new stores and/or store closures.

Therefore, in addition to customer performance measures (which in turn relate to performance of objectives based on critical success factors), we suggest that comparisons be made over time of sales and cost profiles of new, refurbished and existing stores. Topics to be monitored include sales, stockholding costs, occupancy costs, operating costs, distribution costs (together with a comparison of infrastructure utilization, capacity unused and costs). From these

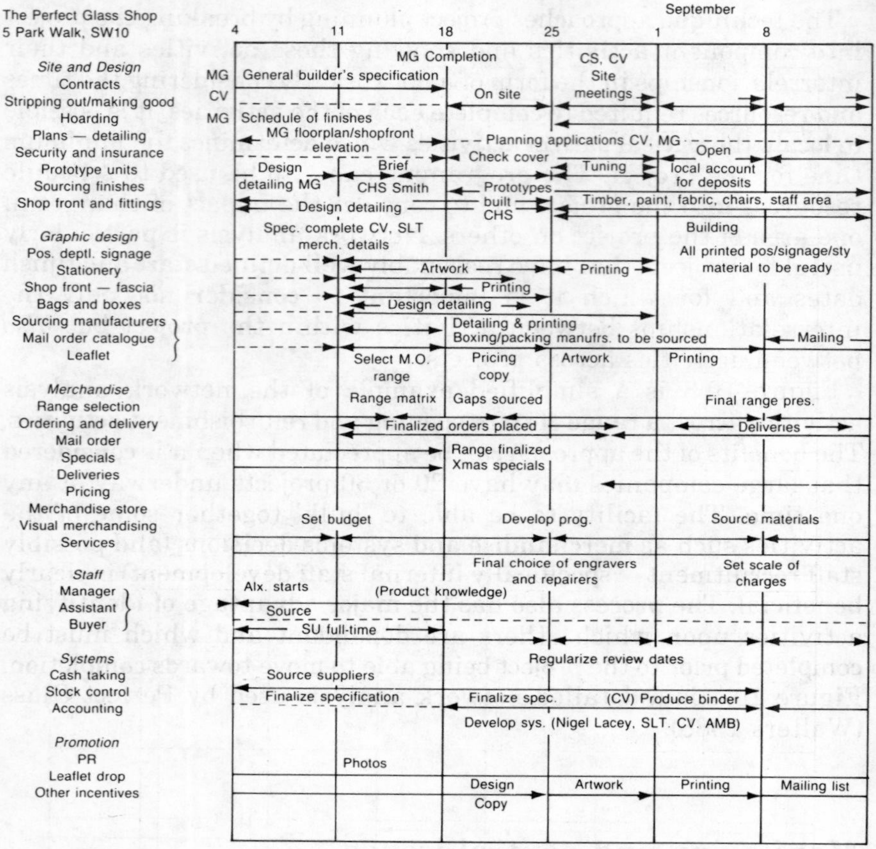

Figure 10.4 *Planning path for opening Perfect Glass*

data a contribution analysis can be produced which will be useful in comparing:

1. Cost-effectiveness (in ROI terms) of the store development undertaken.
2. Extent to which store expansion is putting the infrastructure under pressure.
3. The possible/projected requirement for infrastructure system expansion.
4. The impact on sales and costs of additional stores.
5. The availability to continue to use recycled cash flows to expand the store portfolio.

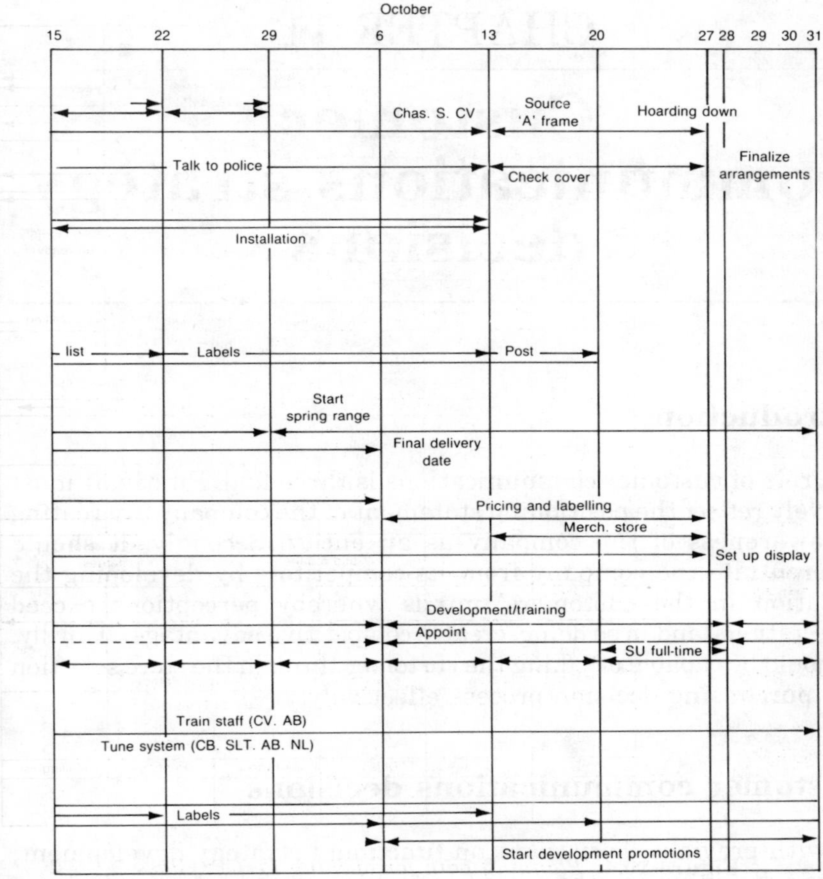

Figure 10.4 *continued*

CHAPTER 11

Customer communications strategy decisions

Introduction

The role of customer communications is three-fold. Firstly, it must actively reflect the positioning statement of the company by creating an awareness of the company as an entity. Secondly, it should differentiate the company from its competitors by developing the situation in the customers' minds whereby perceptions exceed expectations (and in so doing, creates competitive advantage). Thirdly, it should be capable of taking the customer through the store selection and purchasing decision process effectively.

Customer communications decisions

As with previous discussions on functional strategy development, there are two areas to be considered when making communications decisions. These are discussed in Figure 11.1 and comprise marketing considerations and financial considerations. Figure 11.1 offers a framework with which to explore these topics.

Marketing considerations

Customer communications, primarily through advertising, can add emotional values as well as providing the rational reasons that, together with merchandise, format and environment and customer service, create preferential choice, regular visits, high average spend and thereby develops a customer-loyal base.

Recent years have seen the multiples seizing on the opportunity to address specific markets in specific terms and offering specific added-value characteristics. In so doing, they have not *created new*

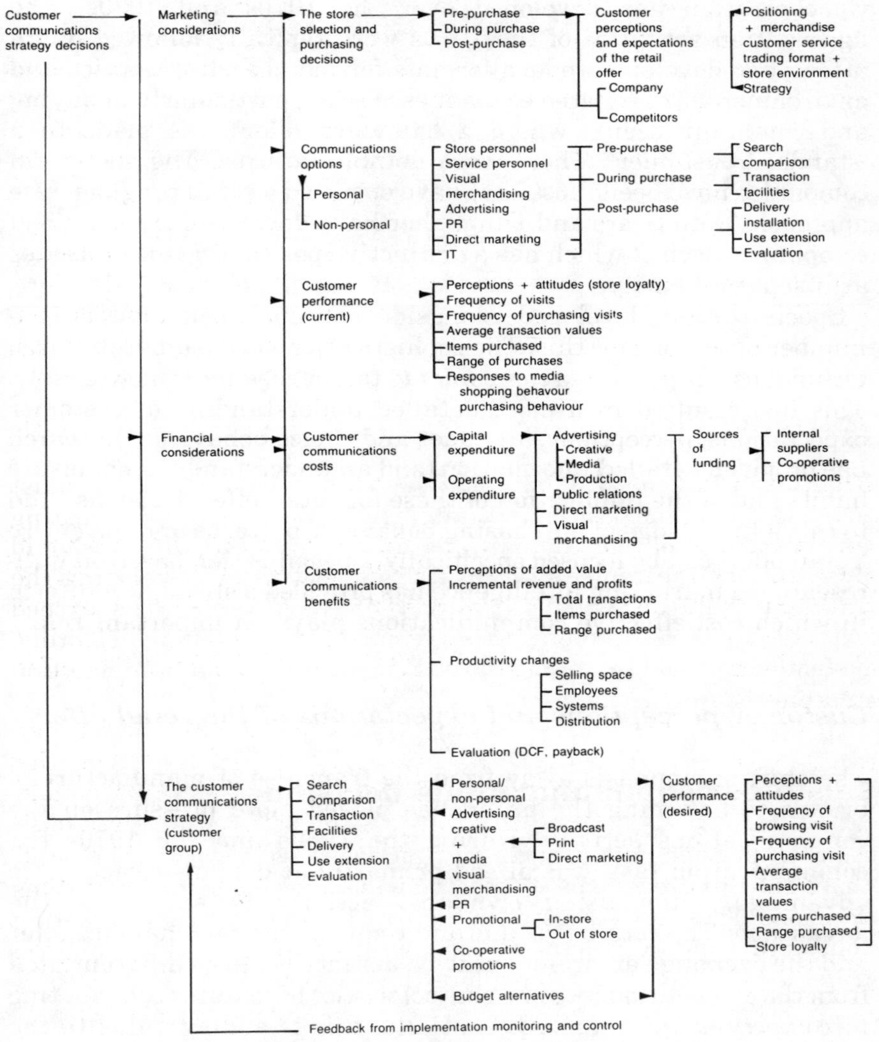

Figure 11.1 *Developing customer communications strategy*

markets and customers, but rather have attracted customers away from competitors' stores.

Central to recent developments is the development of the retail brand. Two structural issues have assisted this: concentration and specialization. A third feature has been the application of marketing research to retail marketing issues with the result that segmentation and customer profiling have become increasingly sophisticated.

Concentration has developed over the 1970s and 1980s. The aggregation activities of the 1970s were typically followed by an attempt to develop standard formats for merchandise, service and environment. This offered economies of scale, particularly in buying and communications, where a 'standard offer' was made to a 'standard customer'. There were notable failures. The successful companies have been those that have operated a retail conglomerate approach. Both Sears and Kingfisher have developed a portfolio of companies, each of which has a distinctive positioning and operates as a separate entity.

Specialization developed alongside concentration. There is a number of reasons for this. The sophistication of consumer research techniques has permitted companies to target customers more closely. This has resulted in a more detailed understanding of customer expectations, perceptions, attitudes and choice behaviour. Research has provided detailed information (and an understanding) on leisure habits and of the implication of these for retail offer decisions. Add to this a knowledge of purchasing behaviour patterns and the entire 'retail offer' can be focused specifically. Specialization based on well-researched marketing intelligence has provided a strategic platform in which cost-effective communications plays an important role.

Customer perceptions and expectations of the retail offer

The shift of emphasis away from the franchise of manufacturers' brands to becoming the brand has placed more pressure on the communications activity. During the 1960s and the 1970s the communication task was aimed primarily at demonstrating price advantage, often using own-label activity to emphasize the advantage. The retailer as a brand requires the merchandise offer and the exchange environment to be distinctive, to be differentiated from the competition by some characteristics or features contributing to *competitive advantage*. Essentially, this is adding value to the customers' perceptions of the overall package and communicating this offer to the customer. Thus the concept of the retail brand expands the role of communications. The benefits to the target customer are those identified by research and combined to create a differentiated offer. This is the basis of the communications task. Often this is easier said than done because many of the benefits sought and offered may be short-term and easily imitated by competitors. Therefore, it is necessary for management to identify long-term customer franchise opportunities and to develop a communications strategy which builds and reinforces an awareness of this with the customer.

This cannot be achieved solely by advertising. If the offer that is advertised is not delivered in-store, then the credibility necessary to establish the 'authority' of the retailer's positioning is never achieved. As an example, consider the communications activities of Sainsbury. The Sainsbury offer has not changed for many years. Their distinctive competence has been used to develop a competitive advantage based on merchandise quality, choice and competitive price within an inviting store environment which enhances the merchandise offer and is supported by knowledgeable and helpful staff. The company continues to improve their positioning by range extension, own-labels and by innovating additional product ranges. Store environments are refurbished and staff training supports these developments. Sainsbury uses four-colour advertisements to communicate these positioning characteristics, which are essentially long-term in their nature, and the advertising reminds customers of the Sainsbury benefits by illustrating how these are transferred into new product and service offers.

We have so far considered the single-brand company. Sainsbury's offer is essentially a single 'product' or end-use offer. Customer targeting is relatively simple, and so too is the task of communications. Much of the communication task can be achieved by a skilful blending of merchandise and store environment through the medium of visual merchandising. Press, television and direct marketing media can be utilized in directing a closely targeted message to the selected customer group to reflect the visual merchandising theme. Because it is a 'single brand' it can be selective and distinctive. Other retail companies that typify this approach are Laura Ashley and, in its early days, Next.

However, multi-brand companies, such as department stores, have problems. It is much more difficult to co-ordinate the 'branding' of a range of product groups or merchandise concepts. This is likely to become increasingly difficult if, as the Henley Centre suggests, segmentation becomes complicated by the fact that people behave differently in different markets and, of increasing importance, there is the need to recognize that these same people behave differently on different occasions within the same market!

This suggests that the multi-concept brand will require a brand theme that identifies those features that have endured. Thus exclusivity, style, quality and choice may prove to be basic positioning characteristics upon which the customer franchise has been built over time. The successful companies are those that identify and blend these characteristics of distinctive competence into a co-ordinated communications strategy. This is difficult to achieve for companies offering a range of merchandise and services, and requires careful research to identify the precise interpretation of exclusivity, style, quality and choice by the customer *across* the company's retail offer.

The fundamental objective of the customer communication strategy is to create favourable attitudes within the target customer group so that they:

- Visit frequently with high average transactions.
- Spend across the range.
- Make return visits.
- Become brand-loyal.

To achieve these tasks the communication strategy should be designed such that it is capable of guiding the customer through the store selection and purchase decision process effectively. This requires detailed knowledge of customers' selection and purchasing processes, together with information concerning their media leisure habits in order to use appropriate media types at relevant reception times with messages that reflect the positioning strategy of the store (in order to reinforce customer empathy), identify needs and wants and offer solutions to consumer problems.

Communications options

The communications task is extremely varied and requires close direction and control. To this end, a clear statement of objectives will be helpful. We have established an overall objective: that is to assist the customer through the store selection and purchasing decision process. This suggests that the communications strategy should be capable of:

1. Creating the awareness of a need.
2. Identifying alternative solutions capable of satisfying the need.
3. Persuading the customer that one particular solution (i.e. that of the company) is most suitable: evaluating the offers.
4. Persuading the customer to make a decision to purchase.
5. Demonstrating alternative product uses.
6. Developing a strong customer franchise such that the customer will consider the company a 'first choice' for related future purchases.

Essentially, communications in retailing comprises either personal or non-personal media. This is not surprising as the majority of transactions are interpersonal activities. The use of technology both to initiate and to complete a transaction remains quite small as a proportion of total transactions. In any event, the most likely strategy will require a flexible approach in its use of media. Not only are customers likely to be at differing stages of the store selection and purchasing decision process, but they will also vary concerning their attitudes towards the store.

Personal communications

Personal contacts and communications have a strong influence on customer attitudes towards a retailing company. Consequently, all members of staff have a responsibility to ensure that their efforts in selling and service roles enhance the image of the company. Often customer perceptions of a company are developed by non-point of sale activities; a chance contact with a helpful service department can be responsible for developing long-term customer relationships. (Equally unhelpful service will result in an opposite effect.)

Thus, the conduct of staff and the content of the 'messages' delivered by them is an important aspect of positioning. It can only be *developed* by all personnel sharing the philosophy that puts customer care uppermost in their minds. It can be *reinforced* by training, but essentially staff must believe in and share an ethos of customer care. It follows then that *all staff* should receive training in customer care and for it to be shown to be important.

An important activity is that of *personal selling* which can range in its influence on the positioning statement from a very high input (e.g. a service lead offer in an exclusive department store) to one of low importance (e.g. a catalogue-based offer). Recent trends have moved towards a reduction of the personal selling content in almost all retail offers. The pressure on operating and occupancy costs has directed even the most service-minded retailers towards reducing the content of personal selling and towards more elements of self-service. Manufacturers have co-operated in this move by offering well-supported (in advertising terms) brands. The emphasis on price competition during the 1970s and early 1980s focused consumer interest on price rather than service-based competition. The return towards service in the second half of the 1980s was difficult for many retailers and, as a result, their attempts to 'motivate' sales staff have been made difficult by:

1. A lack of experienced available staff.
2. Lack of the perception of the role of sales/service.

3. An unwillingness to accept what is perceived as a low-status occupation.
4. Hitherto, the availability of employment opportunity in higher-status, better-paid occupations.
5. Lack of application by salespeople to acquire product knowledge.

There are many other explanations that could be added to this list. It would appear that to create a successful sales activity a number of issues require to be considered:

A 'service' ethic should be promoted by the board such that selling involves:

- Helping customer identify needs and helping them solve them by demonstrating the benefits and attributes of merchandise (and services sold).
- 'Educating' customers in all of the uses and applications of new and existing merchandise (and services).
- Making customers feel that shopping with the company is a pleasant experience, that they are welcome and that their patronage is appreciated, so that they want to return.

Training programmes should be designed to include:

- *Customer buying behaviour processes*: a description of the buying process stages and illustrations of how personal selling can help customers progress through the process.
- *Merchandise knowledge*: application, alternatives, sourcing, purchasing options, competitive offers and merchandise availability and location.
- *Service support facilities*: maintenance, storage, etc.
- *Customer contact*: approaches to customers, asking and using names, identifying their needs, demonstrating solutions and alternatives, asking for the order diplomatically but positively.
- *Customer follow-up*: building a 'data-base', which can be used for subsequent customer contact to ensure satisfaction with purchases and to identify further needs.

Motivation and incentive programmes should offer:

- A facility to progress within the company.
- A means of increasing job satisfaction.
- A means of increasing financial rewards.

Personal selling can have a major role in influencing customer store selection and purchasing decisions, and for this reason it is possibly the most important aspect of customer communication. Its importance is not minimized by the extent or amount of selling activity within the retail offer. The view taken by successful retailers is that everyone in the company has a responsibility to ensure that customers are made to believe that they are the most important person *in that company* – that they are, in fact, part of it.

Non-personal communications

The growth of concentration in retailing and the increase in specialist retailing has required development in the use of non-personal communications. The multiple retailer has both the requirement and the financial ability to use national broadcast (press and electronic) media in developing the business. There is also the increase in competition which both concentration and specialization have brought with them. Therefore, not only does the multiple retailer need to identify ways and means by which the business can be expanded and extended, it must also consider how communications might be used defensively.

The role of communications in extending the business is also significant. The increasing sophistication of information technology, together with decreasing capital and operating costs, offers numerous opportunities to increase both the assortment offer and the geographical range over which the offer may be made available. The work that Kays (the catalogue company) has undertaken in establishing the feasibility of globalizing their catalogue offer such that purchases can be made, using IT, anywhere in continental Europe is an indication of the increasing impact of communications.

There are five major elements of non-personal communications that typically form a major part of the communications mix:

1. Visual merchandising.
2. Advertising.
3. Public relations.
4. Direct marketing.
5. Information technology applications.

Visual merchandising (together with store ambience, store layout and design)

Visual merchandising was discussed in Chapter 9, together with store ambience, store layout and design. We need not repeat that discussion here. However, it must be quite clear to the reader that, together, these four activities should be combined into a powerful communications activity.

They have the advantage of being able to influence the customer in the store, with the benefit that part of the process (i.e. store selection) has been completed. Thus, the emphasis can be placed on progressing the potential customer through the purchasing decision process and eventually into becoming an actual customer. They also have the benefit that, because visual merchandising can reflect life-style issues and present merchandise co-ordinated in combinations that reflect customer purchasing patterns, they are very effective in their role of influencing the purchasing decision at the point of sale.

Advertising

Advertising has been, and remains, a major element in any communications programme. We referred to the role taken by advertising in creating and reinforcing positioning. There has been a change in emphasis over recent years: from an advertising stance of providing product exposure and price comparison — with price being used as the prime reason to generate demand — to a *brand* proposition for the retailer in its own right. Essentially, the role of advertising is the *differentiation of the equally acceptable.* Competition has intensified and, as a result, many outlets offer similar appeal to the consumer. Advertising can emphasize the added value of the offer by adding emotional or theatrical values which, with environment and merchandise, can create preferential choice, regular choice and thereby customer loyalty.

Within the communications task role, advertising can have a number of objectives. The basic requirement is for advertising (indeed, all communications activities) to take customers through the store selection and purchasing decision process such that purchases result and the store becomes adopted in the consumer's choice set. However, underlying this requirement are two basic objectives, which contribute to or facilitate:

1. The creation of awareness of the main institutional positioning factors (exclusivity, variety, availability, competitive pricing) as marketing-led differentiation with a specific customer group.
2. The development of circumstances by which productivity-led differentiation may be increased (e.g. by building volume markets in selected merchandise areas in order that buying margins may be increased or that source markets may be dominated).

Both objectives, if realized, will create a situation or set of circumstances that will influence customer decision-making. Marketing-led differentiation will identify the company's expertise in meeting store selection and purchasing criteria. Within these, productivity-led differentiation will reinforce the competitive price offer.

The purpose and application of advertising will vary according to the needs of the company and we shall return to the detail of these decisions subsequently. Clearly, it is quite possible for two levels of advertising to be running concurrently. In recent years we have seen Sainsbury conducting a corporate campaign aimed at creating awareness for the features of its selected positioning in the market and, at the same time, price-reminder advertising or price-led advertising at volume spending times, i.e. public holidays.

Numerous media options, each having particular strengths and weaknesses, include:

- Press.
- Television.
- Radio.
- Cinema.
- Outdoor (posters, transport, etc.).

Press advertising is used extensively by retailers. It has a number of strengths. One important one is the fact that it offers the user the results of extensive readership research, thereby facilitating selection by readership type or target customer interest. This suggests another advantage — the ability to select media for specific targeting. An example of the effectiveness of press media is illustrated by Tables 11.1, 11.2 and 11.3. Table 11.1 illustrates the readership profiles of a range of magazines read by women. As the table indicates, there is a considerable age difference across the readership, which is important for targeting. Table 11.2 shows social grade differences for the same media. It follows that both age and social grade are important considerations when selecting media to carry an offer message. There are many examples of retail offers with large empathy with some media alternatives and not with others. A high fashion, exclusive, ladies' wear offer, supported by very high levels of service, is more likely to reach a target audience in *Harpers & Queen* or *Vogue* if the customer age and social grade profiles are 15–34, and A, B and some C1. Table 11.3 illustrates a media selection application example. Here attitudes are used, as well as age and social grade. The target group penetration is improved for a number of journals. Typically, production costs are considerably lower than television. However, depending upon the creative strategy, they can be considerable, particularly if colour processes are used.

Press advertising also has the advantage of being able to carry 'long' messages. Unlike television it is 'permanent' and can be read

Table 11.1 Readership profiles – women by age

Estimated percentage of population ages 15+	15–24 (18%)	25–34 (17%)	35–44 (16%)	45–54 (13%)	55–64 (13%)	64+ (22%)
Weekend Colour Magazines						
Sunday	26	19	15	14	11	15
Sunday Express Magazines	12	12	14	17	17	28
You/Mail on Sunday Magazine	23	20	20	14	11	13
Sunday Times Magazine	19	20	22	15	13	11
Observer Magazine	18	22	18	14	13	15
Women's Weekly Magazines						
Bella	27	22	18	11	10	11
Woman	18	23	18	15	11	14
Woman's Own	20	21	17	15	11	15
Best	29	23	17	12	10	8
Hello	26	24	17	16	8	10
Women's Fortnightly Magazines						
More	74	14	10	2	1	—
Women's Monthly Magazines						
Essentials	32	25	17	13	10	4
Company	48	32	11	6	1	2
Cosmopolitan	38	27	16	12	6	1
Prima	26	29	20	12	7	5
Options	32	28	20	10	6	4
19	73	14	8	3	—	2
Harpers & Queen	19	21	22	16	4	9
Vogue	36	17	18	11	9	8

Source: NRS, Jan.–Dec. 1988.

at leisure, and thus complicated aspects of an offer can be explained in detail. It also has the benefit of longevity and as such can be referred to as well as read by a number of different people in different situations.

The weaknesses of press advertising are three-fold. It can be expensive on a cost per 1,000 basis (i.e. the cost of the space divided by 1,000 readership). Table 11.4 illustrates the cost, coverage and cost per 1,000 alternatives when attempting to target A, B and C1 women aged 20–35. The choice depends on what the offer is, and is attempting to do, as well as considering budget constraints. Press advertising has limitations concerning creativity. It is difficult to demonstrate 'offers', particularly the exclusivity of an offer across an extensive range of merchandise, unless, of course, a considerable amount of media space is used, which will prove to be expensive.

Table 11.2 Readership profiles — women by social grade

Estimated percentage of population aged 15+	A (3%)	B (15%)	C1 (23%)	C2 (25%)	D (17%)	E (17%)
Weekend Colour Magazines						
Sunday	1	6	19	32	25	17
Sunday Express Magazine	12	12	14	17	17	28
You/Mail on Sunday Magazine	23	20	20	14	11	13
Sunday Times Magazine	19	20	22	15	13	11
Observer Magazine	18	22	18	14	13	15
Women's Weekly Magazines						
Bella	1	12	22	31	22	11
Woman	3	14	27	28	17	12
Woman's Own	2	13	25	29	18	13
Best	2	11	27	31	20	8
Hello	9	18	32	26	9	6
Women's Fortnightly Magazines						
More	3	21	32	29	10	5
Women's Monthly Magazines						
Essentials	3	17	28	29	17	7
Company	6	22	37	21	11	3
Cosmopolitan	5	21	35	21	13	5
Prima	3	16	29	29	16	7
Options	8	25	32	21	10	4
19	2	16	30	31	18	4
Harpers & Queen	17	27	35	13	6	2
Vogue	8	25	29	21	11	6

Source: NRS, Jan.–Dec. 1988.

Finally, press advertising has long copy dates and cancellation deadlines, particularly for colour.

Television advertising has two major weaknesses. It is an expensive medium with respect to time (advertisement exposure) and production of the advertisement. However, it has considerable strengths. It has high coverage and high impact and permits a wide creative scope. As a medium it can be used to address the audience at specific times of the day and can be designed so that the message and its time of delivery are pertinent to the activities (almost moods) of the audience.

Television advertising has a well-documented history in building brand-awareness. These strengths were used by fast-moving consumer goods manufacturers in the 1950s and 1960s to build large market share and to dominate retailers' buying and stocking decisions.

Table 11.3 A media selection example

Publication	Profile 1 %	Profile 2 %	Index
Cosmopolitan	24.9	21.1	84.7
Company	37.6	35.4	94.1
Essentials	22.1	18.6	84.2
Vogue	20.8	18.9	90.9
Marie Claire	26.4	25.6	97.0
Bella	16.1	13.9	86.3
Options	23.1	19.9	86.1
Woman's Own	13.6	12.0	88.2
Independent Magazine	30.2	21.6	71.5
Woman	15.3	13.3	86.9
Prima	19.8	16.0	80.8
Best	19.7	17.7	89.8
You/Mail on Sunday	16.4	14.8	90.2
Elle	18.2	17.6	96.7
Harpers & Queen	20.8	19.3	92.8
Sunday Times Magazine	21.6	18.8	87.0
Sunday	9.6	8.8	91.7
19	15.5	14.2	91.6
Observer Colour Magazine	19.9	16.8	84.4
More	17.6	15.8	89.9
Sunday Mirror Magazine	7.6	7.4	97.4
Sunday Express Magazine	7.9	7.4	93.7
Hello	23.2	23.2	100.0

Profile 1: All A, B, C1 women aged 20–35.
Universe: 2,730,700.

Profile 2: All A, B, C1 women aged 20–35 who agree with the following statements:
I like to stand out in a crowd.
It is important to me to look well dressed.
I have a very good sense of style.
I like to keep up with the latest fashions.
I really enjoy shopping for clothes.
Universe: 2,359,000.

Source: TGI, 1988/9.

An example of television advertising rates is given in Table 11.5.

Radio advertising has a number of advantages. It offers a rapid build-up of coverage among its audience. It usually does so with immediate results; for example, radio advertising promoting store openings and promotions is usually met with a rapid response. Lead-times for booking radio advertising 'spots' are quite short, with 24 hours not being unusual. Because of its relatively low cost (in comparison with press and television), frequency can be quite high.

Table 11.4 Cost, coverage and cost per thousand against a target of all A, B, C1 women aged 20–35

Publication	Cost full-page colour (£)	Cover %	Cost per thousand (£)
Cosmopolitan	8,100	12.2	24.24
Company	5,040	7.6	24.37
Essentials	8,400	11.4	26.88
Vogue	8,900	10.4	31.24
Marie Claire	4,800	5.6	31.53
Bella	16,500	19.2	31.53
Options	4,950	5.5	32.71
Woman's Own	19,600	19.9	35.98
Independent Magazine	6,300	6.2	36.92
Woman	16,800	16.2	37.98
Prima	16,560	15.9	38.18
Best	18,000	16.5	40.05
You/Mail on Sunday	18,200	16.4	40.57
Elle	5,400	4.7	41.74
Harpers & Queen	4,500	3.7	44.69
Sunday Times Magazine	19,000	15.2	45.75
Sunday	31,000	21.8	52.14
19	4,015	2.8	52.59
Observer Colour Magazine	11,700	7.2	59.88
More	5,060	2.6	71.88
Sunday Mirror Magazine	24,750	12.6	72.15
Sunday Express Magazine	24,640	8.3	108.72
Hello	4,800	1.6	109.34
Universise: 2,730,700			

Source: TGI, 1988/9.

Radio has disadvantages and these are reflected in the low costs. It has low overall coverage, range is limited and it is very local. It therefore has limited appeal, a feature that is further diluted by audience appeal and time of day. For example, a typical audience during the middle of the day would not include AB men, but would favour non-working wives and C2 manual workers.

Table 11.6 illustrates the cost of a similar advertising exposure as to that in Table 11.5 (television campaign). The costs are very much lower, but so too is the cover.

Cinema advertising, like television, has a high impact. It also has the advantages of sound and vision and therefore offers considerable creative scope. It has a major advantage over television in that it does allow specific targeting (cinema audiences can be accurately profiled). It is also exposed to a captive audience.

Table 11.5 Television advertising rates and coverage

Costs, coverage and frequency for a two-month campaign of 1,000 women TVR for a 30-second commercial on independent television in March/April 1990

Area	Cost (£)	Women TVR	Coverage	OTS*
Thames	524,718	1,000	96%	10.4
Central	260,890	1,000	96%	10.4
Granada	164,286	1,000	96%	10.4
Yorkshire	142,800	1,000	96%	10.4
Scottish	69,450	1,000	96%	10.4
HTV	111,900	1,000	96%	10.4
TVS	286,000	1,000	96%	10.4
Anglia	133,600	1,000	96%	10.4
Tyne Tees	61,400	1,000	96%	10.4
Ulster	23,720	1,000	96%	10.4
TSW	53,040	1,000	96%	10.4
Border	10,640	1,000	96%	10.4
Grampian	19,360	1,000	96%	10.4
Total	£1,861,804			

* Opportunities to see.

Table 11.6 Radio advertising rates and coverage

Costs, coverage and frequency for a two-month campaign of 1,000 women GRP for a 30-second commercial on independent local radio in March/April 1990

Area	Cost (£)	Women GRP	Cover	OTH*
Anglia	35,088	1,000	47.6%	21.0
London	97,952	1,000	57.5%	17.4
Midlands	49,744	1,000	52.1%	19.2
N. Ireland	9,280	1,000	54.9%	18.2
North West	43,312	1,000	53.0%	18.9
Scotland	30,544	1,000	61.0%	16.4
Southern	40,128	1,000	48.5%	20.6
Tyne Tees	18,016	1,000	56.6%	17.7
Wales & West	30,000	1,000	47.6%	21.0
Severnside	23,920	1,000	46.7%	21.4
South West	6,080	1,000	51.2%	19.5
Yorkshire	29,296	1,000	48.5%	20.6
Total	£546,400			

* Opportunities to hear.

The disadvantages are its low coverage, resulting from specific targeting, but primarily because of the capacity of cinemas. Cinema advertising costs can be very high (but clearly local services can produce low-cost commercials), and typically advertisements produced for cinema use are not interchangeable with television. Not only do audiences differ, but the technical problems are expensive to resolve.

Outdoor advertising (poster and transport) has the exclusive advantage of being able to reach people who cannot be reached by other media. It has high visual impact and the ability to be focused by region and by type of location. However, 'good' sites are not readily available and there is a lack of reliable research on effectiveness. Outdoor advertising requires regular maintenance and this too can be expensive. Production costs can be very high, depending on the visual impact required of it. Furthermore, because of varying traffic flow speeds and use of transportation facilities, the message content interpreted may differ by location.

Public relations and corporate affairs

There are two aspects of public relations to be considered: a public relations activity, which deals with corporate development issues by encouraging press and television journalists to feature the activity in some depth; and corporate affairs, which could be described as a board concern with environmental and community issues such as the 'green' movement and local employment and leisure facilities in some of the company's less affluent trading areas. We suggest these are different in their initial stages, but clearly both should be featured in communications. However, where it may be required to be frankly commercial, as in the developments of a new merchandise range, it may not be appropriate when becoming involved in local community problems, where there are areas of overlap. For example, a corporate view (and corporate action) over food contamination or over product ingredients or components should be publicized through the public relations activity.

Within the context of customer communications we see a role for both activities. Public relations activities should be used to maintain an ongoing liaison with those sections of the media (and with specific journalists) who have interests related to company developments. For example, developments of a range of convenience recipe dishes should be discussed with magazines in the ABC1 home-making areas, the catering press and the 'executive woman' areas. Developments in children's products should be discussed with editorial staff of women's magazines and educational journals (for toys, etc.). There is clearly a role for public relations in explaining the company's activities and views concerning broader issues and, indeed, advertising can be used to broaden the coverage. For example, Tesco managed the communications activities of its views and development of the availability of unleaded petrol — so much so that the campaign attracted a number of awards. The interesting point about this particular development is that the company appeared more visible in the campaign than did the oil companies.

The role of corporate affairs is particularly relevant in the area of employment, youth problems and problems of depressed areas. While the initial impact of activities to relieve problems of this sort is not commercially motivated, it can have a favourable impact on the 'City Press' pages and with organizations concerned with these issues.

Direct marketing

Increasingly, retailers are using a direct approach to customers. By using customers' personal details (e.g. address, interests, family status), together with details of shopping behaviour (e.g. visiting frequency, purchases made, services used), they can readily profile customer behaviour and identify any specific merchandise offer interests they may have.

The benefits of direct marketing are that they enable the retailer to be very specific with either the targeted customer or the merchandise offer (or both). This eliminates considerable wastage of advertising resources. However, the investment in data-base systems and their operating costs are significant, and care should be taken when investigating their application. A number of factors are worthy of consideration:

1. *The nature of the merchandise*: for frequently changing merchandise the cost of tracking customer purchases, which may not be repeat purchase items, may not be seen as worthwhile in cost/benefit terms.
2. *The value of transactions*: the cost of processing customer purchases, expressed as a proportion of the sale value, may preclude item data capture.
3. *The number of transactions*: huge numbers of transactions are very expensive to process and 'store'. Subsequent processing and structuring for reporting purposes can be equally expensive.
4. *The nature of the customer group*: to be effective the data-base should reflect the shopping patterns of store-loyal customers. In this way their shopping behaviour and their preferences may be established and future responses to offers may be estimated.

Essentially, we suggest that while a customer data-base may be considered to be an important part of the communications process, it should be seen in the context of the investment and operating costs it requires. In turn, these should be considered within the context of the contribution made to achieving overall communications objectives.

The central feature of the data-base is the means by which data are generated. Typically, a store credit card is the vehicle used to generate purchasing and visit activities, but this has limitations in as much as non-purchasing visits are not registered. To combat this problem the premium card approach may be used (see page 171).

The application process can provide considerable information on the background of the customer. Usually, there is little resistance shown by customers as they usually accept the need for such information by companies offering financial services. The type of data that may be collected during the application process may include:

- Age, gender, family status.
- Residential information:
  - — location,
  - — type of residence,
  - — ownership,
  - — length of tenure.
- Occupation and income.
- Other store cards held and credit commitments.
- Shopping preferences.
- Estimated value of purchases.

Use of the card will provide data on:

- Purchasing visits (all visits for premium cards).
- Purchases:
  - — value,
  - — merchandise purchased,
  - — date and time of purchase,
  - — price paid.
- Responses to promotional offers.
- Merchandise returns.
- Payment record (conduct of account, type of account).

Over time, a pattern of responses can be used to construct a campaign, which may be as broad or as narrow as the need requires. Repeat purchasing patterns can be monitored and used for remainder mailings. Increasing sophistication brings the facility for identifying customer preferences for competitors' offers by monitoring patterns of sales against competitor offers (and thereby identifying and evaluating the customers' sensitivity to price or other offers).

Structuring the data on the basis of catchment area zones may also identify specific competitive threats by highlighting merchandise either not sold or for which sales are above company average.

Information technology

The role of information technology (IT) within the merchandise, service and format and environment functions was discussed in earlier chapters. Here the role of IT to facilitate and augment communications is considered.

The role of IT in extending merchandise ranges was considered earlier. Here our concern is with extending the communications activity. This may be done in-store by the use of VCR equipment to 'demonstrate' a range of uses of merchandise, or used in-store to communicate the benefits of merchandise with outdoor applications.

Communicatioins outside the store was referred to earlier. The example of Kay (the catalogue company) using IT to extend its catalogue offer throughout Europe is one application among an expanding range of applications. The particular interest in this example is because IT extends across the store selection and purchasing decision process. The Minitel application in France offers an extensive range of products and services from a large number of manufacturers.

The use of IT in supply chain management should not be overlooked. While this is a form of reverse communications, the IT links can be extended to provide customers with order and transaction details.

Customer performance (current)

Any communications programme requires precise and clear objectives. In the introduction to this chapter they were described as three-fold:

1. To make explicit the 'offer' made by the positioning statement.
2. To differentiate the company such that company perceptions exceed expectations.
3. To 'take' the customer through the store selection and purchasing decision process effectively.

This suggests that where at all possible we should attempt to establish a series of objectives against which to measure the effectiveness of the communications campaign. Figure 11.1 suggests a number of topics against which quantifiable objectives might be established. These, we suggest, could be:

1. *Perceptions and attitudes*: quantitative (scaling) assessment of the relative competitive advantages (or disadvantages) of aspects of the offer:
   (a) merchandise features,
   (b) customer service,
   (c) format and environment characteristics,
   (d) communications effectiveness.
2. *Frequency of visits*: a specified increase in store visits frequencies across the range of customer groups.
3. *Frequency of purchasing visits*: a specified increase in purchasing visits across the range of customer groups.
4. *Average transaction values*: a specified increase in the value of transactions per customer.
5. *Items purchased:* an increase in the number of items purchased per customer transaction.
6. *Range of purchases*: as well as an increase in the number of items purchased per customer transaction, we can (and should) seek to increase the range of customers' purchases from the assortment offered.
7. *Responses to media*: each of the above items is influenced by the type of media (broadly, personal and non-personal) used. Consequently, it is essential that the effectiveness of all media used is evaluated and recorded for future decisions.

This information will be a valuable input into the financial considerations of communications decisions and invaluable if monitored over time. Clearly, the changes occurring in customer performance responses when considered against targeted levels of response (*together with* the activity and expenditure levels of the communications programme) provides a very useful planning and control approach.

Financial considerations

If we consider expenditure on customer communications to be similar to that in any other part of the business, it is not surprising that similar expectations concerning results and budgeting are expressed by the board. There are, however, a number of issues, which, because of the nature of the expected results and the difficulty of correlating results with expenditure, are not clearly defined. The issues to be considered are:

1. *The nature of the expense*: here we should consider issues of investment and operating costs and the treatment of the costs (i.e. capital and revenue charges).
2. *The time issues*: clearly lead-times are important; furthermore they differ. For example, an in-store communication of a promotional offer should have as an objective an immediate response from customers; the response from a corporate positioning campaign is likely to have a long-term impact on customer and consumer attitudes.
3. *The media selection*: we have seen earlier that the availability of media types is considerable, and therefore the selection of appropriate media with which to achieve specific objectives is an important feature of the decision process.
4. *The sources of funds*: we shall discuss the advantages and disadvantages of supplier sponsorship later in this chapter. Here the point we wish to raise is that such funding is usually available to supplement communications budgets; too often they dominate the communications output.
5. *The opportunity costs*: most companies operate in situations within which resources are scarce, thus the allocation of cash to a communications programme will prevent its being used elsewhere. This suggests that communications budgets should be set within the context of overall company objectives and initiatives and includes such considerations as:
6. *The issues of make or buy*: the extent to which a company may create and execute a communications programme itself, in-house, is a function of a number of issues:
   (a) its experience in the area,
   (b) the level of competitive sophistication,
   (c) the level of competitiveness in its markets,
   (d) the availability of advice and service,
   (e) the 'tasks' to be achieved.

   Often, the services of some outside agency may be necessary. For most companies the solution is to 'buy in' the expertise they do not have.

Investment considerations: capital and operating expenditures

Almost twenty-five years ago the question was asked: Does advertising belong in the capital budget? (Dean 1986). Much more recently attention has focused on the balance-sheet treatment of brand names.

In Dean's (1986) article concerning the accounting treatment of advertising, he demonstrates similarities between advertising and promotional expenditures with other business expense items. The thesis of the argument — that advertising is in many ways similar to other business investments – suggests that, provided this expenditure is expected to provide a measurable return in terms of its impact on profitability, a case may be made for considering advertising to be capital expenditure. Consequently, the analysis used to measure capital productivity should be the same as for any other investment. Dean suggests that DCF analysis provides the most appropriate financial yardstick. Accordingly, the criterion for rationing scarce capital among competing investments should be the company's cost of capital, market cost of capital or internal opportunity cost, whichever is the highest.

Financially-determined criteria must be used, together with marketing-based issues. For example, in a rapidly growing market the returns may be very high and the opportunity cost also high. The issue then to be resolved is whether or not all available capital expenditure should be allocated to store expansion, or whether long-term issues of positioning and customer communications should be given consideration. This leads us to the time issues. The nature of some expenditure categories is essentially tactical and will be contributory to the overall performance achievement rather than a major component of it. Consequently, it may be both unrealistic and impractical to consider *all* communications activities as 'capital' expenditure and to use investment appraisal methods to evaluate its efficacy. However, we do suggest that corporate campaigns which reinforce strategic positioning are considered to be items of capital expenditure. Other forms of communication, which are essentially short-term in their desired impact, should be considered as operating expenditure.

While we do not wish to deal at length with the accounting issues that arise, we would suggest that any communications activity, which may be planned for a substantial period of time (and can be linked with an identifiable activity of the business), should be considered to be a capital expense. As such, it may be permissible to consider depreciation of the 'asset' which creates goodwill. Activities seen as candidates for such treatment would include: corporate/strategic positioning, store opening promotion and merchandise launches. The cost of establishing a customer data-base is clearly a capital expenditure.

Operating activities, such as price reminder promotions, revised opening hours, short-term promotions, etc., should, we suggest, be treated as normal business revenue expense. Where possible, the expense incurred should be matched with the activity it supports.

This will provide useful input into the cost-effectiveness of alternative approaches when reviewing performance and planning future activities.

Communications expenditure categories

Ideally, any business activity should be matched with the expense it incurs. Thus, while it may be convenient to aggregate communications expenditure, this is limiting when attempting to evaluate the effectiveness of alternatives.

Obvious categories for initial allocation of costs are the communications activities of advertising, public relations, direct marketing, visual merchandising, etc. But it may also be useful for cost-control purposes to allocate costs to a lower level. Here we suggest that creative, media and production are possible considerations. A breakdown of costs by these activities not only facilitates more effective budgeting, it also identifies for management possible areas of economies of scale in media and print-buying.

Sources of funding

The communications budget may be supported by funds from suppliers. These may vary in the form of the funding. Suppliers may offer to provide co-operative advertising funds and design (usually in the form of standard artwork), or possibly simply the design format. Both offer the retailer lower-cost promotion, but dominate the style, frequency and offer made by the retailer.

Sponsorship of events within the store is a popular alternative. The sponsor will, of course, require a communications ‘presence’, but this is likely to offer more flexibility in the content and management of the activity. Furthermore, sponsorship may be more useful when viewed in the context of customer targeting. An accurate customer profile will identify the relevance of particular merchandise, service and format offers to the customer group. Thus, if a particular sponsor’s offer has specific appeal to the customer group, a convincing communication programme may be built around such sponsorship. Furthermore, if it is exclusive to the retailer, it is likely to be very effective.

Many manufacturers (and suppliers) build promotional allowances into discount structures. Allowances of this type are a reaction to pressure exerted by strong retailer customers. Typically, there are no constraints (other than the volume of purchases) and, again, typically the funds are used to promote the ‘retail brand’ rather than the suppliers’ product specifically.

It is not difficult to see why suppliers may become interested in direct marketing initiatives from retailer customer data-bases. Nor is it difficult to see how this may be managed, as direct marketing offers the facility for exclusive promotions. What may be problematic is the lack of control that suppliers may be offered and the high relative costs of this form of communication.

The attitudes of retailers towards suppliers' funding are mixed. They vary from a level of expectation of promotional allowances for which no specific retailer response will be required to a view that refuses co-operative funding at all costs because of the retailers' desire to maintain independence for communications decisions.

Customer communications benefits

Earlier in this chapter we discussed the range of objectives that may be expected of customer communications. It was suggested that the fundamental objective of customer communication is to create favourable attitudes within the target customer group so that they:

- Visit frequently with high average transactions.
- Spend across the range.
- Make return visits.
- Become brand-loyal.

This is achieved by informing, influencing and reminding the customer base about the retail offer. To do this the strategy should be designed so that it is capable of guiding the customer through the store selection and purchase decision process effectively. From this, we can deduce the need to create customer communications benefits. Some of these may be quantifiable but others may be qualitative.

The qualitative benefits are just as important as the quantitative benefits because they create perceptions of the company in the mind of the consumer, which, it is hoped, create favourable attitudes towards the company when the store selection and purchasing decision process commences. To do this effectively, the communications strategy should aim to convince the consumer that there is added value in the offer being made.

Perceptions of added value

Added value occurs in the mind of the customer when perceptions exceed expectations either of the overall shopping experience or of a specific purchase. An example of this could be said to have occurred concerning the customers' selection of one store in preference to another, or perhaps one product over another, similar alternative. The role of communications is to use the aggregate perceptions of added value (identified by qualitative research) to create competitive advantage. Some examples will help to explain. The 'never knowingly undersold' offer of the John Lewis Partnership is very well known and has created perceptions of a low-price/high-quality offer; often the fact that this offer is available in competitive outlets is overlooked. Thus, perceptions exceed expectations and added value is created. Similarly, communications can create added value for quality, variety and exclusivity. The confidence of the quality of Marks & Spencer products is 'communicated' by their attitude towards customers returning merchandise and their 'well-known' quality standards and supplier monitoring. Both of these attributes have been developed by communications activities.

Incremental revenues and profits

One set of useful quantitative measures can be derived from the critical success factors. If the purpose (directly or indirectly) of a communications activity is to increase revenues and profitability, then the *nature* of this increase may differ in the way in which it might be achieved.

For example, a communications strategy in which *an increase in total transactions* is an objective requires a different approach from one in which the strategy is either to increase *the items purchased* or to increase the *range purchased*.

The strategy to increase total transactions can feature all aspects of the retail offer whereas others require a more selective approach. Furthermore, the differences will extend across media, frequency of communication, as well as the creative approach.

Productivity changes

An additional performance measure may be based on productivity increases, whereby sales per square foot and/or employee reflect the increase in physical and human assets.

More important in this context are the activity level changes experienced in the operating and distribution support systems. The impact of the volume increases following Operation Checkout (the Tesco move out of trading stamps and an introduction of a price offer) is well known. The lessons to be learned from this concern the need to plan for such increases and accommodate the shifts by providing capacity in both activities (operations and distribution).

This issue has both short- and long-term implications. In the example used above, it is likely that the volume increases surprised the company and that both short- and long-term planning was affected. The point we emphasize is that support activities can easily reduce the impact of an expensive communications campaign if they are inadequately prepared. Furthermore, the consumer disappointment that may result from the failure to deliver the offer made may have long-term implications.

Evaluation of alternatives

As with the investment in store format and environment, so too we can evaluate the alternative communication strategies open to the company.

We have seen that the benefits accruing will be both qualitative and quantitative in their nature. However, the qualitative benefits can be quantified. Attitudes and perceptions can be measured using scaling techniques and thus quantitative targets may be set for them. Sales, profit and productivity increases are all readily quantifiable; however, it must be remembered that the temporal links between expenditure and impact should be considered.

Evaluation methods that offer effective appraisal are those discussed in an earlier chapter. The discounted cash flow techniques of net present value and internal rate of return offer the most suitable methods. Both allow the consideration of lagged effects and the long-term impact of 'strategic' communications campaigns. Payback has the problem of being unable to consider the impact of benefits accruing beyond the recovery time of the investment.

The investment, the costs, are capital and revenue in their nature. Capital costs include:

- Agency service charges (advertising and PR)

  Design costs
  Production costs
  Research costs
  Media costs
  } Strategic communications (positioning, etc.)

- Operating costs include:

  Design costs
  Production costs
  Research costs
  Media costs
  } Operational communications (promotional activities)

Two issues concern the treatment of communications costs. We discussed the treatment of costs for accounting purposes earlier in

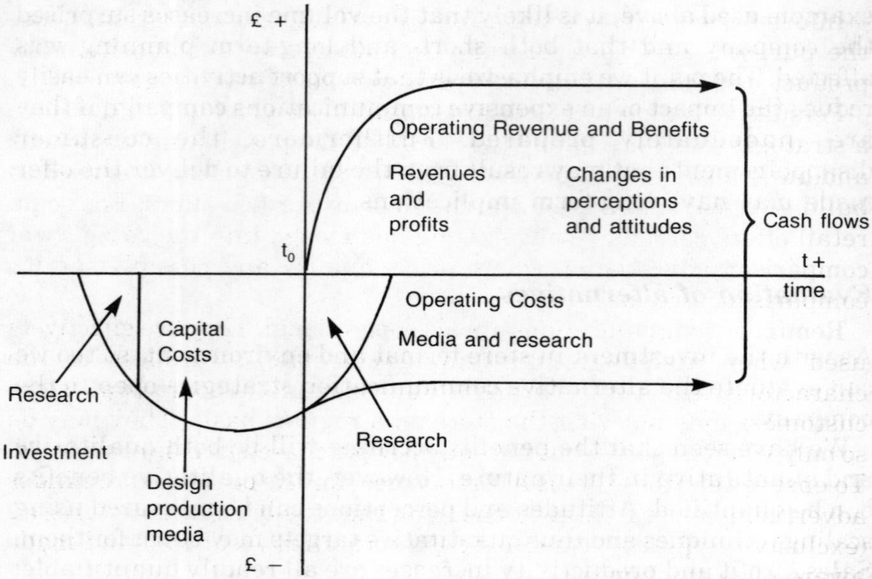

Figure 11.2 *Evaluating communications strategy alternatives*

this chapter. This discussion suggests that the capital costs should be considered as investment costs, while the operating costs should be considered as cash flows for the purpose of investment appraisal of communications alternatives. Figure 11.2 illustrates the suggested procedure.

The communications strategy

To develop the overall strategy for customer communications we should return to Figure 11.1. Three points for attention arise:

1. What it is that is to be accomplished.
2. How this is to be achieved.
3. The costs involved.

What it is that is to be accomplished concerns the objectives of the communications process. We have identified 'performance' criteria which indicate changes in customer perceptions and attitudes, together with store visit and purchasing behaviour seen as desirable. These form a useful basis on which to establish communications objectives. Essentially, the purpose of any communications activity is: to inform, to influence and to remind.

Informative communications may be strategic or operational, and the purposes or objectives vary from 'statements' or positioning, product development or range extension to price changes.

Persuasive communications are typically operational, but can have a strategic role, for example, to reinforce the positioning statement and build a preference for the retail brand. More often it is used to build *selective* demand for merchandise or service offers. For some retail offers persuasive advertising has moved into the category of comparison advertising, where price, quality and possibly service comparisons are made.

Reminder communications are also operational. They are effectively used when aimed at maintaining customer awareness of the characteristics of the 'brand'. For example, department store customers may not visit the store on a regular basis. They may do so only when a specific but infrequently purchased item is considered. To ensure that the store is a 'first choice' for the customer, reminder advertising is used, thereby ensuring that the brand characteristics (exclusivity, quality, choice, etc.) are regularly featured and made aware of to customers.

Each of these objectives has as an overall purpose: to create favourable attitudes within the targeted customer groups so that they:

- Visit frequently with high average transactions spend across the range.
- Make return visits.
- Become brand-loyal.

Earlier in this chapter we identified a range of communications options. Each has particular uses in given application situations. The communications strategy should offer an integrated programme, which is matched to the store selection and purchasing decision process such that it meets the objectives set by the board. Clearly, the strategy will vary with the tasks prescribed by the objectives for each targeted customer group.

The customer groups are likely to vary. One possible classification would be:

1. *The core customer group*: Customers who visit very frequently, have a common customer profile and who spend widely in the store and have very high average transaction values.
2. *Occasional customers in the core customer group*: Customers who have a similar profile to the target customer group, but who use the store less frequently.
3. *Non-customers in the core customer group*: Again these customers have a similar profile, but do not use the store.

Store selection purchasing decision process / *Customer Group*	Core customer group who use the store very frequently		Occasional customers in the core customer group		Non-customers in the core customer group		Occasional customers in peripheral customer groups		Non-customers in peripheral customer groups		Potential customers in related market segments	
	In-store	Ext. to store	In-store	Ext. to store	In-store	Ext. to store	In-store	Ext. to store	In-store	Ext. to store	In-store	Ext. to store
Pre-purchase: Search; Comparison												
During purchase: Product augmentation; Transaction; Facilities												
Post-purchase: Delivery; Installation; Use extension; Evaluation; Repeat visits												

Figure 11.3 *Developing communications strategy by customer group*

4. *Occasional customers in peripheral customer groups*: These are customers who do not form part of the targeted customer group, but who do make some purchasing visits to the store.
5. *Non-customers in peripheral customer groups*: These are potential customers who may become regular customers if changes to the offer were made, which had appeal for them.
6. *Potential customers in related market segments*: These too are of interest. The lack of interest so far may be due to the failure of the retail offer to address their needs. Future developments may prove to be attractive to this group.

Given this approach to the customer opportunities facing the company, the broad direction for a communications strategy may be developed. Figure 11.3 offers a matrix which helps focus the communications requirements at each stage of the store selection and purchase decision process by customer group. Its advantage is that it offers management the facility to focus communications activities (and resources) on both the customer groups and the groups' specific stage in the store selection and purchasing decision process. In the following chapter we shall develop the use of the matrix. However, at this juncture we shall simply suggest that it is helpful in deciding on the direction and emphasis of the communications strategy decisions. For example, the emphasis of any communications activities for the core customer group is likely to be very different from that directed towards non-customers. The former are familiar with the store, visit frequently and spend widely. The communications needs are more likely to be directed towards them when they visit the store rather than to encourage visits. Occasional customers should be encouraged to visit the store more frequently and non-customers encouraged to make an initial visit.

Summary

In this chapter we have identified the elements of the communications process. In addition to this we have discussed the need to develop an integrated communications programme, which can be used to 'move' the customer through the store decision and purchasing process smoothly and effectively.

To do this cost-effectively requires an understanding of the customer profiles of the available customer base. Having ascertained the importance of each group to the growth of the business, it is possible to develop the broad direction of the communications strategy. This is achieved by using the store selection and purchasing decision process model and by considering the suitability of each of the communications options in meeting the overall objectives of the communications activity: to create favourable attitudes within targeted customer groups so that they:

- Visit frequently and make high average purchases across the merchandise range.
- Make frequent return visits.
- Become brand-loyal.

CHAPTER 12

Implementing a customer communications strategy

Introduction

Having considered the role of customer communications in the overall task of positioning the company within the market-place and how communications will address the target customer group, the task of implementation now has to be addressed.

There are eight stages to be considered:

1. A detailed consideration of the strategy.
2. Consideration of campaign planning issues.
3. A review of market dimensions and specific market objectives.
4. Developing the communications objectives for the company and for the branches.
5. Detailing the communications campaign.
6. Campaign pre-testing.
7. Implementation.
8. Monitoring and control issues.

See Figure 12.1.

The customer communications strategy

The previous chapter discussed the process by which the elements and communications options of a communications strategy are combined. The chapter concluded by proposing a planning format which comprised customer groupings and the store selection and purchasing decision process.

We also discussed in somewhat general terms the objectives that communications activities should achieve. In this chapter we develop the strategy so that it may be implemented. Before expanding on the planning format proposed in Figure 11.3, we shall expand on

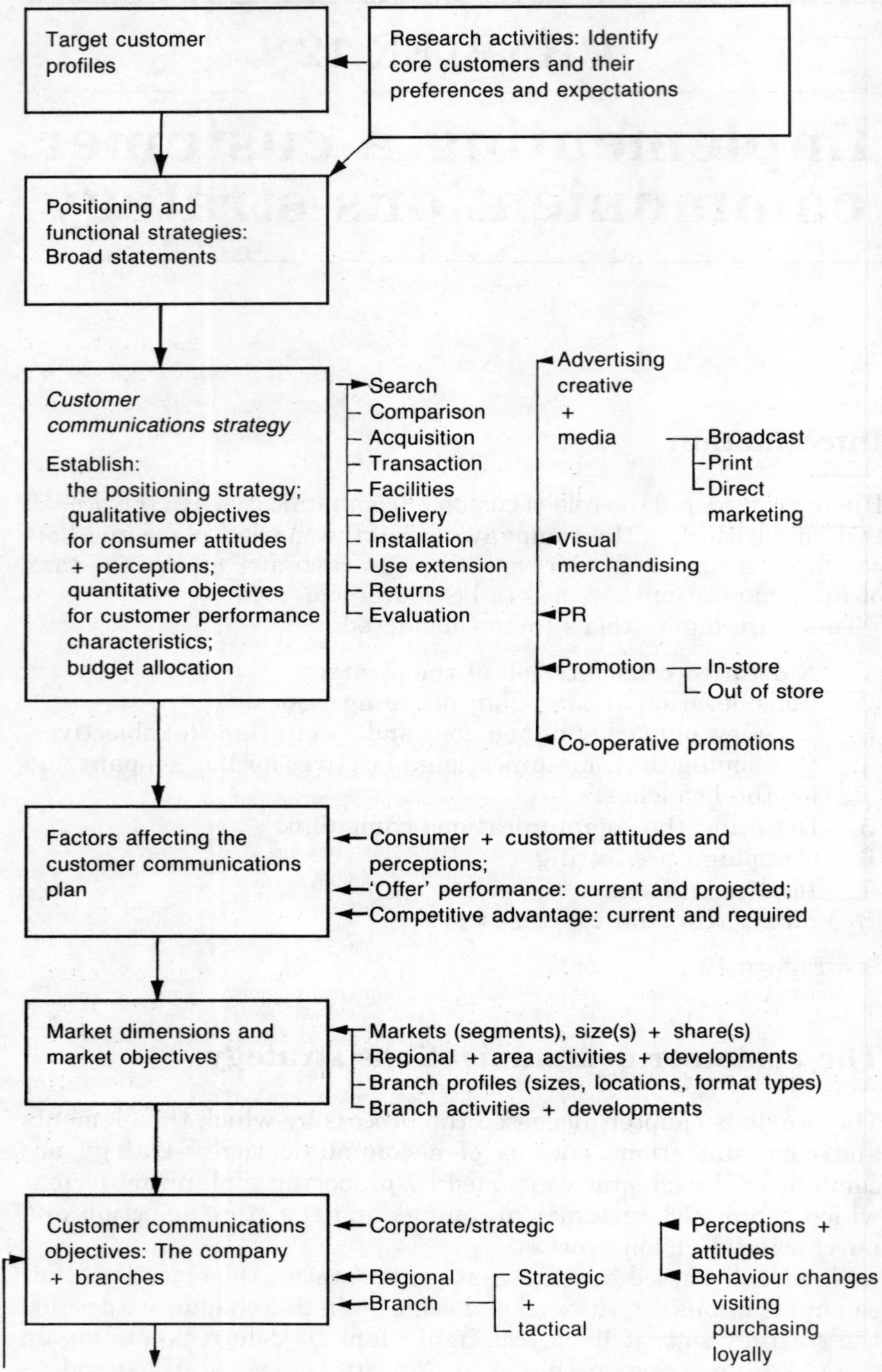

Figure 12.1 *Customer communications: planning and control*

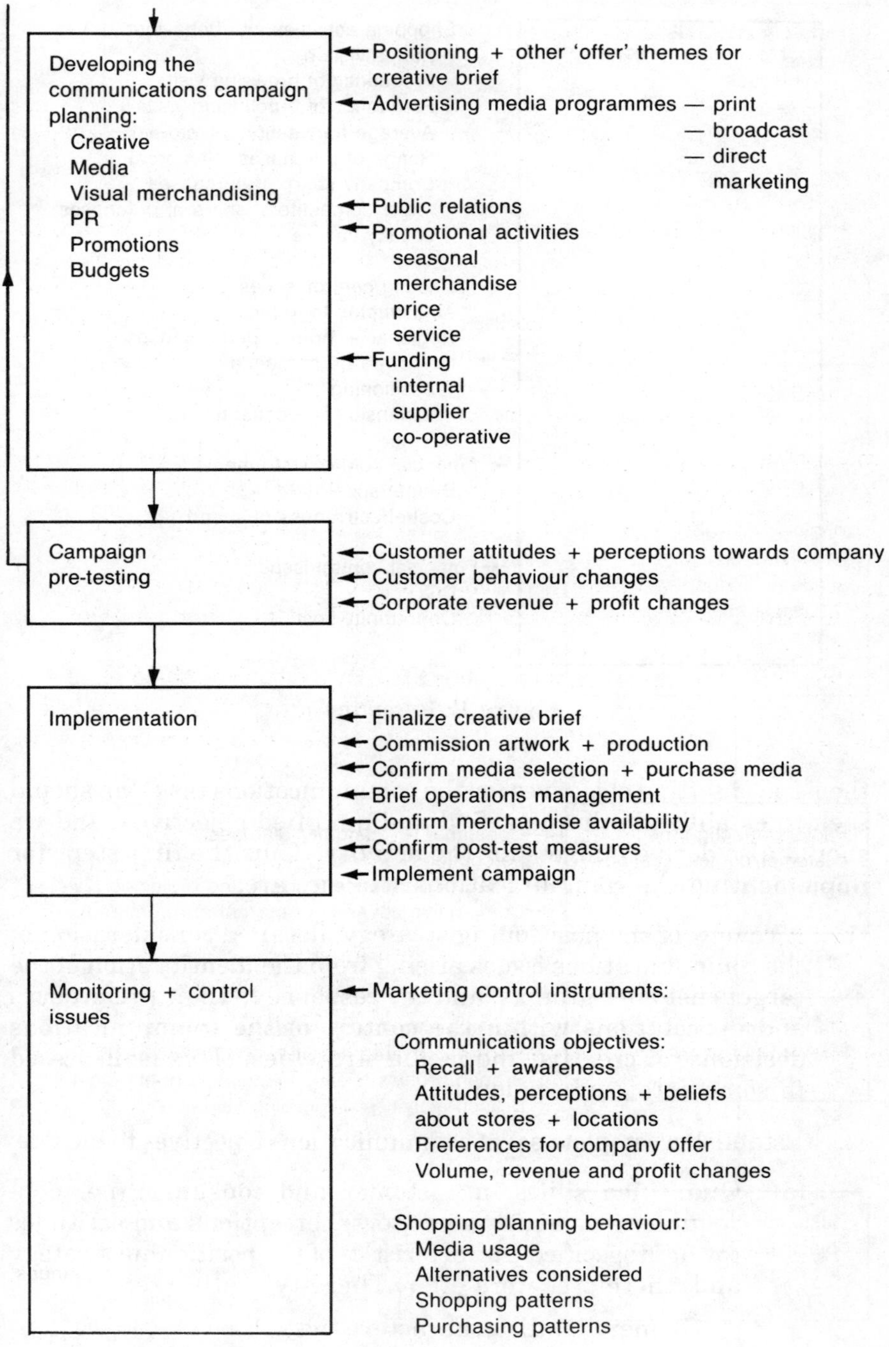

Figure 12.1 *continued overleaf*

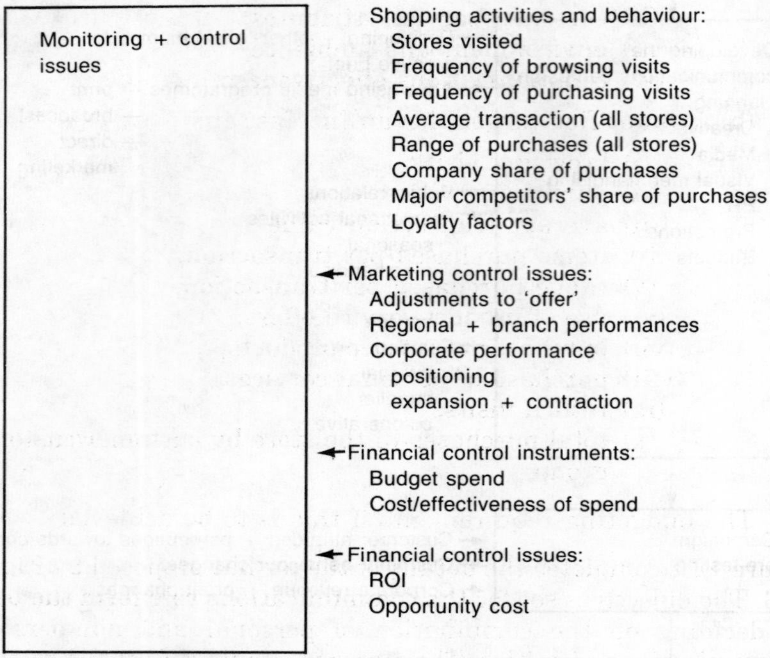

Figure 12.1 *continued*

the issue of setting objectives for the communications task. We should seek to establish both quantified and qualified objectives, and we should also derive budgets for the activity. Thus the first steps for implementing the communications strategy are:

1. A review of the positioning strategy: detailed consideration of the communications issues arising from the identification of the target customer group(s) and the response to their preferences and expectations within the context of the communications decisions for creative and media strategies. (This is disucssed in some detail subsequently.)

2. Establish a complete set of communications objectives to include:

   (a) Quantified shifts in customer and consumer (i.e. non-regular or non-customer users) perceptions and attitudes towards specified characteristics of the positioning strategy and, therefore, store offer. These typically are:

      (i) merchandise characteristics,

(ii) customer service attributes,
(iii) environment and ambience,
(iv) communications effectiveness;

(b) Quantified targets for an increase in:

(i) browsing visits,
(ii) purchasing visits,
(iii) average transaction values,
(iv) items purchased per transaction,
(v) range purchased per transaction,
(vi) use of product-service offers,
(vii) purchases of service-products,
(viii) purchase of personal services,
(ix) return visits,
(x) total purchases in the store by customer/customer group.

3. The budgeting requirements if this is to be achieved.

Figure 12.2 completes the details of the format proposed by Figure 11.3. The objectives set for the communications role form the basis for deciding on the combination of personal and non-personal communications activities. The strategy should reflect the relative importance of each customer group as well as 'tracking' customer and consumer store selection and purchase decision-making processes.

The hypothetical example given in Figure 11.4 assumes that the core customer group is to be the focus of the communications activity. The use of customer personal and shopping behaviour to create a data-base for direct marketing would form the basis of the programme with a strategic campaign designed to strengthen the positioning statement with occasional and non-customer groups. Promotional advertising would be used around high spending times of the year (e.g. Christmas). It would also be used for 'price reminder' and to introduce 'new offers'.

The costs involved in implementing the strategy are broad indications of how the total budget is to be allocated. The budget should be broken down as follows:

- Allocation by customer groups.
- Allocation by customer group activity.
- Allocation of spend between strategic and operational uses.

Figure 12.3 can be helpful in deriving and indicating the budget allocation. A matrix of costs by activities is easily generated and is a useful indication of how the strategy is to be implemented.

Store selection and purchasing decision processes	*Core customer group who use the store very frequently* — In-store	External to store	*Occasional customers in the core customer group* — In-store	External to store	*Non-the group*
Pre-purchase					
Search	Visual merchandising	Direct marketing and	Visual merchandising	Strategic advertising	Strategy with direct
Comparison	Visual merchandising	promotional advertising Public relations	Introductory promotions	Direct marketing Public relatioins	camp public
During purchase					
Product augmentation	Product displays	Promotional advertising	Product displays POS information	Promotional advertising	
Transaction	POS promotion	Direct marketing	POS promotion	Direct marketing	
Facilities	Reminder information		Introductory promotions		
	External to store		*External to store*		
Post-purchase					
Delivery	Delivery information by store liaison staff				
Installation	Operating instructions with store contact number				
Use extension	Direct marketing				
Evaluation	Follow-up call by store liaison staff				
Return visits (store loyalty)	Direct marketing and strategic and operational advertising				

Customers in core customer	*Occasional customers in the peripheral customer group* — In-store	External to store	*Non-customers in peripheral customer groups* — In-store	External to store	*Potential customers in related market segments*
Glc advertising targeted marketing signs	Visual merchandising	Strategic advertising	Strategic advertising		Strategic advertising
Relations	Promotional offers	Direct marketing	Operational advertising		Public relations
		Public relations			
	Visual merchandising		Public relations		
	POS promotion of total store offer at POS points and in facility areas				
	External to store				
	Delivery information by store liaison staff				
	Operating instructions with store contact number				
	Direct marketing				
	Follow-up visit by store liaison staff				
	Direct marketing and strategic advertising				

Figure 12.2 *Developing a customer communications strategy by customer group*

Campaign planning issues

Before campaign planning can be initiated three planning factors should be considered. These are:

1. Consumer and customer attitudes.
2. Offer performance: current and projected.
3. Competitive advantage: current and required.

These are issues that will have been examined during the corporate analysis and strategic planning activities. At this juncture they should be reviewed to ensure that the creative planning for the overall campaign reflects the conclusions of research conducted earlier and strategy decisions developed from it.

Consumer and customer attitudes and perceptions

It is particularly important that attitudes and perceptions of the customer groups discussed in Chapter 11 and featured in Figure 12.2 and Figure 12.3 are ascertained and understood. Specifically, we are interested in the differences that may exist between the core customer group, occasional users of the store and non-users.

Such issues as:

- Who are they?
- Do they differ from users of the competition?
- What does each group perceive the store to be?
- What are their attitudes towards the store?
- What do they expect from the store?
- What is important to satisfy them?
- What are the reasons for becoming store/brand-loyal?
- What are the reasons for rejecting the store offer?

are of concern when developing the communications plan. The answers to these questions should determine the creative and media strategies for the period of the plan. Figure 12.2 suggests how the plan's objectives might be developed and Figure 12.3 how a budget might be allocated. The message content is derived from the answers to these questions.

Offer performance: current and projected

Consumer and customer research (such as that described above) will provide data concerning attitudes and perceptions towards the offer.

Store selection purchasing decision processes / *Customer Groups*	Core customer group who use the store very frequently	Occasional customers in the core customer group	Non-customers in the core customer group	Occasional customers in the peripheral customer groups	Non-customers in peripheral customer groups	Potential customers in related market segments
Per cent of total allocation	35%	20%	10%	15%	6%	15%
Pre-purchase: Search; Comparison	50	60	100	50	100	100
During purchase: Product augmentation; Transaction; Facilities	20	15		20		
Post-purchase Delivery; Installation; Use Extension; Evaluation; Return Visits (Store Loyalty)	30	25		30		
Per cent of total allocation by customer group	100	100	100	100	100	100

Figure 12.3 *Budget allocation for customer communications*

It will identify perceptions of:

- Quality.
- Exclusivity.
- Choice.
- Availability.
- Competitiveness of price.
- Customer services.
- Services facilities.
- Store environment.

It should always be borne in mind that if the consumer perceives that, for example, the 'offer' is comparatively expensive (compared with those of competitors), then it is, for them, expensive. If research proves otherwise, the task of communications is to change the perceptions of the consumer.

The research may identify aspects of the offer that need to be changed, particularly if competitors 'score' highly against the company being researched. The task of communications, then (assuming the changes have been made), is to ensure that the target audience understands that this change (or changes) offers added value.

It is not unusual for the view to be held that advertising's sole task is to generate sales and that in this way the offer performance is enhanced. This is an important role for communications. But, in many instances, the purpose of communications is to create an awareness of changes to the 'offer' from which an increase in sales may then be developed. A moment's reflection on current retail advertising campaigns will confirm this. It is quite usual to see a 'corporate offer' campaign establishing the brand virtues, together with a price reminder campaign to emphasize price competitiveness.

Competitive advantage: current and required

A competitive advantage that is enjoyed by the company should be exploited in the communications plan. In fact, no opportunity should be missed to create an awareness in consumer and customer minds of the benefits offered. The creative strategy and the media strategy decisions should be made such that the communications programme features the competitive advantage features strongly.

Once again, research will identify areas or features of relative strength in comparison to competitors. These should form a major feature of the programme. The John Lewis Partnership price offer was mentioned in this context in the previous chapter. Others of a similar nature include the environmental concern of The Body Shop and the natural product content of the Early Learning Centre, together with the careful merchandise selection that ensures the safety features of their ranges.

Research will also identify emerging issues of consumer concern and preferences for merchandise, service and store environment. These should be developed for the communications programme and increasingly featured as consumer demand intensities. In this way, differentiation is established and reinforced into a strong element of competitive advantage which can prove to be sustainable.

Market dimensions and market objectives

Market segments, sizes and shares

For multiple retailers operating on a national basis, the problem of allocating the communications budget can be complex. Because consumer catchment segments differ in terms of their requirements and expectations, and competitors' strengths vary, the communications decision should consider a number of factors:

1. Regional tasks and preferences that are specific to the catchment.
2. Consumer and customer perceptions of the company and of its competitors.
3. Market shares of company and competitors, and growth rates.
4. Local media constraints.

It is clear that any major differences in one or more of these items requires consideration and treatment for the catchment or region. For example, in a catchment area in which disposable income is below the national average, it is likely that expenditure will be directed towards commodity-based merchandise rather than luxuries, with price featuring strongly in customer requirements. Compare this with a preference for high-added-value items. The need to strengthen market share in a specific catchment may require additional expenditure as well as a different communications approach.

Regional and area activities

Competitors' activities should be considered when deciding on regional communications plans. Often their objectives are quite different, and consequently the frequency, volume and communications messages differ.

It is important to identify these differences. A competitor who is attempting to build a market share may do so with a price-led advertising campaign. This will determine the pattern of local competition and may be in conflict with the plans of the company, possibly requiring a major rethink.

Branch profiles

For the national or regional multiple the profile of local branches is an important influence on communications decisions. We have mentioned earlier the temptation for large multiples to feature their most recently opened store in their advertising. However, if the local branch profile is very different, advertising based around an offer that does not exist locally may alienate customers rather than develop strong links with them.

Branch activities and developments

It follows that a retailer who is expanding (or closing branches) in an area should consider the issues surrounding such activities. The communications plan should reflect branch openings (and closures) and creative approaches and budgets be adjusted accordingly.

It has been known for centrally controlled communications plans to overlook the closure of branches or their relocation. It is wasteful and creates a poor image concerning efficiency in the customers' eyes.

Often specific activities occur that require support. Community fund-raising, local anniversaries and similar activities should be noted and given additional budget and creative treatment. This often improves customer relations by indicating a local empathy with the community.

Customer communications objectives: company and branches

At this point, detailed planning can commence. Clear objectives should be established for both corporate and operational communications.

Research will have established:

1. The number/(proportions) of customers who are:
   (a) the core customer group and who are frequent store users,
   (b) occasional customers in the core customer group,
   (c) non-customers in the target customer group,

   (d) occasional customers in peripheral groups,
   (e) non-customers in peripheral groups,
   (f) potential customers in related market segments.
2. Their attitudes and expectations concerning the company and its outlets.
3. Their attitudes and preferences between the company and its competitors.
4. The reasons for store/brand loyalty among the frequent users.
5. The reasons for rejecting the offer by non-users.

And consequently:

6. The opportunities and problems confronting the merchandise, customer service, store environment and ambience characteristics of the offer and how these are communicated,
7. Specific sales and profit objectives will have been established.
8. The branch opening, closing and refurbishment programme will also have been determined.

Customer communications objectives should be determined on the basis that:

1. Existing customers maintain (or increase) their visiting and spending patterns.
2. Occasional customers become frequent, store-loyal customers.
3. Non-store users and customers in peripheral segments are encouraged to visit the store and make initial transactions.

The extent of this task will determine the initial budget allocation between strategic (or corporate communications) and operational expenditures. It will also determine the creative requirements. Some issues which may influence these decisions are:

Credibility

Any attempt to expand the customer base should consider the reality of the existing offer. Non-store users may not be using the store because of what they perceive to be major deficiencies in the offer. Any attempt to convince them to become customers, without previously making necessary changes to 'correct' the offer, can only be dysfunctional.

The existing customer base

For those frequent customers using the store, the offer is appropriate. Any decision to make changes to the offer and subsequently to promote a 'different' retail offer may result in a feeling of disenfranchisement on the part of the existing customers. This may persuade them to switch to more appropriate offers of competitors.

A sales and profit forecast exists

The communications programme is required to be effective in contributing towards the company's efforts to achieve its sales and profit objectives. Consequently, the allocation of communications effort must be made such that these objectives are achieved. The allocation between strategic and operational expenditures should, therefore, be made with this basic objective in mind.

Regional and branch activities

The multiple retailer has the additional factors of regional and branch developments to consider. Quite often local competition requires specific attention. When making decisions concerning local needs, the overall direction and style of the corporate communications strategy should be considered. For example, price-led advertisements aimed at local competition should be designed to be compatible with an overall company advertising format. In this way, the long-term continuity of the communications activity is maintained.

The characteristics of competitive advantage should be featured wherever and whenever it is possible.

Communications campaign planning

The importance of a customer profile

In Chapter 4 we discussed the importance of market positioning strategy and the need for research to establish customer profiles within alternative segments. Often research will indicate changes that are likely to have major implications for retail offer formats. For example, changes in commuter travel facilities can change the structure of catchment areas.

Recently, one such study (by the authors) showed: 'A new level of *affluence*, higher than the average for the region, and concentrated in the 25–44 age groups (which now accounted for over 50% of the catchment total).' *Anti-functional trends* were noticed among a major sector of the catchment population. Those of interest to retail format design were trends towards:

1. *New romanticism*: the desire to restore romance, mystery and adventure to their lives.
2. *Novelty and change*: the search for constant change, new experiences, reaction against 'sameness' and habit.
3. *Adding beauty to one's daily surroundings*: the stress on beauty in the home and the things people do and buy to achieve it.
4. *Sensuousness*: by placing greater emphasis on a total sensory experience — touching, feeling, smelling; moving away from the linear, logical and visual approaches commonly used.

The customer profile that emerged from the research was identified as:

1. Above-average earnings, from skilled and/or managerial occupations.
2. Age range 25–44.
3. Both male and female and probably married.
4. Aspiring to be 'a little different' in terms of dress and how they furnish their homes. Both are seen as an expression of their personality.
5. Own their own homes.
6. Less concerned with price than with value, expressed as quality, exclusivity, style, rather than 'current fashion' in terms of both merchandise and the store environment from which it is purchased.
7. Remains 'store-loyal' provided expectations are met.
8. Reads quality press and magazines, limited televison viewing, appreciates personal communications.

The expectations of the customer group were for:

1. Store format and environment: modern, bright and nonconformist. Merchandise groups should be presented in a related fashion.
2. Full range of financial services: store credit, major credit cards.
3. Free delivery service operated to meet customers' convenience — not that of the distribution company.
4. Design, advisory and installation service for room interiors.
5. Maintenance service for appropriate products.
6. Staff with extensive product knowledge motivated to help and advise customers.
7. High quality, unique merchandise constantly changing, but with a level of continuity where required, e.g. glass, china and lighting.
8. Wide ranges capable of cross-merchandise group co-ordination

to achieve a 'total' look; lampshades to match curtains and/or wall coverings and/or curtains, etc.
9. Easy access to store with ample car parking.
10. Preview evenings for new merchandise ranges.

The positioning statement addressed these requirements:

> A department store with appeal to the discerning customer who seeks to be an individual and to demonstrate this individuality in their clothes, their homes and their leisure pursuits. They are likely to be in well-paid occupations. They enjoy shopping in stores which offer them exclusive, quality and co-ordinated merchandise presented in a store environment in which the visual merchandising offers ideas for co-ordination of styles and colours. Our offer must be both unique and extensive to ensure their desire for exclusivity, choice and co-ordination is met. And we must support this offer with an extensive portfolio of services to meet with their needs.

Media decisions

Against such a brief it is possible to plan a communications campaign. Assuming the merchandise, customer service and store environment decisions reflect the interests and requirements for the target customer group's store selection and purchasing process, the communications decisions can be supportive.

From the customer profile and expectations the approach to *media decisions* can follow the process suggested by Figure 12.2. The research suggests that once in the store, the customer is likely to be influenced considerably by visual merchandising which appeals to their attraction towards 'romanticism', 'novelty and change' and 'adding beauty to daily surroundings'.

The use of direct marketing will play an important role. The research suggests that relevant and informative mailings are received favourably and actually are read.

The use of newspapers and journals is problematic. It is unlikely that many of the options available could be justified in terms of cost-effectiveness. This decision would be influenced by the number and location of branches. A small business with few outlets is very unlikely to find media that it can afford.

The use of television has similar problems. The advantage it has is its ability to 'demonstrate' the ambience of the store environment and local media time rates (in some areas) are low enough for them to be considered.

Two major decisions confront media planners. How much do we spend and how often should the advertising appear? There is a considerable literature which has developed around the budgeting decision, much of which concludes that the most effective budgeting is that based on what the task is that is to be achieved, and is conditioned by what the company can afford.

The critical success factors can be helpful. The company can ascertain targets for its customer flow and average transaction per customer. It can estimate similar data for major competitors. From the two sets of information it can establish a realistic value for both customer visit frequency and their purchases. The pattern of visits can be ascertained for each customer group (see Figures 12.2 and 12.3) and the days of the week when high-density customer flows occur are also readily identified.

Thus, with sales, visit frequency and average transactions, together with costs, the level of activity required in order that sales budgets may be achieved can be estimated.

The impact of communications on attitudes and perceptions (which when changed will convert non-customers into customers and reinforce the favourable attitudes of the loyal customers) is more difficult to estimate. Here we suggest the use of tracking studies which monitor the *overall* shifts of attitudes and perceptions towards retailing generally; the *relative measures* among competitors with similar offers; and *specific* monitoring of customer/consumer attitudes towards the company. Based on the amount of movement achieved and the time taken to achieve the shift so the amount and frequency of spend (and the media used) can be adjusted.

Public relations activities can also be very effective for a proposition with this type of consumer offer. Perfect Glass was a similar venture. It was launched by using public relations exclusively. The interest generated in magazines in which the company could not afford to buy space was considerable (Walters 1988).

Promotional activities and themes require pre-planning. Within the context of the example above, any promotional activities should be considered against the background of the positioning strategy. The merchandise strategy will include frequent changes (customer expectation) and price is not a major merchandise characteristic. In such a situation the role of the promotion should be to focus on seasonal requirements, e.g. Christmas gifts, at relevant times of the year. The fact that merchandise co-ordination and exclusivity are major features of the offer, then these, together with frequent changes of the merchandise offer, will (or should) maintain a high level of customer flow.

For many retailers the annual (or bi-annual) sale becomes an indulgence for the customer. The Harrods sale, possibly the world's best-known, is in many ways an indulgence for the customers, many of whom plan their holiday activities around it. Furthermore, for the large store (and store groups) it can create considerable public relations activity.

However, the total costs of sales are invariably never included in the communications budget. Many costs, such as buyers' searching time and management time used for planning and co-ordinating the sale activity, are difficult to isolate and typically they are absorbed into other activities.

In more general terms the 'sale' and other promotional activities should be considered against the positioning strategy of the retail company. For a company that offers exclusivity and quality for eleven months of the year, supported by an appropriate store environment and customer service, the decision to move away from that offer, albeit for a short time, cannot or should not be taken without considerable debate within the company.

Issues that arise from funding offers and alternatives were discussed in Chapter 11. Care should be taken when accepting supplier funding, that it is not:

- A broadcast offer which is taken up by all of one's competitors.
- Totally controlled by the supplier or influenced to an unacceptable extent.
- Disruptive to the 'style' of the company and consequently confusing to the customer.

Campaign pre- and post-testing

Prior to making large commitments for communications, a campaign should be tested. If the design of the campaign has been influenced by research, then much of its contents, certainly its logic, should be correct. However, it is not unusual for there to be two or three alternative approaches and therefore pre-testing can be useful.

Pre-testing methods to identify likely effectiveness comprise:

1. *Direct ratings*: A panel of consumers (matched to the target customer profile) are exposed to alternative advertisements (or other forms of communication such as visual merchandising formats) and asked to give a view on which would have most influence on their store selection and purchasing decision. Alternatively, a form of scaling may be used which attempts to evaluate the communication's:
   (a) attention gaining,
   (b) retention strength,
   (c) cognitive strength,

(d) affective strength,
(e) motivating strength.

2. *Portfolio testing*: Again, a structured panel of consumers is used. This test requires them to consider a number of advertisements (or communications). They are asked to recall the material, together with its message content. The results indicate its prominence and its ability to be understood and remembered.
3. *Laboratory tests*: Some advertisers use psychological measures. These tests measure the 'attention-getting' strengths of the communication by measuring changes in heartbeat, blood pressure, pupil dilation and perspiration. While effective for measuring attention-getting, these tests do little to predict intentions or to measure attitudes or perceptions.

Pre-testing can be useful in avoiding wasteful expenditure. It can also be helpful in testing retail concepts which are often the basis of a communications campaign. The purpose of pre-testing is to ensure that the campaign will be as effective as it is possible to be in maintaining (or changing) attitudes and perceptions towards the company. Two issues must determine the eventual content of the campaign: credibility and viability.

Credibility has two considerations. The first concerns the offer made by the communications compared with the reality of the offered that is actually delivered. The second concern is with perceptions and expectations, particularly those of the targeted customer groups. These should be congruent or, better still, perceptions should exceed expectations. There is no credibility to be gained from making *assumptions* concerning consumer expectations; they must be *determined by research*.

Viability also has two considerations. Firstly, the planned offer must be viable in terms of sourcing, presentation and availability. Secondly, it must be commercially viable. The largest problem experienced by niched or focused retailers is that they offer a very narrow range of merchandise. Consequently, unless customer purchasing visit frequencies are very high, the low average transaction values restrict the achievement of revenue and profit targets.

Corporate revenue and profit changes are useful measures to include in the pre-testing stage. The results of pre-testing can be expressed quantitatively as customer visits and transactions, which in turn can be developed as total corporate revenue and profit forecasts. These, when compared with the required performance levels for revenue and profitability, are a positive measure of the likely success of the communications programme.

Implementation

Communications production

The research results from pre-testing exercises will be important inputs in the final decisions concerning creative and media strategy.

Once agreed, artwork should be commissioned and put into production. At all times the agents producing the creative work should be closely monitored. This will ensure that the brief is adhered to rigidly and that no short-cuts are taken.

Media selection and purchasing should be similarly monitored; no substitutions of time, frequency or media (journals, etc.) should be made unless the options are considered against the objectives of the campaign.

A briefing document for all members of staff should be prepared. This should explain the logic of the creative aspects of the campaign and the media selected (and frequencies of use) made known. This action will keep all members of staff both informed *and involved.*

Implications for operations management

It is important that all support activities are well briefed concerning the extent and content of the communications campaign. However, it is vital that operations management are given detailed briefing of the campaign because it is their responsibility to ensure that the total offer is delivered. Hence, they require to know the detail of the campaign to ensure that:

1. Merchandise is available to meet demand, at advertised prices, in all locations.
2. Store environment and design reflect communications themes.
3. Staff are aware of the communication objectives and of the demands placed upon them as part of the delivery process.

Lack of attention to such detail can result in a communications campaign failing. Poor or no availability of merchandise can result in disaffected customers, and attempts to convert non-customers into regular customers may easily fail.

Confirm post-test measures

Prior to commencing the campaign the methods and measurement of results should be clearly established. Furthermore, the frequency of testing should be set so that changes to the campaign can be considered at appropriate times.

The measures may be both qualitative and quantitative.

Attitudes and perceptions are essentially qualitative and they should be monitored against criteria established during the period of campaign planning. They should attempt to measure attitudes and perception changes for each customer group. For example, among the core customer group, which visits and purchases frequently, the objectives should be for their attitudes to remain positive concerning the core issues of the proposition. Possibly, they should show some increases.

However, the less frequent and less loyal users should be expected to show larger and more positive shifts in attitudes if the communications campaign is proving to be successful. The attitudes and perceptions of both regular and non-regular users should be measured against the basic features of the offer, e.g. merchandise, customer service, environment, etc.

Quantitative targets should be established to show an increase in browsing and shopping visits; transaction values and items purchased; return visits and total store purchases.

With these considerations in place the campaign can be implemented.

Monitoring and control issues

The issues here are similar to these discussed in previous implementation chapters. They comprise: marketing control instruments and issues; and financial control instruments and issues.

Marketing control instruments

Here our concern is with:

1. Communications objectives.
2. Shopping planning behaviour.
3. Shopping activities and behaviour.

Communications objectives

While the basic objectives are to achieve changes in attitudes, perceptions and beliefs (and these have been discussed extensively in this and the previous chapter), the objectives should be made specific in terms of:

1. Retail offers generally.
2. Retail offers of competitors.
3. The company's offer and preferences that exist.
4. Time-periods over which the shifts should occur and the extent of the shifts.

However, the objectives should include a measure of the effectiveness of the creative and media strategies used in the communications programme. To this end post-testing measures should include measures of *recall* and *recognition*.

Recall tests are conducted among a structured sample who have been exposed to the media used. They are asked to describe anything remembered concerning companies, products, services, etc. The recall scores indicate the ability of the communications to be noticed and remembered.

Recognition tests are used to develop readership scores (starch scores, named after Daniel Starch). These are:

1. *Noted*: the percentage of readers who have previously seen the advertisement.
2. *Seen/associated*: the percentage who correctly identified offer and advertiser with the advertisement.
3. *Read most*: the percentage who way they read more than half of the written material.

Both tests (and there are others that may be used) are an indication of the *effectiveness* of the campaign. Furthermore, increases in volumes, revenues and profits are sought, together with market share shifts, to indicate the marketing and financial effectiveness of communications.

Shopping planning behaviour

The impact of the company's communications strategy on the store selection and purchase decision process should be monitored frequently. As we have suggested during the earlier discussion, the purpose of the communications activity is to progress customers through this activity so that they ultimately consider the retail company to be the 'first choice company'.

Thus, the media used to reach store selection and purchasing decisions, together with the consumer/customer appraisal of alternatives, should form part of the monitoring process.

Furthermore, the resultant shopping and purchasing patterns should also be monitored. For example, an increase in customer response to direct marketing activities should suggest an increase in the communications activity in this area.

Shopping activities and behaviour

Actual behaviour is the input for modifying the communications strategy and revising future planning.

A diary study or omnibus research can provide information on essential elements of shopping activities and behaviour. Diary studies can offer a useful approach. By structuring the sample to reflect the composition of the customer groups (users, non-users, etc.) a range of information can be obtained concerning shopping behaviour and other relevant topics. The data should include:

- Age and family situation, residence details, etc.
- Socio-economic group.
- Leisure interests.
- Media interests and uses.
- Stores visited for browsing and for purchasing.
- Stores purchased from.
- Frequency of browsing shopping visits.
- Frequency of purchasing shopping visits.
- Average transaction (all stores).
- Range of purchases (all stores).
- Allocation of purchases (company + competitors).

From this information a comprehensive consumer/customer profile can be constructed; it also provides invaluable input to communications planning and control.

Marketing control issues

The performance of the company, its customers' shopping behaviour and customer response to communications can prove to be invaluable for a number of key decision areas:

1. Adjustments to merchandise, customer service and store environment will be indicated by on-going research.
2. Regional and branch performance differences may be able to be explained within the context of customer responses (and attitudes) to communications.

3. Comparison of consumer/customer relative attitudes and perceptions may indicate the need to shift the company's positioning such that a more appropriate (and competitive) response may be developed and communicated.

Financial control instruments

The effective financial control instrument is the budget. Provided that the budget has been developed on a sound basis, and that it reflects all of the communications activities and identifies the executive responsibilities of management, the budget remains a very effective monitoring device.

The effectiveness of the budget should be measured by comparing the amount of expenditure with the qualitative and quantitative results achieved.

Financial control issues

Advertising expenditure competes with other aspects of corporate investment. The board must consider each allocation of resources as an opportunity cost basis. For example, it must decide whether an amount invested in communications is likely to achieve the same (or a better result) as the same investment in increasing the outlet base, or investment in merchandise or customer service.

For this reason we suggested that an investment appraisal process be developed which identifies the efficacy of a communications, location (or some other) investment. It also facilitates the choice *between* investment alternatives. In this way, at least some of the irrational influences may be taken out of communications budgeting decisions.

Summary

This chapter has considered the issues involved in implementing communications strategy. We have discussed the issues that are involved in creating strategy.

The need for a clearly identified positioning strategy, together with an understanding of the implications for communications decisions, is a primary requirement, together with qualitative and quantitative objectives with which to monitor the success of the strategy.

Budgets are an essential feature of the activity. They provide a check on overall expenditure, together with a measure of cost-effectiveness of each component activity.

A crucial input is qualitative and quantitative research on customer attitudes, perceptions and behaviour. A number of alternatives are suggested, such as tracking studies and consumer diary studies.

Communications like any other corporate expenditure competes for scarce resources. To this end conventional investment appraisal methods offer a means by which 'opportunity cost' can be evaluated and alternative expenditure can be decided.

APPENDICES

Case Studies

The following case studies have been written with a number of teaching purposes in mind. They can be used to demonstrate both strategic and operational issues confronting retail marketing management.

At a strategic level they present students with an opportunity to consider the broad issues around which the companies were making decisions concerning the business situations facing them. The questions raised at the end of each of the case studies can be used as a guide for this purpose.

Given more time, the case studies may also be used to investigate the interface between *developing* retail marketing strategy and its *implementation*. This, we suggest, may be achieved either by observation (visiting stores) — where the students are encouraged to use the issues raised in the text as a basis for observing the 'practices' of the case study companies. Alternatively, the case study questions can be posed to students such that they use the text to question the decisions made by the companies. Clearly, both approaches can benefit from observation which offers the student an opportunity to develop a view concerning effective management of retail marketing.

CASE STUDY 1

Betty's

Introduction

In many ways Betty's is a throwback to the 1920s/1930s, the time of the classic English tea room, e.g. J. Lyons Corner House, Fullers Tea Shops. Betty's was started by a young Swiss confectioner, Frederick Belmont. Travelling in England soon after the First World War, he settled in North Yorkshire where the 'air seemed as clear and sweet as his native Alps', and he opened his first Tea Rooms and Cake Shop in Harrogate in 1919. The Tea Rooms quickly became established due to a natural Swiss flair for hospitality combined with excellent tea and mouth-watering cakes.

Mr Belmont saw Betty's as a place to meet, where ladies could enjoy a cup of tea and civilized conversation. To add to the atmosphere and enjoyment of the occasion, a café orchestra was employed to play the appropriate tunes of the day. The business prospered, but it was not until the mid-1930s that a further Tea Room was opened in York. This was quickly followed by the opening of two further outlets in Ilkley and Northallerton. There has been no further expansion in terms of the number of shops and the family business today (1990; run by descendants of Frederick Belmont) is still conducted from the original four outlets. In the late 1980s, each of the four towns in which Betty's trade portrays an image of being traditionally Yorkshire county/spa towns.

Company philosophy

The statements attributed to the founder summarize Betty's philosophy — 'fresh and dainty' and 'if we want things right, we have to make them ourselves'. From the outset, great attention was paid to detail, in the spotlessly clean and neatly designed Tea Rooms and in the quality both of the tea and cakes and courteous service. To guarantee the quality of the cakes and patisseries sold in the Tea Rooms, Frederick Belmont opened a bakery above the Harrogate café. In 1922 the bakery moved to larger premises in Starbeck, Harrogate, where it is today still supplying on a daily basis the merchandise sold in all four outlets, using a fleet of company-owned delivery vans. Sixty staff work in the bakery to produce over 400 different product lines. All Betty's bakers and confectioners are sent to train at the world-renowned Richemont College in Lucerne, Switzerland.

The company is rightly proud of its training record throughout its staff and this has been recognized by the receipt of national training awards and entries in both the Good Food Guide and Egon Ronay's *Just a Bite* Guide.

The Betty's experience

On entering a Betty's Tea Room, it is possible that a customer will be asked to wait in a queue, especially at peak lunch times (11.30 a.m.–2.30 p.m.). Certainly on entry there is a notice asking customers to wait by an appropriate sign until welcomed and seated by the seater. Customers are not allowed to occupy a table until it has been cleared, cleaned and reset, and are asked whether they wish to sit in the smoking or non-smoking area. Table decor is white linen, fresh flowers and three menus contained in a specially designed holder. Orders are promptly noted by a smartly dressed waitress on a traditional order pad. Wherever possible, all items are made to order and are politely and correctly served with tasteful crockery, cutlery and napkins. At an appropriate time, customers are asked if they have any further orders and, when requested, are given a bill, which is paid at the cash desk at the exit.

Atmosphere

The designed atmosphere is one of quietly refined elegance and gentility. Customers are not pressured or rushed, and are served by well-trained, polite and immaculately turned-out staff wearing traditional black and white uniforms. At correct times customers are addressed as 'Sir' or 'Madam'. Newspapers (e.g. *The Times, Guardian, Independent* and *Yorkshire Post*) fixed to reading sticks are available. Café concerts are performed every evening 6.30 p.m.–9.00 p.m. at Harrogate; most evenings, 6.00 p.m.–9.00 p.m. at York; and normally daily at Ilkley. Customers are encouraged to make their views and comments known in the Suggestions Book for, as Betty's acknowledge, 'our best ideas have come from our customers'.

Generally, the atmosphere is the antithesis to that experienced in a fast-food restaurant.

All of the cafés are open seven days a week and on most bank holidays.

Product range

As seen from the menu (Annexes 1.1–1.3 inclusive) a range of teas, coffees, hot drinks, juices, toasts, tea breads, sandwiches and cakes is offered. Specifically to meet the needs of the lunchtime trade, there is also on offer starters, hot dishes, salads and icecreams/desserts. There is also a well-established wine and children's menu.

Finding it difficult to obtain suppliers of good quality teas and coffees in the early 1950s, Betty's acquired a local tea and coffee blender of high repute — Taylor's of Harrogate. Betty's now, as a consequence, offers over fifty different coffees and teas.

A similar idea of vertical integration applies to the wine menu. The Belmont family has had strong links since the mid-1930s with the Alsace region in eastern France. The wines produced there are suited to the fresh, dainty dishes Betty's serves. Consequently Betty's imports a selection of wines direct from the grower, Jean Jacques Miller.

In May 1986, Betty's started a mail order service designed for customers who live outside the Yorkshire area and are unable to make regular trips to any of the shops. Catalogues are on sale in each outlet or customers' names can be added to a mailing list.

Prices

As can be seen from the menu (Annexe 1.1), prices are not cheap. The cheapest pot of tea, served either with milk or lemon, is £1.25. This is deliberately pitched in the upper echelons of the price distribution for tea in the respective trading areas, but is regarded by Betty's as being the entry price for the quality of the service and ambience that is offered.

Promotion

Promotion is essentially that of customer experience, word of mouth and window display. Some items seen delicately displayed in the York outlet include sloe gin cake, Yorkshire delicatessen items, pastries, chocolates, truffles, specialist teas and coffees, morello cherry jam, ginger walnut and York cherry cake.

Staff

Betty's employs, either full- or part-time, 600 + staff, all of whom are well trained and encouraged to participate in the running of the company. Although wages are similar to those paid elsewhere in the catering industry, a group bonus reward system is operated which reflects Betty's emphasis on teamwork.

Market segmentation

Betty's is a thriving family business serving three main groups of customers:

1. Core customers — store-loyal, regular users living in the area and likely to be from the ABC1 socio-economic grouping, who are not price-sensitive.
2. Semi-core customers — store-aware weekend visitors from local and regional conurbations. A treat on the Sunday family day out.
3. Passing trade — store-unaware and likely to be tourists/visitors either foreign (especially from North America or Europe) or the rest of the United Kingdom. All ages seeking something British and unique.

The ratios of the customer groups varies by store location. In Harrogate the local population forms a larger proportion of the business. In Ilkley and Northallerton, urban Sunday trippers predominate, while York thrives on the tourist trade.

Questions

1. Identify and evaluate Betty's retail market position.
2. Contrast your analysis of (1) above with the retail market positioning of a fast-food outlet you know well, e.g. McDonald's, Kentucky Fried Chicken, Wimpy, etc. in terms of merchandise, store environment and customer service.
3. Do you think Betty's would be advised to expand the business to other county/spa towns outside Yorkshire, e.g. Bath, Cheltenham, Buxton? What would the criteria be?

CAKES

All Bettys cakes and pastries are made in our own Bakery, as they have been since 1919 *using a unique combination of Swiss and Yorkshire recipes.*
All the eggs used at our Bakery are pasteurised.

For today's selection, please ask to see the cake trolley.
Please ask for prices of our many seasonal specialities.

Yorkshire Curd Tart & Cream £1.74	Warm Apple Strudel & Cream £1.74
Normandy Apple Flan & Cream £1.88	Chocolate Mousse & Cream £2.06
Normandy Pear Flan & Cream £2.18	Fresh Fruit Torte £2.10
Fresh Cream Chocolate Torte £2.10	Fresh Fruit Meringue £1.68
Fresh Fruit Cheesecake £2.06	Fresh Fruit Flan £1.90
Fruit and Cream Heart £1.85	Chocolate Brandy Roulade £1.78
Fresh Pineapple Tart £1.18	Hazelnut Meringue £1.60
Coffee or Chocolate Cream Eclair £1.25	Coffee or Chocolate Cream Puff £1.40
Vanilla Heart £1.55	Caramel Slice 96p
Vanilla Slice £1.22	Japonaise Fancy £1.08

A selection of Danish Pastries from £1.40

Extra Cream 38p *per portion*

SPECIAL RICH FRUIT CAKES

A Taste of Lemon & Almond and Ginger & Walnut
– *served with either Whipped Cream or Wensleydale Cheese* £2.40

ICES & DESSERTS

All our ice creams are made with double cream, raw cane sugar, & pasteurised egg yolks.
Three scoops of ice cream of your choice – *served with a langue du chat biscuit*
Rich Vanilla, Loganberry or Brown Bread £2.12
– *with homemade raspberry, toffee or chocolate sauce* £2.35

Brandy Snap Fanfare £3.98
– *Brown Bread ice cream, homemade chocolate sauce, flaked almonds & fresh cream, with brandy snap fans.*

Loganberry Meringue Melba £3.36
– *Loganberry ice cream, homemade raspberry sauce, fresh cream & flaked almonds on a base of crushed meringue*

Our sorbets are made with real fruit
Three scoops of sorbet of your choice. Mango or Blackcurrant £2.46

Fresh Pineapple Yoghurt Parfait £2.02

WINE

Served with meals during licensing hours

White Wine – Alsace Edelzwicker 1987 £1.90 *a glass*
Red Wine – Pinot Noir d'Alsace 1986/87 £1.98 *a glass*
Special White Wine – Alsace Gewürztraminer 1987 £2.10 *a glass*
A Selection of Alsace Wines imported exclusively by us is available by the bottle. Please ask for the Wine List.

Bucks Fizz *(for 2 people)* £10.30
– *Half Bottle Sparkling Alsace Crémant & freshly squeezed orange juice*
Carlsberg Lager, 275ml £1.40

BETTYS

At the turn of the century Frederick Belmont, a young Swiss Confectioner, travelled to England, settled in North Yorkshire where the air seemed as clear and sweet as his native Alps, and opened his first Tea Rooms and Cake Shop in Harrogate in 1919.

ROYAL & DISTINGUISHED PATRONAGE

Frederick's natural Swiss flair for hospitality and his mouthwatering cakes brought him both royal patronage and popular acclaim, and during the 1920s and 30s he opened Cafés in other Yorkshire towns.

WHERE THE DALES MEET THE ALPS

Today Bettys is still owned and run by the descendants of Frederick Belmont's family, now half Swiss half Yorkshire, with Cafés in the Yorkshire towns of Harrogate, York, Northallerton and Ilkley. Bettys success has been founded on the principle that "If we want things just right, we have to make them ourselves". Cakes, chocolates, bread, scones, muffins – over four hundred different lines in all are still made by hand at Bettys Bakery. Special blends of tea and the best selection of coffees in the country come from Bettys own tea and coffee importing business. Even Bettys wines are imported direct from family contacts in France.

FRESH & DAINTY

In Bettys kitchens, Frederick Belmont's principle of everything being "fresh and dainty" continues today. All dishes are prepared on the premises and are freshly cooked.

WHO WAS BETTY?

After eighty years, the identity of Betty still remains a family secret, and although many tales are told and explanations offered, some mysteries are better left unsolved . . .

CAFÉ CONCERTS

Harrogate – 6.30pm to 9pm every evening. York – 6pm to 9pm most evenings. Ilkley – varies daily: please telephone for details.

YOUR COMMENTS

Our best ideas have come from our customers, so please make your views known to the manager or in the Suggestions Book. If you would like to know more about careers at Bettys, please ask the manager.
There are more than six hundred staff in the business with many diverse talents.

BETTYS BY POST

If you live a long way from Bettys, then our "Bettys By Post" Service will keep you supplied with tea, coffee, cakes and chocolates until your next visit. Telephone Harrogate (0423) 531211.

OPENING HOURS

All the Cafés are open seven days a week and on most bank holidays.
Harrogate and York 9am – 9pm (inc. Sundays)
Ilkley 9am – 7pm (Monday to Thursday) 9am – 9pm (Friday to Sunday)
Northallerton 9am – 5.30pm (10am – 5.30pm Sunday)
VAT included in the prices. Gratuities are at your discretion.

♦

Souvenir Menus are on sale at the Cash Desk.
HY690

Bettys
ESTABLISHED 1919

MENU

HARROGATE • YORK
ILKLEY • NORTHALLERTON

Annexe 1.1 *Bettys menu*

TEA

We select, import and blend our own Teas.
Served with Milk or Lemon. Teapot for one.
The Tea Room Blend £1.25
Makaibarie Estate Darjeeling £1.60
Special Tippy Assam £1.40 Earl Grey £1.40
Special Scented Blend with Exotic Flowers £1.40
Formosa Oolong 'Peach Blossom' £1.74
Lapsang Souchong £1.40 China Rose Petal £1.40
Yunnan Flowery Orange Pekoe £1.40
Peppermint Tisane with Honey £1.52
Chamomile Flowers Tisane with Honey £1.52

COFFEE

We select, import and roast our own Coffees.
The Café Blend — *served with hot milk or cream*
Pot for One £1.65 Cup 98p Large Breakfast Cup £1.30

French Roast Coffee — *Cafetière for one* £2.15
Swiss Water-Process Decaffeinated Coffee — *Cafetière for one* £2.40

Café Vienna £1.52 — *with whipped cream and cinnamon*
Hot Mokka £1.52 — *coffee and chocolate with cream*
Iced Mokka £1.62 — *coffee and chocolate whisked with ice cream*
Café Glacé £1.62 — *coffee whisked with ice cream, topped with sugar crystals*

CAFÉ COMPLET

Pot of Café Blend Coffee for one with Breakfast Rolls,
Croissants or Brioches, Butter and Preserves £2.98

SPECIAL RARE COFFEES

Prices shown are for a Cafetière for one

St. Helena £2.35
— *a rocky outpost of the Empire in the South Atlantic. St. Helena's entire tiny coffee crop has been bought by Bettys. Full bodied with a subtle perfumed flavour.*

Yemeni "Heights of Araby" Ismaili £2.74
— *a very rare, exotic and winey coffee from the first country to cultivate coffee. Organically grown.*

Celebes Kalossi £2.74
— *the island of Celebes, near Borneo, has produced for centuries this classic, full bodied and silky coffee.*

Hawaiian Kona Kai £2.74
— *a fine fruity flavour and a well-balanced body.*

Sumatra Mandheling £2.46
— *rich and full-bodied, with an almost chocolatey flavour.*

Cuban Sierra del Escambray £2.65
— *rich and slightly smoky, with a full mellow flavour.*

HOT DRINKS & MINERALS

Hot Chocolate with Cream £1.52 Hot Milk with Honey and Nutmeg £1.20
Raspberry, Chocolate *or* Fresh Banana Ice Cream Milk Shakes £1.56
Sparkling Apple Juice 98p Copella Farm-Pressed English Apple Juice 98p
Chilled Milk 90p Highland Spring Mineral Water 98p Coca Cola 98p
Freshly Squeezed Orange Juice *small glass* £1.22 *large glass* £1.90
Fresh Homemade Lemonade £1.45

TOASTS & TEA BREADS

Granary Toast 76p Cinnamon Toast 94p Cinnamon Muffin 98p
Two Hot Buttered Pikelets 84p Toasted Yule Bread 94p
Toasted Currant, Wholemeal *or* Spiced Yorkshire Teacake 94p
Buttered Banana & Walnut Loaf 94p
Warm Yorkshire Fat Rascal and Butter £1.62
Honey or Preserves 38p

TOASTED SCONES

Sultana, Cheese, Lemon and Orange,
Wholemeal Date 76p each *as available*

CREAM TEA

Sultana Scones with Whipped Cream and Strawberry Preserve
Pot of Tea Room Blend for one £3.48

♦

Bettys Biscuits 28p *each*
Bettys Ginger Biscuit Shape 65p Bettys Shortbread Oval 76p

SANDWICHES

— *in Granary, White or Wholemeal Bread*
Egg and Cress £1.94 Cottage Cheese and Fresh Pineapple £2.08
Tuna Fish and Cucumber £2.22 Roast Ham £2.12
Smoked Salmon £3.80 Fresh Poached Salmon £3.40
Roast Corn-Fed Chicken Breast £2.12 Smoked Chicken £2.70
Prawn and Avocado £3.40

Hot Bacon Muffin £2.68
Smoked Salmon Muffin — *smoked salmon, lettuce and watercress* £3.80
Prawn and Egg Mayonnaise Open Sandwich £5.08

YORKSHIRE CHEESE LUNCH

Blue and White Wensleydale Cheeses with Apple Chutney,
Celery and Granary Bread £4.65

CHILDREN

A special Children's Menu is available, along with changing and feeding facilities.
Please ask your waitress for details.

STARTERS

Homemade Soup with Roll and Butter £2.15
Deep Fried Granary Mushrooms £2.58
Smoked Mackerel Pâté £3.08 — *served with Granary Melba Toast*
Cheese and Herb Pâté £3.08 — *served with Granary Melba Toast.*
Welsh Rarebit Taster £2.58

HOT DISHES

Hot Dish of the Day *please ask*
Mushrooms on Toast £3.58
Haddock and Prawns au Gratin £4.98
Deep Fried Granary Mushrooms with Tartare Sauce £4.60
Scrambled Eggs with Smoked Salmon £4.88

RAREBITS

The Speciality of the House. Made with Theakston's Yorkshire Ale, served with Apple or Tomato Chutney
Welsh Rarebit Taster £2.58
Original Welsh Rarebit £4.95 Rarebit with Bacon Rashers £5.54
Yorkshire Rarebit with Ham £5.38

GRILLS & FISH

Pork Sausages and Bacon with Apple Chutney £4.42
Fried Fillet of Haddock with Chipped Potatoes £5.32
Bacon, Tomato and Scrambled Eggs with Toast £4.70

OMELETTES

Cheddar Cheese £4.14 Prawn £4.70 Plain £3.90
Mushroom and Bacon £4.26

SIDE DISHES

Mixed Salad Bowl £1.45 Courgettes Provençale £1.60
New Potatoes £1.45 Jacket Potato £1.45 Chipped Potatoes £1.25
Herb and Garlic Bread £1.35 Granary Bread and Butter 62p

SALADS

Smoked Chicken and Avocado Salad Bowl £6.30
— *with carrot, cucumber and bean salads*
Smoked Wensleydale Cheese and Apple Salad Bowl £5.40
— *with carrot, cucumber and bean salads*
Fresh Poached Salmon £7.22
— *with new potatoes and a cream & cucumber salad*
Roast Ham or Roast Corn-Fed Chicken — *with a salad garnish* £4.42
Individual Quiche — *with a salad garnish*
— *with one quiche* £4.42 *or two quiches* £5.40

Annexe 1.1 *continued*

ALSACE WINES

Alsace is a fairytale of little medieval walled villages set in well manicured undulating vineyards with the dark pine forests of the Vosges mountains rising steeply behind. The wine industry there is pleasantly old-fashioned, with vineyards belonging to many small vignerons rather than being in the hands of big business.

Quality is their prime consideration: all wine is bottled in Alsace rather than being shipped in bulk. Alsaciens shudder at the practice of adding sugar to wine – the fruitiness of their Gewürztraminers and Muscats is entirely natural.

The climate is ideal for white wine rather than red and the varied geology of the area enables the Alsaciens to grow more different grape varieties than any other corner of the world.

We import our wine direct from an old family friend, Jean Jacques Muller. His family have been well respected in the wine business for generations.

By specialising in the wines of Alsace, we hope to bring you more interest, more pleasure and, because we import direct, excellent value.

Our wines can also be purchased in the shop.

690

Bettys

ESTABLISHED 1919

WINE MENU

HARROGATE • YORK
ILKLEY • NORTHALLERTON

Wines served with meals during licensing hours

HOUSE WINES

Bettys own specially imported selection is available by the glass (13cl), ½ bottle or bottle.

WHITE WINE	Glass	½ Bottle	Bottle
Alsace Edelzwicker 1987 *medium dry, fruity and refreshing* *alc. 11.5% vol*	£1.90	£5.48	£9.40
SPECIAL WHITE WINE			
Alsace Gewürztraminer 1987 *medium dry, very distinctive bouquet* *alc. 13% vol*	£2.10	£6.05	£10.40
SPARKLING WINE			
Crémant d'Alsace Brut *made by the 'Champagne method'* *alc. 12% vol*		£8.75	£13.98
RED WINE			
Pinot Noir d'Alsace 1986/87 *fruity and refreshing light red wine* *alc. 12.5% vol*	£1.98	£5.70	£9.80

PRIVATE CELLAR WINES

Alsace wines are named after the variety of grape from which they are exclusively made. Alsace wines are drier than German wines and fruitier than Muscadets and Loire wines, with a lovely fragrant bouquet. Our private selection includes wines from the 1983, 1985, 1986 and 1987 vintages. All these wines except the last, are white.

Pinot Blanc 1987 *dry, fresh and fruity. Alc. 11.5% vol.*	£9.80
Sylvaner 1986 *dry, lively, fresh and fruity. Alc. 11.5% vol.*	£9.65
Alsace Riesling 1986/87 *perfect balance of fruit and acidity with a delicate bouquet.* *alc. 12% vol.*	£9.86
Riesling Gold Medal 1985/87 *(awarded at Colmar)* *an outstanding wine from a vintage year. Alc. 12% vol.*	£11.32
Muscat Cuvée Exceptionnelle 1983/85 *a fantastic fragrance from this increasingly rare Alsace grape.* *alc. 12% vol.*	£14.85
Tokay d'Alsace 1983 *(the red wine drinkers' white wine)* *rich, heady dry wine which complements the richest of foods.* *alc. 12.5% vol.*	£11.90
Gewürztraminer Gold Medal 1987 *an award-winning wine with an intense, spicy bouquet.* *alc. 13% vol.*	£13.30
Crémant Brut Rosé *Alsace's answer to 'Pink Champagne'. Alc. 12% vol.*	£15.05

Annexe 1.2 *Bettys wine menu*

BETTYS

May we remind you that the following facilities are provided for customers with small children:

Our Ladies toilets offer changing facilities and a play pen.

Nappies are available, please ask at the Cash Desk.

♦

Your waitress will give you further information regarding the following services:

Our kitchens supply a range of meatless, preservative-free and additive-free foods for small babies.

High chairs and inserts are available. (Bettys cannot be held responsible for any accidents which occur during their use).

We can supply beakers and bibs.
We are happy to heat up or open your own food or milk.

♦

Bettys have no objection to discreet breastfeeding in the restaurant. However, please be understanding if other customers do object.

690

Bettys
ESTABLISHED 1919

INFANTS' AND CHILDREN'S MENU

HARROGATE • YORK
ILKLEY • NORTHALLERTON

DOUBLE DECKER SANDWICHES

Choose any two of these fillings for your sandwich £1.68
Banana & Honey, Peanut Butter, Lettuce & Tomato, Wensleydale Cheese, Egg, Bacon

SINGLE DECKERS

Any one of the above fillings £1.08

EAT BETTYS CLOWN

An egg mayonnaise hat, tomato ears and a pineapple nose, you can eat every bit of our open sandwich face £2.05

♦

Round of Buttered Toast 58p   Round of Cheese Straws 60p
Bettys Shortbread Oval 76p   Honey Muesli Slice 86p
Buttered Banana & Walnut Loaf 94p
Ginger Biscuit Shape 65p

CHIPS WITH EVERYTHING

Bacon, Sausage, Scrambled Egg, Tomato, *or* Mushrooms 94p *per portion*
One with Chips £1.98 *Two with Chips* £2.56 *Three with Chips* £3.14

EGGS

Two Egg, Cheese or Bacon Omelette £3.25

Small Welsh Rarebit £2.58

All the eggs used in our Hot Dishes are pasteurised.

RASPBERRY & LOGANBERRY SUNDAE

Rich Vanilla and Loganberry ice cream with raspberries and fresh cream £2.10

BETTYS BANANA BOAT

Banana with Rich Vanilla and Brown Bread ice cream topped with a brandy snap sail and fresh cream £2.10

ICE CREAM CLOWN

Rich Vanilla ice cream topped with a sugar cone hat £1.18

A single scoop of Rich Vanilla, Loganberry or Brown Bread ice cream 98p
With homemade raspberry, toffee or chocolate sauce £1.15
A single scoop of Mango or Blackcurrant Sorbet £1.20

REAL ICE CREAM MILK SHAKES

Raspberry, Banana or Chocolate £1.56

MINERALS

Freshly Squeezed Orange Juice £1.22
Natural Orange & Apple Drink 72p
Homemade Lemonade 90p
Copella Farm-Pressed English Apple Juice 98p
Sparkling Apple Juice 98p
Coca Cola 98p   Cold Milk 72p   Warm Milk 72p

In addition to these items, half portions of all our normal Menu dishes are available.

VAT included at 15%

Annexe 1.3 *Bettys infants' and children's menu*

CASE STUDY 2

Sauce Boat Limited

Company background

The origins of Sauce Boat Ltd stretch back to soon after the Second World War when the present chairman's father, Ron Brown, was demobilized. Searching for civilian employment, he decided to open a fish and chip shop in the late 1940s. Being a chemist by training, the father experimented with a range of batter mixes and, via trial and error, developed a recipe which was widely thought to be the best available in his trading area.

As a result, the business developed quickly, especially once the decision was taken to offer the batter mix commercially to other fish friers in Yorkshire. By the mid-1950s, the batter supply side of the business was sufficiently strong that the fish and chip outlet was sold. After a further five years of steady growth, the need for alternative product lines became apparent. And Ron Brown had the germ of an idea. Given that in the process of developing his business he had called on a broad range of food preparers, processors and manufacturers, he gradually became aware of a major problem facing meat pie manufacturers. Their problem was simply that they could not find a gravy that did not boil out of their pies in the cooking process. Consequently, they were forced to place the lid on their meat pies after separate cooking of the pie case and filling, and then the pie lid.

Realizing this was inefficient and costly, Ron Brown developed a gravy mix that did not boil out. This product laid the base for what is now the main line of the company's business, gravy and sauce mixes, supplying both meat pie manufacturers and, since the mid-1960s, the general public via supermarkets and other retail outlets.

The early 1980s

By 1982/3 Ron Brown has been succeeded as chairman by his son, John. Company turnover was now £4.2 million, with the breakdown by product as follows:

1982/3	Sales £m	%
Gravy products	1.8	42.1
Ingredients, including gravy supply to meat pie manufacturers and food processors	0.9	21.4
Crumbs	0.5	11.9
Other mixes and sauces, e.g. parsley, apple, batter, etc.	0.3	7.1
Cake mixes	0.2	4.8
Distributor own-label gravies	0.5	11.9
	4.2	100.0

Although the gravy products, sold at retail, accounted for 42 per cent of sales, they contributed over 60 per cent of the company's contribution figure. Two product forms and three flavours of gravy mix were offered, viz.:

Forms	Approx. %	Flavours	Approx. %
Powder	90	Rich brown	65
Granule	10	Onion	20
		Savoury	15

John Brown agreed that the company's core skill was dry-mix manipulation. Hence he laid great stress on the fact that Sauce Boat Ltd was the only company to offer a range of gravy flavours. Competitors only produced a brown gravy mix.

Chairman's concerns

Despite the undoubted successful growth of Sauce Boat Ltd, John Brown had six major concerns regarding the future:

1. Although Sauce Boat Ltd had 20 per cent of the market in Yorkshire and Lancashire, it was a marginal performer nationally, with only 6 per cent market share. Indeed, the market was dominated by Rank Hovis McDougall with Bisto and a market share of over 70 per cent.
2. Across all of Sauce Boat's activities, it faced large, well-resourced competitors, all with strong R&D activities, e.g. Rank Hovis McDougall, Nabisco, Reckitt & Colman.

3. Sauce Boat itself possessed limited resources, especially for new product development and marketing.
4. Sauce Boat had built up strong relationships with a number of Yorkshire and north-east-based supermarket chains, e.g. Morrisons, Hintons, Hillards. These chains were under pressure as other chains went national.
5. While Asda, with whom Sauce Boat were listed, were experiencing some problems in their diversification policy of moving south, Sainsbury, with whom Sauce Boat were not listed, were being extremely successful in their move north.
6. Market forecasts suggested that there would be a major shift in consumer preference away from powder towards granules. In fact, Sauce Boat had only launched their granule product in the last six months as a 'me too' following Bisto.

Problem/assignment

John Brown is anxious to call a special board meeting to discuss his concerns, but prior to doing so, has asked you to prepare a market research proposal which he hopes will help the company determine an appropriate marketing strategy.

Time of assignment — early 1984.

CASE STUDY 3

Wm Low and Company PLC

Wm Low is a Dundee-based food retailer. The company has focused its activities on Scotland and the north of England. It operates sixty-three stores. Their location and size ranges are:

Under 4,000 sq.ft
Edinburgh Gilmerton
Edinburgh Davidsons Mains
Edinburgh Corstorphine
Gateshead Low Fell

4,000–10,000 sq.ft
St Andrews Market Street
Montrose High Street
Milngavie Douglas Street
Glasgow Halfway
Helensburgh Sinclair Street
Penicuik John Street
Bo'ness East Pier Street
Bathgate South Bridge Street
Edinburgh Boswell Parkway
Edinburgh Pennywell Road
Carnoustie High Street
Monifieth Reform Street
Dundee Barnhill
Dundee Perth Road
Dundee Overgate
Dundee Macalpine Road
Dundee Albert Street
Kirriemuir The Roods
Dalgety Bay Regent Way
Banff Carmelite Street
Fort William High Street
Morpeth Market Place
Bedlington Front Street
Newcastle Jesmond
Newcastle Forest Hall
Rewlands Gill Shotley Bridge Road

10,000–20,000 sq.ft
Rosyth Queensferry Road
Haddington Court Street
Edinburgh Nicolson Street
Grangemouth Baltic Chambers
Linlithgow Regent Centre
Berwick-on-Tweed Walkergate
Kilmarnock Western Road
Stranraer Charlotte Street
Forres Gordon Street
Oban Market Street
Dingwall Tulloch Street
Inverurie Burn Lane
Elgin Batchen Lane
Inverness Tomnahurich Street
Forfar Myre Road
Blairgowrie High Street
Lanark Castlegate
Dunbar Friarscroft
Gateshead Felling High Street

Thirsk Station Road
Driffeld George Street

20,000 sq.ft and over
Perth Crieff Road
Perth Victoria Street
Cumbernauld Teviot Walk
Greenock Inverkip Street
Dalkeith Newmills Road
Kirkcaldy Hunter Street
Wishaw Main Street
Dundee Pitkerro Road
Edinburgh Canonmills
Dumfries Lochfield Road
Consett Delves Lane
Goole North Street

Recent years have seen considerable expenditure on store development and merchandise range extension. Store development has involved Wm Low in a rationalization programme in which the small, non-profitable stores have been closed, with others being extended or relocated as larger stores. The emphasis has been on the opening of larger stores with wider merchandise ranges and customer services and service products. In 1985 the company operated eighty-one stores with an average selling area of 9,500 sq.ft. In 1989 there were sixty-three stores averaging 15,200 sq.ft.

As the business has expanded, Wm Low has developed its distribution infrastructure at a pace that will maintain the demand for service from the branches. Recent expansions to the Dundee and Gateshead warehouses have been completed, and a distribution warehouse for frozen and chilled products is being built in Livingston to replace the Whitburn depot.

A phased introduction of EPOS is underway.

The company is strong in both a financial and marketing context. The balance-sheet is very strong. Despite the extent of the redevelopment, gearing remains low, at less than 10 per cent. The ongoing development programme will mean that borrowings will continue to rise in the foreseeable future, but the strength of the balance-sheet can comfortably support the company's anticipated levels of increased borrowings.

Financial performance for the years 1985–9 is shown in Table A3.1.

Marketing performance is indicated by the growth in turnover and operating profit. The company, being regionally-based, does not have a significant national market share. However, the physical expansion of the business, together with the sales and profit increases, have been achieved in a highly competitive environment; the major national food multiples have been expanding their activities in Scotland and the north of England. However, as can be seen by the branch portfolio, Wm Low have skilfully developed an alternative offer: their stores are on smaller sites than those of the major national multiples but offer choice and variety, quality, service and competitive prices from *convenient* locations.

The repositioning strategy of the past five years has involved the company in an extensive customer communications programme. Media advertising has been

Table A3.1 Financial performance for 1985–9 (£ million)

	1985	1986	1987	1988	1989
Turnover	206.9	233.4	247.3	265.2	304.3
Operating profit	7.1	7.4	9.0	12.0	17.6
Operating profit to sales	3.44	3.17	3.64	4.53	5.8
Sales area (000s sq. ft)	615	583	613	675	713
Size of average branch (sq. ft)	9,500	9,600	11,500	14,500	15,200
Sales per sq. ft (sales area/annum)	£410	413	419	423	441
Increase in sales area (%)	37.9	(5.2)	5.1	10.1	5.6
Average number of staff employed during year (2 pt = 1 ft)	3,995	4,465	4,760	4,990	5,222
Sales per employee (weekly)	£997	1,005	999	1,022	1,121
Operating profit per employee p.a.	£1,780	1,659	1,893	2,410	3,378
Operating profit to sales ratio (%)	3.44	3.17	3.64	4.53	5.8
Sales increase on previous year (%)	34.1	12.8	6.0	7.2	14.8
Sales to stock closing ratio (%)	16.6	17.4	18.0	16.3	16.9

a major component with combined estimated press and television expenditures of:

	£000
1983	562
1984	725
1985	595
1986	1,161
1987	605
1988	640

Two examples of the strategies pursued by the advertising campaign during this period are given by extracts from the Wm Low television campaigns over the years.

The first campaign (illustrated as *Figure A3.1*) was screened in 1985. It featured price exclusively and used major branded products in the commercial. Emphasis was created by the strong visual impact of the price gun and the intensive activity of the store sales assistants.

Figure A3.1

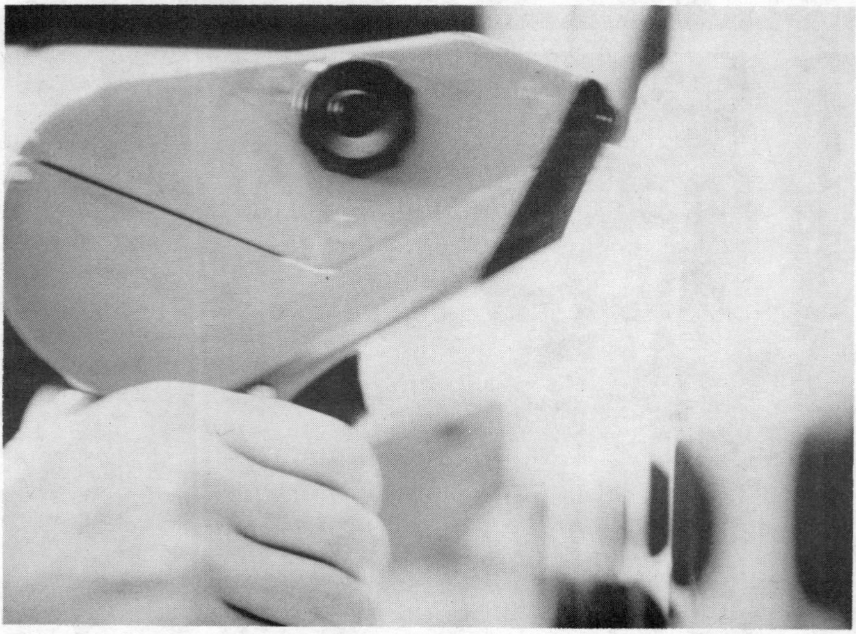

Figure A3.1 *continued*

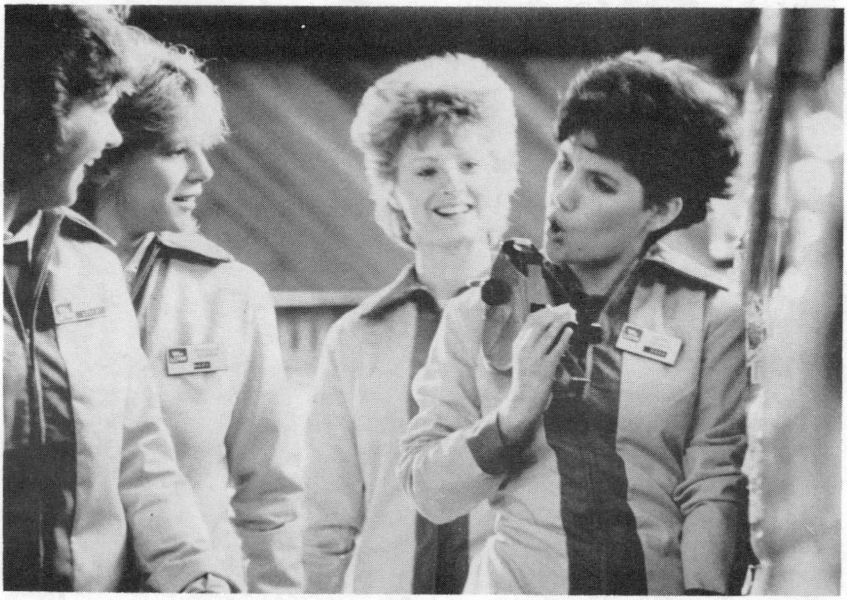

Figure A3.1 *continued*

The second campaign, *Figure A3.2*, appeared in 1987. 'Down Down' was still very much a price-led approach but was expanded to include customers' endorsement of the price offer. The friendly approach of the staff was included to expand the offer.

Figure A3.2

Figure A3.2 *continued*

The 1988–9 campaign shifted away from price. A personality was introduced — Stuart — who describes the offer of wide ranges, fresh food and produce, and larger, spacious stores, between 'confrontational incidents' with a girl called Linda. Stuart and Linda are shown in *Figure A3.3*.

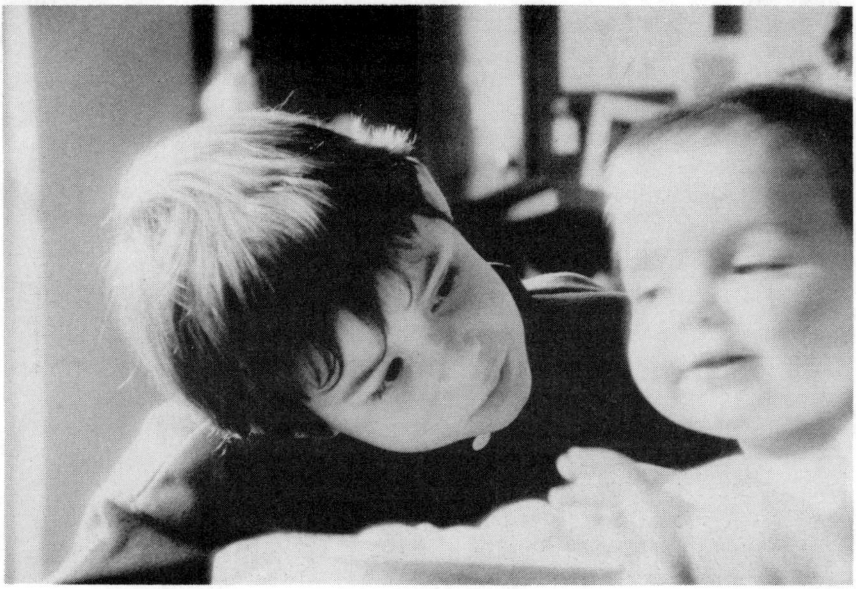

Figure A3.3

Towards the end of 1990 Wm Low announced a rights issue that was to fund further expansion of the store portfolio into the South.

Questions

1. Research and identify Low's positioning strategy in the UK grocery market.
2. Identify and evaluate the alternative creative strategies available to Wm Low. Which approach do you advocate as being the most appropriate?

CASE STUDY 4

Next

J. Hepworth & Son PLC

Hepworths, a manufacturer and retailer of men's clothing, entered the 1970s with great confidence. Despite a clothing strike in Leeds, the company was able to report in its 1970 accounts that, for the first time, pre-tax profits exceeded £2 million, with turnover for the year ended 31 January 1970 at £14.6 million. Indeed, the chairman proudly noted that whereas it had taken 100 years to achieve the first £1 million profit milestone, the second million was earned in six years. The chairman concluded that the customers must like the combination of quality, value and service offered. At a time of such achievement it was appropriate to announce the decision to build a new head office in Claypit Lane, Leeds. Demand was so strong for the young men's made-to-measure styles designed by Hardy Amies, a leading fashion consultant, that the company's buyers were instructed actively to search the world for attractive merchandise that could be made in Hepworth's own factories. Besides the question of designing suitable merchandise, the other major problem facing the company was the identification and development of further sites in the United Kingdom. Although some 320 + stores were operated, it was estimated there were at least a further 100 cities and towns throughout the country that would benefit from a newly opened Hepworth store.

Corporate strategy for the first 3–4 years of the decade incorporated five major thrusts:

1. An active programme of new site acquisition, seeking geographic expansion of the number of corporate outlets throughout the United Kingdom.
2. For existing stores, a policy of refurbishment and, where appropriate, re-siting.
3. The main product offering was designer-styled (Hardy Amies), made-to-measure suits.
4. Vertical integration, with the orders taken in the shops being made in the company-owned factories.
5. Productivity drives in both the retail outlets and factories, to improve efficiency and cut costs.

By the mid-1970s, however, Hepworths was facing a changed retail environment. Following the 1974 Arab-Israeli conflict and the resultant quadrupling of the oil price, the UK economy moved into a period of economic depression and industrial dispute, culminating in a three-day working week. As a result, retailers generally faced severe margin pressure with the twin pincers of increases in inflation, interest rates, wages and salaries, rent and rates alongside depressed demand. The drop in demand was exacerbated for Hepworths because of a number of factors unique to men's wear retailing. In particular, there was a movement away from the wearing of suits, especially by the younger male, in favour of more fashionable and casual wear. It was no longer *de rigueur* that suits were the required dress at work and in the office. Indeed, even if a suit were bought, customers were often no longer prepared to wait the 5–6 weeks while the order was made up, preferring to buy off-the-peg, perhaps on credit.

Hepworth's response to these trends was six-fold:

1. An enhanced economy drive.
2. The experimentation of opening Hepworths 'shop in shops' in a number of Debenhams' department stores.
3. The use of concessionaries and franchises within Hepworth outlets, e.g. Carrington Viyella for shirts and Michelson for ties.
4. The extension of the product range to include *inter alia* knitwear, Lotus shoes and leisure wear.
5. An increased stress on off-the-peg, instant gratification, although made-to-measure suits would continue to be a main offering.
6. Increased credit availability via Club 24, Hepworth's own credit organization.

Basically, the same strategy was followed for the latter half of the 1970s, but by 1980, the chairman was reporting that the company was facing the worst recession since the Second World War. It was recognized that the company was at a watershed because of three factors:

1. A permanent, large decrease in demand for made-to-measure men's suits.
2. A significant increase in demand for leisure wear, which Hepworths was not capable of making in-house.
3. An inability by Hepworths to find outside third party orders for underutilized corporate manufacturing capacity.

With 365 outlets, 1980 pre-tax profits were £2.1 million earned on sales of £60.2 million. By 1981, the number of outlets had been cut to 345 (of which 28 were in Debenhams) and, although sales had increased by some 22 per cent to £73.5 million, profits had been wiped out. In 1981 Hepworths made a loss of £62,000.

In an attempt to restructure the business, four main steps were taken:

1. Four factories were closed, at Colburn, Hetton, Woodlesford and Sunderland.
2. As part of a productivity drive, larger men's wear outlets were sought to replace smaller, uneconomic shops.

3. W & E Turner, a chain of 160 shoe retail outlets with sales of £5.2 million, was acquired in May 1980.
4. In May 1981, Kendalls, a 79-outlet ladies' fashion retail chain, was 'purchased' from Combined English Stores for £1.75 million.

George Davies, previously with Pippa Dee, was recruited to develop the Kendalls outlets in June 1981, initially as ladies' merchandise director. Terence Conran subsequently joined Hepworths, in December 1981, as a non-executive director. The two brought key skills into the organization: Davies, ladies' wear merchandising, and Conran, interior design. The combination led to the genesis of the Next concept, a fusing of Davies' 'eighteen years of thoughts, feelings, aspirations and frustrations' and Conran's flair for atmospherics.

Environmental analysis

The four restructuring decisions noted above emanated from a decision taken in the early part of 1980 to reorient the business. No longer would the company be driven from its manufacturing base but would become increasingly marketing-oriented. Corporate stress would shift from manufacturing to retailing skills, appreciating the need for market segmentation and targeting customers. At the same time, the decision was taken to seek to employ the company's retail skills in the women's outerwear market.

Such a drastic change of strategy was the result not only of poor financial performance in the period 1977–80 but also because of a number of environmental trends forcing adaptation upon Hepworths. In addition to the shift in the men's wear market away from traditional made-to-measure suits towards more casual fashionable clothing, a number of key environmental trends were influential:

1. A dramatic increase in the number of working women, especially mothers, continuing in full- or part-time employment after family formation. Consequences of this phenomenon included both higher levels of disposable income and poverty of time. Implications of this trend included:
   (a) a need to use shopping time efficiently,
   (b) the opportunity for an increase in the importance of individualism and personal identity, especially with 'ego-intense' merchandise,
   (c) the emergence of the need for some duality in clothing use between working and leisure activities,
   (d) enhanced confidence especially among working women with a need to be smartly turned out for work.
2. As the consumerism movement gained pace, it was important for retail staff to adopt a more proactive role in the provision of customer service. This was reflected in the trend away from the idea of viewing retail staff as sales assistants towards the advisory role of fashion consultant mirroring the age and life-style aspirations of the target customers.

Table A4.1 Number of households in the United Kingdom, 1971–91

	(unit = millions)
1971	16.7
1976	17.5
1981	18.4
1986	19.2
1991	19.9

3. For those shoppers with higher levels of disposable income, shopping especially for ego-intensive items could become an exciting leisure activity. Value for money, style and fashion were likely to be more important than price.
4. A marked increase in the number of households (see Table A4.1). Three main factors were thought to explain this trend:
   (a) an increased divorce rate,
   (b) the decline of the 'nuclear family' as young people set up home before marriage and older couples/individuals maintained their own homes in their retirement rather than living with their sons and daughters,
   (c) increasing affluence and education; especially of those passing through the higher education system.
5. The beginnings of the emergence of income polarity, underpinned by unemployment and the North/South divide with the clear implication for retailers to target income groups.
6. The increasing availability and use by retailers of information technology epitomized by electronic point of sale (EPOS), with consequences for speed of customer service, stock levels and inventory policy.

Next — the original concept (Spring 1982)

The growth in the number of working women created a situation where a significant segment of the population experienced enhanced spending power with the need to purchase suitable but smartly fashionable clothes for the workplace. Of the options available in 1980, many found themselves too old for Top Shop, Marks & Spencer too unfashionable and widely available; and Jaeger *et al*. too expensive. Hence there was a strategic window offering the retail opportunity of providing fashionable co-ordinated garments at reasonable prices, complete with a mix of accessories from bags to shoes, at a single location. The target market was identified as the 25–45-year-old, time-poor, fashion-conscious, value-for-money-

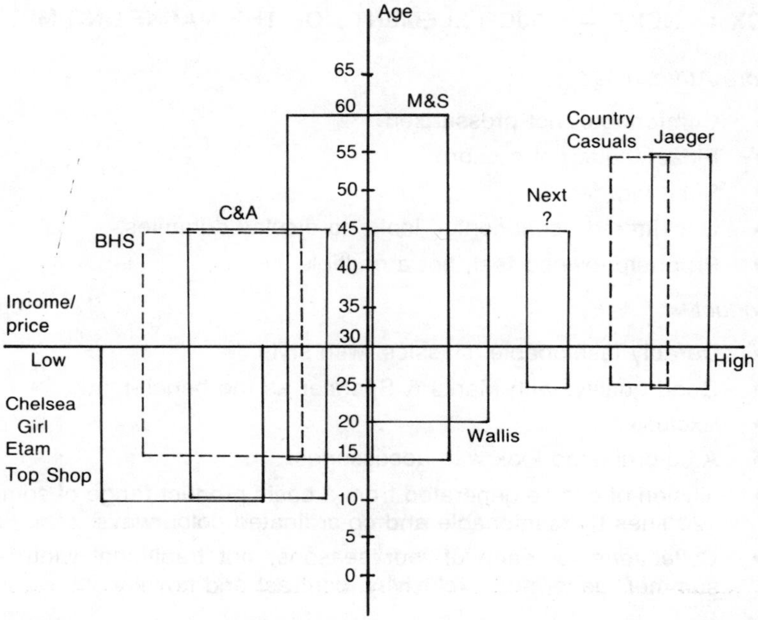

Figure A4.1 *Ladies' outerwear market, United Kingdom, 1982: positioning map of some major retailers*

oriented, increasingly independent, working women (see Figure A4.1). This was the first time a clothing retailer had narrowly segmented the market by life-style, not age. Next's strategy was to retain control over product design, maintain exclusivity and to enable brand image developments. The announced aim was to offer:

> Well-designed products in well-designed environments, at reasonable prices [interpreted as Marks & Spencer + 10 per cent], appealing to people's aspirations and enabling selection of a co-ordinated look to encourage multiple purchase.

Next was launched in the Spring of 1982 with simultaneous opening of seventy stores.

Careful attention was paid to all elements of the marketing mix to guarantee internal consistency, giving particular reference to the target market (see Box 1).

From its launch in early 1982, Next grew rapidly by taking sites from the Hepworth chain and quickly established a strong brand image, customer loyalty and imitators, e.g. Principles and Solo. By the end of 1982, 30 stores had been added and in the next 12 months a further 31 were opened giving 131 stores in operation.

BOX 1 NEXT — MAJOR ELEMENTS OF THE MARKETING MIX

Store Atmosphere

- Comfortable, not pressurized.
- Pleasurable, not a chore.
- Subdued decor.
- Uncluttered, 'continental' look, no display dummies.
- Proprietor-owned feel, not a multiple.

Product

- Durably fashionable 'classics' with style.
- Good quality, with Marks & Spencer as the bench-mark.
- Exclusivity.
- A co-ordinated look with accessories.
- Illusion of choice generated from a basic product range of some 120 lines by fashionable and co-ordinated colourways.
- Collections for each of four seasons, not traditional winter–summer, generated exclusivity, contrast and novelty.

Pricing

- Pitched at level to assure quality yet offer value for money.
- Support exclusivity but not deter target market.
- Marks & Spencer + 10 per cent premium.

Promotion

- Low-key, below-the-line, e.g. sponsorship of show jumping.
- No end-of-season sales.
- Continuous release of merchandise through the season to create customer interest and loyalty.

Merchandising/display

- Mix-and-match principle. Complete wardrobe of clothes, shoes and accessories displayed in co-ordinated ranges helping outfit matching and enhancing multiple purchases.
- Tight computerized stock control minimizing stock outs.

Selling/shop staff

- Consultants not 'sales assistants'.
- Profile target customer age/aspirations.
- Wear-and-display store merchandise.

Next for Men (August 1984)

Because Next had targeted a narrow segment in the UK women's outerwear market, major expansion was thought to be limited. Therefore, in August 1984, Next for Men was launched, drawing heavily on the original Next concept. The basic idea was to target 'the male partner of the Next woman', especially as research had shown that up to 70 per cent of men's wear purchases were influenced by women. The transfer of the Next concept from the women's to the men's market was not thought to be without risk, especially as traditionally men spent less of their disposable income and overall placed less emphasis on clothes than women. However, the Next plan was to replicate, wherever possible, their basic approach in the men's market, segmenting by life-style and age, middle-class aspirations, expectations and to a lesser extent incomes in the 25–45 age group.

Clearly, there was an intention to build upon the authority of the brand already built in the women's market. A product positioning analysis for Next for Men's market entry is suggested in Figure A4.2. As with the launch of Next into the women's market, careful attention was paid to the design of the marketing mix to ensure consistency with the overall market strategy (see Box 2).

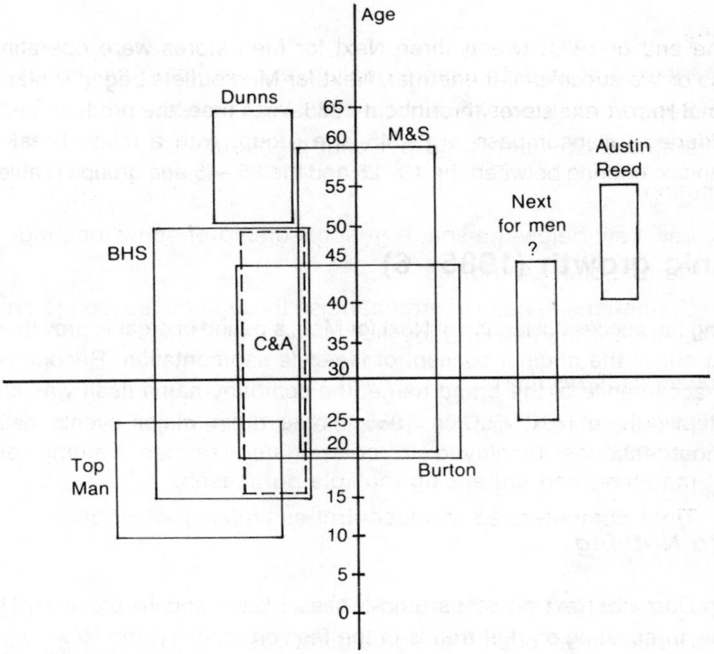

Figure A4.2 *Men's outerwear market, United Kingdom, 1984: positioning map of some major retailers*

Table A4.2 UK population by age group and sex, 1983–98

(unit = %)

	1983		1989		1993		1998	
	Female	Male	Female	Male	Female	Male	Female	Male
0–14	18.8	20.9	17.9	19.9	18.7	20.8	19.3	21.4
15–24	15.6	17.2	14.5	16.1	12.6	13.9	11.4	12.6
25–44	25.8	27.5	27.9	29.6	28.2	30.0	28.3	30.2
45–64	22.1	22.4	21.3	21.7	22.2	22.6	23.0	23.3
65+	17.7	12.0	18.4	12.7	18.3	12.7	17.9	12.6

UK population by sex 1983–98

(unit = 000s)

	1983	1989	1993	1998
Female	28,946	29,042	29,203	29,411
Male	27,430	27,579	27,825	28,121
Total	56,376	56,621	57,028	57,532

Source: HMG Actuary's Department.

By the end of 1984, twenty-three Next for Men stores were operating and, because of the success of the format, Next for Men outlets began replacing the traditional Hepworths stores throughout 1985. With time, the product positioning was widened to encompass a 19–45 age group, with a clean break in the merchandise offering between the 19–25 and the 25–45 age groups (Table A4.2).

Organic growth (1985–6)

Following the successful launch of Next for Men, a period of organic growth ensued, working out of the original concept of life-style segmentation. Recognizing the market acceptance of the brand name, the company name itself was changed from Hepworth to Next PLC in 1985. Three other major events happened throughout 1985.

Next to Nothing

Given the fact that Next did not use end-of-season sales and the problem of buyers' precisely forecasting market trends in the fashion industry, the Next to Nothing format was employed. The basic idea was to use secondary off-pitch sites to solve three problems in fashion retailing:

BOX 2 NEXT FOR MEN — MAJOR ELEMENTS OF THE MARKETING MIX

Location

- Originally analyzed by Acorn classification
- Heavily influenced by Hepworth property portfolio.

Atmosphere

- Similar to original Next conception.
- Subdued sophistication, including spacious changing-rooms, considerable amount of glass and mirrors, music, leather chairs, coffee tables, wooden fixtures.
- Warm, no pressure.

Product

- Exclusivity.
- Good quality/value.
- Formal wear (including off-the-peg and made-to-measure suits) and casual wear (fashion, leisure and active sportswear).

Pricing

- Premium over Marks & Spencer and major department stores.
- Availability of credit via Club 24.

Merchandising/display

- Limited merchandise on display creating illusion of space and exclusivity.
- Restricted range depth and width but create impression of both via co-ordination.

Selling/shop staff

- Reflect target customer profile.
- Wear-and-display store merchandise.

1. End of season reductions: By establishing a separate chain, Next were able to clear out reduced items from the prime locations. Such a move presented clear advantages in terms of releasing scarce retail selling space, allowing new lines to be displayed to maximum effect. Further, the fact that no discounted merchandise was on offer in the prime outlets enhanced the intended image of quality and exclusivity with an overall aura of excitement and customer interest.

2. Buyers' mistakes: Any lines that fail to sell as well as hoped could be removed and discounted without damage to the prime outlet.
3. Broken stock: Similarly, odd sizes, which appear when suppliers have run out and size ratios break down too, could be removed and discounted.

Next Interiors

Launched in August 1985, although a diversification from the traditional clothing base, the new product range was designed to appeal to the existing customer base. Next Interiors represented a transfer of the established brand name and merchandising techniques into home furnishings. The position adopted was to sit between the design/value offering of Habitat and the traditional furniture store. Tight stock control and a limited product range was achieved, with the support of a Home Furnishings Catalogue, which illustrated the some thirty product groups of households goods, furniture and fabrics.

Next Too and Next Collection

In August 1986, the original Next formula was refined by segmenting further into Next Too and Next Collection. As George Davies said: 'we decided to divide and grow. We felt that the fashion market in the mid-1980s was itself splitting, with women wanting to make different statements at different times of the day' (*Financial Times*, 21 August 1986). The catalyst for the move though was probably two-fold: concern at competitive response and imitation, e.g. Principles (Burton Group) and Marks & Spencer; and secondly, worries about the possible loss of exclusivity.

Next Too was developed from approximately half of the original Next outlets. In particular, it was aimed at the high-spending businesswoman. The apparel remained as stylish as before but more limited in quantity, with a higher level of quality and associated price. The remaining half of the original stores were converted to Next Collection, which offered similar prices and quality as before with both formal and casual styles. In some cases, rather than establish separate stand-alone outlets, larger stores, e.g. Newcastle upon Tyne (25,000 sq. ft) were converted to a shop-within-a-shop format offering not only clothing but also cosmetics, fragrances, accessories, hairdressing, lingerie, florist arrangements and a coffee bar. The split into the two formats provided the opportunity to adjust significantly the market offering according to the requirements of a given locality and trading area.

To solve the problem of site acquisition and geographical expansion required of such an organic growth policy, Next acquired 104 Lord John and Werff outlets from Raybeck PLC in September 1985. Alongside the three major events noted above, throughout the two years 1985/6, Next inaugurated and developed a range

Table A4.3 Next PLC — number of outlets

	1982	1983	1984	1985	1986[b]
Next Too	100	131	159	210	112
Next Collection					109
Next for Men			23	114	162
Next Lingerie					5
Next Accessories (stand-alone)					3
Next Interior				14	36
Next Café				5	9
Next Expresso bar				1	6
Next Florist				5	8
Next Hairdressers					3
Next to Nothing				2	15
Hepworths	316	294	204	84	—

a Including shops within shops.
b By August 1986, Next operated 275 stores and 468 outlets.
Source: Company Data.

BOX 3 ADDITIONAL NEXT CONCEPTS

Next Cafe/Expresso Bar

Appeared in 1985 in existing stores giving what Next believed to be an 'aromatic pull' into the store, where space allowed.

Next Accessories

Originally developed to complement and co-ordinate with the apparel portfolio.

Next Lingerie
Next Florists
Next Hairdressers
Next Cosmetics

Life-style segmentation employed to create a total package of related product areas around the core business.

Next Boys & Girls

A targeted range of fashionable children's wear purchased by existing 'Next' mothers and fathers for their progeny.

of further niche concepts working out of the basic principle of life-style segmentation. Four of these additional concepts are described in Box 3. Table A4.3 provides an illustration of the proliferation of Next life-style concepts.

During the summer of 1986, Club 24 was established as a separate entity 'with a credit facility of £400 million'. Although clearly concentrating on the United Kingdom throughout the two years of 1985/6 (Table A4.4), Next did establish a number of franchise operations overseas, e.g. in Oslo, Nicosia, Limassol, Qatar and Antwerp, and also entered discussions with Daido and C Itoh concerning the establishment of a joint venture in Japan.

Growth by acquisition (1986–7)

The twelve months from July 1986 to July 1987 saw Next make three major acquisitions: Grattan PLC (July 1986), Combined English Stores (June 1987) and Dillons (July 1987).

The logic for the agreed acquisition of Grattans for £300 million was explained by George Davies in his CEO's comments, in the 1986 Report and Accounts:

Table A4.4 Regional distribution — population by sex and Next branches, 1986

	Distribution of female population %	Next branches (women's) number	%	Distribution of male population %	Next branches (men) number	%
Scotland	9.4	14	7.5	9.3	11	8.6
North	5.7	6	3.2	5.7	4	3.1
North West	11.7	21	11.3	11.6	14	10.9
Yorkshire & Humberside	8.9	12	6.5	9.0	8	6.3
West Midlands	9.3	18	9.7	9.5	14	10.9
East Midlands	7.0	14	7.5	7.1	7	5.5
East Anglia	3.5	8	4.3	3.5	6	4.7
Wales	5.1	9	4.8	5.1	3	2.3
South West	8.1	23	12.4	8.0	12	9.4
South East	18.7	54	29.0	18.8	30	23.4
London	12.4	27	14.5	12.2	19	14.8
	100.0	206	100.0	100.0	128	100.0

Source: Trade Information/*Retail Business*, 343, September 1986.

> The speed and success of our product development programme caused us to look beyond the High Street for other growth areas. This led us to consider possible retail alternatives and in particular the attractions to our customers in being able to shop from home. Exploring this opportunity brought us to Grattan . . . Both Next and Grattan had enormous strengths . . . that could be cross-fertilized to the benefit of both companies.
>
> We therefore formed a unique marriage, with the ultimate goal of creating an entirely different concept through the medium of home shopping. Our aim is to widen the availability of the Next product range and to broaden people's perception of buying by catalogue.
>
> Grattan has been conspicuously successful not only in expanding its traditional catalogue business through the medium of its agents, but also in developing mail order selling. The company has been able to target particular markets for its smaller catalogues and distributors by virtue of its first class computer and systems expertise. (Company Report and Accounts, 1986)

Table A4.5 Mail order in the United Kingdom — market shares of leading companies, 1980 and 1986

	1980	1986
GUS	36	43
Littlewoods	29	25
Freemans	11	14
Grattan	10	10
Empire	7	6
Others	7	3
	100	100

Source: Trade estimates.

At the time, Grattan was the fourth largest catalogue mail order company in the United Kingdom with a market share of about 10 per cent (Table A4.5). In the early part of the 1970s, Grattans had performed badly as a result of the economic depression and the erosion of the mail order houses' differential advantages of extended credit and a wide range of goods, displayed in the bi-annual 1,000+ page 'free' catalogue. However, in the years immediately prior to acquisition, under new management led by David Jones, performance had improved (see Table A4.6). The reasons for this improvement were three-fold:

1. A significant tightening-up of the traditional agency business, which itself had declined in importance from 75 per cent of company turnover in 1985 to 60 per cent in 1986.
2. The emergence of the profitable growth sectors of direct mail and direct response (20 per cent and 10 per cent of company sales respectively in 1986).
3. The successful launch of a range of specialogues covering particular products and aimed at specific customer target groups.

Table A4.6 Grattan and Combined English Stores: financial performance[a]

Grattan PLC (acquired July 1986)
Year ending 31 January

	1982	1983	1984	1985	1986
Turnover £m	177.1	183.3	219.1	266.0	195.3
Pre-tax profit £m	5.2	(1.1)	3.5	9.6	16.0
Net margin %	2.9	(0.6)	1.8	4.4	6.6

Combined English Stores (acquired June 1987)
Year ending 31 January

	1983	1984	1985	1986	1987
Turnover £m	102.7	110.0	121.9	142.8	189.0
of which retailing £m	67.6	73.4	81.9	97.4	139.7
Pre-tax profit £m	1.8	5.9	9.2	12.4	21.8
Retail profit £m	2.2	3.3	7.5	11.8	21.7

a For the five years prior to takeover.

Source: *Retail Business Quarterly Retail Trade Review*, 3, September 1987.

In addition to the bi-annual main catalogue, other catalogues operated by Grattan in July 1986 included: Look Again, aimed at younger shoppers; You and Yours, offering one catalogue for personal requirements and one for home and family; Streets of London, offering up-market fashion products aimed at the career woman; Second Look; Fashion Plus; Grattan Direct; Scotcade, a direct operation; Kaleidoscope, a direct catalogue offering unusual merchandise and Manorgrove, the clearance catalogue for merchandise selling badly in other catalogues.

The successful operation of such a range of catalogues and specialogues required the development of sophisticated computer systems. Such expertise, it was thought, would be a great potential benefit to Next, using primarily UK suppliers and often carrying small stocks of a limited range of goods. Such a policy demanded both an effective stock control and ordering system.

Next outbid Ratners PLC, the leading UK jewellery retailer, paying £325 million for Combined English Stores in June 1987. The reasons for the acquisition were at the time argued to be two-fold: a number of the acquired retail outlets would be converted to 'pick-up' points for customers ordering from the then-to-be-launched Next Directory and additionally the opportunity geographically to expand the number of Next outlets in the United Kingdom and possibly West Germany would be seized.

At the time of the acquisition, approximately 75 per cent of CES's £189 million turnover was accounted for by retailing, the remaining 25 per cent of the business being generated by wholesale and travel divisions, including Eurocamp and

Table A4.7 Combined English Stores — number of retail outlets, June 1987

Paige	205	Women's fashion chain
Salisbury	150	Handbags and fashion accessory chain
Collingwood	131	Jewellery chain[a]
Zales	112	Jewellery chain
Weir	107	Jewellery chain
Allens	100	Chemists chain
Biba	56	Fashion chain (West Germany)

a Positioned up-market from both Collingwood and Zales.

Sunsites. In the five years prior to acquisition, CES had performed satisfactorily (see Table A4.6), operating seven different retail formats (see Table A4.7).

Plans discussed at the time of the CES acquisition suggested that Next was likely to retain and develop Zales, Salisbury and Biba; the latter, of course, giving access to the European fashion market. The other two jewellery chains, Collingwood and Weir and about half of the Paige outlets, it was thought, would be converted to the Next format.

Of the remaining 100 or so Paige shops, some 50 were likely to be converted to Salisbury outlets, the rest being sold as surplus to requirements. Next announced its intention also to sell off the wholesale business and probably Allens, although there was the possibility of the chemist chain being used as part of Next's mail order plans.

The third major acquisition, in July 1987, was that of Dillons, a CTN (confectioner, tobacconist, newsagent) group with about 270 outlets for £28.5 million. (Analysts suggested this was an inflated price when compared with the price of £16.9 million for the purchase of the larger Finlays CTN chain earlier in 1987.) Dillons' year-end report and accounts at 28 June 1986 showed a net profit of £3 million on some £60 million of turnover. Given that the majority of the Dillon sites were either neighbourhood or suburban, they were thought to be ideal as 'pick-up' points for the imminent January 1988 launch of the Next Directory. The use of collection points was thought to be vital as frequently Grattan had experienced the situation of there being nobody at home to receive orders sent through the post.

Integration and expansion

The Next Directory was launched on 12 January 1988, combining the strengths of Grattan's customer data-base, mailing, IT and distribution skills with Next's merchandising skills and image. As George Davies had noted, it was a case of 'being able to identify an affluent group of customers not currently being catered for by an existing chain'. The Directory offered Next a possible alternative solution to the problem of finding and acquiring expensive retail sites. It moved away from the 'old' mail order philosophy and offered revolutionary quality of both product and service — recognizing that the working woman wanted to enjoy her leisure time with less effort involved in such activities as shopping. The launch was an immediate success with 500,000 copies of the catalogue being sold in the first four weeks and sales of £20 million being made in the first ten weeks. The average order size of £75 was about 50 per cent above the industry average. This probably represented the fact that a high proportion of customers were of the ABC1 socio-economic groupings, rather than the more traditional C1 C2 DE mail order catalogue user. The catalogue itself was exclusive and lavish in quality and layout, with fabric swatches and high-quality professional photography. Some 80 per cent of orders were delivered by Next's own delivery service within forty-eight hours, with a small proportion of orders being delivered by post within three days. Analysis of the customer base quickly established that a high proportion of men were using the Directory, ordering both formal and casual merchandise, and that 48 per cent of customers placed repeat orders. Packaging consisted of high-quality hanging bags and 'chocolate box' packs.

A second integration of Next's and Grattan's operations lay in the area of IT and financial services. Next integrated their Club 24 with the Grattan data-base marketing facility to enhance their credit services. Next also began to offer data-base marketing facilities to marketeers and retailers as well as a complete laser printing and mailing service. Additionally, the Next data-base was developed to achieve highly accurate direct mail-shots, promoting their own financial services. The expansion with financial services allowed Next the opportunity to integrate their own marketing, credit, printing and mailing operations into services that could be offered to third parties and were ultimately used by retailers such as Dixon, Etam, Kingfisher and Granada.

The opportunity to integrate and rationalize the physical distribution management system of Next and Grattan was also seized, to consolidate warehouse and distribution operations. Direct Line instituted a distribution network for both Next retail stores and the Next Directory. Given Next's concern with quality, value for money and design its minimal stock holding and its reliance on UK suppliers, it was company policy to establish close relationships with manufacturers. To this end, it had not only invested in its own tailoring facility in Ashington, Co. Durham, but also acquired a small knitwear manufacturer, Paul James Knitwear.

Dénouement — restructuring

The two-year period between Spring 1988 and Spring 1990 saw a dramatic turn-around in Next's fortune (Tables A4.8 and A4.9). The six years since inauguration in 1982 had, by early 1988, seen significant growth, success and stock-market acclaim. However, in the succeeding two years Next faced major problems on at least three levels:

1. The speed of such rapid growth placed the company under major organizational strain — managerially, operationally and financially.
2. A changed environment with generally depressed demand and increased interest rates and costs.

3. Increased competition from Marks & Spencer, Principles, Solo, Blazer, Zy, Hornes, etc.

These pressures led to a dramatic change of senior personnel, declining sales and profitability, and ultimately the institution of a major restructuring and divestment programme. However, an aura of confidence still permeated the group in January/February 1988. It could be pointed out that:

1. Following the success of Kaleidoscope and Scotcade, four retail shops had been opened.
2. Following the split of Next into Next Too and Next Collection, total sales in any given town or city had increased.
3. The linkage between Salisbury and Next had proved beneficial, especially to the former's sales following the launch of Next shoes.
4. Mercado, CES's wholesale division, had launched a specialist range of Next carpets.
5. The Next Directory launch had surpassed expectations.

Indeed, 1988 was a continuation of the basic Next strategy with four new concept launches:

1. *Next Originals*: Launched in January 1988, this range of merchandise and outlets was initially aimed at ABC1 women in county towns. The range possessed its own 'unique personality and fashion statement'. Indeed, it was argued to incorporate the true essence of the Next philosophy as it encompassed design, style and quality at affordable prices. Because of its success, the offering was extended to the cities and at the same time, the decision was taken to discontinue the Next Too and broaden the Next Collection ranges.
2. *Next Jewellery*: Following the successful introduction in 1987 of fashion jewellery into the product range, it was decided to launch, in May 1988, free-standing Next Jewellers, offering basically fashion jewellery but with some precious stone items. The move represented a deliberate attempt to move away from the atmosphere of the traditional jewellery outlet.
3. *Department X*: With a dual opening in Oxford Street, London and Argyle Street, Glasgow, a dramatically different retail environment was offered in Autumn 1988. The new format offered established clothing ranges but the interior store design deliberately reproduced the working parts of a high technology warehouse, including moving rails, carousels and a paternoster. The two major advantages of the design were argued to be increased store attractiveness and efficiency.
4. *Next 24 Hours*: The concept of the 24 Hour Store was that it would carry no stock, only one of any given item of merchandise and would be restocked on a daily basis before 10.00 a.m. Consequently all stock was displayed giving at least a 100 per cent increase in display over conventional retailing.

Table A4.8 Hepworth/Next PLC, 1980–90: financial performance

Year ended	1980[a] 31 August	1981[a] 31 August	1982[a] 31 August	1983 31 August	1984 31 August	1985 31 August	1986 31 August	1988 31 January (17 months)	1989 31 January	1990 31 January
Turnover £m	60.2	73.5	83.4	98.6	108.3	146.0	190.0	1,119.7	1,135.9	949.2
Pre-tax profit £m	2.1	(0.06)	3.9	8.5	13.6	17.0	23.6	122.5	62.3	(46.7)
Net margin %			4.6	8.7	11.2	11.6	12.4	10.9	5.5	

a Next launched Spring 1982; 1980 and 1981 Hepworth figures only. Hepworth did not change its name to Next PLC until 1985.

Source: Company Report and Accounts.

Table A4.9 Next PLC: financial performance by main activity, 1986–90

	1986[a] Turnover	1986[a] Operating profit	1988[b] Turnover	1988[b] Operating profit	1989 Turnover	1989 Operating profit	1990 Turnover	1990 Operating profit
High street retailing	160.4	13.9	519.4	62.8	289.2	23.2	301.6	10.7
Home shopping	18.4	0.4	529.0	48.9	450.0	18.7	491.6	13.7
Financial services[c]	—	5.3[c]	6.9	11.2	7.0	7.8	9.6	4.0
Property	11.2	4.8	64.4	9.8	52.4	11.8	45.9	11.8
					798.6	61.5	848.7	30.2
Businesses sold					337.3	31.3	100.5	5.8
	190.0	24.4	1,197.7	132.7	1,135.9	92.8	949.2	36.0

a 12 months to 31 August 1986.
b 17 months to 31 January 1988.
c Financial services includes the group share of Club 24 Ltd profit but excludes its turnover.

Source: Company Report and Accounts.

In April 1988, a successful bid of £22 million was made for a further CTN chain, Alfred Preedy PLC, which it was planned would be integrated with the Dillon outlets as collection points for the Next Directory operation. Difficulties however were being experienced with the Directory. Although it was widely acclaimed as a breakthrough by mail order analysts, it was a loss-maker in the first two years of its life. Some problems were initially experienced with meeting delivery promises and the credit clearance of customers. Because of a lack of a trade preview, some merchandise sold badly, with significant markdowns being required. In other areas, though, demand was underestimated, which in turn increased pressure on suppliers.

In its second year of operation, the Directory suffered from a nation-wide postal strike. Estimates suggested Next lost some £15 million of mail order sales because of the postal workers' industrial action.

In the second half of 1988, tensions emerged in the group and particularly at board level, concerning corporate strategy leading into the 1990s, especially given the rapid rate of growth since the mid-1980s. As noted earlier, management strains were appearing, especially concerning operations, finance and the problems of integration. Some critics were arguing that George Davies' skills were more appropriate to the guidance of a smaller 'entrepreneurial flair' company than to the professional management needs of a large organization. The board schism and argument deepened to such an extent that in early December, George Davies and his group product director, Liz Davies, were dismissed. As the *Financial Times* (10 December 1988) cryptically commented: 'cash before flash'. Davies was succeeded as chairman by Michael Stoddart, who had in fact earlier relinquished that same position in October 1987 and as chief executive, by David Jones, who had joined the group with the Grattan takeover in July 1986.

While the company results for the year ending 1 January 1989 were bad with pre-tax profit falling to £62.3 million from £111.5 million the previous year on sales of £1,135.9 million and £1,119.7 million respectively, those for the year ending 1 January 1990 were disastrous, showing a loss of £46.7 million on a turnover of £949.2 million (Table A4.8). Not surprisingly, the newly constituted board conducted a major and urgent review of the group's four core businesses (designated as high street retailing, home shopping, financial services and property, see Table A4.10). As announced in the 1990 chairman's statement, the board conducted 'a major review of the Group's trading activities at all levels to identify profitable growth areas and to reduce the cost base in line with current trading'.

Five major actions were taken as a result of this strategic review:

1. The disposal of peripheral activities and businesses not seen as being central to the group core operations.
2. A large-scale efficiency study conducted with the aid of external consultants, resulting in both a major retraining programme and staff redundancies.
3. A dramatic reduction in corporate selling space.
4. A continuous on-going emphasis on cash control.
5. The transfer of all of the home shopping distribution operation to the newly opened Listerhills depot in Bradford.

Table A4.10 Next PLC: sector breakdown of group companies

At 31 January 1988	At 31 January 1989	At 31 January 1990
High street retailing	*High street retailing*	*High street retailing*
Allens	Biba	Next Retail
Biba	Dillons	Next Originals
Dillons	M Mercado	Directory Shops
Next Accessories	Next Retail	
Next Boys & Girls	Preedy	
Next Collection		
Next Interior		
Next Lingerie		
Next for Men		
Next Originals		
Next Too		
Paige		
Salisbury		
Zales		
Manufacturing division		
New Island Clothing	Van Dyke	Van Dyke
Paul James Knitwear	WVO	
Van Dyke		
W. Van Overdyke		
Home shopping	*Home shopping*	*Home shopping*
Aspect	Grattan	Grattan
Grattan	Kaleidoscope	Kaleidoscope
Kaleidoscope	Look Again	Look Again
Look Again	Next Directory	Next Directory
Next Directory	Scotcade	Scotcade
Scotcade	Streets of London	Streets of London
Streets of London	You and Yours	You and Yours
You and Yours		
Travel division		
Carefree		
Eurocamp		
Sunsites		
Financial services	*Financial services*	*Financial services*
Callscan	Callscan	Callscan
Club 24	Club 24	Club 24
Laser Mailing Services	Perimeter Technology	Time Retail Finance
Precision Marketing International	Wescot	Wescot
Westcot		
Property	*Property*	*Property*
Development Estates	Astonfawn	Astonfawn
Joint Ventures	Next Properties	Next Properties
	Shearwater Estates	Shearwater Estates

Source: Company Report and Accounts.

In his introductory comments to the 1990 Report and Accounts, Michael Stoddart pointed to the figure of £63 million for exceptional write-offs. Then, addressing each of the four core business areas in turn, he outlined plans for the future.

High street retailing

The high street core business activity had suffered from three unique factors since July 1987:

1. The activity had experienced profitability problems for three reasons, viz. the rapid increase in selling space and the number of stores following the CES acquisition with a resultant decrease in sales per square foot, increased competition and lastly increased costs.
2. Although Next Too was discontinued on the launch of Next Originals, a full range of Spring/Summer wear was received because it proved impossible to stop the initial orders placed in 1988. The received merchandise was merged into the Next Collection, but this resulted in an unbalanced range, with poor sales ensuing.
3. The same team was responsible for the merchandise collection for both the retail shops and the Directory. This resulted in overwork, weak merchandise ranges and disappointing sales.

A study of the precise reasons for poor high street performance revealed that the group only traded profitably from medium-sized stores (2,500–6,000 sq. ft) offering a full range of ladies'/men's wear, footwear and accessories, children's wear and fashion jewellery. As a result, it was decided to close sixty-three large and small outlets reducing total retail selling space by 98,000 sq. ft. As the five Next 24 Hour shops had traded successfully, it was planned to increase the number to fifteen, but because of the close link to home shopping to change the trading name to Next Directory.

Home shopping

The group was argued to be unique in the industry because it possessed four major activities incorporating:

1. Direct response retailing in which it was the market leader with Kaleidoscope, Scotcade and one-off joint ventures with a range of magazines and newspapers.
2. A range of direct-to-customer catalogues including Look Again, You and Yours, and Streets of London.
3. A traditional agency catalogue, Grattan.
4. The Next Directory which, although only two years old, introduced new dimensions to the industry of both customer profile and the quality of goods

and services offered. Sales for the year ended 1 January 1990 were £77 million, a £17 million increase on the previous year.

The group was, therefore, strongly argued to be well placed to take advantage of the future, especially given the expectation of the demise of the traditional agent, i.e. the person who ran the catalogue for friends and neighbours. Increasingly, it was being experienced that the majority of home shoppers required a full range of merchandise for themselves and immediate family alone.

Financial services

This area of core business had been expanded to include the full range of credit services, credit rating systems, data-base marketing and telephone marketing information systems.

Property

Following difficulties in the commercial property market, the group would follow selective development with a policy of stressing projects realizing a positive cash flow in 12–18 months.

Divestment

As part of the restructuring process, all those activities not perceived as central to the future of the four core businesses were sold. Major divestments throughout 1989 are indicated in Table A4.11.

The future

Following the major restructuring and divestment programme, the board announced in early 1990 three key future objectives:

- to continue to improve the quality of our product and service
- to continue the efficiency programme to reduce costs
- to continue to control our cash

> We believe that the successful retailers of the 1990s will be those that offer the best product and the best service. This is equally important to all our core businesses. The reputation of Next in the 80s was established by the quality, design and value of its products and by the high standard of service to its customers. We shall build upon this asset in the 90s and we shall take advantage of demographic changes by positioning our products to appeal to a broader range of customers. (Company Report and Accounts, 1990, p.17)

Table A4.11 Divestments in 1989

Activity	Buyer	Price £m
Dillons } Preedy } (majority of stores)	T. & S. Stores	53.9
Preedy (larger stores)	W.H. Smith	7.9
Zales } Salisbury }	Ratner	135.0
Allens	Lloyds	30.0
Eurocamp	Management buy-out	32.0
Next Jewellers	Management buy-out	10.0
Mercado	Management buy-out	20.0
Biba (West Germany)	European consortium	?

Questions

1. Identify and evaluate those factors which you think account for Next's success in the first half of the 1980s.
2. Identify and evaluate those factors which you think account for Next's failure in the second half of the 1980s.
3. In the light of your analysis, what lessons might be learned by the newly incumbent managerial team for the 1990s?

CASE STUDY 5

EPOS in supermarkets — some customer reactions

Introduction

Throughout the 1980s UK retailers, especially in the grocery, do-it-yourself and to a less extent the clothing sectors, as part of their productivity and cost-control drive, increasingly invested in IT (information technology). For the public, the most obvious manifestation of such an investment was the appearance of bar codes on produce and items, initially with a price label on the produce or item itself, and the installation of laser bar code reading equipment at check-outs, viz. EPOS (electronic point of sale).

However, as stores judged customers became used to such equipment and systems, the price label was not put on individual items of merchandise. Prices *per se* were only displayed on the shelves on which the goods were displayed.

Justification

To justify IT investment, retailers cited advantages for both themselves and also the customers:

Advantages to the retailer

By far the most regularly quoted reason for the installation of EPOS was cost saving to the individual retailer. Because EPOS represented the substitution of capital for labour at the check-out, fewer staff were required not just at the check-out itself, but also in the storeroom and warehouse, both marking prices on goods after delivery and ensuring new orders were placed on the shelves to ensure regular availability on the shopfloor. Generally, the tasks of stock ordering and replenishment and the check-out operation were performed more efficiently. As a result of this improvement, less buffer-stock was held throughout the retail organization with under- or over-stock positions only occurring locally, rather than throughout the whole group.

A second category of advantages offered the opportunity to increase both unit sales and total revenue. This could happen in five ways. As immediate implementation of a price change was possible, this meant that a product was no longer for sale at the old price. In a period of inflation, this price change normally meant a price rise. Where store management were given the authority, slow-selling lines could be eliminated, the freed shelf-space being allocated either to faster selling lines or to new product introductions. Line rationalization, however, did not only apply at store level. Improved buying decisions and line rationalization were most readily achieved centrally. In addition to making more effective decisions concerning the product mix, via centralized buying, large concentrated retailers were able to negotiate better terms from suppliers. Because of the increased efficiency of the check-out operation, retailers also anticipated decreased shrinkage rates.

If the first two groups of advantages can be regarded as 'hard', the third represents 'soft' advantages. Four specific advantages were frequently argued:

1. The opportunity to develop more accurate sales data and information.
2. Enhanced central discipline and control on branch management.
3. The development of electronic interchange with suppliers, possibly leading to automatic ordering systems.
4. The development of information collection, retrieval and manipulation skills allowing better strategic decision-making.

Of the advantages listed, those classified as cost-saving or revenue-generating were most frequently used to support EPOS/IT investment decisions.

Advantages to the customer

The three points most frequently mentioned by the retailer as being customer benefits were that the system would involve less queueing and waiting, it would provide an itemized bill that could be studied at home and, because of the reorder facility, a minimum number (ideally none) out-of-stock positions on the shelves would be experienced. Two more marginal benefits were also thought to apply. As the system was fully computerized, it was suggested there would be no pricing mistakes or overcharging. This, of course, was shown not to be true by a number of cases brought against EPOS-based retailers for overcharging in the county courts throughout the United Kingdom during the period 1987–9. Additionally, it was thought that as there were no price labels to fall off merchandise items, there would be no difficult pauses at the check-out while supervisors were asked to ascertain prices. These advantages, together with a bagging facility, were thought to be positive customer benefits, which would significantly assist consumer acceptance of EPOS. Concern, though, was expressed at the impersonality of the system, the fact that the customer would not have a price on a good once at home, and the danger of a breakdown of the total system.

Group interviews

In November 1987, four group discussions were held in Farsley, Bradford. The major objective was to assess customers' reaction to EPOS systems and, in particular, to ascertain whether the benefits as explained by retailers were so regarded by customers. Respondents were recruited by IRB Ltd, a London-based market research agency and the group interviews held at the field recruiter's home. Respondents were asked to participate in a group discussion on 'shopping' which would last approximately $1\frac{1}{2}$ hours. Prior to being invited, respondents had to meet the requirement of doing one major grocery shopping trip per week during which they would spend between £30–£50. Eight respondents participated per group. Taxi transport was provided where required to collect and return respondents to their homes and each was paid £7 for their time. Two groups were composed exclusively of Sainsbury shoppers, while the other two groups were primarily composed of Asda shoppers. However, in each of the latter two groups, one and two participants respectively most frequently shopped at Morrisons. Groups were controlled by socio-economic classification. All respondents had shopping experience of EPOS and non-EPOS grocery supermarkets.

Findings

J. Sainsbury PLC

Company image

Before discussing in any detail reactions to EPOS, respondents were asked to consider their overall impression of the supermarket they used most frequently, viz. Sainsbury and Asda/Morrisons. (Figure A5.1 shows a perceptual map of food outlets in the Bradford area prepared in the Spring of 1984. The study was repeated two years later but no significant changes were identified.) Generally, both groups possessed a highly favourable image of Sainsburys. There was general agreement that compared to other supermarkets in the area, Sainsburys was bigger, brighter and friendlier, especially where young children were concerned. Not surprisingly, this was of concern to mothers with pre-school children. Staff were always smiling, never unhappy or miserable, always helpful, regularly showing customers where difficult-to-find items were located in the store. Respondents liked what they perceived to be an extended product range offering unique items. Ranges noted included food, cosmetics and household items. Especially liked was the availability of a packer at the check-out and free carrier bags. (With no prompting, a number of participants pointed out the Asda policy of charging for a bag irrespective of spend.) Some thought the in-store bakery created a 'lovely atmosphere'. One respondent supported this thought strongly by reporting the situation of where she thought she had been overcharged for a reduced bakery item and was refunded

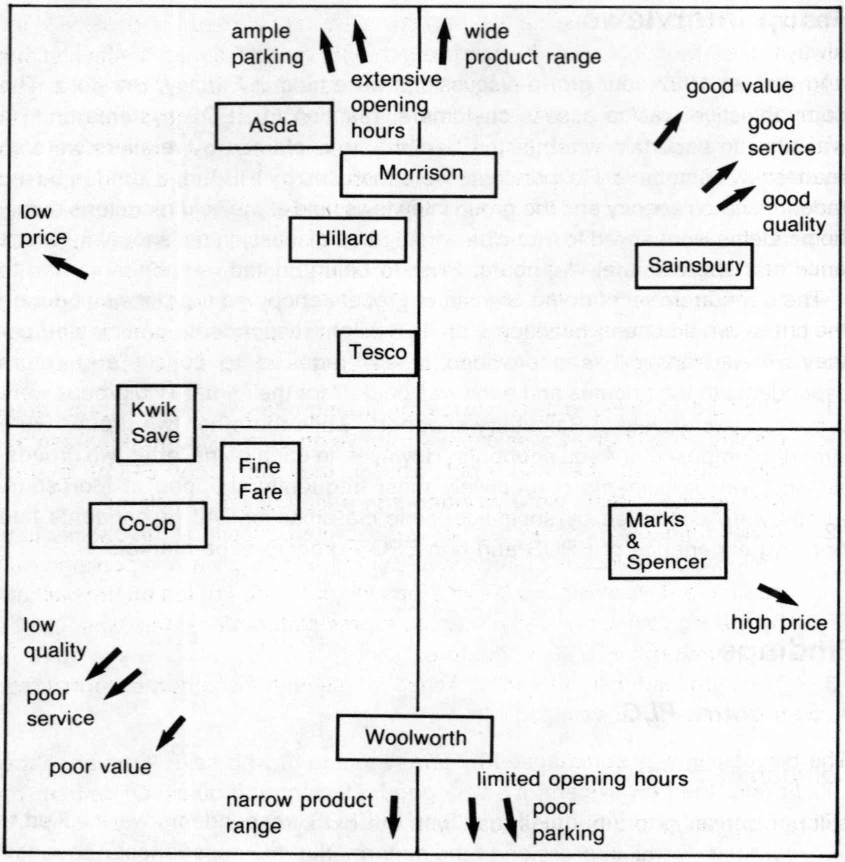

Figure A5.1 *Perceptual map with dimensions identified*

not only the difference between the two prices but also the cost of the telephone call on her next visit.

It was difficult for the groups to identify dislikes and complaints, but when pushed, identified waiting at the delicatessen (thought to be understaffed), accessibility from the road, and a lack of a one-way system in the car park as problem areas. One respondent requested a fresh fish bar.

Overall, both groups possessed strong positive images of the identified Sainsbury outlet, with one accolade receiving general approval — 'the Marks & Spencer of groceries . . . Sainsbury seems the cream of everything to me.'

Reactions to EPOS

When compared to the two Asda groups, Sainsbury respondents had much less to say about their reactions to EPOS and beyond two possible criticisms, all reaction was positively favourable. The two problem areas concerned the possibility (not always was it true) that squashy items, e.g. bread, would not read on the first pass and that as no prices were displayed on tins especially, it was not possible to compare prices on the pantry shelf at home. It should be pointed out that there was no worry within the discussion, that if an item were passed across the laser reader more than once, a customer would be charged for more than one item. Indeed, some members of the groups rejected the need for price comparison at home as they were given an itemized bill and were always able readily to see the price of any given item clearly displayed on the shopfloor shelf.

The general acclaim for the Sainsbury EPOS system evolved around speed at the check-out and the availability of an itemized bill. Customers generally thought they were spending less time waiting at the check-out for three reasons:

1. They did not have to queue twice for greengrocery produce — once at the display area to allow a salesperson to weigh and price the purchase and then again at the check-out. Under the Sainsbury EPOS system, greengrocery items were weighed and priced at the check-out.
2. A well-trained and skilful cashier was more productive at the check-out as it was easier to locate a bar code as compared to a price ticket on any given purchase. This was because whereas the bar code printed on the package by the manufacturer was always in a predictable place, this was not true for items priced by hand in store.
3. The itemized bill offered a sense of security whether or not it was subsequently scrutinized.

The discussion was summarized by one respondent who said: 'I'm very happy . . . I prefer the new system; it's very good, efficient and quick. Of course, you still get human errors but less than with the old system.'

Asda/Morrisons

Company image

Overall, the two Asda/Morrisons groups had a much less favourable image of the store(s) they most regularly used, as compared to the Sainsbury shoppers. Whereas the Sainsbury customers were highly satisfied and loyal users, it was certainly not true of the Asda shoppers, who tended to express views of only partially satisfied and slightly reluctant shoppers. The major reasons for using the Asda store were convenience in terms of location, product range, especially electrical items and children's clothing and value for money. (A number of resondents thought Asda offered the cheapest prices available in the neighbourhood.) Initially, the three Morrison's shoppers argued similar reasons for using their selected outlet; but once it was pointed out that a recently opened Morrison's state-of-the-art technology supermarket, which they had all visited, was not dissimilar to a Sainsbury store, general confusion emerged among the three concerning Morrison's image.

Reactions to EPOS

In both of the appropriate groups, Asda shoppers were by far the more articulate in expressing their views and experiences of EPOS. Whereas the Sainsbury shoppers welcomed the EPOS experience, the opposite was true of the Asda customers. A number reported that if they had the choice they would revert back to a non-EPOS, 'normal' store. It is possible to classify customers' complaints and concerns about EPOS under six headings:

1. A lack of trust and loss of confidence/control.
2. Problems of price identification and awareness.
3. The danger of overcharging.
4. Difficulties in estimating spend per supermarket visit.
5. Time pressures at the check-out.
6. Concerns about value for money and price comparisons with previously bought merchandise.

The initial reaction was that customers felt a loss of control, and indeed wondered whether they could trust a laser reading code system. As one respondent said:

> I just do not trust them [the EPOS system] . . . It's almost illogical because I somehow feel a computer should be more trustworthy, more reliable than having a cashier sitting there punching a number in . . . she might be tired or have something else on her mind. I would have thought she would be more likely to make a mistake, but actually, psychologically, I don't feel like that. I do not know what she's doing. I do not know what she's interpreting. I do not understand the system.

This view was firmly supported by another participant:

> You can't trust these codes because you do not know what they relate to in the machine . . . you lose control.

Discussions led on to worries about price identification, awareness and the danger of overcharging. Respondents much preferred the existence of a price ticket on an item of merchandise whether or not, in addition, it was bar-coded. The worst scenario was for an item to be bar-coded only. Often, it was pointed out, there were difficulties in establishing the price of an item either because the price card on the shelf was wrong, not there, or inaccurately positioned. A consequence was that it was impossible to relate price cards/data to merchandise displays. Often, it was said, that staff, once found, were unable readily to establish/locate the correct price.

Many stressed the need to be aware of prices not just to make a judgement as to whether or not to purchase an item, but to keep an approximate idea of spend to ensure that the weekly budget was not exceeded. Some dreaded the thought of being asked for more money than they physically had available in a purse or wallet. After all, it was said, 'it's your money you are spending.'

The problems of keeping track of prices were exacerbated by the practice of some stores charging different prices for the same item, e.g. baby food, according to store location. Special promotions too made it difficult to monitor price changes. Hence the broadly-held view was that it was much preferable for merchandise to be price-labelled.

A strong fear of being overcharged was expressed. Respondents reported the main ways in which they thought this might occur:

1. An item is wrongly 'priced within the computer', despite the fact that the correct price is displayed on the shopfloor.
2. When merchandise is passed over a laser reader more than once because of failure to read the first time.
3. A single item from a multiple pack (e.g. yogurt, which theoretically should not be split into individual items) will read off the multiple pack and not the single item price. Hence, on this point, respondents argued it was possible to be overcharged by a factor of 4 or 6.

As under the EPOS system, a cashier required less time to ring a trolley basket full of groceries through the till, the speed with which items were cleared/read was too fast for the individual customer to cope, if she wished to monitor the flow of individual prices across the laser reader. Hence, it was likely that in the absence of a packer, a customer would be confronted with a jumbled collection of shopping at the end of the check-out chute and the final total spending simultaneously. It was not physically possible both to watch prices ring up on the till and pack at the same time.

Customers, generally, felt under great time pressure, especially if there was a queue of five or six people, each with full trolley loads, waiting. The presence of a packer did little to help the customer as many people liked to pack their merchandise in their own way. The advantage lay, it was thought, with the retailer as generally the check-out process was speeded up.

Another major worry was the difficulties encountered in estimating the total spend per visit, not only because of the thought of spending too much but also the embarrassment of asking for items to be withdrawn from the buy because of insufficient available cash. It was not possible to estimate the precise cost of self-selected loose produce, e.g. greengrocery, unless items were priced per unit, e.g. oranges or pineapples. One respondent recounted the experience of one elderly shopper who had filled a plastic bag with peanuts, expecting to pay 75p. When asked for £6, he did not have the presence of mind to explain that he had grossly underestimated the cost. Consequently, he paid the bill but felt cheated.

The final major worry expressed by the Asda shoppers concerned value for money and the difficulty of making price comparisons at home with previously purchased items. Although itemized bills were received, these were regularly lost in the bottom of a bag or car boot and possibly thrown away with the multitude of small plastic bags acquired on a grocery shopping trip. Consequently once placed alongside previously bought items in the cupboard at home, it was not possible to track price movements nor readily identify older stock. Normally, with inflation, newer stock would bear higher prices. Hence, by looking at price labels alone, it was possible to ensure that the older stock was used first.

All but one of the Asda/Morrisons respondents preferred, on balance, the non-EPOS-based shopping system. It was conceded though that, under EPOS, the time spent waiting in the check-out queues was reduced.

Questions

1. As the Sainsbury and Asda supermarket store manager respectively, what recommendations would you make to your senior management concerning the launch of an EPOS-based store?
2. Privy to the results of all four group discussions:
   (a) as Sainsbury store management, how would you take advantage of the Asda results?
   (b) As the Asda management, how would you take advantage of the Sainsbury results?

CASE STUDY 6

Gateway Corporation PLC

Problem

At the end of 1988, the main board of Gateway Corporation PLC faced a number of problems. Headed by chairman Alec Monk, the corporation had grown dramatically for the previous 5–6 years via a policy of acquisition. Because of the speed of growth, the company faced particular problems of integration and the management of a retail grocery group with highly disparate store sizes, ranging from superstores to small neighbourhood shops, all trading under the one name 'Gateway'. In addition, although No. 3 in the UK grocery market, Gateway faced fierce competition especially from Sainsbury, Tesco, Argyll (including Cordon Bleu, Galbriath, Liptons, Lo Cost, Presto and Safeway) and Asda (see Box 1).

With little growth in the overall UK grocery market and a large number of small technically inefficient outlets, Gateway was looking for progress in terms of both effectiveness and efficiency. Many senior executives and indeed some main board directors were of the view that the company did not possess any differential advantage.

The position was subsequently encapsulated by trading director, Bob Willett:

> As you get bigger, sales per square foot go up. Ours was just the reverse; our sales per square foot were higher in our smaller stores than in our bigger ones. We were attempting to be all things to all men. We were trying to run superstores, big food markets, medium sized food markets and small ones. We presented a disparate picture to the customer and he was confused.

Company history

The story of how Gateway became a major player in UK grocery retailing is one of acquisition and began in May 1983 when Dee Discount, based in the north-east of England, merged with the southern-based Gateway. Within three months, Key Markets had been taken over, an event that set the tone for the next five years.

BOX 1 COMPETITITION — SOME PEN PORTRAITS

Asda

Sales £2.28 billion. After returning to basic food retailing by selling the MFI furniture chain and its food manufacturing business, 12 per cent increase in pre-tax profits to £215.3 million (1988). Increased margins as a result of increased own-label (now 35 per cent sales) and increased sales of fresh foods, clothing and footwear.

Argyll

Sales £3.24 billion with pre-tax profit £132.1 million. Converting Presto stores to Safeway format (seven converted during 1987 with plans to convert a further 60 during 1988/9). By 1991 hope to operate 400 Safeway stores. Smaller Presto stores unsuitable for conversion will become Lo Cost discount stores, of which there will be 400.

Sainsbury

Sales £5.01 billion with pre-tax profit £308.4 million (1977/8). UK's largest retailer. For third year running headed Marplan poll assessing the most effective marketing strategy. Own label 50 per cent + of turnover.

Tesco

Sales £4.12 billion with pre-tax profit £224 million (1987). Acquired Hillards (1987). Margin improvement via the increased sale of fresh foods. Chairman committed to large-scale retailing.

At least ten major acquisitions took place in this period, ensuring that, by 1988, Gateway possessed more retail outlets than Sainsbury and Tesco together and, because of the consequent geographical spread, could truly claim to be a genuinely national food retailer.

As Table A6.1 shows, two of the major acquisitions were in Spain and the United States.

In 1988 with a 12 per cent share of market generating £3.6 billion of sales, Gateway was clearly in the No. 3 position, although Argyll did possess fifty-six more outlets. However, when the top five UK food retailers are compared by sales per store per week, it can be seen that the top three are Asda, Sainsbury and Tesco, with both Gateway and Argyll lagging a considerable way behind (Table A6.2).

Such a wide disparity of sales per store per week is explained by the size of store. Gateway's distribution of stores by size in shown in Table A6.3.

The large number of small stores was a major problem, accounting for 70 per cent of the number of stores and yet generating only 40 per cent of total trade. These

Table A6.1 Acquisitions: Gateway Corporation PLC, 1983–8

	Stores/outlets	Price (millions)
June 1983: Key markets	98	£45
F.A. Wellworth (N. Ireland)	20	£22
Lennons (supermarkets)	43	£23
(off-licences)	95	
International Stores (ex. BAT)	380	£180
Lonsdale & Thompson Cash & Carry		£8
Fine Fare and Shoppers Paradise	435	£686
Woolco Hypermarkets	12	£26
		£990
Spanish Supermarkets	38	4
Medicare Drug Stores (UK)	49	20
Herman's Sporting Goods (US)	131	£278
		£1,294

Source: *Retail Business Review*, December 1988.

smaller neighbourhood stores relying upon convenience were losing out to the larger, out-of-town, one-stop shopping superstores and hypermarkets. Gateway were attacking the problem by seeking out-of-town sites and using some of the smaller stores, especially those acquired from Medicare, as drug stores, but as can be seen, this still left them with a large number of small outlets often operating as supermarkets.

Table A6.2 UK grocery market, 1988

	Sales £ (billions)	Number of stores	Market share %	Sales per week per store £000
Sainsbury	5.01[a]	283[b]	15	340
Tesco	4.12	379	14	209
Gateway	3.6	831	12	83
Argyll[c]	3.24	952	8	65
Asda	2.28	120	7	365

a Including Homebase but excluding Savacentre.
b Including Savacentre.
c Including Cordon Bleu, Galbraith, Liptons, Lo Cost, Presto, Safeways

Source: *Retail Business*, 8, December 1988.

Table A6.3 Store size (sq. ft): Gateway Corporation PLC

<5,000 sq. ft	323	571 stores or 70% of stores produce 40% of trade
5,001–10,000 sq. ft	248	
10,000–15,000 sq. ft	98	260 stores or 30% of stores produce 60% of trade
15,001–25,000 sq. ft	87	
25,001–50,000 sq. ft	54	
> 50,000 sq. ft	21	
	831	

Source: *Retail Business*, 8, December 1988.

Integration and rationalization

With the intention of bringing all trading units under a Gateway banner, a five-prong integration and rationalization programme was followed. The intention was that by April 1989 all outlets will be trading under the Gateway fascia. The programme involved:

1. Store refurbishment, including all fixtures and fittings according to the Gateway format.
2. The rationalization of all buying offices with a purpose-built head office in Bristol at the cost of £20 million.
3. The overhaul of the physical distribution system in a rolling three-year programme at a cost of £3.7 million. This has involved the building of two new 200,000 sq. ft distribution centres.
4. A major management training programme for 800 store managers to explain the Gateway culture and philosophy.
5. A training programme for 68,000 employees, again to explain the Gateway culture and philosophy.

Alongside the integration and rationalization programme, Gateway began in 1986 to become heavily involved in advertising, spending £710,000. By 1988 they were by far the largest advertiser in the UK grocery market, spending over £10 million (Table A6.4). The impact of this advertising can be seen in Table A6.5.

Performance

As a result of the strategy of acquisition supported by refurbishment, rationalization, management restructuring and staff retraining, group turnover in the five years

Table A6.4 UK grocery market: advertising expenditure by selected company, 1983–8 (£000)

	1983	1984	1985	1986	1987	1988
Asda	8,505	13,464	9,945	8,842	11,613	8,691
Bejam	1,325	2,097	2,575	1,888	2,900	3,559
Fine Fare }[a]	3,503	3,327	4,318	3,176	1,247	—
Gateway }[a]	—	—	—	710	3,917	10,826
Hillards }[a]	302	1,189	564	420	145	—
Tesco }[a]	11,593	11,176	9,614	9,022	8,313	6,008
Kwik Save	2,560	2,810	2,631	2,213	2,404	2,289
Presto }[a]	3,669	3,213	3,270	4,476	2,532	1,528
Safeway }[a]	949	1,281	1,009	1,653	3,123	5,498
Savacentre }[a]	1,125	78	1,113	332	—	273
Sainsbury }[a]	5,883	5,616	5,617	3,670	3,013	3,731
Total[b]	67,245	70,251	64,159	62,852	66,852	70,642

}a Companies bracketed together indicate either one company has taken over the other (e.g. Gateway, Fine Fare; Tesco, Hillards) or that they operate broadly under a joint corporate banner, e.g. Argyll took over both Presto and Safeway, while Sainsbury has a 50/50 share with British Home Stores in Savacentre.

b All chain grocers, co-ops, off licences, etc.

Source: MEAL.

Table 6.5 Percentage of shoppers who have heard of Gateway

	January–March 1987	March–July 1988
Total Great Britain	60%	82%
London	57%	82%
Midlands	56%	87%
Tyne Tees	59%	86%
Yorkshire	58%	61%
Lancashire	51%	82%
South	76%	86%
East of England	74%	86%
Scotland	33%	87%
South West	90%	97%
Wales and West	80%	79%

Source: *AGB Retail Image Monitor*.

Table A6.6 Financial performance 1983–7, some key indicators: Gateway Corporation PLC

	1983	1984	1985	1986	1987
Turnover £m	910.1	1,387.0	2,434.1	4,008.5	4,838.6
Profit before tax £m	17.0	28.3	64.3	126.5	192.2
Net margin %	1.9	2.0	2.6	3.1	4.0

Source: Company Report and Accounts.

Table A6.7 Main considerations when choosing to shop at Gateway

Convenience	65%[a]
Everything under one roof	41%
Good parking	30%
Clean/hygienic Store	25%
Stocks well-known brands	21%
Cheapest prices	21%
Opening hours	20%
Good quality fresh food	16%
Pleasant place to shop	16%

a Percentages add to more than 100 per cent because respondents rated more than one variable.

Source: PWA Image Study.

1983–7 increased five-fold. In the same period pre-tax profits increased by a factor of 10 and net margin per cent doubled, essentially because of the acquisition of Fine Fare with its large efficient stores in 1986 (see Table A6.6). Indeed, in 1988 Gateway was voted top UK retailing company by the *Director Magazine*. In addition to its acquisition programme, size and national coverage, it was pointed out that the company achieved £1 million of food trading per hour, with takings representing £1.30 for every man, woman and child in the United Kingdom each week. The national coverage point was emphasized when Gateway commissioned a PWA Image Survey probing why customers shopped at Gateway (see Table A6.7). By far the most important reason was convenience (65 per cent), followed by a distant second, everything under one roof (41 per cent). The remaining seven factors received a score of 30 per cent or below.

Exclusive brands

Aware of the need to build and create a differential advantage, which would enable the company to compete on more than just price in a highly competitive market,

Gateway introduced the concept of exclusive brands in 1987/8. The idea was to offer the consumer an alternative to the manufacturers' national brand, the retailers' own-label and indeed to generics. The proposition was that unique brand names and positionings would be generated for selected product groups and lines that were exclusively available from Gateway. The individual brand/product would be capable of promotion with the brand identity and personality being the foremost consideration. Retailer identity would conspicuously be a secondary consideration.

By the end of 1988, exclusive brands accounted for 17 per cent of turnover with 2,000 lines among fifteen brands. Within the period of 12–18 months 'exclusives' were:

1. The largest UK private bread brand (Wheatfields £36 million p.a.).
2. The largest UK milk brand sold through multiples (Fresh £50 million p.a.).
3. Pasta, which had gained 13 per cent of dry pasta sales (Bella £4 million p.a.).
4. A chocolate brand with a meaningful annual sales target of £2 million (Thistleton).

It was hoped that, by the end of 1990, exclusive brands would account for 30 per cent of group turnover with some fifty brands and 2,000 lines.

Management argued that exclusive brands offered six major advantages to Gateway:

1. The opportunity to generate exclusiveness and long-term differentiation as the product and brand were only available at Gateway outlets.
2. The opportunity to generate improved margins.
3. Exclusive brands had the potential to possess more personality than own-label.
4. Controllability, especially in terms of manufacturer relationships.
5. A relatively easy and inexpensive way of expanding a grocery shopper's evoked set of acceptable brands as Gateway controlled both promotional effort and space allocation.
6. Increased variety and choice for the consumer.

Questions

1. Evaluate the acquisition strategy Gateway pursued throughout the 1980s.
2. Do you agree that the exclusive brand concept will play a key role in achieving a long-term differential advantage for Gateway in the UK grocery market?

CASE STUDY 7

Rumbelows

Industry background

By the mid-1980s the UK electrical retailing industry had reached a watershed position in a largely mature and saturated market. The number of specialist outlets had fallen dramatically from a peak in the early 1970s by about 30 per cent to 13,000 in 1986 (see Table A7.1). The prime reason for this decline was the rationalization in the industry throughout the 1970s, as newly emerging national retailers, often from the basis of a strong TV rental business, e.g. Granada, Telefusion, DER, Thorn-EMI, acquired smaller regional chains. As part of the consequent integration process, small uneconomic outlets were closed, with possibly four or five small units being replaced by one enlarged and maybe re-sited shop.

Not surprisingly, therefore, by 1985 national multiples sold more electrical goods than any other type of outlet. Multiples possessed a 35 per cent share of the market as compared to the 25 per cent of the independents. Throughout the preceding fifteen years, multiples had been experiencing an increasing market share at the expense of the declining share possessed by the independents. Electricity boards held a 10 per cent share, largely, it was thought, because of the convenience to customers of paying one combined bill for both electricity used in any given time period and any instalment credit/higher purchase payment required to meet the purchase of a large electrical appliance, e.g. cookers, and to a lesser extent, fires.

Table A7.1 Number of retail electrical outlets, 1961–86

1961	16,500
1971	19,000
1976	18,000
1982	14,000
1986	13,000

Source: *Retail Business*, July 1986.

Table A7.2 Sales of electrical goods by type of organization, 1985 (%)

Multiples[a]	35
Independents	25
Electricity boards	10
Department stores	10
Co-ops	5
Other[b]	15
	100

a Includes Comet, Curry, Dixon, Lasky, Rumbelow and Tandy.
b Includes Boots and W.H. Smith, both of whom expanded the product range available in their record departments to include brown goods, e.g. stereo and hi fi equipment.

Source: Retail Business, July 1986.

Surprisingly, department stores too had a 10 per cent market share, but were under strong pressure on price from the national discounters, e.g. Comet and Curry (see Table A7.2).

For the period 1980–4, sales of electrical goods in total had struggled to show any real growth in value terms (see Table A7.3). Indeed, in some product areas as products reach the mature and decline stages of the product life-cycle declining real prices were the order of the day:.

With high UK penetration rates, the demand among white goods for large pieces of equipment (e.g. cookers, refrigerators and freezers) was essentially replacement,

Table A7.3 Sales through household goods and radio and electrical retailers, 1980–5 (Figures for 1980 sales in £m)

(Index weekly average sales, 1980 = 100)

Year	Household goods retailers	Electrical and music goods retailers	Television hire businesses	Electricity showrooms	Gas showrooms
1980	9,146	2,057	945	386	240
1981	107	109	109	103	102
1982	114	123	117	113	107
1983	128	137	129	136	113
1984	137	141	135	148	115

Source: Adapted from *Retail Business*, July 1986.

although some opportunities existed because of the social trend for an increase in the number of single-unit households.

Despite the overall pattern, some sectors were reasonably buoyant (e.g. microwaves and dishwashers). Additionally, demand for certain small electrical appliances (e.g. food processors and coffee machines) was becoming more fashion- and prestige-conscious to the detriment of functional requirements. Demand for television sets within the brown goods sector had not been as depressed as the overall performance in white goods. Despite high levels of household penetration of television ownership/usage, sales had been stimulated by a stream of innovations (e.g. teletext and VCR equipment) and the tendency for multiple television set ownership/usage per household. It was not uncommon for three or four television sets to be used in a household, one in the sitting room, one in the kitchen, with the remaining one/two being located in the children's bedrooms. Sales of VCRs too were boosted by the trend away from rental to outright purchase. This phenomenon had earlier been experienced by the industry both with the initial introduction of black and white TVs and then subsequently with the conversion to colour. The industry was also optimistic concerning the future of compact discs and compact disc players.

The major players

The major UK electrical retailers by 1985 are shown in Table A7.4.

Table A7.4 National chains: number of outlets, 1985

Currys[a]	527
Rumbelows[b]	404
Dixon	290
Comet[c]	161
Connect[d]	67
Ultimate/Supreme[e]	60

a Acquired by Dixon, December 1984.
b Owned by Thorn EMI.
c Acquired by F.W. Woolworth, April 1984.
d Owned by Telefusion rental shops and Trident discount stores.
e. Harris Queensway, a major furniture retailer, launched the Ultimate Chain subsequently expanding the operation via the acquisition of the 32-branch Rayford Supreme in the south east.

Source: *Retail Business*, July 1986.

Of the six major companies, only Dixons was not part of a larger parent group. The distribution of outlets by retailer is shown in Table A7.5. From the table it can be seen that all of the companies are relatively over-represented in London and the south-east, probably because of the higher level of disposable income in this area. Comet was particularly strong in Scotland because of it acquisition in 1977 of both the Philips discount chain, Eclipse and the local independent retailer, James McOnomy. Rumbelows only entered Scotland in 1983 and was over-represented in the north-west because of its 1960 acquisition policy. Large independent retailers not shown in Table A7.5 included the 100 outlet-strong Clydesdale operation in Scotland and the Vallance & Wigfall groups based in Yorkshire. Vallance based in Leeds operated thirty outlets while Sheffield-based Wigfalls was about three times larger, operating 100 shops.

In the latter part of the 1970s and the first half of the 1980s, the industry was actively searching for larger sites both to move out of town because of a rapid rise in high street rents, and also to increase productivity via the replacement of smaller uneconomic sites with enlarged, refurbished and possibly re-sited outlets. This was particularly true of Currys developing its out of town Bridger Chain, Comet and Connect trading from warehouse-style outlets in cheaper locations, and Harris Queensway with Ultimate operating sixty edge-of-town discount stores. The average Ultimate store size was 10,000 sq. ft, of which 75 per cent was designated as sales area. Indeed, in 1985, large edge- and out-of-town stores accounted for 5 per cent of industry turnover. By 1990 it was estimated this figure would quadruple to 20 per cent.

Throughout the period 1980–5, those companies which operated both a rental and retail business from the same site were increasingly recognizing the incompatibility of the two types of business. In the early 1970s, Donald Curry had

Table A7.5 National chains: regional concentrations by number of outlets, 1985

	Comet	Curry	Dixon	Rumbelows	% of population
Scotland	22	44	18	12	9
North	5	21	11	23	6
North West	16	48	36	75	11
Yorkshire	16	31	21	21	9
West Midlands	15	43	29	35	9
East Midlands	9	41	22	20	7
East Anglia	6	22	5	11	3
Wales	6	38	7	11	5
South West	12	55	18	24	8
South East	36	122	71	109	18
London	18	62	52	63	12
Total	161	527	290	404	100

noted:

> You cannot rent and sell successfully. The two operations are incompatible. Purchasing, marketing, stocking, financing, servicing — all these key functions are different.

As a result of this realization, Telefusion announced a plan to reorganize its method of operation with the intention to halve the number of retail outlets in a bid for survival. Similarly, Dixon had agreed to sell Comet's rental business to Granada should its bid for F.W. Woolworth prove successful.

Competitive strategies

Box 1 sets out the essential characteristics of Comet's and Dixon's strategies.

Environmental change

In the period 1984/5–1987/8, four major environmental changes occurred:

1. There was an increase in the number of young people (15–25) with relatively high levels of disposable incomes who were prepared to buy. With increased levels of self-assuredness, possibly because of education and exposure to foreign travel, the demand was for fashionable often state-of-the-art brown goods, e.g. hi-fi systems, videos, personal stereos and 'ghetto blasters'.
2. With an increased rate of new product development, a flow of innovations and revolutionary product features was generated with major implications for buying, stocking and particularly for the pricing of older or obsolete products in the latter stages of the technology life-cycle.
3. Enhanced aggressive competition, especially from Dixons.
4. An identifiable movement away from the high street in favour of out-of-town locations.

Rumbelows — a brief historical note

In the early 1960s Thorns, a UK-based electrical goods manufacturer, adopted a policy of forward integration, buying up local chains of electrical and rental shops. The group injected capital into each acquired operation but essentially allowed the incumbent management to continue to run the business with the minimum of constraint or intervention. By 1966 Thorn operated some 200 retail outlets. The same forward integration policy was continued throughout the 1970s so that at the end of the decade 525 outlets were operating under some 25 different names, including: Rumbelows, Radio Rentals, HMV, Focus, Multi Broadcast and DER.

BOX 1 STRATEGIC COMPARISONS — COMET *vs.* DIXON

Comet

- Edge/out-of-town locations operating from warehouse-style outlets.
- Discount prices using television and newspaper promotion; no own-label.
- Product range; white goods; large and small appliances and brown goods especially televisions, VCRs and hi-fi.
- Target market C1, C2, DE family-oriented unit.

Dixon

- Operates a three-prong parallel retailing approach with three different trading formats.

1 Dixons

- Range of original high street outlets offering high-technology electronics and optical products, e.g. cameras.
- Price-competitive, availability and exclusivity of own-label; Chinon for camera equipment and Saisha for brown goods.
- Target market young male, relatively up-market innovators.

2 Currys

- Essentially high street/shopping mall location.
- Product range white goods, small appliances, family-style brown goods with own-label Matsui.
- Target market older, more down-market family-oriented customer.

3 Power City

- Edge/out-of-town discount chain.
- Product range similar to Dixon and Curry, but hope both to extend and broaden.
- Not carrying Saisha and Matsui own-label goods, but may develop its own range.

The forward integration policy was followed to guarantee an outlet for group products. Only manufacturer brands were stocked with the major emphasis being upon UK-made products. Some Japanese brands were carried. Appreciating the benefits of consolidation under a single national chain, the decision was taken in 1979 to rationalize the retail operation with all outlets trading under the one name Rumbelows. Some five years later, the group operated about 400 retail shops. The majority of the outlets were relatively small high street located. The market target could be reasonably described as middle-aged or the less well-off

Table A7.6 UK electrical retailing industry by share of market, 1986 (%)

Dixon	14
Comet	5
Rumbelows	4
Connect	3
Lasky	2
Wigfall	2
Other	70
	100

Source: Trade estimates.

younger couples in the C1/C2 socio-economic category. Overall store design was rather dowdy, but stressed the corporate colours of brash blue, yellow and orange.

Within the marketing mix, price was emphasized, with regular promotional offers and events.

By 1986 Rumbelows was No. 3 in the UK electrical retailing industry as shown in Table A7.6.

Position as of mid-1980s

A brief SWOT analysis of Rumbelows as of the mid-1980s would indicate the following situation.

Strengths

1. Rumbelows had 400 high street branches representing a strong asset base.
2. The name Rumbelows had high awareness and was well respected as an electrical goods retailer.
3. Rumbelows possessed its own service network likely to be a crucial asset concerning customer care.
4. Rumbelows had their own distribution system servicing all their retail outlets.
5. Rumbelows were part of a major group, Thorn EMI.

Weaknesses

1. Rumbelows' image was out of date. It had not adapted sufficiently quickly to keep pace with the times.
2. In some instances it had been argued that senior management was highly conservative.

3. With significant competitor growth (Dixon, Comet and Curry especially), Rumbelows possessed a small market share (4 per cent).
4. The television and video recorder rental business was in decline.

Opportunities

1. Move into own-label products offering uniqueness and exclusivity as Curry — Matsui and Dixon — Saisha.
2. Diversify into products beyond Rumbelows' traditional lines (e.g. cameras, computers).
3. Increase market share by either attacking the industry leaders or acquiring smaller competitive companies (e.g. Clydesdale, Vallance, Wigfall).
4. Stress out-of-town sites moving away from the high street location.
5. Re-target the business aiming at perhaps the youth or the older, more conservative market.
6. Reposition the business laying greater emphasis on non-price factors.

Threats

1. The major threat was competition, especially Dixon, Comet and Curry.
2. General environmental turbulence, including rapid technological life-cycles and changes in socio-economic and demographic variables.

Repositioning 1985–7

Of the options available, Rumbelows decided in 1985 both to re-target and reposition the business. The new market target was identified as the 18–35-year-old 'Next'-type of shopper in the ABC1 socio-economic categories seeking good quality products, offering value for money. Product ranges demanded were likely to be more up- than down-market with before-sales service being important for both brown and white goods. Rumbelows' intention was almost to become the 'Sainsburys of electrical retailing', stressing service, help and advice in a pleasant, non-pressurized shopping environment. It is possible to hypothesize the objective was to move the business from a price-oriented hard sell to a non-price-oriented soft-sell dimension as shown in Figure A7.1.

The specific changes enacted under the repositioning strategy can be classified under seven headings:

1. *Store design and location*: Appreciating the need to adjust the retail shopping environment to meet the needs of the newly targeted market segment, in

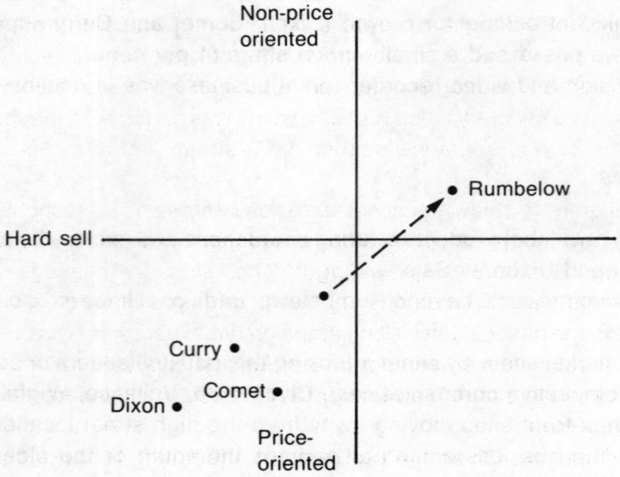

Figure A7.1 *Rumbelows' selling dimension*

1986 a major programme was begun to update, refit and, where appropriate, re-site existing stores while at the same time opening new sites. By the end of 1987, 200 branches had been revamped to a new design, Module 90. This design, proposed by McColls, a specialist design agency, incorporated timeless features using subtle shades of grey but is amenable to fashion changes. The 200 refits cost approximately £5 million. A further £5 million was spent on the acquisition and development of new sites. As the property team had been instructed to seek quality square footage in new towns or alternative sites for poorer, smaller branches, many of the new sites were out of town.

2. *Product offering*: To meet the needs of the perceived more discerning customer, Rumbelows enacted a general upgrading of the product range. A wide range of well-established brand names was introduced, including for brown goods, Sanyo, Hitachi and Toshiba, and for white goods, Zanussi, Indesit and Hotpoint. A revolutionary payment system, Option 3, was introduced whereby customers pay an ordinary instalment/hire purchase type payment each week/month for three years, after which the customers own the appliance concerned. The customer benefits of this system were thought to be three-fold: convenient and easy payment, the back-up of Rumbelows' repair/breakdown service throughout the payment period, and eventual ownership.

3. *Advertising*: In the early 1980s Rumbelows' advertising both on national television and in the national press featured a cartoon family, stressing a price appeal. Such an approach was considered inappropriate for the new

market target. Seeking a different style, a light-hearted approach using Michael Barrymore, a TV games host and personality, was tested in the Thames TV area. The slogan used was 'nobody cares more'. However, the experiment was rejected as, on reflection it too was considered inappropriate for the new market segment, neither did it stress any of the benefits of Option 3.

Consequently, in 1986, a national television campaign was launched using a simpler but more sophisticated approach, with an animated arm highlighting Rumbelows' new logo. The closing message of the advertisement was: 'Rumbelows . . . we'll keep you in touch.'

Alongside the national television campaign, an experiment was conducted using a full colour advertisement in the *Sunday Times* magazine with an invitation to readers to ring a number to purchase the illustrated 'designer washing machine'.

4. *In-store promotion*: Given the problems of attempting to run a combined rental and retail business from the same site and the general decline of the rental business, Rumbelows sold the rental part of their business to a sister company, Radio Rentals. The released display/selling space was used to show a wider and more sophisticated product range. The old HP system was revamped and launched as a company credit card. However, the card was quickly withdrawn as it was attracting the wrong type of customer and, in November 1987, was reintroduced as a debit, rather than as a credit card.

   Monthly special promotions too were introduced stressing particular products, models or features. These were not always a success as when overemphasis on Option 3 gave the impression to some customers that the company was more of a money-lender than an electrical retailer, and also when a major sale campaign with large 'SALE' notices emblazoned in shop windows inferred in some minds liquidation. The result in the latter situation was a decrease rather than the expected increase in sales.

5. *Staff training*: A four-pronged major staff training programme was initiated and included:

   (a) training within individual branches but organized at regional level, covering branch selling, product and procedure familiarization,

   (b) central conferences for major introductions, e.g. Option 3 and Rumbelows credit card run at appropriate hotels,

   (c) every employee attended a one-day customer care programme 'Putting People First', which was organized by Time Management Consultants,

   (d) an in-company video was made explaining in detail the company's repositioning strategy.

   Centrally organized events and conferences were followed up and reinforced at the local area.

6. *Customer service*: Overall the philosophy of the new customer service programme was to move away from a hard, price-oriented, push approach to one stressing a soft sell, emphasizing customer benefits and advice. To support staff in their efforts, specialist advice leaflets and a quarterly 'On Line' customer magazine were prepared. The leaflets, prominently displayed and available free of charge, concentrated on product features, dimensions, design and, where appropriate, safety. With the aid of such information and photographs, customers were better able to select the correct appliance for their home. The quarterly magazine promoted special products and carried general interest articles.

   Customers were able to subscribe to Rumbelows' Coverplan insurance plan.

7. *Information technology*: The use of IT enabled the company to offer a 90 per cent stockholding with next-day delivery. In chronological order, four major steps were taken in the period 1985–7:

   (a) STARS (Stock Transfer and Reservation Systems) was introduced in 1985. An IBM-based stock control system, it enabled all branches, delivery centres and head office to be linked. It was therefore possible to establish whether an item was in or out of stock at a given point in time. If an item was available at the delivery centre, it was booked for delivery. If this was not the case, it was possible to establish whether the item was available elsewhere in the distribution network. The two major benefits to flow from STARS were for the company a decrease in stocks and for the customer detailed knowledge of availability and delivery.

   (b) AUTOSCORE — a computer-based credit rating system was introduced in 1986. Using this system a credit request could be accepted or rejected within twenty minutes of application.

   (c) BOSS (Branch Offering of Shop Stock) introduced in 1987 facilitated direct inter-branch stock transfer.

   (d) EPOS (Electronic Point of Sale) was initially adopted in December 1987.

Questions

1. Of the options confronting Rumbelows' management in 1985, do you agree that radical repositioning was the appropriate one to follow?
2. Do you think that the repositioning strategy followed by Rumbelows in the mid-1980s will enable the company to achieve a long-term sustainable competitive advantage in the UK electrical retailing market?

CASE STUDY 8

Harry Ramsden's PLC

Introduction

Harry Ramsden's specializes in the sale of high quality fish and chips prepared in the traditional Yorkshire manner, using only the purest beef dripping, to both restaurant and takeaway customers.

It operates from a freehold site of approximately 2.6 acres in Guiseley. The restaurant attracts nearly one million customers a year and is open seven days a week, only closing for Christmas Day and Boxing Day. No restaurant reservations are taken.

History

Harry Ramsden's was started from humble beginnings in 1928 and has grown to such an extent that it features in the *Guinness Book of Records* as 'the world's largest fish and chip restaurant'.

Harry Ramsden had been a successful Bradford fish fryer when he was advised to move to the country due to his wife's ill health. He selected a site at White Cross, Guiseley, 7 miles north of Leeds, as it was the terminus for the city's trams and gateway to the Yorkshire Dales. He bought a small wooden hut for £150 and commenced trading. The reputation of Harry's fish and chips quickly spread far and wide to the point where he decided to expand. Accordingly, in 1931 he moved across the road to the current site, borrowed the funds from his suppliers and built, according to a journalist of that time, 'the largest and most magnificent fish and chip emporium in the land'.

The business went from strength to strength and its reputation spread throughout the north of England. On 7 July 1952, to celebrate twenty-one years on the same site, fish and chips were sold at 1912 prices — 1d per portion.

In 1952 Harry retired and leased the business to his manager, Eddie Stokes, and his wife. The business continued to grow, maintaining the high standards set by Harry. A complete refurbishment of the premises was undertaken and the famous 'cut glass' chandeliers were introduced. In 1965, the business was acquired by Association Fisheries PLC. Such was the popularity of the business by then that in 1968 the restaurant's seating capacity was doubled to its present size of 186 seats. The business was acquired by Merryweathers in April 1988.

Merryweathers was established in 1985 to provide traditional high-quality fish and chips while taking advantage of up-to-date financial controls, operations, training and marketing. The company was founded by a group of entrepreneurs combining the best of traditional standards, based on the 'fish and chip industry' personality of Carol Merryweather, together with the best modern managerial techniques and skills. Merryweathers is dedicated to ensuring that fish and chips remains Britain's favourite fast food.

In May 1988 a detailed review of key operational standards at Harry Ramsden's was carried out by Merryweathers and, as a result, significantly higher quality specifications were instituted, particularly in the quality of haddock, the main selling line. Food and labour costs were reduced through tighter controls and better labour scheduling. The effect of these changes has led to a significant improvement in profitability which is estimated to increase, for the year ended 1 October 1989, by 41 per cent over the previous financial year.

On 5 July 1988, a liquor licence was obtained. As a result, Harry Ramsden's Yorkshire Ale, which is sold exclusively in the restaurant, and a range of wines, have been introduced. These have proved very popular with customers.

In October 1988, a week-long major marketing event was organized to celebrate Harry Ramsden's 60th anniversary at Guiseley. The climax took place on the Sunday when fish and chips were sold at 1928 prices equivalent to 2p per portion. A record 10,182 customers were served. Widespread publicity was generated with features on national and regional television, radio and newspapers. This has led to a significant rise in consumer awareness of Harry Ramsden's, which has increased nationally from 31 per cent to 39 per cent (source: National Telephone Survey) and also in sales which are estimated to increase, for the year ended 1 October 1989, by 17 per cent over the previous financial year.

Prospects and future plans

Plans are afoot to increase company sales and profitability by both the expansion of the existing site at Guiseley and also by opening further Harry Ramsden outlets both in the United Kingdom and overseas.

Existing site development

Increased seating capacity

During peak periods throughout the summer months and on weekends in particular, the existing restaurant capacity has been insufficient. While customers are prepared to queue it can be uncomfortable and a deterrent in unplesant weather. A new 70-seat extension is planned to be built to the rear of the existing restaurant to increase overall seating capacity to 256. It is planned to use this extension as a facility for corporate functions, private parties and other social occasions.

Plans are in hand to build the extension in time for May 1990. In addition, a major refurbishment of the restaurant exterior and interior is planned for 1991. Planning permission has been granted to restore the original façade of the exterior frontage and the interior will be redecorated in the original blue and gold colour scheme.

Theatre bar

The group believes that many visitors, particularly coach customers, would welcome a facility where they could enjoy a drink before or after their meal with live entertainment. The idea of live entertainment was successfully tested during the 1988 Diamond Jubilee when several events featuring the 'Mr & Mrs' Show, Old Tyme Music Hall and comedian Charlie Williams were successfully staged in a marquee in the car park. It is proposed to construct a permanent 'Theatre Bar' to meet these customer needs on the existing site.

Branded merchandise shop

An opportunity exists to increase sales of branded merchandise which currently account for less than 2 per cent of total sales. Revenues will be increased through the provision of a purpose-built and well-displayed souvenir shop. The branded range will be redesigned and extended to feature items which not only have popular appeal, but also further promote 'Harry Ramsden's' and will include crockery, cutlery, tablemats, pen/pencil sets and T-shirts.

It is proposed to open the Theatre Bar and souvenir shop in mid-1990 and, in the longer term, to develop other family entertainment facilities.

New sites in the United Kingdom

Customer research has indicated that there is the potential to open a number of Harry Ramsden's outside Yorkshire. It is proposed that these restaurants will be modelled on the original site and will be located in the United Kingdom as follows:

1. *Blackpool*: Negotiations are in progress for a prime site in Blackpool and it is planned to open a restaurant in time for the 1990 summer season.
2. *Glasgow*: An option has been granted to open a Harry Ramsden's, under a franchise, to D. J. H. Leisure Limited, a company run by two local entrepreneurs, Harry Davis and Derek Statt. Negotiations for a prime site have reached an advanced stage. These proposals have been well received

by the Glasgow authorities and have been given a considerable amount of publicity from the Scottish media. The group intends to acquire a minority interest in D. J. H. Leisure Limited. It is expected that the restaurant will commence trading in the Summer of 1990.

Sites are being examined for Harry Ramsden's restaurants in the Midlands and in the south-east of England.

International development

It is believed that there are major opportunities to exploit the popularity of British fish and chips allied to the international reputation of the Harry Ramsden's name.

Interest in opening a Harry Ramsden's has been received from a number of countries and negotiations have commenced with potential local partners in New Zealand, Australia and Singapore with a view to developing these markets on a franchise basis. In 1986, a demonstration team from Harry Ramsden's visited Singapore for a week and served fish and chips in one of the principal hotels. It was a great success with both the local population and tourists.

Financial performance

The financial performance for the period 2 October 1987–1 October 1989 is set out in Table A8.1.

Note

The preparation of this case has extensively used the prospectus document issued in November 1989, offering for sale 4,000,000 ordinary shares of 10p at £1 per share before Harry Ramsden's flotation on the Third Market of the London Stock Exchange. The offer was 2.6 times oversubscribed.

Table A8.1 Ramsden's financial performance, 1987–9

(£000s)

	Year ended 2 October 1988	9 months ended 2 July 1989	Year ended 1 October 1989*
Sales	1,476	1,171	1,720
Pre-tax profits	327	280	460

* Estimate.

Questions

1. To what extent do you think it is advisable for a company such as Harry Ramsden's PLC to enter the international market? In making your judgement, it would be useful to consider the experiences of companies in not dissimilar situations, say Sock Shop and Bodyshop.

2. Conduct a programme of cross-cultural desk research to assess whether openings in Australia, New Zealand and Singapore are likely to prove successful.

CASE STUDY 9

Boots Company PLC — Retail Division

Early history

Jesse Boot (1850–1931) was born in Nottingham, the only son of John Boot a medical herbalist and Wesleyan preacher, who used his itinerant lay ministry as a vehicle to bring his herbalist medicines to the poor. When he was ten, Jesse's father died, forcing him to leave school to help his mother and sister run a small 'medical botanist's' shop that had been established in Goosegate, Nottingham. The shop prospered slowly until Jesse was in his mid-twenties, when it was decided in 1874 to enter the proprietary medicine business. This decision was, in many ways, forced upon the Boot family as the working-class customers they were serving were switching their allegiance from herbal to well-advertised patent medicines.

Because of a lack of capital, the Boots were not able to develop their own products and consequently decided to sell others' medicines at cut prices. Placing heavy advertising in the Nottingham *Daily Express*, they experienced a five-fold increase in takings to £100 per week. The influence of the main tenets of the 1874 policy can be traced to Boots' strategy today. The five main aspects of the policy enacted in 1874 were:

1. Popular advertising.
2. A direct challenge to old-fashioned retailers.
3. High turnover.
4. Low profit margins.
5. Regular attempts to establish Boots' proprietary brands.

It was not until three years later in 1877, following judgment in the *Pharmaceutical Society* v. *London & Provincial Shipping Company Ltd*, that limited liability companies were allowed for the first time to employ qualified pharmacists. Boots immediately entered the dispensing trade employing pharmacists. A major consequence of this diversification was the creation of a cadre of well-educated managers able rapidly to expand the number of branches.

While on holiday in Jersey during the summer of 1886, Jesse Boot met and subsequently married Florence Anne Rowe, the daughter of a St Helier bookshop owner. After marriage, Florence maintained her business interests by building up what became known as the 'Number 2 Department' in Boots' shops. Among other things, the product range included books, stationery, fancy goods and pictures.

Via a process of organic growth and acquisition, Boots operated 251 outlets in 1901, the figure increasing to 560 at the outbreak of the First World War, which provided the opportunity for Boots to manufacture fine chemicals for medical and military use. As Jesse Boot had no faith in his only son's abilities, he sold the controlling interest of his company to the United Drug Company of America in 1920. Ironically, it was two years after his father's death that the son, John Boot, the second Lord Trent and second chairman of Boots, in 1933 bought back control from the American Corporation.

At that time Boots had 1,000 retail outlets thoughout the United Kingdom.

Acquisition of Timothy Whites

Boots' policy noted earlier was pursued throughout the Depression of the 1930s and wherever possible for the duration of the Second World War and the subsequent period of austerity in the 1950s. By the early 1960s, Boots was operating some 1,300 branches throughout the United Kingdom. The number of outlets declined slightly each year during the 1960s, until in 1969 Boots took over a competing chemist chain, Timothy Whites Ltd. This meant that the number of branches increased from 1,256 in 1968 to 1,817 in the newly formed and enlarged organization.

The arguments in favour of the merger were basically two-fold:

1. To obtain extra geographical coverage generally throughout the United Kingdom, but especially in the major conurbation areas of London, Birmingham, Leeds, Manchester and the north-east.
2. To allow Boots to establish a second but complementary chain of outlets, under the Timothy White name, specializing in housewares. Boots' outlets were to trade essentially as chemists, dispensing ethical drugs as well as selling proprietary products and other lines initially introduced by Florence.

Immediately following the merger, the basic task was, via the process of rationalization and integration, to incorporate as many Timothy Whites outlets as possible into the Boots chain. Any duplicate or redundant outlets were sold or closed. By 1972 there were 1,400 outlets trading as Boots and 196 as Timothy Whites in the group. As a consequence of the merger, the company name was changed from Boots Pure Drug Company to The Boots Company and it was reorganized into four main subsidiaries:

1.	Boots Pure Drug	Non-retail operatioins.
2.	Boots Farm Sales	Fertilizers, herbicides, etc., sold to the agricultural industry.

3.	Boots the Chemist	Retailers of pharmaceuticals, toiletries, photographic equipment, films, electrical products, etc.
4.	Timothy Whites	Retailers of housewares including kitchen and tableware, garden and leisure products.

In terms of properties and store development, both retail operations then separately began a policy, basically continued throughout the 1970s, subject to the exigencies of the state of the economy and the availability of sites, of:

- The closure of small uneconomic outlets.
- Refurbishment, extension and modernization.
- The opening of new and normally significantly larger outlets.

The 1970s

Boots the Chemist

Throughout the 1970s, the keystone for Boots the Chemist was agreed to be the pharmacy, both dispensing ethical and selling proprietary products. Therefore, although it might have been necessary to close smaller, uneconomic units, wherever possible they were replaced with larger outlets with the stated objective of ensuring no reduction in the overall national representation. The general tenor for the decade was clearly established in the early years when Boots explained its policy as possessing a number of key thrusts:

1. The growth of the core pharmacy business via competitive pricing, an increasing product range, attractive shops and the convenience of location.
2. Skilled merchandise presentation.
3. Aggressive pricing and promotion.
4. Value for money, with slogans like 'Boots for Value' being used.
5. The increased use of own-label products offering quality, design, value and uniqueness. Own-label was especially considered where Boots encountered availability and quality problems concerning manufacturer national brands.
6. An increase in the total selling area. By the end of the 1970s, Boots were operating a number of departmental store-type outlets of at least 40,000 sq. ft in selling area.
7. Improved service and working conditions.
8. A modest profit margin.

However, in response to changes in shopping habits, as early as 1971 Boots were conducting a number of experiments, e.g. the introduction of self-service and the operation of two specialist outlets operating as Babyboots concentrating, as the name suggests, on baby wear and equipment. A survey conducted in 1973 established that two-thirds of all women in the United Kingdom visited Boots at least once a week and that in response to the increased product range including electrical, audio, film and camera products, there was an increasing number of male shoppers. Approximately one year later, the decision was taken to switch the basis of merchandise groupings. Traditionally merchandise was grouped and consequently displayed on a product basis (e.g. chemist, surgical, toilet, fancy and stationery) but with the two-fold objective of achieving more even sales of merchandise over the total sales area and offering customers a more logical service — four 'concept groups' were introduced: chemist and baby; home; fashion and beauty; and leisure.

Each of the newly established merchandise departments was responsible for its own development, buying and promotion. By the mid-1970s the own-label product range had been dramatically increased away from the traditional pharmaceuticals, cosmetics and toiletries to include electrical, beauty and shaving products, photographic equipment and more general household items. Although it was not possible to offer all of the new own-label ranges in all the outlets, especially the smaller shops, it was hoped that as the new store development programme stressed departmental store-sized new shops, the increasing own-label product range would extend into product groupings where Boots possessed nationally a relatively small market share.

The earlier experiments with Babyboots departments had been so successful that by 1976 there were some 200 in operation selling the complete range of children's clothing for the 'up to fives', as well as a comprehensive range of nursery equipment and feedtime, change and bath items. Problems, however, were being encountered with the store development programme, particularly building costs, general uncertainty concerning government legislation, site availability and a likely slowdown in major shopping centre developments.

Concern was also being expressed as to the profitability of the dispensing business with there being little reward for professional services given the twin pincers of rising ingredient costs and DHSS control. Given these pressures, the number of Boots' dispensing chemists had declined, but the smaller, unprofitable outlets were closed reluctantly, with the objective being to maintain representation wherever possible and to open new outlets whenever the opportunity profitably presented itself.

The centenary year of 1977 saw Boots reiterate four aims, which had been used as guiding foundation stones 100 years earlier:

1. To serve all sections of the community through offering the widest selection of merchandise at competitive prices.
2. To make shopping easier through well-laid-out shops.
3. If it was not possible to find the appropriate quality at a given price, to make in-house thereby augmenting an own-label product. Hence in 1,247 branches one third of the product range and more than one third of sales was of own-label products.

   Initially own-label products were normally of a restricted product list (e.g.

cosmetic, toiletries, household products and pharmaceuticals manufactured in Boots' own factories), but with time the list had been extended to include *inter alia* children's clothing and accessories, electrical products, photographic and audio equipment, etc., and manufactured in third-party factories.

4. To maintain a presence in areas suggested initially by Florence Boot which are not traditionally regarded as being the domain of a chemist shop.

In the late 1970s, because of overall pressure on retail profitability given a number of years of inflation, increasing costs and decreasing margins, constraints were placed on the number of full-time employees. As a result, adjustments were made on the level of service offered with some products requiring personal advice being dropped and wherever practically feasible, self-service being adopted. By and large, the majority of Boots products were capable of being sold via the self-service technique. 1977 saw the opening of a shopfitting factory to cope exclusively with Boots' branch opening and refitting programme.

Reviewing the decade in 1979, the chairman, Dr G. I. Hobday, noted that the previous five years had generally been ones of high real sales growth, but at the same time, because of increasing costs, a period of pressure on margins. However, he was pleased to report market research findings that the public had a highly favourable image of Boots, particularly liking:

- Boots' national coverage whereby the chain was accessible to 97 per cent of the population.
- Reasonable prices.
- The wide selection of goods.
- The high quality and range of own-label.
- Value for money.
- A pleasant shopping environment.

Timothy Whites

For the whole of the decade Boots struggled to find a profitable role for a separate specialist chain. In the early 1970s, after the initial period of rationalization, Timothy Whites operated an autonomous chain of some 200 outlets, specializing in housewares (e.g. kitchen and tableware, electrical and garden equipment and leisure items). A similar shop development programme to Boots the Chemist was followed, with particular attention being paid to the introduction of own-label products, which offered increased value and complemented national brands. Attempts were made to trade up, increase margins and hold costs. Gradually, the product range was extended to include glass, china and large electrical appliances, including freezers and refrigerators.

To encourage sales of the higher ticket items, both Access and Barclaycard were accepted. By the mid-1970s, though performance was still not as expected, dramatic action was taken such that in the search for the correct formula and image, the product range was rationalized to create a specialist identity based on kitchen and tableware, homecare and electrical merchandise. At the same time a closure programme was initiated to eliminate some forty outlets. By the end of the decade, it was argued that the narrower specialist range was sufficiently well received for consideration to be given to a new store decor and fascia in an attempt to increase Timothy Whites' high street authority.

Other bids and acquisitions

As the Boots Company moved through the 1970s there was an increasing realization of the need to diversify/merge with other organizations. At various times, particular reasons for such a policy were explained:

1. With the trend to globalization, the need to operate on a wider basis than the United Kingdom alone.
2. For the non-retail side of the business Boots had always regarded the world as the appropriate market, depending primarily on the marketing of research-based products. The UK market alone, it was thought, was not sufficiently large to justify the heavy investment required to guarantee the required new product flow.
3. With UK entry to the European Community (1973) it made sense to seek ways to exploit the new opportunity.
4. Although it would be possible to broaden the company base by either acquisition/merger or organic growth, the second route would be much slower.

When the 1970s opened, Boots, already regarding the non-retail business as worldwide, possessed a small retail operation (ten shops) in New Zealand. Two major events occurred in 1972: the acquisition of Crookes Laboratories and the bid for Glaxo, which was subsequently refused by the Monopolies Commission in 1973. Boots had argued the need to establish a larger international base with another research-based company. The bid was disallowed, the Monopolies Commission maintaining that if the acquisition were successful, there would be an overall decline in UK research activity and investment.

In November 1973, a bid was made for the House of Fraser, a 100 per cent retailer group with headquarters in Edinburgh. Broadly similar arguments were used to those put forward in the Glaxo bid, but it was also pointed out that the increased merchandise range offered by the House of Fraser had a first-class reputation, would not blur Boots' image and would complement Boots' existing product range with the minimum of overlap. However, because of changes in the UK economic and political environment, the Boots' main board subsequently attempted to renegotiate the terms of the bid, a move rejected by both the House of Fraser board and the takeover panel. Boots maintained that the balance between the 100 per cent retail House of Fraser and the joint retailer/manufacturer Boots had changed for three reasons:

1. A less optimistic retail forecast.
2. Arbitrary government action to decrease retailers' gross margins.
3. The strong international business element in Boots' portfolio.

Even after the bid had floundered, the Boots board was still expressing expansion hopes, but placing short-term stress on organic growth.

The next significant move on the mergers and acquisitions front was three years later in 1976. Recognizing the law in the majority of EC countries prohibiting the dispensing and sale of medicines by a company owning multiple outlets, discussions were held with Nouvelles Galeries in Paris and subsequently a single shop, Sephora, opened. Regarded as an experiment, Sephora offered a similar product range to a medium-sized Boots, but not medicines. The concentration was cosmetics, perfume and toiletries.

One year later, appreciating the need to be less reliant upon the vicissitudes of the UK economy, three purchases were made. Tamblyns, a 93-store Ontario drug chain, was bought for £4 million. The intention was to remodel the chain to mirror Boots' UK image and use it as a springboard for entry into the United States.

Two specialist chemical manufacturers were also acquired: Rucker of the United States and Technochemie of West Germany. In each of the following two years further Canadian acquisitions were made: fifty Isaac Pharmacy outlets in British Columbia, Alberta, Saskatchewan and Manitoba in 1977; and seven McDermott Drug Marts in 1978. The intention was to convert all outlets to the Boots format, including name, product range (including own-label manufactured in Canada) and operating systems.

Overview of the 1970s

It could be argued that throughout the 1970s Boots had:

1. Struggled to run two separate autonomous concerns in parallel.
2. Dramatically increased the selling space and average shop size of Boots the Chemist.
3. Significantly increased the product range in Boots the Chemist, especially own-label, supplied both in-house and from third parties.
4. Acquired a substantial international retail base in Canada, while maintaining a small operation in New Zealand and conducting a limited experiment in Paris.

The 1980s

If one of the main thrusts of Boots in the 1970s could be said to be a drive to extend both the base of corporate operations and total selling area, the 1980s saw a change of emphasis with greater attentions being paid to productivity, profitability and margins.

Timothy Whites

Under the severe competitive environment of the early 1980s, Timothy Whites managed a small increase in sales and was announced, along with Boots, 'The Electrical Retailer of the Year' in 1982, but neither of these achievements was reflected in increased profitability or return on investment.

It was therefore decided, in 1983, following a strategy review, that it was no longer sensible to operate two retail chains in housewares. Therefore it was announced that by 1985 all Timothy Whites outlets were to be closed and 130 'Cookshops' were to be established in larger Boots the Chemist. The Cookshops were to operate as shops in shops with a product range including saucepans, cutlery and specialist equipment (e.g. coffee percolators/filters, carving and preparation knives, etc.).

Boots the Chemist

Certainly for the first half of the decade Boots, like many other high street retailers, faced a number of problems. Those of particular concern included:

- A slump in consumer confidence.
- High inflation and interest rates.
- Increasing costs, particularly energy charges and business rates.
- Increasing unemployment.
- A decline in real disposable income.
- Deepening world recession.
- Increasing high street price competition from departmental stores, discount operations (e.g. Superdrug, Tip Top, etc.), traditional chemist outlets and supermarkets.
- Constrained demand often in product areas where Boots was a brand or market leader (e.g. records, toiletries and cosmetics).
- Government moves to control the NHS budget, especially the amount spent on prescribed drugs both via general practitioners and hospital specialists.

It was recognized that the company was not achieving sufficient value-added but the main board argued these were precisely the conditions in which Boots could display their retailing skills. One objective clearly stated in 1982 was to achieve real sales growth while reducing the level of expenses over which some control could be exercised. As a result, in order to shift stock, the level of promotional activity was increased, e.g. the SuperSaver Campaign, prices and margins on a broad range of merchandise decreased and a number of initiatives were taken to decrease costs and increase productivity with investment funds being transferred from the shop development programme to specialist projects, e.g. the opening in 1982 of a £10 million warehouse in Beeston, Nottingham enabling the release of a number of leased facilities. It was not a matter of the shop development programme of refurbishment and relocation being stopped, but of a switch in the allocation of resources.

Alongside the drive to increase sales and productivity, a number of decisions were also taken concerning the product range in the period 1980–5. These included:

1. An early decision to move into higher priced merchandise (e.g. audio equipment, 35 mm cameras and jewellery). To help the movement of such merchandise, Boots introduced their own credit card and, in larger stores, personal loans.
2. The relaunch of both the No. 7 and No. 17 cosmetic ranges.
3. An extension of Boots 'An Original Recipe' range of high-quality preserves, chutneys and mustards made with natural ingredients.
4. The launch of specialist own-label products, e.g. Boots Aids — a product range aimed at personal disabilities; Boots Second Nature — a product range of dietary supplement high-fibre foods.
5. Efforts to increase Boots' share of the photographic processing market.
6. The opening of specialist sports departments offering a range of clothing and equipment in an effort to strengthen the company's position in the leisure market.
7. Entry into the home computer market with the subsequent introduction of the sound and vision concept whereby photographic, audio and home computing equipment and recorded music were offered under one banner.
8. After experimentation the decision to go national with in-store optical practices to take advantage of impending changes in legislation.
9. A continued but increasing use of own-label merchandise to seek long-term differential advantages, particularly concerning value, quality, availability, uniqueness and, where supplied in-house, margin.

As a result of these decisions, Boots was in a strong position to take advantage of the upsurge in UK consumer spending when it occurred throughout 1985/6. Initially the main increase in spending was in areas (e.g. clothing) in which Boots had little activity but they were able to record a good performance in the core business areas of cosmetics, fragrances, toiletries and photographic processing. Indeed, overall an increase in gross margin was achieved largely attributable to an improved product mix, skilful buying, the increased use of own-label and a determination to be price-competitive, especially on the core business products. Despite this stress, however, it was argued that 'long-term competitive advantage is founded upon merchandise and service' (Company Reports and Accounts, 1987). During the mid-1980s, developments continued apace. By 1986 Boots were able to announce:

1. Sixty-eight optical practices had been established in the larger stores and the concept would be extended to similar outlets.
2. Supporting the health care concept, a number of in-store food centres were to be established concentrating on healthy and nutritious foods.
3. Sixty-three sound and vision departments had been established in the larger stores.
4. Mother and baby rooms were established in larger stores following successful experimentation.
5. In the larger stores 120 in-store mini labs were to be established offering a one-hour film processing service.
6. As the refurbishment of the larger stores was nearly completed, attention would now be turned to the smaller stores, concentrating on the health and beauty tradition.

The last three years of the 1980s also saw dramatic changes in the company's activity. The process of departmentalization of the core business areas was continued such that, *inter alia*, Bath Shops offering co-ordinated ranges to enhance the appearance of existing bathrooms and Play & Learn departments offering an own-label range of educational toys, were established. However, the most significant moves in the late 1980s were:

- The creation of a new subsidiary, Boots Opticians Ltd, in 1987.
- The establishment of a range of out-of-town Children's World hypermarkets.
- The takeover of Underwoods the Chemist, in 1988.

Following the success of in-store opticians, the separate subsidiary was established both via the incorporation of these in-store operations and also by the acquisition of freestanding competitive practices (e.g. Clement Clarke, Edmund Wilkes and Curry & Paxton, both in 1987). One year later the company was operating some 260 practices with 40 optical laboratories offering a two-hour service. Sales were £50 million with profits, £3.7 million.

Building on experience gained via operating both Babyboots and Mother & Baby departments and concerned with the development of the high street, Boots entered the edge-of-town retail developments via Children's World. The intention was to establish a chain of thirty to forty outlets, approximately 30,000 sq. ft in size, offering one-stop shopping for the needs and requirements of the under-tens. The product range includes clothing, toys, furniture and equipment, maternity wear and concessions, e.g. Dash, Benetton, Snips Hairdressing, Clarks and Start Rite shoes. Facilities offered included changing-rooms, toilets and a restaurant. It was claimed the concept has no direct competitor but clearly individual competitors will include Mothercare, Marks & Spencer, Adams, W. H. Smith and McDonald's.

In line with the strategy of concentrating investment, Underwoods — a fifty-outlet chemist chain mainly located in central London — was acquired in November 1988. When floated on the Stock Exchange in October 1985, Underwoods was twenty-two times over-subscribed but had subsequently experienced major problems of stock control and shrinkage. Underwoods held abortive takeover talks two years later with F.W. Woolworth in 1987. The advantages to Boots of the acquisition were thought to be three-fold:

1. They obtained outlets in an area in which they were under-represented.
2. Forty-eight of the fifty outlets possessed pharmacies.
3. Those outlets not readily turned into Boots shops were ideal for the alternative health and beauty format.

As part of a productivity drive, Boots — like many other UK retailers — invested heavily in IT particularly EPOS and DPP, thereby generating better management information which in turn it is argued will enable:

- An improvement in gross margin.
- The rationalization of inventories.
- The elimination of unprofitable lines.
- The better use of the existing sales area.

Overseas

Throughout the decade, problems were experienced with the Canadian activity. In one attempt to control costs, two separate operations in the east and west were created in 1980, but overall little progress was made, with losses being generated each year until the sixty-one Boots Drugstores in western Canada were disposed of in 1988, followed by total withdrawal from Canada with the disposal of the remaining 116 outlets in Ontario in 1989.

Developments in France have been steady throughout the decade such that Sephora in 1989 operated a twenty-eight strong chain throughout the country.

Boots still has a small operation in New Zealand.

Overview of the 1980s

In contrast to the 1970s, the 1980s saw a significant shift in resource allocation. Rather than a drive to increase sales, selling space and geographic coverage, greater emphasis was placed on longer-term strategic thinking epitomized in the Canadian withdrawal followed by investments in the establishment of Boots Opticians Ltd, Children's World and the acquisition of Underwoods. As well as the ongoing store refurbishment and extension programme, the expansion of own-label, the investment in in-store mini laboratories for film processing and the establishment of specialist product groups (e.g. Vision and Sound, and Photographic) considerable attention was paid to an improvement in productivity and profitability. Hence major investments were made in IT especially EPOS and DPP. In the late 1980s a general consolidation programme was being followed in France.

Questions

1. Contrast and evaluate Boots' marketing strategies for the two decades, the 1970s and the 1980s.
2. During the second half of the 1980s, Boots was frequently rumoured to be the target for a takeover bid. Do you think the company will continue to remain high on the Stock Market's potential takeover list?

Annexe 9.1

Boots Company PLC Retail Division: sales and trading profit, 1970–89

(£m current)

	Sales			Trading profit		
	UK	Overseas	Total	UK	Overseas	Total
1970–1974	Not available from company report and accounts					
1975	435.9	1.2	437.1	39.7	—	39.7
1976	528.2	1.2	529.4	45.7	0.1	45.8
1977	628.4	1.7	630.1	54.9	—	54.9
1978	743.0	14.2	757.2	60.3	(0.1)	60.2
1979	858.5	48.5	907.0	69.1	(1.8)	67.3
1980	980.5	63.0	1,043.5	73.4	(3.2)	70.2
1981	1,134.7	74.6	1,209.3	79.6	(2.4)	77.2
1982	1,237.3	98.7	1,336.0	65.9	(2.1)	63.8
1983	1,351.1	127.8	1,478.9	73.1	(3.0)	70.1
1984	1,456.9	146.2	1,603.1	82.8	(0.1)	82.7
1985	1,564.6	194.3	1,758.9	107.1	1.6	108.7
1986	1,644.9	187.1	1,832.0	112.0	(0.6)	111.4
1987	1,799.6	205.4	2,005.0	124.8	(1.4)	123.4
1988	1,980.2	225.0	2,205.2	130.8	(4.1)	126.7
1989	2,159.9	145.2	2,305.1	182.8	1.5	184.3

Source: Company Report and Accounts.

Annexe 9.2

Boots Company PLC Retain Division: relative performance of group and Industrial Division, 1975–89

	% Group sales	Sales % change previous year: Group	Industrial[a]	Retail	% Group trading profit	Trading profit % change previous year: Group	Industrial	Retail
1975	86.9				64.4			
1976	86.6	+ 1.9	+ 24.5	+ 21.1	59.5	+ 25.0	+ 42.5	+ 15.4
1977	85.7	+ 20.2	+ 28.2	+ 19.0	58.3	+ 18.2	+ 25.6	+ 19.9
1978	85.7	+ 20.2	+ 20.9	+ 20.2	59.9	+ 6.8	+ 2.8	+ 9.7
1979	86.1	+ 19.1	+ 15.3	+ 19.8	62.0	+ 8.0	+ 2.2	+ 11.8
1980	86.8	+ 14.2	+ 8.6	+ 15.1	62.1	+ 4.2	+ 4.1	+ 4.3
1981	88.0	+ 12.5	+ 3.6	+ 13.7	64.3	+ 5.7	− 1.2	+ 10.0
1982	89.8	+ 8.3	− 0.5	+ 10.5	53.5	+ 0.5	+ 16.5	− 17.4
1983	88.6	+ 12.3	+ 11.3	+ 10.7	59.9	+ 18.5	+ 17.2	+ 15.9
1984	87.5	+ 9.7	+ 15.1	+ 8.4	63.0	+ 11.4	+ 7.6	+ 17.3
1985	82.1	+ 10.4	+ 13.7	+ 9.7	61.8	+ 12.6	+ 3.0	+ 18.5
1986	81.9	+ 4.4	+ 5.7	+ 4.2	66.2	+ 8.5	+ 3.7	+ 11.1
1987	81.1	+ 10.5	+ 15.4	+ 9.4	63.1	+ 16.0	+ 26.9	+ 10.5
1988	80.9	+ 10.2	+ 11.1	+ 10.0	59.2	+ 9.1	+ 20.5	+ 2.5
1989	81.5	+ 3.9	+ 1.0	+ 4.5	67.4	+ 6.5	(6.7)	+ 32.4

a Including sales to retail division.

Source: Calculated from Company Report and Accounts.

Annexe 9.3: Chemists and drugstores

Introduction

Chemist shops are defined by the Department of Trade and Industry as shops which dispense drugs, medicines, pharmaceutical preparations, surgical and orthopaedic appliances, toiletries and cosmetics. The category contains drugstores (i.e. outlets with no prescription dispensing business) and cosmetic houses as well as traditional chemists.

It follows that there are two kinds of business carried out through this shop sector — the sale of prescribable drugs (which requires by law the presence of a qualified pharmacist) and the sale of what are called over-the-counter (OTC) products. Until about ten years ago, the number of chemist shops in the country was in decline. Since then, however, the emergence of so-called drugstores has meant that there has been a reversal of the trend. These shops do not normally dispense ethical pharmaceuticals but concentrate on the discounting of mainly OTC goods and toiletries. Ranges have been expanded into merchandise in the household sector not normally stocked by the traditional chemist.

Another reason for the growth in the number of chemist shops during the past year or so has been a rush to open pharmacies to beat a legal deadline. Paradoxically, the new DHSS legislation is designed to limit the proliferation of dispensing chemists as part of the Treasury's plan to curb spending on the NHS.

Sector performance

Two factors complicate the numerical assessment of the sector performance. The most important is the classification of shops perceived as chemists but in fact by nature of their overall trade classified as mixed businesses. This means that the turnover of Boots — the largest dispensing chemist in the country — is not counted in the sector total and neither is that of Underwoods. The second complication is NHS receipts. These are a guaranteed source of revenue for pharmacies at prices that are subject to review and adjustment and tend to rise roughly in line with inflation. An indication of the importance of NHS receipts in chemists' turnover is given by the difference in total turnover for the sector shown by Business Monitor monthly retail sales indices which specifically exclude NHS receipts and those in the bi-annual Retail Inquiries which include them. For 1984 the Retail Inquiry put sales by chemist shops at £2.46 billion while turnover for the same year derived from the Business Monitor indices was £1.1 billion.

Another point is that the turnover of Boots' retail operation and of Underwoods would add some £1.9 billion to the sector size.

Table A9.1 shows that chemist shops have outperformed the retail industry generally over the past six years. This growth has nothing to do with increases in the values of NHS prescriptions (which have been known to account for up to

Table A9.1 Sales by chemist shops compared with all retailing, 1980–6

1980 = 100

	All retail		Chemist shops		
	Index	% change	Index	% change	Turnover[a]
1981	108	8.2	116	16	776
1982	117	8.2	134	15	896
1983	128	9.0	145	8	970
1984	138	7.8	160	10	1,070
1985	150	8.7	185	16	1,238
1986	162	8.2	205	11	1,271

a Excluding NHS receipts.

Source: *Business Monitor*.

70 per cent of a retail chemist's turnover) since NHS prescription business is excluded from turnover figures but largely by increases in sales of toiletries, cosmetics and similar goods as the country moved out of its recession, from which the growth sector of drugstores benefited (Figure A9.1). Some actual indications of progress in the drugstores sector comes from their most recent results which generally show net profit increases of the order of 20 per cent and similar increases in turnover (margins in some cases have been constrained by new openings).

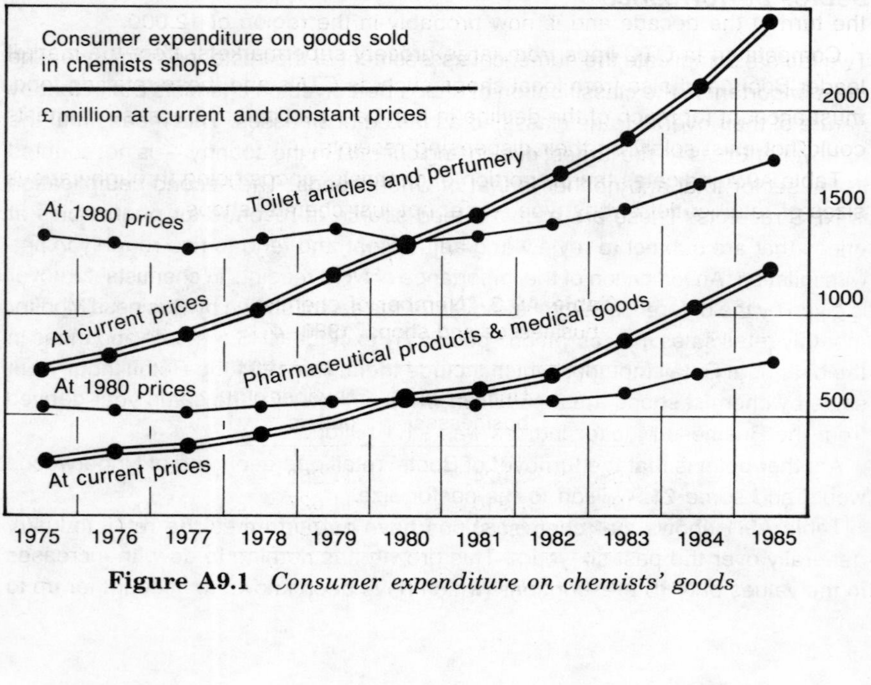

Figure A9.1 *Consumer expenditure on chemists' goods*

Table A9.2 Average weekly household expenditure on chemist products, 1985

	Medical and surgical goods		Toilet requisites/ cosmetics	
	Value £	% of total expenditure	Value £	% of total expenditure
1981	0.56	0.4	1.26	1.0
1982	0.57	0.4	1.36	1.0
1983	0.68	0.5	1.53	1.1
1984	0.71	0.5	1.69	1.1
1985	0.83	0.5	1.90	1.2

Source: Family Expenditure Survey.

Table A9.2 indicates that average family expenditure on medical and surgical goods, toiletries and cosmetics was almost £142 in 1985. The proportion of total household expenditure spent on these goods rose from 1.4 per cent in 1981 to 1.7 per cent in 1985. The sector is, therefore, experiencing something of a boom.

Sector structure

The 1961 Census of Distribution showed there to be over 18,000 chemist shops in the United Kingdom (Table A9.3). This figure dropped to around 14,000 by the turn of the decade and is now probably in the region of 12,000.

Competition in OTC lines from large grocery supermarkets, from the market leader Boots and also from local shops such as CTNs and those retailing food, must account for much of the decline in numbers particularly because chemists could not exist solely on their dispensing receipts.

Table A9.4 indicates the proportion of chemists' goods going through various sizes of retail outlet of any type — i.e. not just chemist shops.

Table A9.3 Number of chemist businesses and shops, 1980–4

	Number of businesses	Number of outlets
1980	7,924	11,252
1982	7,910	11,627
1984	8,060	11,756

Source: *Retailing Inquiry*.

Table A9.4 Sales distribution by form of organization (%)

	Drugs, medicines, etc.	Toilet preparations, cosmetics, etc.
Single outlet retailers	44.2	15.5
Small multiple retailers (2–9 shops)	23.0	10.4
Large multiple retailers (10–99 shops)	9.1	15.0
Large multiple retailers (100 or more shops)	23.7	59.1
Total	100.0	100.0

Source: *Retailing Inquiry*.

While independent retailers still had 44 per cent of the market for drugs, medicines and pharmaceutical products in 1984 they had only 15.5 per cent of the toiletries and cosmetics markets (Table A9.4). Large chains of over 100 shops have nearly 60 per cent of the toiletries and cosmetics trade and nearly 24 per cent of the drugs, medicines and pharmaceutical products trade.

Chemist shops are, as might be expected, paramount in sales of drugs, medicines and pharmaceutical products of which they account for nearly three-quarters. They are still significant in toilet preparations and cosmetics with over one quarter of that market. Their presence in other merchandise areas is minimal.

What might be termed the classic products mix for chemist shops is shown in Table A9.6. This shows an extremely high dependence on drugs, medicines and pharmaceutical preparations, prescribed and otherwise.

Table A9.5 Market share of chemist shops by main merchandise sectors, 1984 (%)

Drugs, medicines, pharmaceutical products	73.9
Toilet preparations, cosmetics, etc.	25.4
Photographic and optical goods	4.3
Household cleaning products, kitchen paper products, etc.	2.8

Source: *Retailing Inquiry*.

Table A9.6 Chemist shops product mix, 1984 (%)

Drugs, medicines, pharmaceutical products	70.0
Toilet preparations, cosmetics, etc.	22.5
Household cleaning products, kitchen paper products, etc.	1.9
Other products	6.6
Total	100.0

Source: *Retailing Inquiry*.

Major retail participants

The sector has for long been dominated by Boots the Chemist which still has some three times more outlets than the next largest group. Some substantially sized drugstore chains have been built up over recent years, however, as Table A9.7 shows. Once again the classification of Boots outside the specialist chemist sector complicates analysis but in this instance Boots is shown with the other major chains within the sector.

The firms named in Table A9.7 suggest that the multiple chains contain only about 10 per cent of the number of outlets, excluding Boots which alone adds some 8 per cent to numbers. In addition supermarket companies are entering the sector. Tesco has four franchises in stores currently and is planning drugstores in superstore developments. Safeway has thirty more chemists in operation already.

Table A9.7 Major sector participants and branch numbers, 1987

Boots the Chemist	1,025
Superdrug (Woolworth)	300
National Co-operative Chemists	164
Lloyds Chemists	154
Share Drug	133
Billingtons	123
Gordon Drummond Chemists	112
Tip Top	100
Harry S Allen	83
Savory & Moore	63
E Moss	53
Underwoods	50
Medicare (Dee Corporation)	46
Total	2,406

Source: Published sources.

Wholesalers and voluntary groups

The major wholesalers in the pharmaceutical sector are AAH, which purchased Vestric from Glaxo and has an estimated 27 per cent of the market, Unichem, which has 24 per cent and Macarthy Pharmaceutical, with 10 per cent. Unichem was (June 1987) interested, along with Macarthy, in the purchase of the 112-strong Gordon Drummond Chemist chain from Guinness. In the former case, the chain would be sold off to independents. According to *Chemist & Druggist* any independent would be eligible although Unichem members would receive priority. Purchasers would be expected to become Unichem customers if they were not already. Macarthy wants the Gordon Drummond shops to add to its Savory & Moore chain. Macarthy has also recently purchased both the Lifecycle retail chain of health food shops and Nature's Stores, a wholesale supplier of health food.

Most wholesalers in the sector keep a more hands-off approach to retailing through the voluntary group system. The big three voluntary, or symbol, groups are Numark, Vantage and Pointer to Value whose total membership adds up to 8–9,000, indicating that nearly every independent shop and some of the multiples belong to one or the other (or even to two). The pharmacy symbol groups offer services to retail members similar to those provided by grocery voluntary groups. There is evidence to suggest that many independents could capitalize on the benefits of membership more than they do.

Sector developments

Boots has been under pressure from the drugstores in recent years particularly in the toiletries ranges and, latterly, from the new pharmacy openings which compete with its NHS business. Boots has responded to these pressures in a number of ways both to streamline the organization and generate new business:

- A new tier of retail management has been inserted and eight new business centres have been established to help focus buying and distribution, which are already producing positive results.
- The Children's World venture has been launched, with five units open by the autumn of 1987. It is envisaged that forty stores, each with around 27,000 sq. ft of sales area, will be open by the end of the decade. The stores are basically theme shops selling all sorts of children's merchandise from clothing to furniture. (Woolworth is doing something similar with Kidstore.)
- A new subsidiary, Boots Opticians Ltd, was created in January 1987. With 240 practices (107 in Boots stores and 133 free-standing), it is now the second largest optician chain in the United Kingdom.
- Some 300 small Boots stores will be refitted by March 1988 and the number of in-store photo mini labs will double (91 were introduced last year). Sports departments are being removed from stores but new initiatives on the shop-within-a-shop theme will be introduced including gift shops, bath shops, fashion accessories and men's shops.
- The experimental sale of newspapers has begun at the Hoxton branch.

Woolworth made an agreed £233 million bid for Superdrug in March 1987 as part of its plans to extend into specialist sectors of retailing. Woolworth is rationalizing and refurbishing its chain stores and will be able to help Superdrug realize its expansion plans by offering high street sites. Superdrug plans to double its chain to 600 units within the next three to four years. Previously, Woolworth had been in abortive talks with Underwoods.

Midlands-based Lloyds Chemists is one of the fastest growing chains, having recently purchased a nine-branch South Wales chemist group, Andrew & Courie.

Lloyds also operates a number of drugstores under the Drugstore name and these are designed to reduce this quoted company's dependence on NHS business. The company is planning to increase its range of own-label products and to open seven more chemist shops and five more drugstores by the end of its financial year 1986–7.

Share Drug is a Southampton-based chain of drugstores but it has expanded rapidly. The company recently took over twenty branches of the Midlands-based Billingtons group, all located south of the M4 and therefore outside the latter group's planned development area. Share Drug hopes to open a further twenty-five units by August 1988.

Tip Top Drugstores is based in the north of England and has already expanded into the Midlands. The company is considering a move into the south. During 1986, Tip Top along with other drugstores, faced the Boots retailing campaign of 'You can't buy it cheaper'. This showed that as the drugstore concept matures, the traditional drugstore focus on price alone needs to be broadened. Tip Top has moved to heighten the company's image and introduce more own-label and higher value products. Eventually, own-label is planned to make up 20 per cent of sales.

Gordon Drummond Chemists, like other retail interests owned by the Guinness Group, is up for sale. There were (July 1987) several potential buyers. Unichem, the wholesale group and wholesalers Macarthys are two of them.

Underwoods is a central London-based chain with fifty branches. Recently the company has expanded into out-of-London stores and it intends to maintain its developments in towns in the southern half of England as well as in central London and the suburbs. Ten new stores were expected to open during the current year, adding 35,000 sq. ft to selling space.

The Harry S. Allen chain was previously owned by Combined English Stores, which has, of course, just been taken over by Next.

Medicare, one of the smallest of the drug store chains, was acquired by Dee Corporation, the grocery group, in late 1986. This could be a significant move because it links Medicare to substantial buying power and retailing skills.

Two other grocery groups which are developing in the chemist/drugstore area are Tesco and Safeway (now owned by Argyll). Tesco is planning to set up its own drugstores on superstore sites, and it seems likely that pharmacies will be part of new operations but these, like four pharmacies currently open in Tesco stores, would be franchised.

Argyll Group has announced that there will be over 350 Safeway stores in Britain by 1990, possibly involving an increase in their pharmacy services. Safeway operates over thirty pharmacies currently.

Prospects

There will be continuing decline in the market share of the sector held by independently owned chemists as competition continues to grow. The better managed of these shops will attempt to become more community-oriented on the same lines as convenience stores.

The drugstore element in the sector will grow apace, both through acquisition and organic development. There may occur territorial clashes (as in grocery superstores) as northern and Midlands-based firms move southwards and the London and south-based companies look north. In the determination to become national chains (like Superdrug) further takeovers cannot be ruled out.

The marketing mix in the sector will be refocused away from price and on to extended and value-added offerings, not precluding a much greater development of own brands. As distribution becomes countrywide for many companies national television advertising will become more likely.

Boots, as the largest multiple involved, will continue to restructure its retail division by developing specialist chains and by focusing its product offerings more tightly to specific market segments. Existing branches will be refurbished and upgraded.

Three of the four major grocery groups (Tesco, Argyll and Dee) have already gained a foothold in the chemists' market in varying ways and this commitment will increase. It will be interesting to see if Sainsbury — less of an innovator in respect of 'bolt-on' facilities — will follow this route.

More forward integration by wholesalers into chemist shop chains will occur, led by the revived Macarthy and, possibly, Unichem.

On the consumer side, the real increases in spending of maybe 5 per cent a year are likely to continue for the next year or so aided by the steady movement to self-medication and the stream of new products emerging which range from slimming to keep fit.

Annexe 9.4: Trade Review 5: Chemists

Summary

- Turnover increased by 15 per cent in 1988, to reach £1.7 billion. Volume sales increased by 9 per cent.
- More than 414 million prescriptions are dispensed annually; this business is worth up to £1.9 billion to retail phamacists, bringing turnover of the chemists's sector up to £3.6 billion.
- Boots is the leading advertiser, with £8.6 million spent in 1988.

A 13 per cent turnover increase is forecast for 1989, which would bring sector sales to £1.9 billion.

Turnover

The largest dispensing chemists, such as Boots and Underwoods (now part of Boots) are classified as mixed retail businesses and are not, therefore, included in official statistics for specialist chemists. Neither are NHS receipts included in the retail sales data, although separate information on prescriptions is available and is included later in this report.

The chemist shops sector has experienced buoyant trading throughout the 1980s, and 1988 saw a further significant increase in sales. Turnover in 1988 was £1.7 billion, a 15 per cent increase over 1987.

Table A9.8 Sales by chemists, 1981–8

(£ million 1980 = 100; % change)

	1981	1982	1983	1984	1985	1986	1987	1988
Total	776	896	977	1,077	1,224	1,331	1,465	1,679
Index	116	134	146	161	183	199	219	251
% change	16	15	9	10	14	9	10	15

Source: Based on Department of Trade and Industry Indices.

Comparative progress

Chemist shops continue to show better increases than both retailing in general and the miscellaneous non-food sector. Growth by non-food specialists was 11 per cent in 1988, and the all retailer average was just under 10 per cent compared with the 15 per cent increase registered by the chemists.

Seasonal sales

1988 started very promisingly for chemist shops, with 15 per cent more sales than in the first quarter of 1987. The second and third quarters saw slightly smaller gains but the final quarter showed an increase of 17 per cent, five points ahead of the specialist non-foods sector as a whole.

Volume sales

Volume sales trends are shown in Table A9.10; 9 per cent growth was recorded in 1988, compared with 7 per cent for the sector as a whole. Since 1981, volume sales by chemists have increased by 26 per cent, compared with 17 per cent for the non-food specialists sector in general.

Table A9.9 Quarterly progress by chemists, 1986–8

(% change on previous year)

	1986 1 Qtr	2 Qtr	3 Qtr	4 Qtr	1987 1 Qtr	2 Qtr	3 Qtr	4 Qtr	1988 1 Qtr	2 Qtr	3 Qtr	4 Qtr
Chemists	12	11	8	7	8	7	12	11	15	14	13	17
Miscellaneous non-food retailers	7	7	8	8	8	8	9	9	11	11	9	12
All retailers	9	8	9	9	7	8	8	9	10	9	9	10

Source: Department of Trade and Industry.

Table A9.10 Volume of sales by chemists and miscellaneous non-food retailers, 1984–8

(Index = 100; % change on previous year)

	1984	1985	1986	1987	1988	1987 1 Qtr	2 Qtr	3 Qtr	4 Qtr	1988 1 Qtr	2 Qtr	3 Qtr	4 Qtr
Miscellaneous non-food retailers													
Index	103	105	107	113	121	99	106	111	137	107	113	117	148
% change	3	2	2	6	7	3	6	6	7	8	7	5	8
Chemists													
Index	121	127	132	140	152	123	132	141	162	134	143	151	181
% change	4	5	4	6	9	4	3	8	6	9	8	7	12

Source: Department of Trade and Industry.

Table A9.11 Prescriptions dispensed by chemists and other suppliers, 1982–8

(million; % change on previous year)

		1982	1983	1984	1985	1986	1987	1988[a]
England & Wales	Total	335.3	339.9	345.5	343.7	347.6	361.3	373.6
	% change	3.7	1.4	1.6	−0.5	1.1	3.9	3.5
Scotland	Total	35.0	35.7	36.4	36.4	36.7	38.4	38.9
	% change	3.2	2.0	2.0	—	0.8	4.6	1.3
Northern Ireland	Total	13.1	13.6	13.7	13.3	13.2	13.9	14.2
	% change	3.0	3.8	0.7	−2.9	−0.8	5.3	2.0
United Kingdom	Total	383.4	389.2	395.6	393.4	397.5	413.6	426.7
	% change	3.6	1.5	1.6	−0.6	1.0	4.1	3.2

a *Retail Business* estimate, based on nine months' figures.

Source: DHSS; Common Services Agency for the Scottish Health Service.

Table A9.12 Cost of prescriptions, 1982–7

(£million; % change on previous year; £)

	1982	1983	1984	1985	1986	1987
Cost of prescriptions	1,468.7	1,628.5	1,749.8	1,875.1	2,030.5	2,261.7
% change	14.9	10.9	7.4	7.2	8.3	11.4
Average cost per prescription	3.83	4.18	4.23	4.77	5.11	5.46

Source: DHSS; Common Services Agency for the Scottish Health Service.

Prescriptions

The trends in prescription dispensing in the United Kingdom are shown in Table A9.11. The majority of prescriptions are dispensed by retail chemists. The total number rose in the first half of the 1980s, but large increases in charges meant that there was a decrease in 1985. 1986 saw a small increase again, and 1987 and 1988 much larger ones, of 4 per cent and 3 per cent respectively, bringing the total number to almost 427 million in 1988.

The costs of prescriptions are shown in Table A9.12. Between 1982 and 1987 the average cost of each prescription rose by 42.6 per cent. Boots, although not officially classified as a chemist, accounts for a substantial proportion of prescription business; trade sources suggest up to £300 million; this leaves chemist shops with perhaps £1.9 billion of prescription business, compared with £1.7 billion of retail sales. This would give total turnover for chemist shops of up to £3.6 billion.

Retail prices

During 1988, price increases for household consumables were just ahead of inflation. Chemists' goods price increases were just below inflation, and personal articles prices increased by only 2.3 per cent. The trends are shown in Table A9.13.

Retailing inquiries

The summary results of the 1986 Retailing Inquiry do not separately detail chemist shops. The latest data relate to 1984 when there were 11,756 shops, controlled by 8,060 businesses. Average turnover per outlet was £209,100 and gross margins were 23.7 per cent of turnover. Some 92.5 per cent of sales were accounted for by drugs, medicines and toiletries.

Advertising

Boots's advertising expenditure remained at £8.6 million. The Numark and Vantage voluntary groups both recorded reduced expenditure (see Table A9.14).

Leading participants

Boots dominates this sector and having acquired Underwoods in 1988 has over 1,000 outlets. Lloyds is the next largest retail chemist with 464 branches, although Kingfisher (Woolworth) with 600 drugstores is also important (see Table A9.15).

Table A9.13 Index of retail prices, 1987–9

(1987 = 100)

	1987 Mar.	Jun.	Sep.	Dec.	1988 Mar.	Jun.	Sep.	Dec.	1989 Mar.
Household consumables	100.2	102.6	103.3	105.5	106.2	107.6	111.3	111.8	113.9
Personal articles	100.1	99.3	99.5	100.9	100.9	101.3	102.1	103.2	103.3
Chemists goods	101.1	103.3	102.1	104.7	105.9	107.8	108.6	110.1	112.2
All items	100.6	101.8	102.4	103.3	104.1	106.6	108.4	110.3	112.3

Source: Department of Employment.

Table A9.14 Advertising expenditure by major chemists, 1983–8

(£000)

	1983	1984	1985	1986	1987	1988
Boots	9,287	6,503	6,387	8,923	8,620	8,602
Numark	408	515	441	522	317	212
Underwoods	—	—	—	—	71	520
Vantage	179	115	277	620	345	272

Source: MEAL.

Table A9.15 Leading chemists retailers, 1988

Trading name	Company/parent	Number of outlets
The Body Shop	Body Shop International	107
Kingswood Chemists	Booker McConnell	92
Boots the Chemist, Underwoods	The Boots Company	1,000+
Drummond Savory & Moore John Bell	Macarthy Retail	175
GK Chemists Chalmers	GK Chemists	55
Lloyds, Lloyds Supersave, Scotts, Allens	A & J Lloyd (Investments)	464
Medicare Drugstores	Gateway	102
Moss Chemists	E Moss	79
Cooperative Societies	National Cooperative Chemists	156
Selles	Molescroft Holdings & Investments	39
Share Drugstores Superdrug Tip Top Stores	Kingfisher Holdings	600
Yves Rocher	Yves Rocher (France)	45
Body & Face Place	Alan Paul PLC	46

Source: Trade information.

Table A9.16 Forecast sales by chemist shops, 1989

(£ million; % change)

	1982	1983	1984	1985	1986	1987	1988	1989
Turnover	896	977	1,077	1,224	1,331	1,465	1,679	1,897
% change	15	9	10	14	9	10	15	13

Source: Based on Department of Trade and Industry Indices and *Retail Business* forecasts.

Recent developments

Lloyds retail chemist group acquired Bannister and Thatcher, with twenty-four outlets in the Midlands and it purchased 107 Allen Chemists from Next (acquired when CES was bought). The company has grown rapidly since its flotation in 1986, and 1988 turnover is estimated at £135 million.

Underwoods' profits for 1987/8 fell from £3.11 million in the previous year to just £628,000. Underwoods' managing director said, 'management and systems had not kept pace with the rapid growth of store numbers, staff and turnover'. 'Shrinkage' was at unacceptable levels and staff turnover was as high as 100 per cent. In the half-year to July 1988, Underwoods reported a pre-tax loss of £1.3 million.

In November 1988, Boots bought the Underwoods chain of fifty outlets for £40.8 million. All but two of Underwoods' outlets have pharmacies and following a change in the law in 1986/7 it has become much harder to open new pharmacies with NHS contracts, so this acquisition has provided Boots with valuable new pharmacy locations. All but a few located close to existing Boots branches are to be converted to the Boots format and name.

Body Shop International showed a 56 per cent rise in pre-tax profits from £6 million to £9.43 million in the twelve-month period to 30 September 1988. Turnover increased by 62 per cent to £46.2 million. In the United Kingdom 18 new stores were opened, bringing the total to 107; overseas, 46 stores were opened, bringing the total to 232.

Macarthy, pharmaceutical retailer, manufacturer and distributor, put its manufacturing division up for sale early in 1989.

The W. Jamieson chain of franchise chemists is to double its size to fifty outlets following its £14 million takeover by AAH which runs voluntary group Vantage, with 2,500 chemist shops. Vantage is currently introducing 200 more own-label product lines, making a total of over 300.

The Secret Garden aromatics and herbal beauty products retailer which opened its first store in London in 1987 opened two shops in 1988 and plans further expansion.

UniChem, the United Kingdom's largest pharmaceutical wholesaler, has begun its first programme of consumer marketing, starting with promotion of its own-brand baby care range in 5,500 outlets. The Monopolies and Mergers Commission recently ruled that the share incentive scheme introduced by UniChem was anti-competitive and against the public interest. The scheme, which is credited with increasing UniChem's share of the pharmaceutical wholesale market from 30 to 35 per cent, will be discontinued.

The cost of prescriptions to consumers rose by 20p in April 1989, slightly higher than the present 7.5 per cent inflation rate. Prescriptions now cost patients £2.80 but three-quarters are provided free of charge.

Prospects

The chemist sector is expected to have another good year (see Table A9.16), though growth is forecast at a slightly slower rate than during 1988. A 13 per cent increase would bring retail sales to £1.9 billion. (EIU Retail Business Quarterly Trade Reviews, no.10, June 1989.)

Annexe 9.5.1 High street chemist with the scent of success (By Carol Ferguson)

Boots presents interim £132 million

Christmas came early for shareholders at Boots, the pharmaceutical group and high street chemist, when a 20 per cent increase in profits for the first half of the year was announced. The interim dividend was increased from 3.1p to 3.5p.

Although Sir James Blyth, the chief executive, admitted that Boots could not be immune from the downturn in consumer spending, he said that there had been no sign of any adverse impact in Boots the Chemist.

'Christmas started three weeks ago for us,' he said yesterday. 'There are still several weeks to go, and fog or snow could change everything, but we are very happy with the way it is going.'

With retail margins growing strongly, pre-tax profits rose to £132 million.

Excluding property profits, the trading margin rose from 8.7 per cent in 1987 to 9.9 per cent and is still rising. Sir James said that Boots the Chemist was generating significant cash, allowing the cash pile to grow by £56 million to £188 million.

He said that there had been a complete restructuring and reorganization at Boots the Chemist. 'We have attacked costs, reduced shrinkage, widened margins and made staff more accountable,' he said. 'And we have improved the stores and improved the merchandise.'

The average size of transaction value has risen by 8 per cent to more than £3, helped by new products such as Natural Collection, to compete with Body Shop products, and a new collection of up-market cosmetics to rival names like Estee Lauder.

Childrens World outlets grew to 13, but Mr Robert Gunn, the chairman, said that he did not expect a profit unitl 18 to 20 shops was reached. 'We are not absolutely certain when we will have them open because we are only going for the best edge-of-town sites. We will need 50 stores to make the profits we want.' Childrens World lost £2.6 million in the half year.

The industrial division, which had sales of £255 million, saw sales and profits adversely affected by currency movements, the new transfer pricing arrangements with the retail side and the disposal of non-core businesses. Adjusting for these, profits grew by 4.2 per cent on sales up 6.6 per cent.

Total group turnover was up 5 per cent to £1.3 billion. Earnings per share rose 22.5 per cent to 9.8p and the interim dividend was raised by 0.4p to 3.5p. (*The Times*, 25 November 1988, © Times Newspapers Ltd.)

Annexe 9.5.2 Cold comfort for Boots

There has hardly been an analyst in the whole Square Mile of London with a good word to say for Boots. Its pharmaceuticals business has entered a fallow period, with several ideas in the pipeline but no contribution to profits expected until the early 1990s.

Meanwhile, the retailing story has sounded a bit like a cracked record. Each year, the strategy was outlined, yet no real benefits seemed to flow through to the bottom line.

This year, Boots is trumpeting a 1.5 percentage point improvement in margins, and a

£16.4 million rise in profit from the retail business. Can it be that the strategy is at long last paying off?

Mr Zak Keshavjee, stores analyst at SBCI Savory Milln, thinks not. In fact an analysis of exceptional factors in the make-up of the retail profit suggests that margins may have improved very little.

Of the £16.4 million profit improvement, £3 million was due to the absence of stock write-downs and a further £6.5 million from a change in the method of internal transfer pricing. Shrinkage fell from the high level of 2 per cent to 1.6 per cent, saving some £3.8 million, and there was an unquantified refund on prescriptions from the NHS. Add these items up and the margin improvement is seen to be more apparent than real.

To be fair to Boots, it could be argued the reduction in shrinkage is related to the installation of electronic point of sale in the stores, and the lack of stock write-downs could be due to better stock control.

In fact, these results have created a dilemma for a market which has regarded Boots as little more than a potential takeover situation. What the speculators do not want to hear is a good trading result. The shares were marked up 4p to 233p, but in the cold light of day the market may change its mind.

Over the Christmas period, investors may be inclined to give Boots the benefit of the doubt. However the shares are likely to be held back by the realization that any growth in the retail side will need to carry the pharmaceuticals business for up to three years until the new heart drug starts generating profits.

Full year pre-tax profits are expected to nudge £300 million, including property profits. The prospective multiple of 11.2 still has an element of bid premium in it. Evidence of a sustainable rate of growth will be needed to underpin the shares at this level. (*The Times*, 25 November 1988, © Times Newspapers Ltd.)

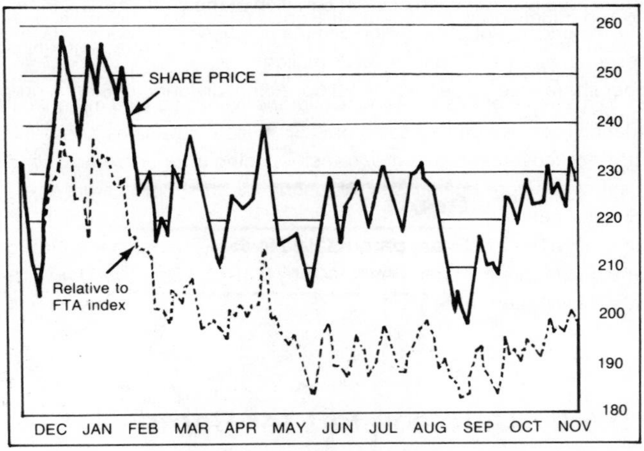

Annexe 9.5.3 Boots profits beam expectations (By Maggie Urry)

Profits from Boots, the retail chemist and pharmaceutical group, have beaten brokers' forecasts, showing a near 25 per cent rise at the pre-tax level to £295 million, against £236.3 million, excluding property profits of £1.7 million (21.3 million).

The City had been looking for around £285 million and the shares rose 9p to 296p. The profit excluded gains on property sales of £11.7 million (£21.3 million).

Mr Robert Gunn, chairman, attributed the success to a 'quiet revolution which started some years ago.' He said the group had redesigned stores, made the assets work harder, increased efficiency, and concentrated resources. These changes were now coming through to the bottom line, he said.

The current year would see a tougher retail environment, Mr Gunn said, but added that Boots usually fared less badly than other retailers in stringent times.

Group sales rose 4.5 per cent to £2.7 billion (£2.59 billion) and net margins, excluding property profits, were up by 1.8 percentage points to 10.9 per cent.

The retail chemists division had been the main engine of growth, showing a 30.5 per cent rise in pre-tax profits on a comparable basis, to £184.8 million. The increase was achieved on a sales gain of 8.1 per cent to £2.1 billion.

Sir James Blyth, the chief executive who joined the group 18 months ago, said that gross margins in the retail business were up 1.8 percentage points. Two-thirds of the group's 1,050 Boots the Chemists stores had been refurbished, and the rest would be done by the year end.

More higher added value merchandise had been brought in, with own brand goods now 39 per cent of sales. The chain of 50 Underwoods stores acquired in January had either been converted to Boots stores or sold, with the 37 converted producing higher sales than the 50 shops used to.

Boots Opticians was facing a tougher period following the ending of free health service sight tests, but Sir James said this would provide an opportunity to buy more opticians shops. The Childrens World chain had doubled to 16 shops and made a loss of £5.7 million (£4.9 million).

A revaluation of the group's properties had added nearly £569 million to assets in the balance sheet. There was net cash of £209.6 million at the year end, a £44 million increase despite capital expenditure of £118 million and the purchase of Underwoods for £40.8 million. Interest receivable was £15.7 million (£7.8 million).

Earnings per share rose 15 per cent to 22.6p. A final dividend of 6.5p is proposed to give a total of 10p (8.8p).

Boots

Share price relative to the FT-A Stores Index

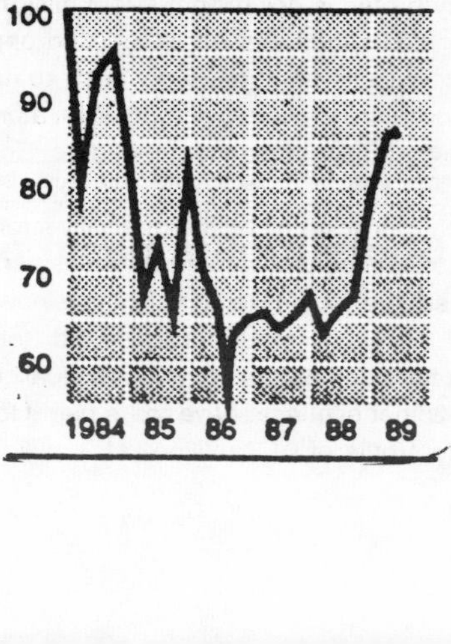

Boots

Not every retailer has out-performed the market by 20 per cent in the past nine months; but then, the market had Boots all wrong. Its dowdiness and inefficiency are fading from memory and it has a tradition of doing better than its sector when consumer spending turns down. It also risks being embarrassed by its cash mountain — a net £210 million at the end of last year and due to rise sharply next year when the refurbishment programme is complete.

The cash seems chiefly destined for the pharmaceutical division, where Boots is acutely conscious of its lack of distributive muscle in Continental Europe. All this is by way of preparing the path for the new heart drug; and if Manoplax disappoints, there is a clear possibility that the division could be sold off in the next few years.

This is partly at odds with Boots' defensive claim that its industrial and retail sides are too intimately linked to be broken up. But though the proportion of retail sales supplied by the industrial division is still increasing, the pure ethical side is detachable and could fetch a fancy price even in the absence of a glamorous new drug.

The puzzle is in deciding how much further the shares have to go. On the basis of £330 million before tax and ex-property this year, the price of 296p represents 12 times earnings. On the basis of almost static floor space, there is a limit to how far retail margins can be cranked up without the customer noticing. But Boots is now a management story and there could be a little further to go. (*Financial Times*, 4 June 1989).

Annexe 9.5.4 Efficient Boots

Boots has come a long way on both the profits and products front since it started out in 1877 as a little shop, dispensing herbal remedies and headache powders.

With Sir James Blyth as its chief executive, it is now Britain's second largest sandwich seller, has a 26 per cent share of the national photo-processing market and has just reported a 19.1 per cent rise in pre-tax profits for the year ended March to £306.7 million.

Such a leap in times of tough retailing conditions, and the improvement of 1.8 percentage points in net margins to 10.9 per cent, illustrate two significant investment points.

That Boots has an air of immunity to the cold bugs that other retailers catch and that Boots is becoming more efficient and better managed.

The element of property profits is down from £21.3 million to £11.7 million, but that is more to do with held-over deals than missed or reduced opportunities.

Boots from here on is to turn its hand more seriously to its property assets in order to make them tick as a profits centre in their own right. With a property portfolio which shows a £568.9 million surplus over book at balance sheet date, Boots is in an especially sound position.

Last year's profits growth was powered by an especially strong retail division, where Boots The Chemists showed a 30.5 per cent advance, with sales per sq metre 7.6 per cent ahead.

The Underwoods acquisition is going well and Boots is now taking as much money from a slimmed-down chain of 37 outlets as Underwoods did from 50.

The Boots Opticians chain made profits of £3.7 million (£2.8 million), though the current year could be tougher now that eye tests have to be paid for. The Boots Childrens World chain last year doubled to 16.

Boots' secure market position and its keener nose for profit opportunities make the shares a core holding.

Pre-tax profits, excluding property, could reach £330 million this year, to put the shares, up 9p at 296p, on a prospective price/earnings ratio of 12.2. (*The Times*, 9 June 1989, © Times Newspapers Ltd.)

CASE STUDY 10

Index — The Catalogue Shop

Business concept

The basic idea of a catalogue showroom is six-fold:

1. To offer merchandise for sale via high street or out-of-town locations at prices lower than established high street competitors.
2. A reasonably wide choice of goods is offered within a restricted range of product classifications. The product classification would include sports, health and leisure items, including photographic equipment; garden, DIY and car accessories; jewellery, watches, clocks and gifts; lighting, furniture and household textiles; kitchen equipment, particularly small electrical appliances and crockery; nursery items, toys and games and finally sound and vision, e.g. personal stereos, television, hi-fi, etc.
3. A bi-annual catalogue (Spring/Summer, Autum/Winter) is used to present product ranges clearly showing price information, which allows customers to pre-select merchandise.
4. Orders are placed either in-store with the completion of customer selection/order form, or over the telephone.
5. A free home delivery service is offered for designated items, e.g. bulky and normally more expensive products, which would be difficult for the customer to carry home (tents, furniture, larger items of outdoor play equipment such as swings and slides).
6. The lower prices offered are supported via bulk purchases direct from the supplier and cost-effective operations, particularly concerning ordering, delivery, stockholding and in-store activity.

Index — Littlewoods' market entry

Littlewoods, the largest privately-owned UK company, with major activities in chain department stores, mail order and football pools, opened their first catalogue showroom on 11 October 1985 in Altringham. The operation was rather basic and

Table A10.1 Market shares of catalogue mail order houses

	1983/4	1984/5	1985/6	1986/7
GUS	42	41	41	40
Littlewoods	29	32	31	32
Empire	7	6	5	
Freemans	12	12	13	
Grattan	9	8	9	
Other	1	1	1	
	100	100	100	

Source: *Retail Business*, August 1986 and September 1987.

labour-intensive but was followed by three further experiments before the end of 1986. At the time, Littlewoods Group was in the process of reviewing its corporate strategy, especially the role of its department chain stores. Established in 1938, as of the mid-1980s, Littlewoods operated some 120 retail outlets and was No. 2 in the UK mail order industry (see Table A10.1), operating six major catalogues, viz. Brian Mills, Janet Fraser, John Moores, Burlington, Peter Craig and Littlewoods.

Catalogue retailing was seen as a major opportunity, combining the corporate core skills and experience of high street retailing and home catalogue shopping. It was argued that the opening of a chain of catalogue showrooms, both in-store and free-standing, would be consistent with the emergent plans to move the chain stores more up-market. Consistent with refurbishment plans, it would also be consistent with plans to upgrade the corporate image and offered the opportunity to provide a more pleasing shopping environment without alienating the existing customer base.

Following the experimentation of 1985 and 1986, the major launch took place early in 1987 with generally a higher standard of shop fittings than those used in the four experimental stores, supported by a sophisticated, computer-based management information system allowing efficient stock replenishment. As part of the logistics network, two new distribution centres were established, at Heywood (Bury) and Oldhill (Birmingham) both within ready access of the motorway system.

Following an aggressive rapid expansionist policy throughout England and Scotland, 33 outlets were opened in 1987 (17 within chain stores) and a further 42 (25 within chain stores) in 1988. Consequently, by December 1988, Littlewoods were operating 75 catalogue showrooms, 33 'stand-alones' and 42 in-store. Sales were estimated at £20 million and £100 million for 1987 and 1988 respectively. Forecasts as of late 1988 indicated a turnover of some £140 million for 1989.

In August 1988, Littlewoods Catalogue Shop was renamed to Index — The Catalogue Shop. Late in 1988, because the operation was not proving as successful as had been planned, there was significant senior management blood-letting. The inaugural management team, largely recruited from Argos, was replaced by executives from other parts of the Littlewoods organization.

Particular problems that the new team faced included:

1. The non-achievement of the 90 per cent stock availability objective. Indeed over the Christmas 1987 period, the availability figure for some items in specific outlets had been as low as 30 per cent.
2. Ineffective supplier management.
3. Operational MIS difficulties.
4. Response from a well-established market leader — Argos.

Competition — Argos

At the time of Littlewoods' entry into the catalogue showroom business, Argos was clearly established as the UK market leader with over 200 stores nationwide. Argos had begun operations in 1974, working out of the original Green Shield Stamp redemption sites and, since 1979, had been part of BAT industries. By 1988 Argos had sales of over £700 million and was the UK's largest small electrical goods retailer, second largest jeweller and third largest toy retailer. Distribution of the Argos catalogue was of the order of 19 million and it prided itself on a 92 per cent merchandise availability in store.

Argos offered its own store credit card, gift vouchers, free home delivery service (on selected items) and a generous returns policy — although few items of merchandise were returned!

Argos responded to Littlewoods' entry to the market in four main ways:

1. Extensive showroom refurbishment of its 208 outlets, each carrying 3,500 lines.
2. The development of superstores in larger towns and cities, e.g. Birmingham, Bristol and Gateshead.
3. The introduction of the 1,500 best-selling catalogue lines to smaller towns using the vacated Jeweller Guild outlets, a discontinued BAT experiment.
4. Investment in new computer technology to enhance cost-effectiveness, stock replenishment and availability.

Questions

1. Identify and evaluate Littlewoods' marketing strategy in its decision to enter the UK catalogue showroom market.

2. On the assumption of Littlewoods Group main board support, what advice would you offer the newly incumbent management team (December 1988)?

3. Visit your nearest Index and Argos catalogue showroom outlets to collect the respective catalogues. Compare and contrast the two companies, store atmospheres and catalogue offerings. To what extent does one company offer a differential advantage over the other? In the light of your analysis, what advice would you offer the two companies?

CASE STUDY 11

Fastframe Franchises Limited

Background — UK franchising

In the United States during the late 1980s approximately $1 in $3 of retail sales were accounted for by franchise operations. The British Franchise Association, established in 1977 with the objective of encouraging but monitoring the growth of the franchise industry in the United Kingdom, hopes that this might be the position one day in the United Kingdom. However, even after a period of dramatic growth for the period 1985–9, the industry is still relatively small when compared to total UK retail sales (Table A11.1).

Table A11.1 Franchise sales in the United Kingdom, 1984–94 (£ billion)

1984	1.22
1985	1.62
1986	2.15
1987	2.86
1988	3.80
1989	4.73
1993 (est.)	9.90
1994 (est.)	11.00

Source: BFA and author's calculations.

In the second half of the 1980s, growth rates of 33 per cent p.a. were experienced (Figure A11.1). It is forecast that over the period 1990–5 the industry, as measured by retail sales, will be at least double in size. In 1989, the number of franchise units operating was 16,600 from a base of 295 franchise systems. On average, therefore, it can be seen that each franchise system operated 56 operating units. Employment in the sector was 185,000.

In the five years to 1989, the number of operating units had not grown as quickly as franchise retail sales (1984 £1.22 billion *vs.* 1989 £4.73 billion). Indeed, the increase in the number of operating units during 1984–9 was 600 from a base of 16,000. Three main reasons were put forward to explain such an increase:

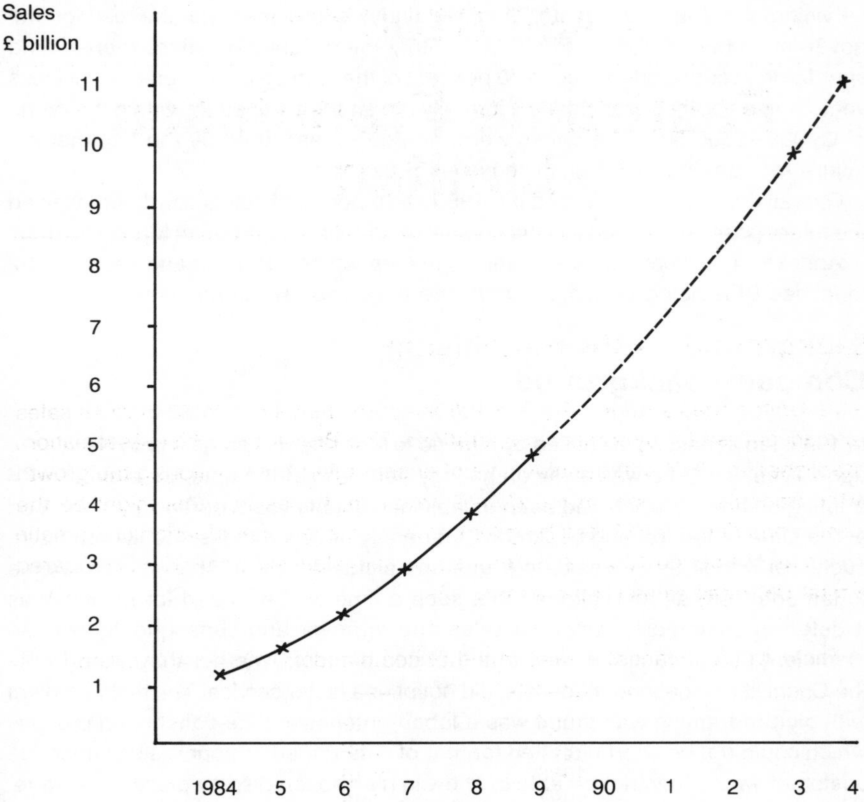

Figure A11.1 *Franchise sales, 1984–94 (Source: British Franchise Association)*

1. Franchisors only accept 4 per cent of all applications.
2. The more mature franchising systems were reaching saturation.
3. The downturn in the UK housing market in the late 1980s, combined with high interest and mortgage rates, meant that franchisees found it difficult to free up their resources to finance franchise investments.

The BFA hoped that, to some extent, as a result of its guidance and experience over the previous ten years, by 1989 approximately 50 per cent of franchisees were reporting sales of between £100,000–£500,000 p.a. and also, 50 per cent were experiencing increasing market shares. Only 10 per cent of franchisees reported making losses.

By the late 1980s the majority of the UK clearing banks had specialist skills servicing the franchise sector and regularly, sometimes via the use of the government-backed Small Firms Loan Guarantee Scheme, where there was a shortfall in security, offered up to 70 per cent of the total cost required of a business venture to a potential franchisee. Normally the amount loaned fell within the range of £5,000–£500,000. The banks were, no doubt, reassured by the fact that the failure rate among new franchisees was 5 per cent.

Overall the industry regarded the 1980s as a period of solid growth and viewed the future positively, especially the creation of the Single European Market in 1992.

Annexe 11.1 offers the BFA definition of a franchise operation and Annexe 11.2 identifies BFA noted benefits to both the franchisor and franchisee.

Company background

In 1983, Ian Johnson was asked by a friend to look after his art gallery in Newcastle upon Tyne, while he was away on holiday. Ian, who at the time ran a successful printing business, which had been established twenty years earlier, was horrified at the state of the framing backroom. Generally, it was a mess and ill-organized, such that it took three weeks to frame any picture or print. This was anathema to Ian Johnson, as he reckoned that such a time wait was bad for business as it deterred customers, restricted sales and turnover and consequently was an inefficient use of capital. It was true that competitors, whether they were Boots the Chemist or independent outlets, did not offer a faster service. The main problem with picture framing was that it was a labour-intensive, time-consuming process which could not be short-circuited for fear of a damaged or poor result, which the customer would then not be able to show in his chosen display place. The trade, indeed, possessed all the hallmarks of a craft. This difficulty was exacerbated by the fact that the picture framing business rarely generated any passing trade as, more often than not, outlets were located in out-of-the-way places — up backstairs and down passageways.

The question was how to transform a craft-based backroom activity into a modern high street-based business. While considering the situation, Ian Johnson thought there had to be a way of deskilling the craft job using modern labour-saving equipment, offering almost instant framing or certainly a same-day service and relocating away from the back street and garret into the main shopping areas and precincts. In fact, the same-day service offered by specialist retail film developers for holiday snapshots and increasingly, opticians for spectacle prescriptions, acted very much as a model.

The breakthrough came with the discovery and subsequent refinement of a mitreing and framing device that would enable a trained operative to produce a framed picture from print or painting to completion, in about 15–20 minutes. This meant that a customer could wait, just as in a heel bar repairing shoes, or at worst, return for the completed order after finishing the rest of the shopping or drinking a cup of coffee. On the strength of this breakthrough, two pilot shops, financed by a bank overdraft on the security of the successful printing business, were opened in Newcastle upon Tyne in 1983.

Growth

The two Newcastle upon Tyne pilot shops were sufficiently successful to persuade Ian Thomson to establish with a co-partner, Maggie Hewison, Fastframe Franchises Ltd, in 1984. Exceptionally fast growth was experienced. By 1985 30 franchisees were operating; a further 16 outlets were added in 1986 and 39 more by 1988. At the same time as major growth was being managed in the United Kingdom, Fastframe was the first UK franchisor to enter the United States where it currently has twenty-eight outlets. Two franchises have also been opened in Australia. As can be seen from Table A11.2, it can be argued that Fastframe's growth has been, as measured by the number of outlets, about twice as fast as that of Bodyshop.

Table A11.2 Comparative growth rate

	Fastframe	Bodyshop
Established	1983	1976
Franchised	1984	1977
Number of outlets (United Kingdom)		
1985	30	71
1986	46	
1988	85	117

In 1988 Fastframe was joint winner of the BFA Franchise of the Year award. The average turnover per store in 1988/9 was reported to be £100,000 per year, with a range of £70,000–£170,000 p.a. The average order took about fifteen minutes to complete and was priced at £25.00. It was estimated that if the £8,000 of framing equipment in each franchise was worked flat out, it would generate sales of £250,000 p.a. Turnover of the company for 1988 was reported as £4.7 million and firm hopes have been expressed that this figure will double in 1989. Although the franchisees are spread reasonably throughout the country, as yet Fastframe does not have an outlet in central London. This reflects franchisees' desire to live near their work and so far, no suitable candidate living in central London has applied. Ian Thomson has estimated that there is potential in the United Kingdom for 170 outlets.

Mr Johnson and Mr James McGreal, managing director and finance specialist, say that all the franchisees appointed to date have been well-motivated people wanting to get into self-employment or small business. They range in age from 26 to 60 and many are husband and wife teams. Some of the outlets have been sufficiently successful for the original franchisees applying to open another store. It is not unknown for there to be a waiting-list of approved applicants wanting to join the network. Mr Johnson has said: 'Only the shortage of good retail sites is holding us back. We wait and pick and choose very carefully. You have to be where everyone can see and find you easily. Nevertheless, we are expanding as fast as we can.'

Expansion in the United States has been largely organized by John L. Scott, a former marketing director of Tyneside-based Prontaprint, one of the first all-British franchise chains. Mr Scott has the US master franchise licence. Turnover per outlet in a US franchise is 1.75 times larger than in the United Kingdom.

Indeed, Ian Johnson argues that Fastframe is the only British company franchising its operation in the United States. He points out that the Bodyshop, Tie Rack and Sock Shop stores are company-owned and not franchised. Hopes are high that the operation will expand into Europe. A search is presently being conducted to find master franchisees, who would partly own and run the operation in their own national markets.

The package

From a written application, short-listed candidates are interviewed for approximately two hours and once approved and the initial monies paid, Fastframe then sets up the selected franchisees in business.

The immediate task, after approval, is site location. Clearly, the area needs to be one that is acceptable to the franchisee, but it is vital that the selected site is both visible and accessible. Fastframe's property manager recommends what he estimates as the most profitable site, as defined by population density and based, to avoid too much overlap, on postal codes. Not only do Fastframe locate the most appropriate site, but also negotiate the lease, lease back to the franchisee at cost, and help devise any financial package and loans required.

Fastframe's management also designs the layout and atmosphere of the new store, paying particular attention to the size and location of the framing area itself. Attention too is given to training. Normally the franchisee undertakes a three-week training programme. The structure of the programme is as follows:

Week 1 Training in framing techniques using the Fastframe method.

Week 2 Training on product range, price structures and customer relations.

Week 3 Skills put into practice in the shop.

Other shop staff are offered a two-week training course mainly in the picture-framing area. The cost of the training, £1,500–£2,000, is included in the franchise fee.

Franchisees are, though, expected to meet their own hotel costs during the training programme.

Fastframe's product range is extensive (Annexe 11.3), allowing the customer to select his/her own particular combination from hundreds of stocked mouldings and mounts. Where help or advice is required, staff are trained to concentrate on the customers' requirements, especially identifying where it is intended to hang or display the finished item. Not only are the expected paintings, prints, cards, certificates and photographs framed, but also three-dimensional items including jewellery, packs of cigarettes for ex-smokers and even a tarantula (dead!). Indeed, this momento segment is a growth area.

To ensure a consistent corporate image, each franchisee is supplied with a detailed in-store promotional package including point of sale material, stationery, even coffee cups and vacuum cleaners. The corporate colours of blue and red were selected intentionally to make local replacement of breakages easy. Fastframe undertake national and local advertising using Yellow Pages, national trade press, national newspapers (e.g. *Sunday Times*) as well as mail-shots, leaflet distribution and local newspapers. Franchisees are expected to make a contribution to the use of local media.

Once in operation, franchisees are supported by visits from Fastframe personnel, regional meetings, an in-house news publication and an annual meeting of all franchisees.

Because of the size of annual purchases, Fastframe have negotiated a deal with suppliers whereby franchisees buy direct at preferential prices. Because of the dramatic increase in business to suppliers, mouldings are now manufactured in shorter lengths than the traditional 11 feet, so that they fit below the standard 9 feet shop ceiling.

Finance

As of early 1989, franchisees pay £49,000 to join the network. To ensure franchisees are not over-geared, a minimum of £16,000 personal capital is required. To cover working capital requirements, an overdraft facility of £4,000–8,000, depending on rent and rates, is required. Fastframe has arranged with four clearing banks, National Westminster, Lloyds, Barclays and the Bank of Scotland, a special finance scheme whereby the respective bank may provide up to 66 per cent of the total investment required. Clearly the precise amount loaned depends upon the individual circumstances of a particular application.

Annexes 11.4, 11.5 and 11.6 provide details of estimated start-up costs, two illustrative bank schemes (Barclays and National Westminster) and operating projections for the first three years of operation.

Questions

1. Why do you think Fastframe has experienced such a strong UK growth rate in the last half of the 1980s?
2. What advice, cautionary or otherwise, would you offer concerning the hope for expansion in both the United States and Europe?

Annexe 11.1

Definition of a franchise operation

The owner of a business (the franchisor) grants a licence to another company or individual (the franchisee) to use the trade name and proven business method. In return the franchisee is provided with a package containing all the elements necessary to establish the business and run it profitably . . . The franchise often states that the business is carried out within a pre-determined geographical area and that the franchisee pays a management service fee and/or a payment for goods supplied by the franchisor. (British Franchise Association)

Annexe 11.2

Benefits of franchise operation

Franchise Benefits

For the Franchisor include	For the Franchisee include
— an excellent way to create a national presence	— being one's own boss
— enables a rapid expansion within a given market	— tried and tested business format
— a relatively low capital expenditure	— management assistance and advice
— a managerial service fee and/or profits from goods supplied to franchisees	— national image and name backed by advertising, marketing and promotion
— property investment — in some cases	— lower risk and potentially higher returns
	— easier access to finance

Source: British Franchise Association.

Annexe 11.3: Fastframe literature

Annexe 11.3 *continued*

Annexe 11.3 *continued*

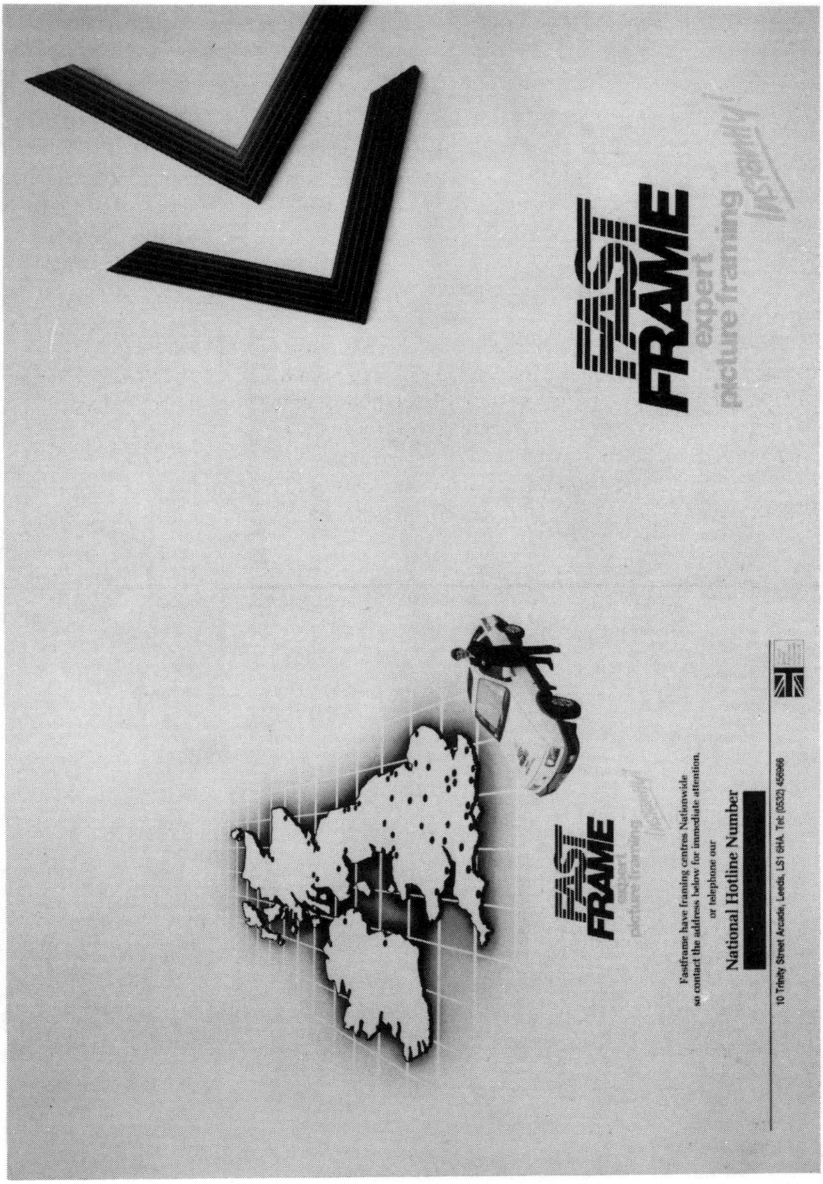

Annexe 11.3 *continued*

Annexe 11.3 *continued*

Annexe 11.4: Estimated start-up costs

FAST FRAME

SETTING UP COSTS

Fastframe Franchises Limited has created a totally inclusive package which sets you up in a completely equipped shop, fitted out in the distinctive FASTFRAME livery – ready to trade.

The Package includes:

- Site selection and negotiation.
- Franchise and launch programme.
- Trading insurances for first year (excluding building insurance).
- A provision for legal fees.
- Printed stationery kit.
- Staff recruitment assistance.
- Training for yourself and your staff.
- Shopfitting, plans, design and liason.
- Fastframe external sign.
- Framing equipment and tools.
- Electronic cash register.
- Office equipment and furniture.
- Operating manual.
- Packaging and merchandising materials.
- Fastframe management costs.

TOTAL COSTS	**£49,000**
PLUS V.A.T. (Recoverable)	**£7,350**
Minimum Capital Required	**£16,000**

NOTES:

1. Barclays and National Westminster Banks have each prepared special Franchise Finance Schemes for FASTFRAME. Up to ⅔rds of the total capital requirement can be funded.
2. A short term facility should be arranged to cover working capital. This will be in the order of £4,000/£8,000 but varies according to rent and rates levels.
3. V.A.T. is recoverable and can usually be separately funded by way of a temporary bank facility.
4. You should provide for hotel accommodation and meals during your training course.
5. Shopfitting is carried out by approved shopfitters to our pre-specified format. Cost may vary according to size and condition of premises or if major structural alteration or electrical re-wiring is required.

   A full quotation will be submitted if costs are likely to be exceeded. An external sign is included.
6. Initial stock is paid for over 6 months by 6 interest free payments built into your trading cash flow.
7. You will be notified immediately of any extraneous costs (such as major structural work, total rewiring or if a premium is payable on the lease, etc.) prior to final commitment on your part.
8. Scale fees will be payable if an Agent other than the Retained Agent secures the property.

N.B. The above schedule is based on costs prevailing as at April 1989. Fastframe Franchises Ltd. reserve the right to change the costs to those are appertaining when the franchise is taken up.

BRITISH FRANCHISE ASSOCIATION 1988

FRANCHISE OF THE YEAR

4.89

Annexe 11.5: Finance schemes

FASTFRAME
instant picture framing

FINANCE SCHEME FOR FASTFRAME FRANCHISEES.

Barclays Bank PLC has designed a special finance scheme for Fastframe franchisees.

This scheme is available to those who are suitably qualified and are about to enter into a franchise agreement with Fastframe Franchises Limited.

A general outline of the scheme is as follows:

1. Up to £30,000 (min £15,001) available by way of overdraft, or branch loan, or a combination of the two.
2. Bank may provide up to two-thirds of total requirement.
3. Interest rate 3%–4% above base rate (depending on security given).
4. Repayments up to five years.
5. Security is subject to individual negotiation.

The above points are obviously only a general guide and the scheme will differ according to individual circumstances.

For anyone to be considered for the above scheme an initial financial assessment and approval must be given by Fastframe Franchises Limited. Arrangements have been made for Fastframe Franchises Limited to introduce you to the Bank should you require assistance.

Further details of the scheme can be obtained from:

Franchise Unit
Barclays Bank PLC
Corporate Marketing Department
Ground Floor
168 Fenchurch Street
London EC3P 3HP
Telephone: 01-283 8989

BANKING FOR + + + BUSINESS
BARCLAYS

Published by Barclays Bank PLC, Corporate Sector Marketing Department, Reg. No. 1026167.
Reg. Office: 54 Lombard Street, London EC3P 3AH. BB161982 PS.71121. Nov. 1988. AC. Member of IMRO.

NatWest Franchisee Finance Scheme

FASTFRAME
instant picture framing

National Westminster Bank in conjunction with Fastframe has arranged a finance scheme designed to assist franchisees to start up and develop their Fastframe business.

Fastframe will advise you of the total investment necessary to commence and run your business.

National Westminster Bank is willing to consider assistance with finance of up to ⅔rds of the total, with the balance coming from your personal resources. Facilities are subject to local Branch Manager's agreement, the Bank's conditions and applicant's status.

Our assistance will be provided by a loan with repayments over 5/7 years, together with an overdraft facility to meet your working capital needs.

In the normal course of events we would expect security to be provided, but here again this scheme has been designed to be flexible to fit the individual's own financial situation and requirement.

In the event that our assistance is required, we have made arrangements for Fastframe to introduce you to the Bank. Nevertheless, it is strongly recommended that you seek the advice of your solicitor and accountant before entering into any franchise arrangement.

The Franchise Managers
Small Business Sector
Commercial Banking Services
8th Floor, Finsbury Court
101/117 Finsbury Pavement
London EC2A 1EH

NatWest
The Action Bank
Small Business Service
Registered Office 41 Lothbury London EC2P 2BP

Annexe 11.6: Operating projections

FAST FRAME

OPERATING PROJECTIONS – FIRST YEAR

Turnover (Net Vat)	£75,000	£100,000	£125,000	£150,000
Management Fee (6¼%)	4,687	6,250	7,812	9,375
Marketing Services Fee (6¼%)	4,688	6,250	7,813	9,375
Cost of Sales (Materials)	16,875	22,500	28,125	33,750
Credit Card Charges	525	700	875	1,050
Gross Profit	**£48,225**	**£64,300**	**£80,375**	**£96,450**
Wages & N.H.I.	9,310	13,910	13,910	18,190
Rent, Rates & Insurance	18,750	25,000	31,250	37,500
Gas, Water & Electricity	1,200	1,200	1,500	1,500
Postage, Stationery & Telephone	1,200	1,200	1,500	1,500
Accountancy	500	500	500	500
Sundry	1,200	1,200	1,500	1,500
Net Profit (before Depreciation and Interest, Drawings and Tax)	**£16,065**	**£21,290**	**£30,215**	**£35,760**
	(21.42%)	(21.29%)	(24.17%)	(23.84%)

IMPORTANT NOTES:

1. The above estimates are based on existing operating shops. They are intended for guidance only and should not be interpreted as a guarantee that any specific franchise will make a profit. Adjustments may be required according to location.
2. Up to ⅔rds finance of the total capital requirement can be funded through National Westminster and Barclays Franchise Finance schemes e.g. £10,000 borrowed over 5 years costs approx. £230.00 per month repayment. This should be taken into consideration when calculating potential returns.
3. Wages: those franchisees who operate husband and wife teams may reduce costs accordingly.

BRITISH FRANCHISE ASSOCIATION 1988
FRANCHISE OF THE YEAR

10 88

FAST FRAME

TYPICAL RESULTS FOR FIRST THREE YEARS

	Year 1	Year 2	Year 3
Turnover (Net Vat)	£85,000	£105,000	£120,000
Management Fee (6¼%)	5,312	6,562	7,500
Marketing Services Fee (6¼%)	5,312	6,562	7,500
Cost of Sales (Materials)	19,125	23,625	27,000
Credit Card Charges	595	735	840
Gross Profit	**£54,655**	**£67,515**	**£77,160**
Wages & N.H.I.	9,310	14,980	16,478
Rent, Rates & Insurance	21,250	22,250	23,000
Gas, Water & Electricity	1,200	1,260	1,323
Postage, Stationery & Telephone	1,200	1,260	1,323
Accountancy	500	1,000	1,200
Sundry	1,200	1,500	1,800
Net Profit (before Depreciation and Interest, Drawings and Tax)	**£19,995**	**£25,265**	**£32,036**
	(23.52%)	(24.06%)	(26.69%)

IMPORTANT NOTES:

1. The above estimates are based on existing operating shops. They are intended for guidance only and should not be interpreted as a guarantee that any specific franchise will make a profit. Adjustments may be required according to location.
2. Up to ⅔rds finance of the total capital requirement can be funded through National Westminster and Barclays Franchise Finance schemes e.g. £10,000 borrowed over 5 years costs approx. £230.00 per month repayment. This should be taken into consideration when calculating potential returns.
3. Wages: those franchisees who operate husband and wife teams may reduce costs accordingly.
4. The above assumes no review of rent level.

BRITISH FRANCHISE ASSOCIATION 1988
FRANCHISE OF THE YEAR

CASE STUDY 12

Harris Furniture Limited

Background and development

Harris Furniture is a family business established by the present chairman's grandfather in Leeds during the 1880s. The original concept was for the company founder to sell furniture, essentially chairs and some tables, to individual households on a credit basis, the payments being made weekly to a collector calling at the house. Gradually the business developed, but it was not until after the First World War that a new thrust of the business emerged.

Given the company's increasing reputation as a furniture supplier, a number of retailers around Leeds asked if it would be possible to obtain supplies direct from Harris Furniture. Throughout the 1920s this aspect of the business grew more rapidly than house-to-house credit sales, so much so that, in 1932, Harris established itself solely as a wholesale furniture supplier. Other than for an expanding geographic base, an extended customer list and an increased product range, the nature of the business did not change until the mid-1950s when an import subsidiary was established, importing chairs from Europe to take advantage of both lower cost on basic items and on some lines, superior design. This new source of product both complemented and competed with the traditional supply base for the UK furniture market — the large number of small, often family-run companies located in the south of England, but especially around High Wycombe.

The 1970s

In terms of a small family firm, the company prospered throughout the 1960s but began experiencing problems in the 1970s for a number of reasons including:

1. Economic depression following the Yom Kippur war and the resultant quadrupling of the oil price.
2. The emergence of national furniture retailers, e.g. MFI, Times Furnishing, Waring & Gillow, obviating the need for a furnishing wholesaler serving smaller regional retail chains or indeed individual outlets.
3. The establishment of an effective UK motorway system whereby large national retailers, buying direct from the manufacturer, were able to accept delivery at the retail outlet bypassing the need for items to be held at a separate wholesale depot.

4. A loss of market share of the UK furniture retail market by the small independent retailer in favour of the emerging national multiples.
5. Difficulties experienced by the established mail order companies, e.g. Empire, Littlewood and Freeman because of increasing costs, delivery problems and declining demand.

(Harris did not do any business with either GUS or Grattan because these two companies insisted on returning any slightly damaged items for repair or replacement, a process which greatly increased Harris's costs and rendered the business unprofitable.)

The current position

During the early 1980s, the company realized it could classify its business under four main headings:

1. A declining traditional wholesale business serving small independent retail outlets in Yorkshire and Lancashire.
2. Sales via the major mail order companies but these too were experiencing problems.
3. Direct sales to working men's clubs and similar organizations based in Yorkshire and Lancashire.
4. Sales direct to small businesses and partnerships, e.g. local companies, doctors, solicitors, etc.

In none of these four areas was there considered to be any growth prospects. Indeed, for the three years 1982/3–1984/5 sales had been static in current terms at about £1.5 million.

Anxious to find sources of extra business and aware of what may be regarded as a major opportunity in contract furniture, the chairman negotiated exclusive UK rights for a range of Modres furniture from Yugoslavia to run for twelve months as from July 1985. (Within the contract furniture segment, large organizations wishing to equip, refurbish or redesign their offices, restaurants, waiting areas, etc., bought centrally from one source. It is thought that the estimated life of a given design is about five years. Illustrative examples might include Trust House Forte, Berni Inns, police authorities, airport authorities and perhaps local authorities.)

In an effort to pursue this opportunity, the company had:

1. Registered on an electronic suppliers' index whereby architects and designers could dial in to find out the names and addresses of suppliers of products and services in which they were interested.
2. Advertised locally via the medium of Yellow Pages.
3. Encouraged its nine to ten commission agents to establish contact with potential contract furniture users.

4. Asked an office junior to work through the local Yellow Pages to see if any business enquiries could be generated.

The problem

The chairman firmly believed that his only problem was that of generating leads as he had total confidence in his ability to convert leads into sales. However, he was a little concerned that by October 1985 not only had he made no sales, but had elicited no genuine enquiries for the Modres range.

What advice would you offer?

CASE STUDY 13

Asda Stores

Senior marketing staff at Asda Stores (a Leeds-based supermarket chain) met in 1985 to review marketing strategy. The company, formed as an offshoot of Associated Fresh Foods, an association of local dairy farmers, had gone from strength to strength during the past few decades and now had a £2 billion turnover with pre-tax profits of £105 million. There were 107 superstores, primarily in the north of the country, with an average selling space of 40,000 sq. ft.

Background

The Asda position had been built on a strategy of offering a wide range of lowest-priced branded goods with minimal own-label products (88 per cent of goods sold were branded). Heavy consumer advertising stressed low price savings through the phrase 'Asda Price'. The product range covered food, clothing and footwear, toys, household and leisure. The operation emphasized low cost, no frills, service primarily based in out-of-town sites with good parking availability. Asda had built a substantial regional following in the north of England.

This strategy had worked well in the 1970s which had been characterized by high inflation, low levels of growth, low levels of unemployment, branded product dominance and growth in car and freezer ownership. There had been ample and cheap out-of-town sites for expansion and the regional competition encountered had been weak and fragmented.

The early 1980s saw a severe world recession, high unemployment and an increasing 'north–south divide' between the prosperous south and the less prosperous north. The grocery market experienced little or no growth. The plentiful and cheap sites for out-of-town shopping of the 1970s became harder and harder to find.

Competition too was hotting up among the major grocery multiples. Kwik Save and Fine Fare were becoming better established nationally with the emphasis on low-priced branded and own-label products. Sainsbury, the largest grocery chain in the country, long established in the south, was now expanding north and clashing with Asda as it attempted to expand south.

The Sainsbury strategy had been very different from that adopted by Asda. The Sainsbury focus had been on high quality, high value for money food items with a particular emphasis on own-label. Indeed the Sainsbury label had become synonymous with high quality at a reasonable price. Currently (1985) own-label accounted for about 60 per cent of Sainsbury sales. Sainsbury also employed, wherever possible, town centre sites for supermarkets. The regional strength of Sainsbury was in the south of England.

The shoppers

As the starting point to re-examining marketing strategy the marketing group commissioned a consumer attitude study of over 14,000 women shoppers.

Overall the study showed that shoppers were becoming more independent, better educated and had less time available for shopping. They shopped less often in more concentrated shopping trips and were less brand-loyal than in the past. In addition they were more quality and health-conscious but less price-conscious. In 1984, for example, consumption of butter was 29 per cent down on 1980 levels, red meat 23 per cent down and salt 22 per cent down. In contrast fruit juice was 71 per cent up, yogurt 38 per cent up, brown bread 18 per cent up and poultry 9 per cent up.

The study also showed a clear segmentation of the market into what were termed the 'conservatives' and the 'experimental-acquisitives'.

The 'conservatives' were the traditional Asda shopper concerned primarily with low-price purchases of reliable, branded, products. They were not particularly adventurous in their shopping or eating habits. They made up 60 per cent of all housewives and 55 per cent of Asda shoppers though the value of their purchases was less than 50 per cent of Asda turnover.

The 'experimental-acquisitives' were a surprising find to Asda management. They were characterized as 'young at heart' irrespective of chronological age, independent, casual, liberal, experimental, innovative and adventurous. Their demand was for 'value for money' which was not always associated with 'cheap'. These shoppers made up 40 per cent of all housewives but 45 per cent of Asda shoppers. While there was a slight demographic skew (towards the higher socio-economic classes) there was no strong geographic bias.

The problem

In early 1985 the marketing group at Asda sat down with the results of the consumer survey to develop a marketing strategy that would take the company into the second half of the 1980s and beyond.

Questions

1. What is the problem facing Asda?
2. What advice would you offer Asda as of early 1985?
3. Research, compare and contrast the marketing strategies of Sainsbury and Asda today. What conclusions do you draw?

Bibliography

In addition to the references made throughout this book we suggest the following articles and books will be useful for the reader wishing to pursue specific topics in depth. The readings selected below represent a wide range of views and approaches to the subject areas discussed by the authors. They offer the reader the opportunity to consider a number of differing views.

Abell, D. and J. Hammond (1979), *Strategic Market Planning*, Prentice Hall, Englewood Cliffs, NJ.

Anderson, E.E. (1979), 'An analysis of retail display space: theory and methods', *Journal of Business*, 52(1), 103–18.

Anderson, W.T. (1972), 'Convenience orientation and consumption behaviour', *Journal of Retailing*, 48(3), 49–71, 127.

Ansoff, H.I. (1987), *Corporate Strategy*, Penguin Books, Harmondsworth.

Arnold, D.R., L.M. Capella and G.D. Smith (1983), *Strategic Retail Management*, Addison-Wesley, Reading, MA.

Arnold, S.J., T.H. Oum and D.J. Tigert (1983), 'Determinant attributes in retail patronage: seasonal, temporal, regional and international comparisons', *Journal of Marketing Research*, 20(2), 149–57.

Bass, F.M. and W.W. Talarzyk (1972), 'An attitude model for the study of brand preference', *Journal of Marketing Research*, 9(1), 93–6.

Bates, A.D. and J.D. Didion (1985), 'Special services can personalise retail environment', *Marketing News*, 12 April, 13.

Beaumont, J.R. (1987), 'Retail location analysis: some management perspectives', *International Journal of Retailing*, 23, 22–35.

Berman, B. and J.R. Evans (1979), *Retail Management: a strategic approach*, Macmillan, New York.

Berry, L.L. (1969), 'The components of department store image: a theoretical and empirical analysis', *Journal of Retailing*, 45(1), 3–20.

Berry, L.L. (1979), 'The time-buying consumer', *Journal of Retailing*, 55(4), 58–69.

Blackwell, R.D. and W.W. Talarzyk (1983), 'Life-style retailing: competitive strategies for the 1980s', *Journal of Retailing*, 59(4), 7–27.

Bliss, M. (1988), 'The impact of retailers on financial services', *Long Range Planning*, 21(1), 55–8.

Bolen, W.H. (1988), *Contemporary Retailing*, Prentice Hall, Englewood Cliffs, NJ.

Bond, C. (1984), 'Own-labels vs the brands', *Marketing*, 6(10), 24–7.

Bowring, J. (1985), 'Different strokes for different folks: the case for developing advertising concepts from consumer typology', *Journal of the Market Research Society*, 27(4).

Britoon, N. (1988), 'Next puts its fashions on the screen', *Marketing*, 14 January, 1.

Brown, B. (1979), 'Using design as a strategic function', *Retail & Distribution Management*, 7(5), 30–2.

Brown, S. (1987), 'Retailers and micro-retail location: perceptual perspective', *International Journal of Retailing*, 2(3), 3–21.

Buckling, L.P. (1981), 'Growth and productivity change in retailing', in R.W. Stampfl and E.C. Hirschman (eds), *Theory in Retailing: Traditional and non-traditional sources*, American Marketing Association, Chicago.

CACI (1989), *ACORN User's Guide*, CACI Market Analysis, London.

Caulkin, S. (1987), 'The fall and rise of brands', *Management Today*, July, 45–9, 104.

Chadwick, L. (1984), 'Comparing financial performance: ratio analysis and retail management', *Retail & Distribution Management*, 12(3), 35–7.

Clark, I.M. (1981), *Retailer Branding: Profit improvement opportunities*, Management Horizons.

Corporate Intelligence Group (1988), *The Retail Rankings*, Corporate Intelligence Research Publications, London.

Cronin, J.J. and S.J. Skinner (1984), 'Marketing outcomes, financial conditions and retail profit performance', *Journal of Retailing*, 60(4), 9–22.

Dalrymple, D.J. and D.L. Thompson (1969), *Retailing: an economic view*, Free Press, New York.

Darden, W.R. and R.F. Lusch (1983), *Patronage Behaviour and Retail Management*, Elsevier, North-Holland, New York.

Dash, J.F., L.G. Schiffman and C. Berenson (1976), 'Risk- and personality-related dimensions of store choice', *Journal of Marketing*, 40(1), 32–9.

Davidson, W.R. and A.F. Doody (1966), *Retailing Management*, Ronald Press, New York.

Davidson, W.R. and N.E. Johnson (1981), 'Portfolio theory and the retailing life cycle', in R.W. Stampfl and E.C. Hirschman (eds), *Theory in Retailing: Traditional and non-traditional sources*, American Marketing Association, Chicago, 51–63.

Davies, G.J. and J.M. Brooks (1989), *Positioning Strategy in Retailing*, Paul Chapman, London.

Dawson, J.A. (1989a), 'Retailer differentiation through service', paper presented at the Food Choice and Opportunity Conference, 5–6 January.

Dawson, J.A. (1989b), Unit 13: Locational strategy, site utilization and store design. Module 7. MBA distance learning programme, Institute of Retail Studies, University of Stirling.

Dean, J. (1986), 'Does advertising belong in the capital budget?', *Journal of Marketing*, October.

Diamond, J. and G. Pinel (1985), *Retail Buying*, Prentice Hall, Englewood Cliffs, NJ.

Donovan, R.J. and J.R. Rossiter (1982), 'Store atmosphere: an environmental psychology approach', *Journal of Retailing*, 58(1), 34–57.

Doyle, P. (1975), 'Measuring store image', *ADMAP*, 11(11), 391–3.

Doyle, P. and D. Cook (1985), 'Marketing strategies, financial structure and innovation in UK retailing', in J. Gattorna (ed.), *Insights into Strategic Management*, MCB University Press, Bradford, 75–88.

Doyle, P. and I. Fenwick (1975), 'An experimental design for measuring advertising payoff', *Operational Research Quarterly*, 26(4), 693–702.

Durhan, R.C. and R.J. Kopp (1987/8), 'Obtaining retail support for trade deals: key success factors', *Journal of Advertising Research*, 27(6), 51–60.

Engel, J. and R. Blackwell (1982), *Consumer Behavior*, Dryden Press, Chicago.

Engel, J.F., R.D. Blackwell and P.W. Miniard (1986), *Consumer Behavior*, Holt, Rinehart & Winston, New York.

Enis, B.M. and G.W. Paul (1970), '"Store loyalty" as a basis for market segmentation', *Journal of Retailing*, 46(3), 42–56.

Epstein, B.J. (1984), 'Market appraisals', in R.L. Davies and D.S. Rogers (eds), *Store Location and Store Assessment Research*, John Wiley, Chichester, 195–214.

Fishbein, M. (1967), *Attitude Theory and Measurement*, John Wiley, New York.

Fletcher, K. (1987), 'Consumers' use and perceptions of retailer-controlled information sources', *International Journal of Retailing*, 2(3), 59–66.

Fulop, C. (1987), 'The role of advertising in the retail marketing mix', Fourth International Conference on Distribution, CESCOM, Milan.

Gabor, A. (1977), *Pricing, Principles and Practices*, Heinemann, London.

Gabor, A. and C.W.J. Granger (1961), 'On the price consciousness of consumers', *Applied Statistics*, 10(1), 170–88.

Gabor, A. and C.W.J. Granger (1964), 'Price sensitivity of the consumer', *Journal of Advertising Research*, 4(4), 40–4.

Gabor, A. and C.W.J. Granger (1966), 'Price as an indicator of quality: report on an enquiry', *Economica*, 33, 43–70.

Gabor, A., C.W.J. Granger and A.P. Sowter (1970), 'Real and hypothetical shop situations in market research', *Journal of Marketing Research*, 7(3), 355–9.

Gilman, A.L. (1988), 'The benefits of looking below gross margin', *Retailing Issues Letter*, 1(6), 1–4.

Goldman, A. (1977), 'The shopping style explanation for store loyalty', *Journal of Retailing*, 53(4), 33–46, 94.

Grafton-Small, R. (1987), 'Marketing or the anthropology of consumption', *European Journal of Marketing*, 21(9).

Grant, R.M. (1987), 'Manufacturer–retailer relations: the shifting balance of power', in G. Johnson (ed.), *Business Strategy and Retailing*, John Wiley, Chichester, 43–58.

Green, P.E., A.M. Krieger and J.D. Carrol (1987), 'Conjoint analysis and multidimensional scaling: a complementary approach', *Journal of Advertising Research*, 27(5), 21–7.

Green, W.R. (1986), *The Retail Store: Design and construction*, Van Nostrand Reinhold, New York.

Gripsrud, G. and O. Horverak (1986), 'Determinants of retail patronage: a "natural" experiment', *International Journal of Research in Marketing*, 3(4), 263–72.

Gutman, J. and M.K. Mills (1982), 'Fashion life-style, self-concept, shopping orientation, and store patronage: an integrative analysis', *Journal of Retailing*, 48(2), 64–86.

Hansen, R. and T. Deutscher (1977), 'An empirical investigation of attribute importance in retail store selection', *Journal of Retailing*, 53(4), 59–73.

Harris, D. (1987), 'DPP takes off with new technology', *Retail & Distribution Management*, 15(2), 9–12.

Hirschman, E.C. and M.B. Holbrook (1982), 'Hedonic consumption: emerging concepts, methods and propositions', *Journal of Marketing*, 46(3), 92–101.

Hofer, C. and D. Schendel (1978), *Strategy Formulation: Analytical Concepts*, West Publishing Co., New York.

Hooley, G.J. and D.E. Cook (1984), 'SIMS: a store image monitoring system', *International Journal of Advertising*, 3, 129–38.

Hornby, D. (1989), 'Battle for Britain: BIM sounding board', *Management Today*, November.

Howard, J.A. and J.N. Sheth (1969), *The Theory of Buyer Behavior*, John Wiley, New York.

Huff, D.L. (1981), 'Retail location theory', in R.W. Stampfl and E.C. Hirschman (eds), *Theory in Retailing: Traditional and non-traditional sources*, American Marketing Association, Chicago, 108–21.

Humble, J. and D. Randell (1988), 'Service in retail', *Retail*, 5(4), 39–41.

Hummel, J.W. and R. Savitt (1988), 'Integrating customer service and retail strategy', *International Journal of Retailing*, 3(2), 5–21.

Humphreys, F. (1987), 'Retail designers or designer retailers: who's briefing whom', *Retail*, 5(2), 42–3.

Johnson, G. (1987), *Business Strategy and Retailing*, John Wiley, Chichester.

Jones, G. (1987), 'EPOS and the retailer's information needs', in E. McFadyen (ed.), *The Changing Face of British Retailing*, Newman, London, 22–32.

Kenny-Leverick, C. (1969), 'Customer motivations: examples from the grocery trade', *British Journal of Marketing*, 3, 208.

King, C.W. and L.J. Ring (1980), 'Market positioning across retail fashion institutions: a comparative analysis of store types', *Journal of Retailing*, 56(1), 37–55.

King, S. (1985), 'Another turning point of brands?' *ADMAP*, 21, 480–4, 519.

Knee, D. and D. Walters (1985), *Strategy in Retailing: Theory and application*, Philip Allan, Oxford.

Kotler, P. (1988), *Marketing Management: Analysis, planning, implementation and control*, Prentice Hall, Englewood Cliffs, NJ.

Kristenson, L. (1983), 'Strategic planning in retailing', *European Journal of Marketing*, 17(2), 43–59.

Lessor, J.A. and M.A. Hughes (1986), 'Towards a shopper typology', *Business Horizons*, 29(6), November/December.

Likert, R. (1932), 'A technique for the measurement of attitudes', *Archives of Psychology*, 140.

Lipstein, B. (1981), 'A review of retail store experiments', in R.W. Stampfl and E.C. Hirscham (eds), *Theory in Retailing: Traditional and non-traditional sources*, American Marketing Association, Chicago, 95–107.

Livesey, F. (1976), *Pricing*, Macmillan, London.

Livesey, F. and P. Lennon (1978), 'Factors affecting consumers' choice between manufacturer brands and retail own labels', *European Journal of Marketing*, 12(2), 158–70.

Lucas, G.H. and L.G. Gresham (1988), 'How to position for retail success', *Business*, 38(2), 3–13.

Lucas, M.D. (1986), 'Changing stores to suit the changing customer', in ESOMAR (ed.), *Retail Strategies for Profit and Growth*, ESOMAR, Amsterdam, 59–77.

Lusch, R.F. (1982), *The Management of Retail Enterprises*, Kent Publishing, Boston, MA.

Market Place (1986), 'Design update', *Market Place*, 4, 28–9.

Martineau, P. (1958), 'Personality of the retail store', *Harvard Business Review*, 36(1), 47–55.

Maslow, A.H. (1970), *Motivation and Personality*, Harper & Row, New York.

Mason, J.B. and M.L. Mayer (1987), *Modern Retailing: Theory and practice*, Business Publications, Planto, TX.

May, E.G. (1981), 'Product positioning and segmentation strategy: adaptable to retail stores?', in R.W. Stampfl and E.C. Hirschman (eds), *Theory in Retailing: Traditional and non-traditional sources*, American Marketing Association, Chicago, 144–54.

Mazursky, D. and E. Hirschman (1987), 'A cross-organisational comparison of retail buyers' information source utilisation', *Internatonal Journal of Retailing*, 2(10), 44–61.

McClelland, W.G. (1961), 'Address to the British Association', in P.J. Barker *et al.* (eds), *Case Studies in the Competitive Process*, Heinemann, London.

McClelland, W.G. (1966), *Costs and Competition in Retailing*, Macmillan, London.

McFadyen, E. (1981), 'Getting away from the curse of the average', *Retail and Distribution Management*, 9(4), 22–6.

McFadyen, E. (1985), 'How good merchandising has transformed the retail scene', *Retail and Distribution Management*, 13(4), 16–21.

McGoldrick, P.J. (1979), 'Store image: how departmental images differ in a variety chain', *Retail and Distribution Management*, 7(5), 21–4.

McGoldrick, P.J. (1987), 'A multi-dimensional framework for retail pricing', *International Journal of Retailing*, 2(2), 3–26.

McGoldrick, P.J. (1989), 'Department store concessions — strategic decisions and consumer reactions', in L. Pellegrini and S.K. Reddy (eds), *Retail and Marketing Channels*, Routledge, London, 287–310.

McGoldrick, P.J. and R.A. Douglas (1983), 'Factors influencing the choice of a supplier by grocery distributors', *European Journal of Marketing*, 17(5), 13–27.

McGoldrick, P.J. and H.J. Marks (1987), 'Shoppers' awareness of retail grocery prices', *European Journal of Marketing*, 21(3), 63–76.

McNair, M.P. and E.G. May (1957), 'Pricing for profit — a revolutionary approach to retail accounting', *Harvard Business Review*, 35(3), 105–22.

Michman, R.D. (1984), 'New directions for lifestyle patterns', *Business Horizons*, 27(4), July/August.

Mintel (1987), 'Retail practices', *Mintel Retail Intelligence*, 5, 3.25–3.28.

Mitchell, A. (1983), *The Nine American Life Styles: Who we are, where we're going*, Macmillan, New York.

Mitchell, A. and C. MacNulty (1981), 'Changing values and lifestyles', *Long-Range Planning*, 14, April.

Monopolies and Mergers Commission (1981), *Discounts to Retailers*, HMSO, London.

Morris, D. (1979), 'The strategy of own brands', *European Journal of Marketing*, 13(2), 59–78.

Myddleton, R. (1988), *Financial Decisions*, Longman, London.

Nicosia, F.M. (1966), *Consumer Decision Processes*, Prentice Hall, Englewood Cliffs, NJ.

Nooteboom, B. (1986), 'Costs, margins and competition: causes of structural change', in ESOMAR (eds), *Retail Strategies for Profit and Growth*, ESOMAR, Amsterdam, 186–98.

Norkett, P. (1985), 'A financial approach to supermarket success', *Retail and Distribution Management*, 13(6), 53–8.

Ody, P. (1987), 'The growth in private brands', *Retail and Distribution Management*, 15(3), 9–11.

Office of Fair Trading (1985), *Competition and Retailing*, OFT, London.

Oxenfeldt, A.R. (1979), 'The differential method of pricing', *European Journal of Marketing*, 13(4), 199–212.

Penny, N. and D. Brown (1988), 'The Tesco approach to store location', in N. Wrigley (ed.), *Store Choice, Store Location and Market Analysis*, Routledge, London.

Pessemier, E.A. (1980), 'Store image and positioning', *Journal of Retailing*, 56(1), 94–106.

Pinnok, A.K. (1986), *Direct Product Profitability: An introduction for the grocery trade*, Institute of Grocery Distribution, Watford, Herts.

Pope, M.P.R. (1984), 'Developing a strategic planning data base', in R.L. Davies and D.S. Rogers (eds), *Store Location and Store Assessment Research*, John Wiley, Chichester, 181–94.

Porter, M.E. (1980), *Competitive Strategy: Techniques for analyzing industries and competitors*, Free Press, New York.

Porter, M.E. (1985), *Competitive Advantage: Creating and sustaining superior performance*, Free Press, New York.

Retail Business (1987), 'Credit and charge cards', *Retail Business*, 356, 36–46.

Retail Review (1988), 'DIY majors on customer services drive', *Retail Review*, 142, 9.

Rosenbloom, B. (1981), *Retail Marketing*, Random House, New York.

Rosenbloom, B. and L.G. Schiffman (1981), 'Retail theory: perspectives and approaches', in R.W. Stampfl and E.C. Hirschman (eds), *Theory in Retailing: Traditional and non-traditional sources*, American Marketing Association, Chicago, 168–79.

Salimans, R.W.J. (1986), 'Brands and own brand in Europe', in *Strategies for Retailer Growth*, ESOMAR, Amsterdam, 125–51. Note: ESOMAR seminar papers available from the ESOMAR Secretariat, J.J. Viottastraat 29, 1071 JP Amsterdam, The Netherlands.

St Pierre, R. (1989), 'A treat in store', *British Midland Voyager*, November.

Stern, L.W. and A.I. El-Ansary (1987), *Marketing Channels*, Prentice Hall, Englewood Cliffs, NJ.

Steward, D. and N. Hood (1983), 'An empirical examination of customer store image components in three UK retail groups', *European Journal of Marketing*, 17(4), 50–62.

Tigert, D.J. (1983), 'Pushing the hot buttons for a successful retailing strategy', in W.R. Dearden and R.F. Lusch (eds), *Patronage Behaviour and Retail Management*, Elsevier, North-Holland, New York.

Tse, K.K. (1989), 'Marks & Spencer: a manufacturer without factories', *International Trends in Retailing*, 6(2), Fall.

Tull, D.S. and D.I. Hawkins (1987), *Marketing Research: Meaning, measurement and method*, Macmillan, New York.

Uncles, M.D. and K. Ellis (1987), 'Own labels: beliefs and reality', Fourth International Conference on Distribution, CESCOM, Milan.

Urban, G.L. and Hauser, J.R. (1980), *Design and Marketing of New Products*, Prentice Hall, Englewood Cliffs, NJ.

Verdict (1987), *Verdict on Retail Market Segmentation*, Verdict Research, London.

Walters, D. (1986), 'Direct product profitability: cost-led or market-led retail management?' *Retail*, 4(2), 44–8.

Walters, D. (1988), *Strategic Retailing Management*, Prentice Hall, Hemel Hempstead.

Walters, D. and D. White (1987), *Retail Management*, Macmillan, Basingstoke.

Ward, J. (1985), 'Retailers and advertising: who's changing who?', *Retail*, 3(3), 8–9.

Williamson, J. (1986), 'Department stores in Japan', *Retail & Distribution Management*, 14(4), 14–17.

Wingate, J.W. and J.S. Friedlander (1978), *The Management of Retail Buying*, Prentice Hall, Englewood Cliffs, NJ.

Woodman, B. (1987), 'EFTPoS in the UK', Proceedings of the EPoS87 with EFTPoS87 Conference, RMDP, Brighton, Q1–Q24.

Worthington, S. (1986), 'Retailer credit cards and direct marketing — a question of synergy', *Journal of Marketing Management*, 2(2), 125–31.

Wrigley, N. (1988), *Store Choice, Store Location and Market Analysis*, Routledge, New York.

Zimmer, M.R. and L.L. Golden (1988), 'Impressions of retail stores: a content analysis of consumer images', *Journal of Retailing*, 64(3), 265–93.

Index